ENERGY SUPPLY AND
GOVERNMENT POLICY

ENERGY SUPPLY AND GOVERNMENT POLICY

EDITED BY

ROBERT J. KALTER and
WILLIAM A. VOGELY

CORNELL UNIVERSITY PRESS

ITHACA AND LONDON

First published 1976 by Cornell University Press.
Published in the United Kingdom by Cornell University Press Ltd., 2–4 Brook Street, London W1Y 1AA.

International Standard Book Number (cloth) 0–8014–0966–7
International Standard Book Number (paper) 0–8014–9159–2
Library of Congress Catalog Card Number 76-15836
Printed in the United States of America by Vail-Ballou Press, Inc.
*Librarians: Library of Congress cataloging information
appears on the last page of the book.*

Contents

Contributors

MARTIN L. BAUGHMAN is Director of Systems Analysis, Center for Energy Studies, at the University of Texas at Austin.

STEPHEN G. BREYER is Professor of Law at Harvard University.

RICHARD L. GORDON is Professor of Mineral Economics in the College of Earth and Mineral Sciences at The Pennsylvania State University.

ESTEBAN HNYILICZA is a Research Assistant in the Energy Laboratory, Massachusetts Institute of Technology.

WILLIAM A. JOHNSON is Professor of Economics and Director of the Energy Policy Research Center at George Washington University.

ROBERT J. KALTER is Professor of Resource Economics at Cornell University.

ALVIN KAUFMAN is Director of the Office of Research for the New York State Public Service Commission.

JOHN V. KRUTILLA is a Senior Fellow at Resources for the Future.

PAUL W. MACAVOY is Henry R. Luce Professor of Public Policy, Sloan School of Management, Massachusetts Institute of Technology, on leave 1975–1976 as a member of the President's Council of Economic Advisers.

WALTER J. MEAD is Professor of Economics at the University of California, Santa Barbara.

STEPHEN L. MCDONALD is Professor and Chairman of the Department of Economics, University of Texas at Austin.

JOHN F. O'LEARY is Energy Resources Administrator for the Energy Resources Board of the State of New Mexico.

R. TALBOT PAGE is a Senior Research Associate for Resources for the Future.

JOHN E. TILTON is Professor of Mineral Economics at The Pennsylvania State University.

NICOLAI TIMENES, JR., is Deputy Assistant Director for Energy, Environment, and Natural Resources in the Congressional Budget Office.

WALLACE E. TYNER is a Research Associate in Resource Economics at Cornell University.

WILLIAM A. VOGELY is Professor of Mineral Economics at The Pennsylvania State University.

ENERGY SUPPLY AND GOVERNMENT POLICY

1

Introduction

**Robert J. Kalter and
William A. Vogely**

The energy economy of the United States is based on petroleum and natural gas, and domestic production of both is declining. At the same time, environmental constraints have restricted increases in the use of coal and have limited the expansion of nuclear power facilities. A combination of factors including environmental constraints, economic considerations, and the lack of demonstrated technology have inhibited development of other sources such as oil shale and solar and geothermal energy. As a result, imported crude oil and petroleum products have steadily increased their relative share of the U.S. energy market in recent years, and natural gas shortages are widespread.

The reasons for this rapidly developing shift in U.S. energy dependence are numerous and complicated. It is clear, however, that the federal government plays a unique role in setting the rules of the game within which the energy market functions. In no other industry, with the possible exception of agriculture, has the public sector been so long and so pervasively involved. That involvement is complex, often subtle, and varies in many ways with the different energy sources and end uses.

Governmental involvement, both direct and indirect, in this industrial sector has resulted from a myriad of past circumstances brought about by often conflicting and changing pressure groups, not the least important of which is the energy industry itself. With our growing dependence on foreign energy sources, the United States has now entered a period in which government energy policy will be at the center stage of public debate. Appropriate consideration of the issues requires a wide-ranging review that must, by definition, cover many aspects of our production, distribution, and consumption of energy. In this volume we attempt to provide the interested public with information and analysis on one facet of this complex subject—that of energy supply.

The degree to which the United States should depend on imported energy supplies in the future is a societal decision which transcends the analytical scope of any one discipline. However, as we grope toward an appropriate dependence level, numerous alternative approaches to achieve the changes that will be necessary in our market mechanisms must be considered.

The debate that has developed over the dependency question since the 1973–1974 Arab oil embargo has tended to center on two polar solutions. On the one hand, many have advocated conservation of energy (reduction in the rate of demand growth) both to avoid exhaustion of our scarce energy resources and to defer or eliminate major exploration and development programs that they view as environmentally unacceptable. Advocates of this strategy argue that conservation is the only immediate solution to our energy dependence problems and has the additional benefit of being environmentally preferable.[1]

Others argue that the United States should develop a large-scale program to tap our unknown and undeveloped energy resources for future use, and that energy production and use can be environmentally acceptable. Although recognizing the time lags involved in developing increased domestic supplies, they feel that the lags would be no greater than those entailed in implementing an effective conservation program. Moreover, they conclude that an adequate program of energy conservation may have adverse effects on domestic economic growth.[2]

Neither polar solution may be adequate by itself. Solutions to substantial problems often involve an amalgamation of alternative strategies. A rational analysis of the energy problem seems to yield the conclusion that action on both the supply and the demand fronts is necessary if national security, environmental, and economic considerations are to be balanced. Therefore, the authors of this volume, while not necessarily advocating a supply based strategy, do believe that greater understanding of the domestic energy supply sector will assist in the construction of a rational and comprehensive national energy policy.

Society cannot afford to ignore the implications of modifying the rules of a game that has evolved over the past fifty years. Since energy supply

1. Energy Policy Project of the Ford Foundation, *A Time to Choose: America's Energy Future,* Final Report (Cambridge, Mass.: Ballinger, 1974).

2. Federal Energy Administration, *Project Independence, A Summary* (Washington: U.S. Government Printing Office, November 1974); M. A. Adelman, et al., *No Time to Confuse* (San Francisco: Institute for Contemporary Studies, 1975).

takes place within a private market constrained by government regulations, however, these linkages must be investigated in order to understand the potential for action. The various regulations governing alternative energy supply sources are far from uniform, and any overview of this area must analyze both aggregate policy impacts and interactions, as well as the situation of individual fuel sources.

The editors asked highly qualified authors to address these issues in their own terms and frames of reference. Thus the chapters of this book are written from a variety of perspectives. This is as it should be—a subject as complex as energy supply does not lend itself to a rigid, simple framework of analysis. Since each chapter is self-contained, some duplication of basic facts and statistics is essential. We have made no attempt to reconcile differences in policy postures among the authors. Our objective is to present the reasoned arguments of experts. It is the duty of the reader, and of society, to sort out these arguments and move toward policy decisions.

Basic Concepts in Energy Supply

Most of our energy now comes from depletable resources in the earth's crust. This fact distinguishes energy supply functions from those of a reproducible commodity, in that supply cannot be increased by replication of producing plants. To increase the supply of energy involves investments at four quite different stages of the production process: exploration, development and production, refining or other methods of treatment and transportation.

This investment procedure differs from that for reproducible resources in its first and second stages. It is their unique characteristics which have lead to government intervention in energy supply. To understand these first two stages, we must consider the fundamental determinants of energy resource availability.

Energy Supply

The primary energy supplies of the United States and the rest of the world come from the fossil fuels—oil, natural gas, and coal. Growing amounts are coming from atomic power, which is currently based on uranium and, to a lesser extent, thorium. Significant supplies to some areas within the United States come from hydropower, using falling water of major river systems.

Petroleum, including natural gas liquids, supplied 45.8 percent of the total energy inputs in the United States in 1974. Natural gas supplied 30.4 percent, coal 18 percent, hydropower 4.2 percent, and nuclear power only 1.6 percent in the same year.[3] Estimates made for Project Independence [4] and for the Federal Power Commission's Natural Gas Survey [5] indicate that even with extremely rapid rates of growth in nuclear power over the next twenty-five years, the United States will still have a fossil fuel economy for many decades to come. Thus, the availability situation of the fossil fuels is of primary importance for public policy decisions.

Reserves and Resources

The measurement of stocks of recoverable fuels in the earth's crust is highly imprecise. Vincent E. McKelvey, director of the U.S. Geological Survey, poses the problem in these terms: "The focus of most of industry's concern over the extent of mineral resources is on the magnitude of supplies that exist now or that can be developed in the near term, and this is of public interest also. Many other policy decisions, however, relate to the much more difficult question of potential supplies, a question that to be answered properly must take account both of the extent of undiscovered deposits as well as deposits that cannot be reproduced profitably now, but may become available in the future."[6]

To meet this problem, McKelvey has proposed the classification of resources shown in Figure 1. The upper left-hand box of this figure includes deposits which are classified as reserves. In the case of petroleum and natural gas, these are the "proved reserves," figures on which are published yearly, representing a working inventory of known oil and gas. Such an inventory covers only a few years of projected demands at any one time. For coal, as Richard L. Gordon discusses in Chapter 8, the reserve figure is of a fundamentally different nature. It covers the entire block of identified resources, much of which cannot be made available without substantial investments in exploration and development. The data on uranium, as reported by the Atomic Energy Commission, also belong in the identified resources portion of the McKelvey diagram.

Increasing the supply of domestic fuels involves moving either to the

3. U.S. Department of the Interior, News Release, Washington, April 13, 1975.

4. Federal Energy Administration, *Project Independence,* p. 46.

5. Federal Power Commission, *Natural Gas Survey,* Vol. 1, ch. 6, "Total Energy Supply and Demand" (Washington, 1974), p. 87.

6. V. E. McKelvey, "Mineral Resource Estimates and Public Policy," in U.S. Department of the Interior, *United States Mineral Resources,* Geological Survey Professional Paper 820 (Washington, 1973), p. 11.

Figure 1. Resource classification

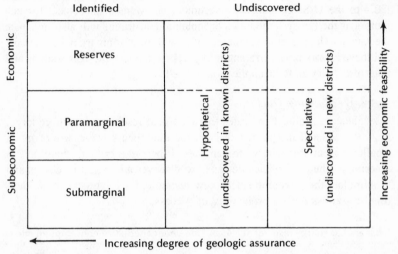

Source: Adapted from V. E. McKelvey, "Mineral Resource Estimates and Public Policy," in U.S. Department of the Interior, *United States Mineral Resources,* Geological Survey Professional Paper 820 (Washington, 1973), p. 12.

right in the diagram to discover new economic deposits, or toward the bottom of the diagram to develop resources which are now identified, but which are economically paramarginal or submarginal.

Policy Decision Areas

The government plays a major role in both approaches to increasing domestic fuel supplies. Most of the major undrilled areas for U.S. petroleum development—the outer continental shelf and the public domain lands of the West and in Alaska—are under the direct control of the federal government, and the rate of development of these lands through exploration is controlled by federal leasing policies. The same situation exists for coal: most of the identified coal resources lie west of the Mississippi and are under the ownership of the federal government, and the pace of development of these resources is also a matter of leasing policy.

Movement down the resources diagram to develop deposits which are now paramarginal and submarginal involves the development of new technologies and/or higher prices for energy fuels. Thus, government decisions on prices, and government, along with private, expenditures for research and development play a major role in the availability of these fuels to the U.S. economy. Government decisions with respect to such factors as the tax system and environmental constraints will also influence the rate and degree of development of new or now submarginal resources. All these factors have differential impacts for the specific fuel sources and may often vary in their application as well.

Are We Running Out?

A glance at Table 1 indicates that identified reserves of coal are large. For oil, gas, and uranium, however, the identified reserves are of much smaller magnitudes relative to demands. It becomes critical, therefore, to determine whether policies designed to discover additional resources and to stimulate the development of new technologies for uneconomic identified resources have a probability of success.

Table 1. U.S. energy reserves, 1974, and life under alternative consumption rates

	Reserves	Life in years at 1974 production rates	Life in years at 1974 consumption rates	Life in years with consumption growing at 5% per year
Coal (tons)	434×10^9	735	804	74
Oil (bbl.)	35×10^9	10	8	6
Natural gas (cu. ft.)	250×10^{12}	11	11	8
Uranium (tons)	340×10^3	29	29	17

Source: U.S. Bureau of Mines, Commodity Data Summary, 1975.

In the case of uranium, the major effort required is to develop new technologies for generating increased amounts of energy from the basic fuel. The breeder reactor program is based squarely on this need, and its success would essentially remove the resource constraint in the uranium area. There appears to be ample time for such development to proceed, if it proves technically and environmentally feasible, as the identified resources in the paramarginal and submarginal categories within the United States are quite large. Thus, ample resources of uranium exist to support a rapidly growing nuclear energy industry, with very moderate fuel-based increases in the cost of the electricity generated.[7]

The case of oil and natural gas, however, is quite different. The ul-

7. U.S. Department of the Interior, *United States Mineral Resources*, pp. 456–468.

timate size of the oil and gas resource lying within the control of the United States is uncertain. This issue was thoroughly examined by T. H. McCulloh [8] of the U.S. Geological Survey in 1973 and was the subject of a recent report of the National Academy of Sciences.[9] McCulloh identifies two fundamentally different methods of estimating the potential economic oil and gas resources within an area. The first of these (the volumetric) involves determining the cubic volume of "host" rocks in the area, and comparing to that cubic volume the amount of oil and gas that has been discovered in fully exploring similar geologic areas. An alternative method (the mathematical), employing the same basic historical records, has been used by King Hubbert.[10] His method takes the rates at which petroleum has been found and produced through time, not the amount of petroleum found per cubic mile, as the estimating parameter.

The two methods give different estimates of the ultimately recoverable amounts of oil and gas in the United States. Using the first method, an analyst at the U.S. Geologic Survey estimated the potentially recoverable barrels of petroleum at around 458 billion. As a contrast, Hubbert's latest estimate of potential reserves is 72 billion barrels. Table 2 presents the range of estimates. Thus, if Hubbert is right, no government policy with respect to opening new areas of exploration will substantially increase the availability of oil in the United States. There is simply very little domestic oil remaining to be found.

Natural gas availability presents the same kinds of questions. Studies done for the Federal Power Commission on natural gas supply [11] indicate that some geologists are extremely pessimistic concerning its remaining availability in the United States, and others are highly optimistic.

The extent of undiscovered oil and gas resources in the United States has become a matter of high public concern. Over the space of a year the U.S. Geological Survey has sharply reduced its estimate of recoverable oil from 200–400 billion barrels to 61–149 billion barrels, and of natural gas from 1,000–2,000 trillion cubic feet to 322–655 trillion cubic feet.[12] Virtually no new information of a geologic nature has become available

8. T. H. McCulloh, "Oil and Gas," in *ibid.,* pp. 477–496.

9. National Academy of Sciences, *Resources and the Environment* (Washington, 1974).

10. M. K. Hubbert, "Energy Resources," *Resources and Man* (Washington: National Academy of Sciences, 1969), pp. 157–242.

11. Federal Power Commission, *Natural Gas Survey,* Vol. 1, ch. 9, p. 14.

12. B. M. Miller et al., *Geological Estimates of Undiscovered Recoverable Oil and Gas Resources in the United States,* Geological Survey Circular 725, prepared for the Federal Energy Administration (Washington, 1975).

Table 2. Estimates of undiscovered recoverable oil and gas resources of the United States

	Oil & natural gas liquid (million bbl.)	Gas (trillion cu. ft.)
Oil companies		
Company A (1960)	168	
Company C (1973)	55 *	
Company D (1974)	89	450
Company E	90	
U.S. Geological Survey		
Hendricks (1965)	346	1,300
Hubbert (1967)	24–64 †	180–500 †
Theobald et al. (1972)	458	1,980
McKelvey (1974)	200–400	990–2,000
Hubbert (1974)	72	540
McKelvey (1975)	61–149	322–655

Sources: National Academy of Sciences, Resources and the Environment (Washington, 1974), p. 89; U.S. Department of the Interior News Release, April 13, 1975.
* Estimated discoverable between 1973 and 1985.
† Exclusive of Alaska.

during this period. The revisions, therefore, are solely the result of applying different methods of estimation to the same data base. The most that can be said is that we simply do not know what the ultimate recoverable resources of oil and gas in the United States are. In the words of Mc-Colloh, "All estimates of petroleum and natural gas resources depend upon prior exploration results and are unreliable." [13]

Moreover, current production technology recovers only about one-third of the oil in any given reservoir. Hence, a large portion of the already discovered petroleum is in the paramarginal and submarginal categories. In addition, identified resources of very large magnitude exist in the so-called heavy oil fields of the United States, but are currently unrecoverable. Improved production techniques could be applied to this substantial resource base to increase the availability of petroleum. The same, however, cannot be said of natural gas, since the production efficiency of a natural gas reservoir approaches 90 percent. There are, however, identified deposits of natural gas in tight reservoirs where the porosity will not

13. McCulloh, "Oil and Gas," p. 477.

permit development now, but which may be amenable to new technologies, such as hydraulic fracturing of the host rocks.

The United States has very large identified coal supplies which can be produced with known technologies. As subsequent chapters discuss, however, these resources carry environmental and social costs which are of serious public concern.

Energy Supply and Policy Focus

Although public policies toward the energy industry have frequently been contradictory, resulting market inefficiencies and adverse environmental and/or equity considerations have not given rise to frequent public outcry. To a large extent, this may have been so because historically energy prices have fallen relative to our general price indices and supplies have been abundant. Only within the past several years have these phenomena reversed themselves. The reversal coupled with our growing dependence on insecure foreign energy sources and increasing environmental problems, has lead to a reexamination of the ways in which public policy impinges on energy production and consumption.

Although most experts concede that *worldwide* resources for energy are abundant and should not be a concern through the end of the century, a substantial possibility of shortages within the United States exists if current consumption rates are maintained. In conjunction with institutional considerations which have led to the absence of a free market in such supplies, the possibility of major disruptions owing to failures in energy markets over the next fifteen years is a substantial economic danger to the United States.

Although shortages in energy supply will generally lead to higher prices, the resulting incentives to find new domestic sources and/or to develop replacement technologies operate only with long lead times. As a result, forward planning has now become a prerequisite for federal energy policy. With respect to supply, the government has traditionally employed six types of policies to control and modify private market relationships. These include taxation policy, disposal policy for energy resources in the public domain, environmental policy, research and development expenditures, control over market prices, and policies pertaining to foreign trade in energy commodities. The growing debate over such policies has also engendered concern for the manner in which the public sector organizes to administer energy policy.

Taxation

Special tax privileges have long been a feature of our public policy toward the energy sector. Such privileges have led to market distortions that, over the long term, have exacerbated our dependency situation. In the words of Stephen MacDonald in Chapter 2, "The general effect of these special tax provisions applying to income from minerals production is to lower the effective tax rate and the long-run supply price in the affected extraction industries." However, differential effects with respect to competitive energy sources are engendered by nonuniform treatment of the different segments of our energy supply sector. The various ramifications of such policies are considered in detail in Chapter 2.

Federal Lands

Although energy resources located in the public domain have been an important marginal source of domestic supply in the past, that situation is now changing dramatically. As private on-land sources are depleted, the focus of the search for future supplies of crude oil and natural gas has shifted to our outer continental shelf. These areas and those in our Naval Petroleum Reserves, on land, will become the primary focus for exploration and development of future liquid hydrocarbon supplies. In general, these areas are controlled by the federal government. The long lead times that are required to obtain production from such regions necessitate long-range government planning. In addition, the major market uncertainties associated with exploration on our outer continental shelf have raised a host of issues regarding the sharing of risks among the interested parties, the impacts on the onshore environment, and the return of fair market value to the public. Undeveloped coal resources, geothermal energy potential, and oil shale reserves are likewise largely located on public lands. The schedule and strategy designed for leasing such resources to the private sector for exploration, development, and production thus raise a set of issues which urgently require attention. Decisions made on these issues will affect not only the supply of domestic energy which can be produced over the next fifteen to twenty years but also the environmental and regional ramifications of such production. The problems involved for individual energy sources as well as the entire range of domestic energy supply possibilities are investigated in Chapter 3. Coal resources and the public domain are also discussed in Chapter 8.

Environmental Policies

A relatively recent phenomenon affecting energy supply is the complex of rules and regulations governing environmental aspects of economic activity. The passage of clean air and clean water legislation has had progressively increasing impacts on the consumption, transportation, and production of energy supplies. By attempting to internalize what were previously considered to be external costs, those regulations have altered the comparative economics of alternative energy supply sources and thus have had major impacts on the level of investment in various segments of the industry. In addition, increasing environmental regulation has had the corollary effect of substantially lengthening the time required to make investment plans operational. Witness the long litigation over the Trans-Alaska Pipeline question and the more recent proposals for baseline environmental information prior to OCS exploration and development activity. On the other hand, the environmental disadvantages of many energy supply options provide the best set of arguments for increasing our emphasis on methods for reducing the growth rate in energy consumption. Of perhaps longer range importance, however, are the intergenerational issues involved in many of the energy supply alternatives currently being proposed. Perhaps the most visible and controversial of these are the potential health and containment problems associated with the use of nuclear power options. A number of chapters in this volume relate to topics which must incorporate an implicit or explicit environmental constraint. Chapter 4, however, attempts to give the reader an overview of the relationships between environmental and energy policy. A definitive set of answers to the problems raised by this complex and often emotional issue has not yet been and may never be written. What the authors of Chapter 4 point out is the need for considering the environmental-energy interface in decision making and the importance of such options as energy conservation and technological change. The necessity of fostering increased public participation in these decisions and the need to provide a mechanism for considering factors that affect future generations is emphasized.

Research and Development

Because today's decisions will shape the nation's energy markets over the next decade and beyond, research and development activity becomes of crucial importance. Chapters 5, 10, and 14 address questions relating to the public's role in energy research and development. The reasons for, and means and limitations of, public research and development funding are discussed. The fact that stands out, however, is the pervasive and often misguided influence which governmental activity in this area can have on the future course of events. "Excessive" funding of nuclear energy programs is but one example of this situation. The importance of research and development expenditures within a specific institutional context (i.e., tax laws, regulatory policy, foreign trade policy) must be better understood before improved decisions in this area will be forthcoming.

Price Policy

An understanding of the pervasive influence that government policy has on energy markets requires consideration of its direct interference with the principal information signal linking the various aspects of those markets—price. For whatever reason, whether it be perceived monopoly power, equity, or noneconomic considerations, public policy makers have a long history of intervention in private market operations. From wellhead price regulation of natural gas to the regulation of so-called monopolies like the electric utility industry and the imposition of price controls during crisis situations, market interference remains an important means of government control over energy production and use. As a result, several authors in this volume (see Chapters 7, 9, and 11) deal, some exclusively, with the factors, problems and limitations of governmental action in price determination.

Trade Policy

Finally, all policies influencing supply are to some extent affected by public policy regarding foreign energy dependence. Import quotas, tariffs, questions of foreign tax credits, and policies regarding transportation of energy supplies all have a major influence on the portion of total supply that will come from domestic sources. These policies, in conjunction with other trade policies, set the long-run context within which domestically oriented policy actions (discussed above) will be taken. Since petroleum has been, and undoubtedly will remain, the major energy source traded in foreign markets, it is the focus of the debate on our degree of dependency. Historical and current factors relevant to this debate and possible policy mechanisms are considered in Chapter 6. The direction of future policy, however, will depend on far more complex considerations than those that governed past actions. As we point out below, it may hinge on a now apparent problem regarding the physical availability of domestic energy resources.

Administrative Organization

Issues relating to administrative organization are important to an understanding of how energy policy is formulated and implemented, to the efficiency with which these tasks are performed, and to their successful execution. An optimal institutional mechanism for handling the somewhat diverse objectives involved may not be attainable. Yet both recent and historical experience with government organization indicate useful directions in which to proceed. Now seems to be a most auspicious time at which to reflect on our recent experience and to attempt the design of a better structure for the intermediate future. Organizational proposals affecting both the executive and legislative branches of government must be considered in any such overview, if our system of checks and balances is to function efficiently. In Chapter 12, the contradiction between the announced objectives of energy policy administration and the reality of recent actions is explored in depth. Drawing from our recent experience with policy making, the author points out the conflicting goals facing policy makers and demonstrates that these conflicts have been resolved by not focusing on either energy conservation or resource supply. In a word, regulatory functions have tended to dominate policy considerations. In Chapter 13, current features of energy organization are summarized and proposals for future change made. By taking these in conjunction with each other and with the chapters relating to specific industries, the reader can obtain an overview of a major element forgotten by most modern economic studies—institutional considerations.

The Policy Dilemma

Future public policy with respect to energy supply cannot be made in isolation. Precise guidelines will depend, at least partially, on decisions concerning the demand side of the equation and perceptions of possible constraints on any action. Yet all decisions may fundamentally depend on assumptions regarding the future availability of crude oil and natural gas. Alternatives under the hypothesis of resource exhaustion in the near term are markedly different from those available under that assuming ample physical supplies over the intermediate term.

If, in fact, higher prices, government and industry research and development, and the opening of public domain lands to exploration will not substantially increase the supply of oil and gas or slow the decline of production domestically, then the policy issue becomes how to ration existing supplies—through the price system or through direct government intervention in these markets—and develop appropriate new energy sources over the long run. On the other hand, if the geologic optimists are correct, the domestic supplies will exist to meet demands at whatever level of foreign dependence is chosen (assuming that we are willing to pay the resource costs).

Unfortunately, there appears to be no way to test these assumptions without a very large expenditure of money for exploration efforts. Oil cannot be presumed to exist or not to exist until reservoir rocks have been tested with the drill. Petroleum reservoirs are highly skewed in their distribution. Sixty-five percent of all oil and gas ever discovered has been found in only one percent of all oil and gas fields. Fifteen percent of the discovered oil occurs in only two giant fields in the Middle East.[14] Thus a discovery of a very few giant fields in the unexplored regions of the United States would radically change the resource posture of this nation.

The question, then, is whether or not supply policy should be based upon the possibility of finding very substantial hydrocarbon resources in the unexplored portions of the ocean floor and of the continental United States. Adoption of a strategy that forecloses supply development and allocates existing supplies will immediately bring about the economic results of resource exhaustion. Concentration on the development of alternative supply technology may be excessively costly to current generations and involve considerable uncertainty (concerning possibilities of success, as well as in environmental terms). But to assume ample resources of conventional fuels will also subject society to substantial economic and environmental risk.

In any economic system, the solution to problems such as those generated by this question of resource availability will depend on the weights that society places on possible alternative objectives and its risk preference. That is, how the trade-offs between economic efficiency (given the current distribution of income), equity, and environmental quality, in the context of various degrees of perceived risk, are determined will influence policy choices.[15] The problem is that these trade-offs are probably

14. *Ibid.*, p. 481.
15. R. M. Solow, "The Economics of Resources or the Resources of Economics," *American Economic Review,* 64 (May 1974), 1–15.

influenced by the rate of future economic growth that is expected at the time they are decided upon.

Given the values and current standard of living in the United States, expectations of low growth rates will probably tend to shift policy emphasis toward a consideration of equity questions and reduce our concern with environmental issues. This will promote increased reliance on regulatory actions and direct government (nonmarket) solutions and place a reduced emphasis on the price system. On the other hand, in times of rapid growth, society can afford to place more emphasis on efficiency solutions and environmental preservation. Equity problems can be handled by specific programs designed for that purpose. The danger faced by the United States at this juncture is the premature introduction of regulatory inefficiencies because of possibly false impressions concerning our capability to sustain long-term economic growth.

2

Taxation System and Market Distortion

Stephen L. McDonald

Since 1918 producers of minerals in the tax jurisdiction of the United States have been favored by some degree of differential treatment under federal income tax laws and regulations. As this differential tax treatment has evolved over the years, it has come to include (a) provision for depletion allowances calculated as a percentage of gross income, these in no way limited by actual investment outlays, and (b) the privilege of treating as a current expense certain outlays for exploration and development that would otherwise be capitalized and written off for tax purposes over the life of productive mines or wells.[1] The general effect of these special tax provisions applying to income from minerals production is to lower the effective tax rate and the long-run supply price in the affected extractive industries, and, since the special provisions are not uniform among the different mineral industries, to alter relative supply prices of such competitive minerals as crude petroleum, natural gas, coal, oil shale, and uranium. It is the purpose of this chapter to explain the operation of these special tax provisions, to discuss their probable market-distorting or misallocative effects, and to estimate the likely consequences of their elimination.

We shall be concerned only with the minerals from which energy is derived: oil, gas, coal, oil shale, and uranium. Emphasis will be placed on the case of oil and gas, partly because oil and gas together account for approximately three-fourths of total energy consumption in the United States, and partly because there have recently been major changes in the

1. The evolution of differential tax treatment of income from minerals may be traced in the following publications: Joint Committee on Internal Revenue Taxation, *Legislative History of Depletion Allowances,* 81st Cong., 2d sess. (Committee Print, 1950); Joint Economic Committee, *The Federal Tax System: Facts and Problems,* 1964, 88th Cong., 2d sess. (Committee Print, 1964), pp. 107–118; Bernard P. Herber, *Modern Public Finance,* rev. ed. (Homewood, Ill.: Richard D. Irwin, 1971), pp. 180–181.

tax law affecting them. The nature and importance of these changes will be best understood following a general explanation of the special tax treatment historically accorded income from minerals production. It should be pointed out here, however, that the Tax Reduction Act of 1975 [2] almost entirely eliminated percentage depletion for major integrated producers of oil and gas and provided for gradual reduction of the effective allowance for independent producers and royalty owners over a ten-year period. (Percentage depletion for other minerals producers was unaffected by the act.) The immediately following discussion of special tax provisions affecting minerals producers is subject to these changes, which will be explained in more detail in a later section.

The Special Tax Provisions
The Percentage Depletion Alternative

In computing his income subject to tax at either corporate or personal rates, as appropriate, the owner of an interest in minerals production is permitted to deduct from his gross income an allowance for depletion presumably representing the current consumption of a capital asset, minerals in the ground. In concept, depletion stands to mineral deposits as depreciation stands to man-made capital assets. Current law provides that the deduction for minerals depletion in a tax period shall be computed for each productive property or operating unit (e.g., oil lease or coal mine) as the larger of (1) a pro rata (unit-of-production [3]) fraction of the capitalized costs of the property, or, for those still eligible under the 1975 act referred to above, (2) a percentage of the gross value of the production, not to exceed 50 percent of the net income, of the property during the tax period. (The maximum percentage of gross income allowed in the second alternative is 22 percent for oil, gas, and uranium,[4] 15 percent for oil shale, and 10 percent for coal.[5]) The first alternative, known as cost

2. Public Law 94–12, 94th Cong., H.R. 2166, March 29, 1975, amending the Internal Revenue Code of 1954.

3. To compute the unit-of-production depletion deduction for a given year, the adjusted basis of the property which would be used to determine the gain upon its sale is divided by the total remaining units to be produced over the life of the property, estimated as of the beginning of the year, and the result is multiplied by the number of units produced and sold during the year.

4. Prior to the Tax Reform Act of 1969, the allowance was 27.5 percent for oil and gas and 23 percent for uranium. The lower rates became effective in the 1970 tax year.

5. For the percentages allowed for all other minerals, see Herber, *Modern Public Finance*, p. 180. Generally, they range from 22 percent for certain strategic metals to 5 percent for such common minerals as brick clay and gravel.

depletion, does not differ in principle from the usual treatment of capital consumption in other industries: the total to be recovered through tax deductions is the initial capitalized cost, and recovery is made in a reasonable, systematic way over the life of the productive property. However, under the second alternative, known as percentage depletion, the total tax deductions that result are not limited to the initial capitalized cost of the depletable asset and, in the nature of the case, ordinarily exceed the initial capitalized cost. Subject to the constraints of the 1975 act, the cost depletion and percentage depletion alternatives are available to all those having direct ownership shares in the mineral being produced, including operating interests, royalties, and other shares in production, and without distinction between foreign and domestic location of the production.[6]

For operators of mines and oil and gas wells, who are usually lessees, the gross income on which percentage depletion is based is exclusive of royalties paid, since the royalty owner is entitled to depletion (cost or percentage) on his share of production. The operator's net income pertinent to the 50-percent-of-net limitation on percentage depletion for a property [7] is computed as the difference between gross income after royalties and all costs except depletion attributable to that property in the tax period. Such costs include production expenses (inclusive of production taxes and an apportionment of overhead), ad valorem taxes, allocable interest, depreciation of tangible investment in wells and equipment, intangible expenses of drilling productive wells on the property, and mine development expenses on the property. (More on development expenses below.) Costs not attributable to producing properties, such as the costs of surrendered leases, dry holes, and other unsuccessful exploration activity on nonproducing properties, as well as interest, taxes, and overhead allocable to such properties, do not act as potential limitations on allowable percentage depletion under the 50-percent-of-net rule but are otherwise fully deductible for tax purposes.[8]

6. Certain strategic minerals are allowed higher percentage depletion rates if produced domestically, but this group does not include any of the mineral fuels under discussion here. Percentage depletion on foreign production of oil and gas is effectively eliminated by the 1975 act.

7. Since percentage depletion may not exceed the specified rate on any property but may be reduced by the 50-percent-of-net limitations on some, the average effective percentage depletion rate tends to be less than the statutory maximum.

8. Since the costs pertinent to the 50-percent-of-net rule do not include all tax-deductible costs, that rule does not necessarily mean that the effective tax rate for a firm or industry is at least 50 percent of the nominal rate. The effective rate may be less than 50 percent of the

The Expensing Alternative

With respect to the current expensing of certain costs, it is necessary to make a distinction between the oil and gas industry and other minerals industries. In the oil and gas industry, operators are given the option of either capitalizing the intangible expenses of drilling and equipping productive wells [9] and recovering them through depletion deductions or treating them as ordinary operating expenses, fully deductible as incurred.[10] Those choosing to capitalize such expenses have the further option of capitalizing or expensing dry hole costs.

In mining other than oil and gas production, operators likewise have the option of expensing or capitalizing exploration expenses—defined as "expenditures to determine the existence, location, extent, and quality of mineral resources" [11]—but deductions are limited to $100,000 per year per taxpayer and to a total over time of $500,000 per taxpayer. Similarly, costs of developing a mine, such as the costs of mine shafts and tunnels, may be expensed currently or capitalized, but there is no limitation on the amount of such deductions by a taxpayer per year or in total over time.

There are two advantages to expensing the eligible costs, provided the taxpayer has sufficient otherwise taxable income to cover them. First, their current expensing yields an imputed interest saving in comparison with capitalization and recovery over an extended period of time. At any positive rate of interest, the present value of an immediate tax saving of given size is greater than the present value of the same tax saving spread over a number of years. Second, the capitalized costs pertaining to pro-

---

nominal rate, especially in the oil industry where unsuccessful exploration expenses figure so largely in total deductible expenses. However, the 1975 act limits percentage depletion in the oil and gas industry to 65 percent of taxable income computed without allowance for depletion. Thus in this industry allowable depletion under current law may be limited by any cost, whether attributable to producing properties or not.

9. Intangible expenses of drilling and equipping productive wells include costs of labor, fuel, power, materials, supplies, tool rental, and repairs of drilling equipment. They typically account for about 75 percent of the costs of drilling productive wells. The remaining costs of drilling such wells, called tangible costs, include expenditures for pipe, pumps, tanks, and other equipment. The latter must be capitalized and recovered through depreciation allowances.

10. The choice of capitalizing or expensing, once made, is binding thereafter on the operator with respect to all his properties, including those acquired subsequent to the choice. In contrast, an operator may employ cost depletion on some properties and percentage depletion on others at a given time, and may switch from one to the other at any time in the life of a given productive property.

11. Herber, *Modern Public Finance*, p. 181.

ductive properties can be recovered only through depletion allowances; but expensed costs are recoverable in addition to depletion allowances. The expensing of eligible investment outlays interferes with or limits percentage depletion only where their total amount in a tax year brings into play the 50-percent-of-net limitation.[12] Thus the *net* benefit of percentage depletion—the allowable depletion in excess of alternative cost-basis depletion—is usually enhanced by opting to expense eligible exploration and development outlays.

It is important to note also that the expensing privilege may combine profitably to the taxpayer with differential taxation of capital gains. If the taxpayer has sufficient otherwise taxable income, he may expense eligible exploration and development expenses, enjoying tax savings at the ordinary income tax rate, corporate or personal, and then when production is established sell his mineral property for a long-term capital gain subject to a maximum corporate rate of 30 percent or a maximum personal rate of 35 percent.

Combination of Percentage Depletion and Expensing

It should be clear from the above that where oil and gas or mine operators combine percentage depletion with the expensing of eligible outlays, and given the depreciation of equipment, they are permitted to make depletion deductions *in addition to,* rather than in lieu of, deductions for actual costs of earning gross income. Percentage depletion is thus an artificial tax deduction, reflecting no genuine costs of earning income, that simply reduces the effective tax rate on actual economic income. To this generalization there are two minor exceptions in the oil and gas industry. Lease acquisition costs and predrilling exploration expenses on properties later proved productive must be capitalized and are recoverable only through depletion allowances. It is estimated that these typically amount to 1 to 3 percent of gross income,[13] so only about 20 percentage points of the 22 percent allowance may be regarded as a deduction in excess of actual costs.

There is one further consideration. The Tax Reform Act of 1969 provided for a "minimum tax" of 10 percent of the excess of "preference items" among tax deductions (including percentage depletion allowances,

---

12. Or, in the oil and gas industry since the 1975 act, the 65-percent-of-taxable-income limitation.

13. Stephen L. McDonald, *Federal Tax Treatment of Income from Oil and Gas.* (Washington: Brookings, 1963), p. 17.

but not expensed capital outlays) over the sum of the unused cost basis, ordinary tax liability, and an exemption of $30,000 per taxpayer. This, too, for the typical minerals producer reduces the net benefit from percentage depletion.

To sum it up, the distinctive tax provisions applying to income from minerals production usually allow the affected taxpayer to make deductions from gross income that in total exceed actual costs incurred and to treat some major categories of costs as current operating expenses even though they are incurred to acquire assets of long productive life. These provisions may be viewed, then, as devices for reducing the effective rate of taxation on income from minerals production relative to that applying to ordinary income earned in other pursuits. This point is illustrated in the following hypothetical, but not unrealistic, example representing a taxpayer in oil and gas production.

An Example from Oil and Gas Production

Refer to Table 1 and assume an independent operator in oil and gas production with two producing properties, A and B, each with a gross income after royalties of $500,000 in the given tax year. For the purpose of computing allowable percentage depletion, which is subject to the 50-percent-of-net limitation, he must make separate calculations for each property. He first deducts from the gross income of each property the costs attributable to that property, including expensed intangible development costs, to get the relevant net income. He then computes allowable depletion for each property as the smaller of 22 percent of gross income or 50 percent of net income. (The allowable rate on property B is only 20 percent due to the 50-percent-of-net limitation.) After deducting allowable depletion from net property income in each case, the operator may combine the remainder ($290,000, line 7) for purposes of further computation. He now deducts total costs of doing business not attributable to producing properties (line 8), such as dry hole costs on nonproducing properties, to get a taxable income of $140,000 (line 9). This is assumed to be subject to a tax rate of 48 percent, yielding an ordinary tax liability of $67,200.

The operator must now compute his "minimum tax" or tax on excess preference items. From total allowable depletion, the only relevant preference item, he deducts his unused cost basis to get "excess" depletion, and then further deducts the exemption of $30,000 and his ordinary income tax liability to get the base of the preference items tax ($82,800,

Table 1. Illustrative computation of effective tax rate of hypothetical oil and gas producer

	Properties		
	A		B
1. Gross income after royalties	$500,000		$500,000
2. *Less* costs attributable to property	−200,000		−300,000
3. Net property income before depletion	300,000		200,000
Less allowable depletion, the smaller of:			
4. 22% of gross income	−110,000		
5. 50% of net income			−100,000
6. Net property income after depletion	190,000		100,000
7. Total		$290,000	
8. *Less* all other costs of doing business (assumed)		150,000	
9. Net taxable income		140,000	
10. Ordinary income tax, 48%		67,200	
Additional tax on net "preference items"			
11. Percentage depletion allowed		210,000	
12. *Less* unused cost basis (assumed)		−30,000	
13. Excess depletion		180,000	
14. *Less* exemption		−30,000	
15. *Less* ordinary tax liability		−67,200	
16. Base of tax on net preference items		82,800	
17. Tax on preference items (10%)		8,280	
18. Total tax liability (15 plus 17)		75,480	
Economic income and effective tax rate			
19. Net before taxes per tax return		140,000	
20. *Add back* excess depletion (13)		180,000	
21. *Add back* excess intangible expenses over amortization charge (assumed)		45,000	
22. Economic net before taxes		365,000	
23. Total tax liability (18)		75,480	
24. Effective tax rate (23/22)		20.7%	

line 16). With the latter taxed at 10 percent, the total tax liability comes to $75,480 (lines 15 plus 17).

Since excess depletion does not reflect an actual cost and expensed intangible development costs overstate costs allocable to current income, the operator's economic income, as he would ordinarily record it for internal purposes,[14] is larger than his taxable income. To find economic in-

14. Most oil and gas companies do not expense intangible development costs for purposes of internal records. They recognize that these costs are incurred to acquire long-lived

come before tax we add to net before taxes per tax return (line 19) both excess depletion and the assumed excess of intangible expenses over amortization charges allocable to the present tax year (lines 20 and 21), getting a figure of $365,000 (line 22). The effective tax rate on economic income (line 23 divided by line 22) is then 20.7 percent.[15]

Although the foregoing example represents oil and gas production, the same principles of tax computation, with different percentage depletion rates and slightly different treatment of exploration and development costs, apply to other minerals producers.

Unneutrality and Misallocation of Resources

Since percentage depletion and the expensing privilege lower the effective tax rate on income from minerals extraction relative to that on income from other activities (e.g., manufacturing), they lower the long-run supply price of minerals and attract a greater application of resources to minerals extraction than would be the case if all sources of income were taxed at the same rate. This rather obvious effect suggests the standard economic criticism of such differential tax treatment—that it results in a misallocation of resources and a lower level of economic welfare in the country.[16]

The argument may be stated as follows: suppose that the tax in question is a flat-rate tax on net income, such as the corporate income tax in the United States approximates, and that the tax is not shifted but is borne by the equity investors in the taxed industries. Assume that before the tax

assets (productive wells) and that such costs are logically distributed over time in accordance with the receipt of income from these assets.

15. This figure is probably on the low side of a typical effective tax rate today. Leonard G. Rosenberg ("Taxation of Income from Capital, by Industry Group," *The Taxation of Income from Capital,* Arnold C. Harberger and Martin J. Bailey, eds. [Washington: Brookings, 1969]) estimated the average effective corporate income tax rate for firms engaged primarily in domestic oil and gas production in the period 1953–1959 to be 19.2 percent, in comparison with 51.5 percent for all corporations (pp. 126–127, 155). In that period the maximum percentage depletion rate was 27.5 percent, the tax on preference items did not exist, and the maximum nominal corporate tax rate was 52 percent. On the other hand, profit margins are presently (summer, 1975) higher than in 1953–1959, so that the effective percentage depletion rate is less depressed by the 50-percent-of-net rule. We may note in passing that Rosenberg found the effective tax rate in bituminous coal production to be 36 percent. No figures are reported for uranium production (or for shale oil extraction, a then nonexistent activity).

16. See, as a leading example, Arnold C. Harberger, "The Taxation of Mineral Industries," *Federal Tax Policy for Economic Growth and Stability,* a compendium of papers presented to the Joint Committee on the Economic Report, 84th Cong., 1st sess. (Committee Print, 1955), pp. 439–449.

is imposed two industries, minerals extraction and manufacturing, are earning an equilibrium rate of 10 percent on investment at the margin. Note that in the absence of the tax this is both the private and the social marginal rate of return. Now suppose that a 50 percent net income tax is imposed on both industries, so that the marginal private rates of return fall to 5 percent. Since by assumption the tax is not shifted, and since the relative marginal rates of return are unchanged, the before-tax (social) rates of return remain at 10 percent and the allocation of resources between the two industries is unchanged. Such a tax, applying equally to all sources of net income, is *neutral* and does not lower the level of national income or its growth rate.

Compare this result, however, with the consequences of taxing the two industries at different rates. Suppose income from minerals extraction is taxed at the rate of 25 percent while income from manufacturing is taxed at the rate of 50 percent, as before. Now on impact the marginal private rates of return fall respectively to 7.5 percent and 5 percent. At the margin, investment in minerals production becomes relatively more attractive. Consequently, capital flows out of manufacturing into minerals extraction until equilibrium is reestablished with the marginal private rates of return equal at, say, 6 percent. The differential tax treatment is *unneutral,* having induced a reallocation of resources; and the new allocation makes the country as a whole worse off. In minerals extraction the before-tax (social) rate of return at the margin is 8 percent, while in manufacturing it is 12 percent. Some capital that might have yielded society, say, 11 percent has been diverted to uses that yield society only, say, 9 percent. Put another way, starting with the new equilibrium situation, society can be made better off if capital that yields society 8 percent at the margin in minerals extraction is transferred to manufacturing where it yields society 12 percent at the margin; but this will not occur through voluntary private action.

It should be noted that the reallocation of capital (and probably other resources) associated with differential taxation implies that supply increases (supply price decreases) in minerals extraction while the opposite occurs in manufacturing. Therefore, in a closed economy or in an open economy where imports are supplied at rising marginal cost, the price of minerals falls relative to that of manufactured goods. Under the conditions specified, unneutral taxation implies alteration of relative prices in favor of the less-taxed industries—"favor" in the sense of leading to greater output and consumption of these industries' products. In an open economy with imports supplied at constant marginal cost, unneutral taxation of the sort described tends to decrease imports of minerals and increase imports of manufactured goods as their supply prices fall and rise, respectively, relative to the supply prices of imports.

The foregoing example assumes a flat-rate tax on business net income similar to the corporate income tax in the United States. The same principle applies, however, when there is differential treatment under a personal income tax with a progressive rate structure. Percentage depletion and the expensing privilege in minerals production lower the relative effective tax rate of a person or partnership engaged in such production, whatever the level of income, and induce a reallocation of capital and other resources in the direction of minerals production. And since tax deductions are worth more to persons in high marginal tax brackets, these special tax features tend to shift minerals production from those in lower tax brackets to those in higher, and to reduce the effective progressiveness of the personal tax rate structure. The expensing privilege combined with capital gains taxation is also relatively attractive to those in high marginal personal tax brackets, so this combination, too, tends to attract capital into minerals production (e.g., from movie stars) and reduce the effective progressiveness of the rate structure.

The argument concerning tax treatment of minerals production versus manufacturing applied equally to oil and gas production versus coal or other mineral production prior to 1975. As was noted earlier, the statutory percentage depletion allowance for oil and gas production is 22 percent of gross income, and prior to 1975 applied to all producers, but for coal production it is only 10 percent. Even allowing for possible differences in the significance of the 50-percent-of-net limitation and of capitalized costs undeductible in the two industries, it is apparent that oil and gas production was more favorably treated. Thus under the assumptions of the unneutrality argument the allocation of resources between these two mineral fuel industries was probably distorted by the then existing tax system in favor of oil and gas production. The same may be said about oil and gas versus oil shale, the maximum percentage depletion rate on the latter being 15 percent. Data are not available to the writer that would allow a conclusion concerning neutrality of the expensing privilege among the mineral fuels.

One difficulty in comparing the tax treatment of the several mineral fuels is that different degrees of processing occur after the application of special tax features and before the resulting fuels enter competitive uses.

Coal and natural gas need only be transported to users before being burned. Crude oil must be transported and refined into several different products, the principal one of which, gasoline, is not competitive with coal and gas. Oil shale must be retorted before yielding a product competitive with crude oil. Uranium must be processed to yield usable fissionable materials, and then is competitive with the other fuels only in the generation of electric power. About the best that can be done is to ask, as Gerald M. Brannon did,[17] "If all the savings from the natural-resource tax provisions were passed along to the consumer in the form of price reduction, what would be the percentage reduction in fuel cost for electricity generated from each fuel?" His answers were: oil, 13.2 percent; natural gas, 11.5 percent; coal, 3.4 percent; gas from coal, 1.4 percent; oil from shale, 4.5 percent; uranium, 2.8 percent. These figures suggest substantial unneutrality between oil and gas and the other mineral fuels prior to 1975, but not as much among coal, oil shale and uranium.

If the unneutrality argument is correct, and it seems perfectly valid under the no-shifting assumption, then society pays a price in lost welfare for differential taxation; and one must demonstrate some noneconomic gain (e.g., national security) that outweighs the cost, and which cannot be secured more cheaply by other means, in order to justify such taxation. It is simply naive of the favored industries to argue that there is a net economic benefit to society from artificially cheapening energy sources, for instance, by means of lower effective income tax rates. One such argument goes that growth of per capita income in the past has been associated with substitution of inanimate for animate energy, that cheaper inanimate energy induces more such substitution, that therefore by making inanimate energy cheaper through tax policy we stimulate growth of per capita income. The fallacy in this argument lies in implicitly equating private cheapening with social cheapening. We can effect the former by means of tax policy, but not the latter. And if we accelerate the substitution of inanimate energy for animate energy when the former has not fallen in relative social cost, then we lower the level and growth rate of per capita income, not raise them.

Nor, if the foregoing argument is correct, can the favored industries justify lower taxation on grounds of differential risk. Suppose that due to

17. Gerald M. Brannon, *Energy Taxes and Subsidies,* (Cambridge, Mass.: Ballinger, 1974), pp. 27–28. The derivation of these estimates is given in Brannon, "The Present Tax and Subsidy Provisions Relating to the Energy Industries," *Studies in Energy Tax Policy,* Gerald M. Brannon, ed. (Cambridge, Mass.: Ballinger, 1974).

differential risk, as for instance in the search for oil and gas, the equilibrium marginal rates of return in the absence of tax are 15 percent in minerals production and 10 percent in manufacturing. An unshifted 50 percent tax on each would lower the marginal rates of return to 7.5 and 5 percent respectively, leaving the *relative* rates of return the same and the allocation of resources unaffected. It is the relative rates of return that are relevant since under a proportional tax with full loss offsets the absolute risk, or dispersion of possible incomes, is reduced proportionately with the tax.[18] Thus even allowing for relative risk, under the no-shifting assumption, equal tax rates are neutral with respect to the allocation of resources while unequal ones are unneutral and hence economically wasteful.

The assumption that the tax in question is unshifted is tantamount, as we have seen, to the assumption that the tax itself is neutral. There is general agreement among public finance economists that the personal income tax is unshifted, but there is no such agreement about the corporate income tax, the tax relevant to most of the producers of minerals and other goods in the American economy. Many economists, including the writer, believe that the corporate income tax is largely shifted forward to the consumer in the form of higher prices. It is evident that since the inception of the corporation income tax the after-tax rate of return has been quickly restored after each increase in the tax,[19] but it is possible to interpret this result as the effect of factors other than shifting, such as a rise in economic activity,[20] and in itself it provides no insight into the direction of such shifting as may occur.[21] We cannot settle the disagreement here, of course, but we must consider the effect of possible shifting on the unneutrality argument.

Suppose the corporate income tax is shifted by raising product prices sufficiently to restore the after-tax rate of return on investment in each industry. Assume that rates of return reflect workable competition, so that inter-industry differences imply differences in risk, and that capital/output

18. Richard A. Musgrave, *The Theory of Public Finance.* (New York: McGraw-Hill, 1959), ch. 14.

19. Marian Krzyzaniak and Richard A. Musgrave, *The Shifting of the Corporation Income Tax* (Baltimore: Johns Hopkins, 1963).

20. John Cragg, Arnold Harberger and Peter Mieszkowski, "Empirical Evidence on the Incidence of the Corporation Income Tax," *Journal of Political Economy,* 75 (December 1967), 811–821.

21. For a complete survey of the literature on the problem see George F. Break, "The Incidence and Economic Effects of Taxation," in Alan S. Blinder et al., *The Economics of Public Finance* (Washington: Brookings, 1974), pp. 138–154.

ratios are rigid in the period required for shifting. Under these assumptions it can be shown that the corporate income tax is itself unneutral, tending to raise the relative prices of, and divert resources from, industries that are relatively risky and/or capital intensive.[22]

The argument goes as follows: the profit margin on sales of an industry, $n = N/S$, may be found as the product of the rate of return on capital, $r = N/K$, and the ratio of capital to sales, $k = K/S$. Thus:

$$\frac{N}{S} = \frac{N}{K} \times \frac{K}{S}$$

or:

$$n = rk$$

Accordingly, industries that have relatively high rates of return on investment (implying high risk, under our assumptions) or relatively high ratios of capital employed to sales, or both, will have relatively high margins of profits on sales. Now if a tax at rate t is imposed on profits, the before-tax margin on sales must rise at the percentage rate $t/1 - t$, and unit prices must rise at the percentage rate $nt/1 - t$, if the rate of return on investment is to be restored through forward shifting. It is evident, then, that industries with a high $n = rk$ must experience increases in their *relative* prices if all industries are taxed at the same effective rate. If demands have any price elasticity at all, resources will consequently be diverted from industries whose relative prices rise (high n) to those whose relative prices fall (low n). Equal effective rates are thus unneutral with respect to the allocation of resources among industries.

For example, consider two industries which before imposition of a profits tax have the following characteristics:

	A	B
Sales	100	100
Cost	95	85
Profit	5	15
Investment	50	100
	$r = .10$	$r = .15$

22. Carl Shoup, "Incidence of the Corporation Income Tax: Capital Structure and Turnover Rates," *National Tax Journal,* 1 (March 1948), 12–17; Stephen L. McDonald, "Percentage Depletion and the Allocation of Resources: The Case of Oil and Gas," *National Tax Journal,* 14 (December 1961), 323–336.

Now a 50 percent profits tax is imposed and is shifted forward. The new situation is:

	A	B
Sales	105	115
Cost	95	85
Profit B.T.	10	30
Tax	5	15
Profit A.T.	5	15
Investment	50	100
	$r = .10$	$r = .15$

The percentage increase in the price of A's product (P_a) is:

$$P_a = \frac{n_a t}{1-t} = \frac{(rk)_a t}{1-t} = \frac{.10 \times .5 \times .5}{.5} = .05 = 5 \text{ percent}$$

For B's product it is:

$$P_b = \frac{n_b t}{1-t} = \frac{(rk)_b t}{1-t} = \frac{.15 \times 1.0 \times .5}{.5} = .15 = 15 \text{ percent}$$

If it were desired to limit the rise in B's price to the same percentage as the rise in A's price, B could be allowed a special exemption from gross income (e) equal to 10 percent of the original gross income, found as:

$$\begin{aligned} e &= (rk)_b - (rk)_a \\ &= .15 - .05 \\ &= .10. \end{aligned}$$

Expressed as a percentage of the adjusted gross income (d), the special exemption (depletion allowance) would be approximately 9.5 percent:

$$\begin{aligned} d &= \frac{(rk)_b - (rk)_a}{1 + P_a} \\ &= \frac{.15 - .05}{1.05} \\ &= .095 \end{aligned}$$

Thus:

	A	B
Sales	105	105
Cost	95	85
Special exemption		10
Taxable income	10	10
Tax	5	5
Profit A.T.	5	15
Investment	50	100
	$r = .10$	$r = .15$

It is possible, therefore, that differential taxation could be consistent with neutrality (or more consistent than equal effective taxation) if the favored industry is relatively risky (high r) or relatively capital intensive (high k), or both. I have elsewhere offered evidence that the oil and gas industry in the United States has both these characteristics relative to manufacturing, the latter taken to be the industry where effective corporate tax rate most nearly approximates the nominal rate. Using Internal Revenue Service data for the years 1949–1956 (except for 1952, for which data were unavailable) [23] and excluding oil and gas producers with predominantly foreign or predominantly refining operations, I calculated the following pertinent ratios: [24]

	Manufacturing	Oil & gas production
Rate of return (r)	10.3%	14.5%
Capital intensity (k)	0.52	1.43
Neutralizing exemption (d)		14.5% of gross

The neutralizing exemption of 14.5 percent of gross income was for the period covered well below the estimated effective excess depletion rate of 23 percent (the maximum rate was then 27.5 percent) to say nothing of

23. U.S. Internal Revenue Service, *Statistics of Income, Part 2, Corporation Income Tax Returns, 1949–56;* and *Source Book of Statistics of Income, 1949–56.*

24. The author is indebted to Douglas Eldridge, then of the U.S. Department of the Treasury, for providing the (unpublished) petroleum industry data free of the influence of foreign operations. See Eldridge, "Rate of Return, Resource Allocation and Percentage Depletion," *National Tax Journal,* 15 (June 1962), 215.

the effect of expensing development costs, elsewhere estimated to be the equivalent of a special deduction of about 4.5 percent of gross income.[25] It is also below today's estimated effective excess depletion rate, after allowance for the tax on preference items, of 16 percent, plus 4.5 percentage points as the equivalent of intangibles expensing, a total of 20.5 percent of gross income.[26] Thus the package of distinctive tax treatment of income from oil and gas production is probably more than merely reneutralizing under the assumption of full forward shifting of the corporate income tax.[27]

The foregoing argument that percentage depletion and the expensing of intangibles may only offset in some degree the basic unneutrality of the corporate income tax is subject to a number of criticisms. First, it is widely doubted that the tax is shifted.[28] If it is not, the argument fails; and if it is only partially shifted, the conclusions of the argument must be modified in degree. Second, no one believes that the personal income tax is shifted, so distinctive tax treatment of minerals income is clearly unneutral to the extent that that tax is pertinent. Third, there is some doubt that the observed relatively high rate of return in the extractive phase of the petroleum industry is due to differential riskiness.[29] If it is due to imperfect competition, then it reflects distinctive tax treatment in part, so that the argument is circular. Fourth, one may attribute the relatively high capital intensity of petroleum extraction in part to wasteful overdrilling induced or permitted, in the period covered by the data, by state conservation regulation.[30] An induced inefficiency in the industry can hardly be used to rationalize distinctive tax treatment.[31] Fifth, since the corporate income tax is in effect a tax on capital, relatively favorable treatment of one group of corporations induces them to use relatively more capital per

25. Stephen L. McDonald, "Incentive Policy and Supplies of Energy Sources," *American Journal of Agricultural Economics,* 56 (May 1974), 402.

26. *Ibid.*

27. Data are not available to permit similar calculations for the other mineral fuel industries.

28. See note 21 above.   29. Eldridge, "Rate of Return," pp. 214–216.

30. Alfred Kahn, "The Depletion Allowance in the Context of Cartelization," *American Economic Review,* 54 (June 1964), 301. In the latter part of the period covered by the data there was in fact substantial excess capacity in the domestic oil industry. See Stephen L. McDonald, *Petroleum Conservation in the United States* (Baltimore: Johns Hopkins, 1971), p. 165.

31. Since the period of the data, state conservation commissions have reformed the allowable depth-acreage schedules that tended to induce overdrilling, and for several years prior to this writing operating rates have been close to capacity.

unit of output. Thus to the extent that the above argument rests on an observed high capital intensiveness in an industry with a relatively low tax rate, it is circular. Sixth, some students of the petroleum industry believe that the corporate income tax and the benefits of distinctive tax treatment are at least partially shifted backward to recipients of rent (lease bonuses and royalties).[32] To the extent that such shifting occurs, the relative prices of minerals are unaffected by tax or benefits, and equity rather than neutrality becomes the relevant issue.

But perhaps the most decisive consideration is this: even if the corporate income tax is shifted forward and is therefore basically unneutral, it does not follow that welfare is significantly increased by singling out the particular group of industries (minerals extraction) that enjoys relatively low rates of taxation. Risk and capital intensity differ in every industry; and if there are other more "deserving" industries, in the sense of more risky or capital intensive, then the relatively high tax rate for them implied by a relatively low rate for minerals extraction may make the allocation of resources worse, not better, and total welfare smaller, not greater. Clearly, it is unfeasible to have a different tax rate for every industry, particularly if one relevant characteristic (capital intensity) is affected by the tax rate, and is in any case likely to be changing with changing technology, so it may be best to make no distinctions and tax the incomes of all industries at equal effective rates.

When all is considered—the doubt that the corporate income tax is shifted, the possible weaknesses of the reneutralizing argument, and the unfeasibility of treating every industry distinctively under the corporate income tax—the case for favorable tax treatment of minerals income appears very weak. The weight of evidence and professional opinion would seem to lie with the view that such tax treatment probably induces a misallocation of resources and reduces the level of welfare in American society—that it should be ended. This conclusion is reinforced to the extent that the special tax features apply under an unshifted tax with a progressive rate structure (the personal income tax) and to the extent that royalty owners are beneficiaries of percentage depletion.

---

32. Paul Davidson, "Public Policy Problems of the Domestic Crude Oil Industry," *American Economic Review,* 53 (March 1963), 103–105; and Brannon, *Energy Taxes and Subsidies,* pp. 39–41.

The Problem of Landowners' Royalties

The application of percentage depletion to landowners' royalties and lease bonuses (hereinafter shortened to "royalties") [33] raises issues rather different from those involved in the case of operators who actively search for and produce the minerals. Mineral royalties paid to landowners consist largely of economic rent. [34] Except as they compensate for the income of alternative forgone land uses, such payments, unlike the payments for the use of labor and capital, are not socially necessary to bring forth supplies of minerals. They are a residual income, a "surplus," that accrues solely by virtue of ownership of a nonreproducible good. They could in principle be taxed at rates approaching 100 percent without adversely affecting supplies; and their relatively heavy taxation, by lowering the required rate of tax on income from labor, investment, and entrepreneurship, would tend to increase productive effort and resulting output. Thus there is definite harm to aggregate welfare from taxing royalties at a differentially low rate. [35] In addition, since most landowners' royalties are subject to the personal income tax, differentially favorable tax treatment in the form of percentage depletion creates horizontal inequities and reduces the effective progressivity of the rate structure.

The matter may be carried a bit further. The size of landowners' economic rent is not independent, under present conditions, of the benefits to operating interests of percentage depletion and the expensing of intangibles. Prospective lessees bid against each other in competition for exploration and production rights on promising land. The lower the prospective taxes on income from production (*ceteris paribus,* including the prospective price of extracted minerals) the higher the bids to landowners tend to be. Presently, with the United States a net importer of oil, the price of oil is determined by the marginal cost of imports, [36] which may be regarded

33. Lease bonuses as received may be treated by the taxpayer as advance royalties and hence subject to the percentage depletion allowance. However, if production never occurs on the land for which a bonus was paid, the taxpayer must recompute his tax liability for the years affected and treat the bonus as ordinary income.

34. Where the royalty owner has specifically purchased mineral rights, the royalty may be largely or entirely return on capital. But in this case the seller is the recipient of rent in the form of selling price (capitalized royalties).

35. Note that where a part of a royalty is to compensate for income lost from alternative land uses, such income would be subject to ordinary income tax.

36. Strictly, the price of "new" oil is fixed by the marginal cost of imports. The price of oil in production prior to October 1973 ("old" oil) is fixed by regulation at $5.25 per barrel. The marginal cost of imports is chiefly tax imposed by the OPEC countries; it is

as constant over the relevant range. Thus by lowering long-run marginal costs of domestic production, percentage depletion and the expensing of intangibles shift the margin of domestic production outward without lowering the domestic price and thus increase both the absolute amount of royalties and the share of royalties in the total value of domestic production.[37] Consequently, landowners are doubly benefited by percentage depletion, and the adverse economic consequences of taxing royalties at a differentially low rate are increased. There can be no doubt that, as it applies directly and indirectly to landowners' royalties, percentage depletion is a detriment to aggregate welfare. Percentage depletion should at least be eliminated on landowners' royalties.

Changes Affecting Oil and Gas in the 1975 Act

As earlier noted, the Tax Reduction Act of 1975 significantly modified the applicability of percentage depletion to income from oil and gas production. It is time now to discuss in some detail the changes made by the act.

The approach of the act, specifically Title V thereof, is to disallow percentage depletion on oil and gas production [38] and then to make exceptions to this general rule.

The first exception pertains to certain domestic gas wells.[39] Continued use of percentage depletion at a rate of 22 percent of gross income is permitted with respect to regulated natural gas, natural gas sold under a fixed contract, and any geothermal well in the United States determined to be a gas well. Regulated natural gas (subject to the jurisdiction of the Federal Power Commission) and natural gas sold under a fixed contract are defined as gas the price of which has not been, or cannot be, adjusted to

---

therefore independent of the level of percentage depletion enjoyed, for domestic tax purposes, by American producers in the OPEC areas.

37. This conclusion does not necessarily follow in the case of coal. The United States is a net exporter of coal, and if the foreign coal with which it competes is produced under conditions of rising marginal cost, as seems likely, then percentage depletion lowers the price of coal realized by domestic producers. Unless the elasticity of demand for coal is greater than unity, therefore, the amount of coal royalties is not increased by percentage depletion on income from mining. Natural gas is still another matter. Some gas is imported and interstate prices are regulated by the Federal Power Commission, while intrastate prices are free. Percentage depletion lowers long-run marginal costs of domestic production, and to the extent that additional supplies can find outlet in intrastate markets it lowers domestic prices and does not necessarily increase royalties. To the extent that new supplies must enter interstate markets, however, given the regulated price, royalties are increased by percentage depletion.

38. 26 USC 613A(a).   39. 26 USC 613A(b).

reflect the seller's increased tax liability incident to the repeal of percentage depletion for gas. The premise seems to be that new contract prices will rise to cover increased tax liability, and the present exception to repeal is intended to protect the incomes of those producers whose prices under old contracts cannot rise.

The second and only other general exception is the exemption of certain independent producers and royalty owners from the repeal of the depletion allowance.[40] For these taxpayers, percentage depletion is allowable on so much of the taxpayer's average daily production of domestic crude oil (or domestic natural gas) as does not exceed the taxpayer's depletable oil (or gas) quantity. The depletable oil quantity, according to the act, is the tentative amount given in Table 2, reduced by average daily secondary or tertiary production (which is treated separately). The depletable gas quantity in cubic feet per day is the depletable oil quantity multiplied by 6,000. Where the taxpayer has both oil and gas production, the depletable oil quantity is reduced by the oil equivalent of the depletable gas quantity claimed by the taxpayer. As the table shows, percentage depletion remains at 22 percent through 1980, but on amounts declining regularly from 2,000 barrels per day in 1975 to 1,000 barrels per day in 1980; then, the amounts remain constant at the latter figure while the percentage depletion rate declines to 15 percent by 1984. In 1984 and thereafter the amount and rate are fixed respectively at 1,000 barrels per day and 15 percent.

Table 2. Tentative depletable quantities of oil and gas and applicable rates of percentage depletion, 1975—

Year	Tentative depletable quantity (bbl. oil per day) *	Applicable rate of percentage depletion
1975	2,000	22
1976	1,800	22
1977	1,600	22
1978	1,400	22
1979	1,200	22
1980	1,000	22
1981	1,000	20
1982	1,000	18
1983	1,000	16
1984 and after	1,000	15

* Gas equivalent: 6,000 cubic feet per day per barrel of oil per day.

40. 26 USC 613A(c).

Secondary and tertiary recovery production is treated specially until December 31, 1983, but thereafter like any other production. Until that date the allowable percentage depletion rate is 22 percent on secondary and tertiary recovery production in the amounts given in Table 2 (or their gas equivalents).

Since the amount of production eligible for percentage depletion is limited for any given taxpayer, the definition of "taxpayer" for purposes of the act is critical. The act provides that in the case of partnerships the depletion allowance on eligible production shall be computed separately by the partners and not by the partnership.[41] However, in the case of businesses under common control or members of the same family (spouse and minor children), the allowable depletable quantities in Table 2 shall be allocated among the separate entities in proportion to their respective amounts of production.[42] This latter is obviously intended to prevent large entities from avoiding the limits on depletable quantities by spinning off or creating numerous controlled subsidiaries, each with its own depletable quantity.

Aside from the limit on percentage depletion imposed by the quantities and rates in Table 2, the act further stipulates that the percentage depletion deduction in a tax year shall not exceed 65 percent of the taxpayer's taxable income for the year, computed without regard to percentage depletion and loss carrybacks. However, amounts disallowed in a given tax year may be carried forward as a deduction to the next tax year, subject again to the 65 percent limitation.[43]

Most significantly, subsection (c) of the act, which retains percentage depletion on a limited basis for producers and royalty owners, is inoperative in the case of any taxpayer who, directly or through a related person, sells oil or natural gas or any product thereof through any retail outlet operated by the taxpayer or a related person, or to any person obligated to use a trademark of the taxpayer or related person or given authority to occupy a retail outlet owned by the taxpayer or related person.[44] It is also inoperative in the case of any taxpayer or related person who is a crude oil refiner and whose refinery runs exceed 50,000 barrels per day on any day of the tax year.[45] It is these provisions of the act that effectively abol-

41. 26 USC 613A(c) (7) (D).   42. 26 USC 613A(c) (8).

43. 26 USC 613A(d) (1).

44. 26 USC 613A(d) (2). A person is a "related person" with respect to the taxpayer if either owns a significant interest in the other or if a third person owns a significant interest in both.

45. 26 USC 613A(d) (4).

ish percentage depletion for major integrated companies (except on the exempted categories of gas), since by definition such companies refine large quantities of crude oil and sell gasoline and other products through service stations.

In summary, the Tax Reduction Act of 1975 effectively eliminates the percentage depletion allowance, except on certain classes of gas income, for integrated oil and gas producers; imposes limits, which grow smaller to 1984, on the amount of oil and gas eligible for the allowance and on the percentage depletion rate for independent producers and royalty owners; and restricts the allowance in any case to 65 percent of taxable income computed without allowance for depletion. The categories of production on which percentage depletion is still allowed are all domestic, so the allowance is eliminated on foreign production by American companies. The act does not affect the expensing privileges of minerals producers; nor does it affect the percentage depletion allowance on minerals other than oil and gas.

The Effects of the 1975 Changes

The changes just described, to be effective in the tax year of 1975, were made in the following setting. The price of "old oil" (oil in production before October 1973) is regulated at $5.25 per barrel by the Federal Energy Administration, but the regulation is due to end on August 31, 1975. The price of "new oil" is free of regulation but is limited by the marginal cost of imports, the latter being constant at the OPEC price plus transportation plus tariff. The price of natural gas in interstate commerce is regulated by the Federal Power Commission, while the price of gas in intrastate commerce is free. The regulated price is about one-fourth to one-third of the free price, and the average price appears to be well below the market clearing level.

On impact, the elimination or reduction of percentage depletion adversely affects current cash flow in the oil and gas industry and, more importantly, reduces the prospective rate of return at the current margin of exploration. Consequently, the long-run domestic supply prices of oil and gas rise (the quantities supplied at given prices fall). This means either (1) higher market prices for these minerals or (2) larger imports in the case of oil and greater deficiency of supply (and more severe rationing) in the case of gas.

In the case of oil, since the free price cannot rise above the marginal cost of imports, the reduction of percentage depletion cannot directly raise the price.[46] A rise in supply price (leftward shift in the supply curve) only means that the margin of domestic exploration and production contracts, and imports rise, until the domestic rate of return at the margin is restored to its competitive normal level. The contraction of domestic production and greater dependence on imports could be avoided, however, by increasing the tariff on oil by an amount equal to the increase in supply price due to reduction of percentage depletion. If under his present authority the President pursues a fixed import limitation goal, he will be led to increase the tariff by at least the increase in domestic supply price.[47]

In the case of gas, the average price is limited by the regulation of interstate prices and the inability of producers, due to long-term contracts and pipeline rigidities, to divert supplies quickly from interstate to intrastate markets. Thus an increase in domestic supply price does not necessarily mean an immediate commensurate rise in the average market price. However, it appears likely that the Federal Power Commission, concerned with growing deficiency of supply in the interstate market, will allow price increases in new contracts at least large enough to compensate for the increased tax liability of domestic producers. It is our judgment, therefore, that the reduction of percentage depletion will indirectly result in higher prices of both oil and gas.

How much higher? We estimate about 10–12 percent. This figure is derived as follows. The maximum percentage depletion rate is 22 percent. Due to the 50-percent-of-net limitation, the average effective rate in recent years has probably been about 21 percent. After allowance for alternative deductions sacrificed by opting for percentage depletion,[48] the effective excess depletion rate has probably been about 19 percent. Further allowance for the 10 percent tax on preference items brings the probable past net benefit of percentage depletion down to the neighborhood of 17 percent of gross income after royalties. Assuming an average royalty of 15 percent of the value of oil and gas produced, the supply price of oil and gas would be increased by about 14 percent by the total elimination of percentage depletion. However, the legislation of 1975 totally eliminates percentage depletion prospectively only for the "majors." As they

46. A deregulated "old oil" price could rise only to the level of the marginal cost of imports, which it would do regardless of change in percentage depletion.

47. As this is written (summer, 1975) the President has already raised the oil tariff by $2 per barrel with the stated aim of limiting imports.

48. Capitalized lease acquisition and predrilling exploration costs, estimated to average about 2 percent of gross income.

contract the margin of their domestic operations, rejecting the poorer prospects that formerly appeared barely profitable, the smaller independents will in part take their place. Some of the prospects rejected by the majors will remain attractive to independents retaining the depletion allowance, so the latter group will tend to expand operations (partly through new entrants), taking leases no longer competed for by majors and ultimately finding some of the oil and gas that the majors might have found. Thus the independent sector of the industry will grow relative to the major sector, and supplies of oil and gas will not be reduced as much (supply prices will not rise as much) as if percentage depletion had been totally eliminated for all. Hence our estimate of a 10–12 percent increase in the prices of oil and gas necessary to avoid greater imports or supply deficiencies.

What of competitive relations among alternative fuels? The supply prices of coal, shale oil, and uranium will not be affected by the 1975 legislation under discussion, since their percentage depletion allowances were not changed. But the demand for them, as alternatives to oil and gas in some uses, will be increased by the rise in oil and gas prices. Their prices will also rise, therefore, assuming upward sloping marginal cost curves, but not as much as if percentage depletion had been eliminated for all minerals.[49] The increase in demand for them as substitutes for oil and gas in some uses means that their share in total energy consumption will rise, given the oil import goal and the remaining supply deficiency, if any, in gas markets.

It may be that the recent reduction of percentage depletion in oil and gas production is the forerunner of total elimination of percentage depletion for all minerals. With total elimination, and assuming that the regulators would seek to avoid increases in oil imports or gas supply deficiencies, oil and gas prices would rise another 2–4 percentage points (a total of 14), since there would be no tendency for independents to replace majors at the exploratory margin. If the proportions of net depletion benefits to nominal percentage depletion rates for other mineral fuels were similar to those for oil and gas, the increases in supply price would be 14 percent for uranium, 9.6 percent for oil shale and 6.4 percent for coal. Allowing for the relatively low proportion of electricity costs accounted for by uranium in nuclear power plants, these latter figures suggest some substitution of other fuels for oil and gas, but not as much

49. The prospective price of shale oil will rise with the level of crude oil prices, since shale oil is a near-perfect substitute for crude oil.

as if the elimination of percentage depletion were restricted to oil and gas.

The proposition that the elimination of percentage depletion would raise the supply prices of the affected minerals must be qualified in consideration of the fact that owners of mineral interests, including royalty interests, presently have the alternative of selling their properties for capital gains, which, of course, are taxed at lower rates than ordinary income. Explorers for and developers of mineral deposits might well find that they would pay more taxes than with percentage depletion, but less than if taxed at ordinary rates, if they expensed eligible investment outlays against ordinary income and sold their properties for capital gains.[50] If this were widely true and the law pertinent to capital gains were not changed, then the increases in supply prices would be smaller than indicated above.[51]

Conclusion

Under the assumption that the corporate income tax is not shifted forward in higher prices, percentage depletion and related expensing privileges in minerals production result in significant misallocations of resources, both between minerals production and other activities and among different minerals. This conclusion is only weakly modified under the assumption that the corporate income tax is shifted forward. In addition, horizontal inequities result from the application of percentage depletion and expensing to personal income taxation, as well as from their combination with special treatment of capital gains. It therefore seems likely that substantial welfare gains could be realized from the abolition of these tax provisions applying singularly to minerals production, especially percentage depletion. With suitable increases in the oil tariff and regulated natural gas prices, these gains could be realized without increasing oil imports or worsening the supply deficiencies in gas markets.

50. In the usual case in the oil industry at present, with percentage depletion, the purchaser of a mineral property finds it most profitable to use cost depletion, based on the purchase price, rather than percentage depletion in calculating tax liability on income from production. The exception to this rule obtains when price increases, not anticipated and capitalized in purchase price, occur subsequent to purchase.

51. It may be noted incidentally that the most likely sales for capital gains would be by independent explorer-developers to large integrated companies seeking to insure dependable supplies for downstream processing (e.g., oil refining). Thus production might become more concentrated in consequence of eliminating percentage depletion without tightening capital gains rules.

3

Disposal Policy for Energy Resources in the Public Domain

Robert J. Kalter and Wallace E. Tyner

The effects of government policy on domestic energy supplies are nowhere more apparent than in the disposal of energy resources located on the public domain. With the continuing depletion of proven energy reserves located on private lands, it is now clear that these public areas may become our chief source of supply over the next twenty-five years. Consequently, the strategy and schedule for leasing the millions of acres involved will become increasingly important. An indication of future production possibilities can be obtained from U.S. Geological Survey data. It has been estimated that 65–130 billion barrels of oil and 395–790 trillion cubic feet of natural gas may underlie our outer continental shelf (OCS) areas.[1] Recently, however, these estimates have been reduced to 10–49 billion barrels of oil and 42–181 trillion cubic feet of natural gas.[2] Depending on the estimation technique used, this could mean that between 13 and 50 percent of all remaining domestic oil and natural gas resources is located in such areas. Additional large accumulations are known to exist under onshore public lands. Moreover, the Geological Survey has estimated that over 50 percent of the coal resource, 75 percent of the oil shale resource, 40 percent of the uranium resource, and 60 percent of the geothermal energy lie on public lands.[3] Yet only a small por-

This study is based on research supported by the National Science Foundation.

1. Council on Environmental Quality, *OCS Oil and Gas: An Environmental Assessment* (Washington, 1974), pp. 2–1 to 2–20.

2. B. M. Miller et al., *Geological Estimates of Undiscovered Recoverable Oil and Gas Resources in the United States,* Geological Survey Circular 725, prepared for the Federal Energy Administration (Washington, 1975).

3. U.S. Congress, Senate, Committee on Interior and Insular Affairs, *Federal Leasing and Disposal Policies,* 92d Cong., 2d sess., June 19, 1972, p. 197.

tion of these potential energy reserves has been leased to the private sector for development. On the OCS, for example, leasing has been underway for over twenty years but less than 5 percent of the available acreage has been opened to bid. The proportion of other public energy resources leased is far smaller.

Recognition of the importance of these resources has led to numerous examinations, by the executive, Congress, the public, and the energy industry, of the policies by which public lands are leased or allocated to the private sector for development.[4] Many changes in current policy and statutory requirements have been suggested and debated. The purpose of this chapter is to summarize the background of this debate and to indicate the significance of policy choices for the development of an overall energy strategy. Proposed modifications in our leasing programs will be evaluated on the basis of the impact such changes would have on relevant social objectives. Finally, the need for, and the prospects and consequences of creating, a comprehensive apparatus to make decisions about publicly owned energy resources will be discussed. Although the primary focus of public attention to leasing issues has been on OCS development, on-land hydrocarbon deposits, as well as geothermal and uranium resources, must also be considered. As will be pointed out, understanding the interrelationships among the various resources may be vital to the design of a workable future policy.

Historical Background

The U.S. Department of the Interior has been and will apparently remain the focal point of federal energy leasing. Operating under the authority of numerous statutes, the department initiates and conducts almost all leasing of energy resources, and manages related production.[5] Even those lands where the surface is managed by other agencies usually come under the scope of Interior, with the management agency's concurrence,

4. *Ibid.*, pp. 1–664; U.S. Congress, Senate, Committee on Interior and Insular Affairs, *Outer Continental Shelf Policy Issues,* 92d Cong., 2d sess., 1972; A. P. H. VanMeurs, *Petroleum Economics and Offshore Mining Legislation* (Amsterdam: Elsevier, 1971).

5. The Mining Law of 1872 (30 USC Secs. 21–54) provides statutory authority for leasing public lands for uranium development. The Mineral Leasing Act of 1920 (30 USC Secs. 181–287) and the Acquired Lands Leasing Act of 1947 (30 USC Secs. 351–359) provide legal authority for onshore development of oil, natural gas, coal and lignite, oil shale, and tar sands. The Outer Continental Shelf Lands Act of 1953 (67 Stat. 462; 43 USC Secs. 133–1343) provides authority for offshore resource development. The Geothermal Steam Act of 1970 (30 USC Secs. 1001–1025) provides for geothermal resource development.

for resource leasing purposes. In addition, Indian lands come under the department's oversight.

On the basis of legal mandates stipulated by the various enabling statutes, Interior has generally considered its leasing objectives to be threefold: (1) to insure an orderly and timely development of the resource in question; (2) to protect the environment; and (3) to insure the public a fair market value return on the disposition of its resources.[6] In general, these three goals apply to all resources under public control regardless of location or type. Although the objectives are broadly stated, they serve to highlight social concerns, which a program for leasing public property must take into account. On the other hand, numerous more specific considerations are left unstated. For example, consumer price effects, balance of payments issues, and regional equity impacts all affect the goal of orderly and timely development. Receipt of fair market value can encompass issues ranging from market structure to the government's need for additional revenue. The interdependence of fair market return with processes of timely development is obvious.

Potential conflicts and complementarities among multiple leasing objectives, whether broadly or narrowly stated, can easily be discerned. The relative weights or trade-offs between the objectives are matters of subjective judgment which must be at least implicitly considered before new or changed policies are established. Many believe that protection of the environment should have a very heavy weight in leasing decisions; witness the concern over the Santa Barbara oil spill, strip mining legislation, and drilling off the Atlantic and Alaskan coasts. Others are concerned about revenue generation (for example, the Office of Management and Budget) or public giveaways to the private sector (resulting from excessive leasing relative to market demand or poorly designed leasing systems).[7] Regardless of who conducts leasing policy, some balance of various social objectives is implicit. The degree of emphasis placed on particular goals will, to a large extent, determine the policy mix.

6. In addition to the guidelines provided by the statutes mentioned in note 5, the Mining and Minerals Policy Act of 1970 (30 USC Sec. 21a) describes national minerals policy, and Title 31 USC 483 obligates the federal government to obtain fair and equitable return on resource disposition. Finally, the National Environmental Policy Act of 1969 (42 USC 4321–47) details the environmental protection goals under which government action can take place.

7. Council on Economic Priorities, *Leased and Lost: A Study of Public and Indian Coal Leasing in the West* (New York, 1974); U.S. Congress, Senate, Committee on Interior and Insular Affairs, *Federal Leasing and Disposal Policies,* 92d Cong., 2d sess., June 19, 1972, p. 102.

The broad administrative authority to set the tone of a national leasing program rests with the Interior secretary. It is his department that now decides the sequence of lease sales for various energy sources, the magnitude of each sale and the lease stipulations designed to mitigate adverse environmental or other impacts.[8] Yet, Department of the Interior prerogatives are often severely limited by legislative provisions. In passing enabling legislation, Congress apparently decided both to outline program goals and to establish constraints (or incentives) that would direct leasing behavior toward their achievement. As is now becoming clear, these provisions, passed at various times in history and under different circumstances, are not necessarily consistent for different resources nor applicable to current conditions. Their continued retention reduces flexibility in setting lease terms, affects achievement of current social goals, and makes formation of an overall strategy more difficult.

Table 1 summarizes a number of the leasing rules established by statute for the various energy resources. The method of leasing, applicable royalty rates and rental fees, lease terms and diligence requirements, tract sizes and holding limitations, government revenue sharing provisions, and special tax legislation all influence the behavior of the private sector. As the table shows, these factors vary considerably among resources. In addition, provisions governing specific issues often set lower or upper limits, within which the Interior secretary has discretionary authority. For example, royalty rates on OCS production cannot, by law, be lower than 12.5 percent of market value. The secretary, however, has traditionally set the rate at 16.67 percent.

The discretionary authority, legal limits, and legal mandates have all provoked controversy. Furthermore, key questions such as where, how, and when to lease various resources remain with no comprehensive framework designed to provide the information needed for their resolution. Lack of executive foresight and leadership must share the blame with ineffective legislative oversight for the failure to develop a comprehensive national leasing strategy.

Enlightened government policies will be crucial in balancing the country's need for energy with other national goals such as environmental preservation. Regardless of the degree of foreign dependence that is ultimately decided upon, new sources of domestic supply will be needed.

8. In a lease sale, the right to develop a resource is sold by competitive bid, and a lease on the property is granted to the winning bidder. The lease holder is granted the right to explore for and produce any resources found on the tract.

Reduction in the current rates of consumption will not be sufficient. Declining production from our existing reserves, along with any growth in population and economic activity, will make this need a physical reality. Monopoly prices in the world market will provide the economic incentive for development.

Proposed Changes in Leasing Procedures

For purposes of discussion, we will artificially separate alternative leasing policies into those that directly relate to the economics of a specific leasehold and those that set the scope of an overall disposal program. The former will be the subject of this section. Since such policies directly affect competitive bidding decisions in general and the production profiles on an individual lease, they in part determine our ability to meet social objectives. For example, procedures which derive "fair market value" from a given lease imply that this objective will also be met in an overall program (subject to any market price effects owing to the number of tracts leased). On the other hand, "orderly and timely development" is more dependent on the scope of the program (subject to appropriate economic policies applied to individual leases). Thus, although the leasehold aspects are only one element that must be considered, they can encompass such issues as leasing method, tax policy, tract size and ownership restrictions, and the lease term. Questions of resource information and industry competition are closely associated with a resolution of these issues.

Leasing Method. A review of the second column in Table 1 reveals that the leasing methods or bidding systems used for various publicly held resources vary substantially. Although competitive bidding predominates, it is not universally required. Experience clearly indicates that disposal by noncompetitive bidding fosters speculation, postpones production on leased lands, and fails to capture windfall profits (economic rents) for the government.[9] But a leasing system entails more than the presence or absence of competitive bidding. Given that competitive bidding is preferable, the issue is one of what mechanism is appropriate.

Currently, a cash bonus bid coupled with a fixed production royalty is the system most widely used. In such cases, the winning bidder is the one who offers the highest lump sum payment (the cash bonus) at the time of a competitive sale. A portion of that payment is due on the sale date and

9. Council on Economic Priorities, *Leased and Lost,* p. 7.

Table 1. Statutory provisions applicable to leasing procedures and behavior on public lands

Resource	Bidding system	Royalty rate	Rental fee/year	Lease term
Oil and natural gas				
OCS	Competitive sealed bid—cash bonus *or* royalty basis.	Not less than 12.5% of market value.	Discretion of Interior secretary.	5 yrs. with renewals and amendments.
Onshore	Competitive for Known Geological Structures (KGS)—cash bonus *and* fixed royalty basis. Non-competitive for other areas.	Not less than 12.5% of market value.	$2/acre minimum for competitive lease; $.50/ac. min. for non-competitive.	10 yrs. with renewals.
Coal	Same as onshore oil.	Not less than $.05/ton but may be a percentage based on value.	1st yr.: $.25/ac. min.; 2nd yr.: $.50/ac. min.; 6th+ yrs.: $1/ac. min.	2 yrs. for permits; indeterminate for leases with 20-yr. readjustments.
Oil Shale	Competitive—cash bonus and fixed royalty basis.	Discretion of Interior secretary.	$.50/ac. min.	Same as coal leases.
Uranium	Same as onshore oil for acquired and AEC withdrawal lands; prospecting permit, preference lease, and patent claims on other lands.	None for patent claims; discretionary otherwise.	Same as royalty.	None on patent lands.
Geothermal	Same as onshore oil.	Not less than 10 or more than 15% of steam or other energy value until 35 yrs. after production starts; then max. of 22.5%.	$1/ac. min.	10 yrs. with renewals to 40 yrs. if producing; with a second 40 yrs. term possible.

Table 1. (Continued)

Diligence requirements	Lease tract and holding limitations	Revenue sharing	Percentage depletion allowance	Expensing intangible drilling expenses
Oil and gas production yielding returns in excess of operating costs.	Lease tract limited to 5,760 acs.; no individual limitation on holdings.	None	Not allowed	Yes
Same as OCS.	Lease tract limited to 640 acs. (competitive) or 2,560 acs. (non-competitive); holdings limited to 246,000 acs. total.	37.5% to the state.	Not allowed	Yes
Diligent development and continued mine operation; or payment in advance of annual royalty and rental fees.	Holdings not in excess of 46,080 acs./state.	37.5% to the state.	10% of gross income not to exceed 50% of net income/tax period.	No
Same as OCS.	Lease tract limited to 5,120 acs.; not in excess of 5,120 acs. total holdings.	37.5% to the state.	15% of gross income not to exceed 50% of net income/tax period.	No
None on patent lands.	None	None	22% of gross income not to exceed 50% of net income/tax period.	No
Production of commercially demineralized water.	Leases not in excess of 2,560 acs.; holdings not in excess of 20,480 acs./state to 1985, then 51,200 acs./state.	None	Not allowed	No

the remainder within thirty days. It is nonrecoverable if production does not take place from the tract. If production does occur, a royalty based on a percentage of gross value is also paid (on the OCS, this is currently only 16.67 percent).

Alternative systems have been suggested that would retain the cash bonus as the bid variable but substantially increase the current royalty rate or substitute a profit sharing provision. The result would generally be lower bonus payments and a shifting of development risk to the government. Other proposed systems fix the cash bonus (at a low level) and use the royalty or profit share rate as the bid variable. In other words, the bidding competition is based on the share of production or profits the bidders are willing to turn over to the government. Numerous variations on these themes have also been proposed.

The choice among these and other systems depends on the weights given a number of the specific impacts that result. The selection can affect annual rates of production (through investment), production lifetimes of given deposits, government revenue from the bidding and production process, the extent of resource recovery from a deposit, the allocation of risk, the possibility of speculation in bidding and/or resource holding, and the degree of competition attending the leasing process. Alternative bidding systems affect these factors because, once a lease is granted, a private sector lessee has control over the amount of investment committed, the time horizon for production, and (to some extent) the annual rate of decline in production (when that is a relevant geologic consideration). The leasing method can result in a modification of lessee behavior in these regards. In addition, implicit differences exist among systems with regard to risk sharing and barriers to entry in the bidding process.

The authors have elsewhere evaluated the possible impacts of alternative bidding systems.[10] Table 2 compares several of the suggested systems to the cash bonus approach (assuming the private sector is indifferent to the risk of developing a specific tract). In general, royalty lease arrangements tend to shift production profiles toward the future with lower annual production rates (because investment levels are reduced).

10. Robert J. Kalter, et al., "The Economics of Outer Continental Shelf Leasing," *American Journal of Agricultural Economics,* 57 (May 1975); Robert J. Kalter et al., "Alternative Energy Leasing Strategies and Schedules for the Outer Continental Shelf," A. E. Research Paper 75–33, Cornell University, December 1975; Thomas H. Stevens and Robert J. Kalter, "The Economics of Oil Shale Resource Allocation Policy," *Land Economics,* November 1975.

Table 2. Alternative leasing systems compared to the current cash bonus

Variable	Increase in fixed royalty	Floating royalty bid	Fixed profit share *
Investment	−	−	=
Production time	+	+	=
Annual production	−	−	=
Government revenue	−	−	=
Total recovery	Depends on geological factors		
Possible no bid	Yes	No	Yes
Possible speculation	?	Yes	?
Increased bidding competition	?	?	?

* Associated with a floating cash bonus to capture any excess rents. Assumes no tax distortions and an appropriate tax base. Tax distortions (i.e., the depletion allowance) tend to reduce investment, production, and government revenue while increasing production time.

For hydrocarbon deposits whose production depends on natural or artificial geological pressures (oil and natural gas), resource recovery may also be increased. As a result of these combined factors, the present value of government revenue may be reduced.[11] Profit share arrangements tend to produce behavior similar to that resulting from cash bonus bidding in the absence of other tax distortions. Contingency leasing systems with high fixed charges (royalty or profit share rates) can, in some circumstances, lead to a lack of bids and no production. This occurs when the marginal cost of developing a tract will exceed the marginal revenue from doing so owing to the high fixed per unit charges or to tax code definitions in the case of a profit share system. This problem is substantially alleviated by contingency systems that vary rates with annual production or value (inversely). Contingency lease arrangements also result in greater risk sharing among the involved parties, since ex ante estimates of economic rent are at least partially verified by actual experience prior to

11. Present value is calculated by discounting and summing the stream of future income. This equates the value of future income with present income given a rate of time preference (the discount rate). The formula for discrete discounting is:

$$PV = \sum_{t=1}^{T} \frac{B_t}{(1+r)^t}$$

where B_t is income (or benefit) in year t and r is the discount (or interest) rate. For example, if the discount rate is 10 percent, $100 received one year from now is worth $90.91 today. By using present values, one can evaluate different streams of income on a comparable basis.

the payment of such rents to the government. Thus the government, which now shares only a small portion of the risk (assuming bidders operate on an actuarial basis), would assume a substantially greater amount under a contingency system.

Contingency bidding systems may also lead to increased speculation in bidding and/or deferred production. Diligence requirements in lease contracts could prevent deferred development, but not lease abandonment, which is a potential result of speculative bidding. In such cases, a bidder could make an unrealistically high contingency bid, beat the competition, and explore in the hope that the resource discoveries will exceed mean prebid estimates (leading to economies of scale in development). From the bidder's standpoint this is rational behavior. If the large deposits were not discovered, the lease could be abandoned with only a small investment having been made compared with other bidding systems. Although the tract could then be rebid, production time would be lost and government transactions costs increased. Cash bonus bidding with its large front end payments (sunk costs) also provides an economic incentive to develop greater production capacity than do contingency systems under comparable resource conditions.

Finally, contingency leasing could change the degree of competition in lease sales. It is often argued [12] that, by reducing early capital outlays, contingency lease systems would reduce barriers to entry into the bidding process, permitting smaller firms to participate.[13] Recent analysis of a royalty bidding experiment carried out by the government on the OCS has tended to confirm this hypothesis.[14] Other considerations, such as total liability for environmental damages and high development costs, however, may still limit entry (because of capital requirements) for areas like the OCS. This may be less true for on-land areas.

Firms involved in bidding competition, however, may not be risk neutral as assumed. In fact, the mix of firms involved is likely to hold a wide

12. H. E. Leland et al., *An Economic Analysis of Alternative Outer Continental Shelf Petroleum Leasing Policies,* Prepared for the Office of Energy R&D Policy, National Science Foundation, August 1974; U.S. Congress, House of Representatives, Subcommittee on Activities of Regulatory Agencies, Permanent Select Committee on Small Business, *Energy Data Requirements of the Federal Government,* 93d Cong., 2d sess., April 11, 1974, pp. 377–393.

13. Until recently, on the OCS for example, 62 percent of the leases were held by ten petroleum companies. U.S. Congress, Senate, Committee on Interior and Insular Affairs, *Federal Leasing and Disposal Policies,* 92d Cong., 2d sess., June 19, 1972, p. 199.

14. U.S. Department of the Interior, Office of OCS Program Coordination, *An Analysis of the Royalty Bidding Experiment in OCS Sale #36,* undated.

range of subjective judgments concerning risk. As a result, the firm that is least risk adverse, *ceteris paribus,* is likely to outbid the competition, assuming all firms require the same risk-free profit rate. If larger firms are risk neutral for a given tract, because of their ability to spread the risk over a large number of enterprises, changing lease systems may not increase competition. Competition would increase only if the government totally accepted all types of risk involved or if the range in risk adversion among firms was sufficiently narrowed by changing the bid system to make risks inconsequential.

The results summarized in Table 2 clearly show the economic superiority of cash bonus over royalty bidding in a competitive market. Because royalty payments act as a per unit tax, they modify a firm's behavior in a nonneutral manner, causing changes in production and the amount of government revenue (economic rent) received. The amount recovered may be increased for oil and natural gas reserves (where decline rates affect recovery), but may be equal or lower for other resources where annual production rates are essentially fixed by investment. Also, certain conditions (like lumpy investment or rapid increases in annual production costs) could reduce production time horizons, government revenue, and recovery even if annual production under a royalty system were equivalent to that under cash bonus. This would further reduce the desirability of a royalty system. The increased possibilities of speculation and of leaving a marginal discovery undeveloped are added factors which argue against a royalty bidding system.[15] On the other hand, a profit share system that would provide results equivalent to other systems by proper manipulation of the profit share rate and the associated income base could be designed. Yet a profit share bid system does not appear very different from a royalty approach in regard to possible speculation. Combinations of fixed profit share and bonus bidding could avoid this difficulty and may deserve further evaluation.

In the end, however, the question of which leasing system to adopt may depend largely on issues of risk and risk sharing, the degree of competition in the bidding process, and efficiency in production. It is commonly argued that royalty bidding is more competitive, since smaller firms are excluded from bonus bidding because of the large capital out-

15. The recent experiment by the Department of Interior with royalty bidding on Gulf of Mexico tracts appears to confirm the possibility of speculative behavior. Several tracts whose resource potential was judged low or nonexistent by geologists were, nonetheless, bid for and leased at relatively high royalty rates. *Ibid.*

lays required and the high degree of risk. It can also be argued that the royalty bidding system does not necessarily result in the most efficient firm winning the bid. The same arguments regarding risk and competition are advanced regarding profit sharing. Our analysis has indicated, however, that some forms of profit sharing can be just as efficient as the current cash bonus system in terms of speed of production and government revenue. If risk or lack of competition is a major factor in bidding, a profit share system could be to the advantage of the government, in that production can occur just as rapidly as under the current bonus system but the total government revenue may be higher (because of the elimination of a risk discount from the bonus bid). Profit sharing does require the government to accept much of the risk that the private sector currently bears. Consequently, the amount of government revenue collected from all leasing activity will be heavily dependent on the geological conditions actually found and economic factors obtaining at the time of production. However, if the public's principal interest is in collecting any actual economic rents involved, rather than taking advantage of uncertainty in information to collect government revenues in excess of those that would be forthcoming under certainty, this dependence would be appropriate. More important, a properly designed profit share system for public land disposal would not have the long-term disadvantage normally associated with this form of taxation: that of misallocating resources among industries. Profit sharing designed to capture only economic rent would act as a neutral tax with long-term allocation effects no different than those experienced under a riskless cash bonus system. On the other hand, profit sharing would be more difficult to administer.

In summary, assuming adequate competition and a minimal importance of risk, bonus bidding is an efficient system. If risk is important and/or competition inadequate, it appears that profit sharing is preferable to royalty bidding and at least comparable to bonus bidding. A cash bonus system in which the royalty rate varies with the value of production could also promote risk sharing without major inefficiencies. The empirical importance of the trade-offs involved requires further analysis. One important policy conclusion that evolves from the analysis of leasing systems is that the existing law should be changed to allow profit share systems, at least on an experimental basis. If such a leasing experiment were performed, the administrative problems associated with designing an appropriate profit sharing system could be gauged to provide a clearer indication of the actual trade-offs involved.

Tax Policy. Energy resource extraction industries have historically been granted perferential tax treatment through the use of depletion allowances and the provision for expensing intangible investment costs. As indicated in the final columns of Table 1, only the expensing option is available for oil and natural gas investment while the percentage depletion allowance varies substantially among the various energy sources. Until 1975, for example, percentage depletion up to 22 percent of gross income (not to exceed 50 percent of net income per tax period) was permitted on oil and natural gas production. It is now fairly obvious that this inconsistent pattern of tax advantages has caused some distortions in the development of energy supplies. To the extent that user technology makes possible, final demanders of energy are faced with differentials in long-run supply prices because of differences in effective tax rates. As Stephen McDonald has pointed out in Chapter 2 of this volume, this differential tax treatment has caused "substantial unneutrality between oil and gas and the other mineral fuels." Moreover, it is difficult to justify this differential treatment on the basis of noneconomic arguments such as national security. Technology can and does permit substantial shifts in fuel sources for many uses. Encouraging, rather than discouraging, use of our more abundant domestic energy sources would have reduced our current national security problems. In fact, the opposite approach has been taken.

In general, the special tax provisions applicable to resource extraction industries have the effect of lowering long-run supply prices and thereby increasing consumption, given a demand schedule for energy. The result has been not only distortions in the development of some fuel sources as opposed to others, but a purposeful subsidy which increases consumption of energy at the expense of other sectors. For these reasons most economists feel that elimination of special tax treatment would be in the best interests of the nation since it would lead to a more optimal allocation of resources. At the very least, the resources in question should be consistently treated.

As we indicated above, Congress recently eliminated the depletion allowance provision as it applied to oil and natural gas. Our analysis indicates that for federal leases, this change will have the effect of reducing investment, lengthening the production time horizon, reducing annual production, and slightly reducing present value government revenue. Since the various leasing methods are designed to capture economic rent, removal of a tax distortion such as the percentage depletion allowance will affect government revenue primarily in the present value sense. Any additional income tax revenue received due to the elimination of favorable tax treatment will reduce the direct bids offered for the leased areas (i.e., cash bonus). However, removal of the depletion allowance can also change government revenue by reducing investment. Since the depletion allowance was removed for oil and natural gas only, nonneutrality among possible energy sources continues to exist, though in reverse form. The relative supply prices of the various sources will again be altered by tax distortions, but that alteration will be no less arbitrary and capricious. If national security or other considerations argue for a turnabout in our traditional bias toward oil and natural gas, a more neutral approach, which would not distort domestic production for any resource would be a tariff upon foreign imports.

Tract Size and Ownership Restrictions. As Table 1 points out, existing legislation limits lease tract size in certain areas such as the OCS but is not a constraint on private acquisition of some other fuel sources. Conversely, no restrictions on the total number of tracts which can be acquired exist for OCS oil and gas, whereas many of the other resources are subject to such restrictions. Oil shale is the one energy resource which has both tract size and ownership restrictions connected with its leasing history.

Arbitrary tract size limitations may have the effect of causing nonoptimal development patterns for a given resource and between alternative sources. Tracts of the same size may contain quite different quantities of a resource. Assuming adequate information about resource distribution, tract size limitations can have the effect of requiring an economically nonoptimal scale of development or no development at all. Tract sizes based upon the quantity of a resource present rather than areal extent would be preferable. However, to make such a determination the leasing agency must have adequate information with respect to both the resource presence in particular areas and the economics of scale attainable in production activity. Acquiring appropriate information can be difficult for any public agency, and rapidly changing circumstances add to the problem. The resort has always been to rules of thumb or statutory limitations. Under such conditions, having the private sector bear the burden of proving the need for a change in existing restrictions or limitations seems most appropriate in view of the governmental transaction costs potentially involved in continued evaluation. Thus, provision needs to be made in the tract nomination process for this type of feedback from the private sector, and statutory flexibility must exist to permit appropriate management actions. It needs to be recognized, however, that the possibility of a tract assignment market may mitigate some of the adverse impacts of tract size limitations. If lease assignment between private parties is permitted (the current case), voluntary action will tend to consolidate tracts if an economic incentive is present and if the location of the tracts permits. Rents resulting from such economies of scale would not be collected by the public sector in this case.

Overall ownership restrictions can also have an important economic effect on resource development. Originally established to ensure the attainment of industry-wide competition, these regulations, if too inflexibly imposed, have other impacts as well. For example, the development of new technologies, such as those currently being contemplated for oil shale production, normally involves a substantial learning process. Economies that could be gained through such processes may not be achieved if ownership is limited to only one tract, as was the case with the prototype leasing program. The reasons for imposing restrictive conditions must be balanced against other implications the action has for social welfare.

Lease Terms. The length of time for which a given lease contract is valid provides the government with a management tool that can be utilized to ensure performance by the private sector in meeting social objectives. Although this contract provision is often used as a diligence requirement (that is, if production has not taken place within a given period of time, the lease contract is canceled), it can also be used to ensure compliance with environmental restrictions and as a mechanism for periodic review of economic terms. For example, it is often argued that a royalty bidding system will result in premature termination of production on a given leasehold because it is, in effect, an increase in operating costs, raising per unit costs over time. A short lease term with provisions for renewal and amendment could overcome this disadvantage by permitting a reduction in the royalty rate during the later years of production. Of course, adequate information must be available to the government if unfair advantage is not to be taken of this provision by the private sector.

Unfortunately, in the past, lease terms have often been established for such lengthy periods that they became inoperative as a management tool and/or were unused by the management agency. This has been particularly true of coal leases, for which twenty-year terms have been set by statute. Renewal of lease contracts at the end of that period has been almost automatic even though no production activity has occurred in the interim. Utilization of lease term requirements for management purposes, however, requires a careful and considered set of judgments on the part of the management agency. Substantial uncertainty as to how they will be used can inhibit private sector investments and retard development. A clear set of ground rules laid down at the outset by the agency, with lease renegotiation as a focal point for their review, is important for insuring achievement of objectives in situations of uncertainty.

Unlike a number of other factors relating to leaseholds, however, the determination of lease terms and renegotiation provisions requires administrative flexibility. When they are used primarily as management tools, sufficient latitude must be permitted to accommodate the varying situations that will be met in any comprehensive leasing program. For example, as OCS leasing moves into new frontier areas, a number of production conditions may change substantially. Areas of extreme weather fluctuation such as the Gulf of Alaska or the North Atlantic may require exploration and development periods in excess of the current five-year diligence requirement. Moreover, an interplay will often exist between the development period required for a given tract and the number of tracts (or acreage) leased over time. If the government does a large amount of leasing (relative to private sector capacity) in any given period, equipment and manpower bottlenecks may develop and result in production lags regardless of development intentions.

The Scope of Leasing Activity

To fulfill the three aims established by statute for public land disposal, policy makers must pay attention to the overall scope of leasing activity. What resources, where, when, in what amounts and under what market conditions become important, if not overriding, questions. Until relatively recently, these issues have received little explicit attention from either the executive or the legislative branch of government. Historically, the Department of the Interior has played a relatively passive role in determining which resource to lease, and in deciding the size and frequency of sales. Private sector initiative and the government's need for revenue have appeared to be the major factors motivating sales. Since market and institutional conditions have permitted higher rates of return from petroleum development than from other energy development on public lands, OCS leasing became the principal focus of attention. Only when acquisition and holding costs were low, as for coal resources, did the industry express interest in public lands containing alternative energy sources.

These leases were obtained mainly for purposes of speculation, and little significant government revenue resulted.[16] The bulk of the non-OCS sales that took place prior to 1973 would not have been permitted if proper planning and management policies had been in effect. Even for the OCS, the policy on lease sales was never clear. As a 1969 report of the Public Land Law Review Commission declared: "There has been no affirmative policy and the timing of sales appears to have been a function of industry demand and varying administrative pressures for increasing revenue to meet the fiscal requirements of the Federal Government."[17] In their 1973 book, D. E. Kash and his co-authors concurred in the feeling that sales were paced to keep bonus bids high.[18] Leasing schedules which do exist for the OCS, and for oil shale and geothermal areas, were conceived and implemented in isolation and have been subject to rapid change (depending on the crisis of the moment).

Given a sustained deficit in domestic supply and the problems it poses for national security, haphazard planning and management can no longer be tolerated. As we indicated earlier, an improved analytical and decision-making framework is needed. Such a framework must be capable of yielding estimates of the various costs involved in reducing our foreign dependence, as well as evaluations of the implications of alternative leasing strategies and schedules for all federal lands containing energy resources. The latter issue involves the integration of several policy concerns.

First, as was pointed out in the previous section, the direct impacts of individual leasing actions must be considered. However, these impacts cannot be weighed in a vacuum for each resource or leasing question. Leasing policies need to be tied to national energy policies. Thus a second requirement must be the ability to obtain information on the interactions among leasing, market conditions, and other government policies.

Without both components, any analysis of the long-term implications of leasing alternatives could lead to substantial misestimates. Because long time lags between a leasing action and resource production are common, decisions made now may not influence current supply but may have a pervasive influence in some future period. Consequently, the new element that is rapidly becoming important in planning leasing activity is the

16. Council on Economic Priorities, *Leased and Lost,* p. 7.
17. Public Land Law Review Commission, *Study of Outer Continental Shelf Lands in the United States,* Springfield, Va., 1969, p. 119.
18. D. E. Kash et al., *Energy Under the Ocean* (Norman: University of Oklahoma Press, 1973), p. 171.

design of an overall strategy (with respect to energy resource mix, timing, amount, location, and allocation method) which is interdependent with national market conditions and other public policies bearing on these markets. Such a strategy must recognize the extent and the types of uncertainty in each resource sector and the impacts this uncertainty can have on private sector behavior.

Design of a decision mechanism incorporating these features is a tall order, if not an impossibility at the present time. Yet some attention needs to be directed to the problems involved. The objective function of society should be to make optimal use of existing resources. In a context of economic efficiency, this means that government actions should not simulate those of the monopolist. Receipt of "fair market value" must be defined as a simple capture of the economic rents, not as an attempt to maximize government revenue. Concurrently, orderly and timely development must mean an attempt to release resources in such a fashion that the resource supply schedule is equated with the value of the marginal output schedule in each period. In addition, the marginal value of a resource unit (BTU) should be equated for each fuel source at the burnertip (taking account of utilization costs and external constraints on use). Any move in this direction will require coordination between the leasing sequence for various resources and exogenous factors impinging on either the development or the use of the resources in question. Material and manpower constraints, environmental aspects, regional impacts and dislocations, competition among fuels, monopoly power, import policy, time lags in economic activity, and taxation policy must all be considered.

In making decisions concerning a national energy leasing policy, additional information on these factors would be useful. The availability of information would not, of course, alleviate the necessity of making difficult choices on which strategy would be of greatest benefit to the nation as a whole. For example, the environmental risks of OCS development must be weighed against those of oil imports, shale oil, or coal, and total social values of the resources must be compared. Unfortunately, no comprehensive effort to deal with these questions has been made.

The Future Course of Public Policy

Although the what, where, when type of leasing questions are critical in defining the scope of an overall program, their resolution may come only after society, through the political process, establishes additional ground rules to shape private sector behavior. As Stephen Marglin has pointed out, the political process often has difficulty functioning optimally in view of numerous, and often conflicting, social objectives.[19] The subjective weighting required to implement a multidimensional social welfare function becomes difficult and the overall frame of reference becomes obscure when a series of decisions is made over time. Consequently, the decisions that are made often seek to achieve a single goal or a small group of objectives within a set of established constraints and/or incentives.

It now appears that at least four issues, in addition to a national policy on energy imports, will need resolution prior to or along with consideration of a comprehensive leasing program. These include the question of government subsidies or price guarantees to the private sector, the final establishment of environmental standards pertaining to energy production and use, the approach to acquiring resource information used by the government, and the mechanism designed for handling the regional impacts of energy activities.

Market Uncertainty. Risk aversion on the part of the private sector may necessitate government subsidies or price guarantees to ensure rapid development of resources like shale oil. In addition, the market uncertainty caused by environmental regulations such as the current sulfur emission standards may require resolution if our coal resource is to be significantly developed in the near future. Each of these market factors stems from the relative supply economics for alternative sources and the current institutional situation governing world energy markets. Middle East petroleum, which would be the principal supply alternative to increased domestic energy production, could be landed in the United States at a resource cost of about $1.50 per barrel. Assuming that least-cost sources would be exploited first in a free trade situation, these resources would be preferred for U.S. markets until their exhaustion (even if moderate tax and royalty rates were charged by producing nations).[20] Few sources of domestic supply can be produced as cheaply, even if adequate reserves exist. New offshore petroleum and natural gas production has a resource cost of from two to seven times that of developed Middle East oil. Shale oil costs fall

19. Stephen A. Marglin, "Objectives of Water-Resource Development: A General Statement," in A. Maass et al., *Design of Water Resource Systems* (Cambridge: Harvard University Press, 1962), pp. 67–87.
20. M. A. Adelman, *The World Petroleum Market* (Baltimore: Johns Hopkins, 1973); William D. Nordhaus, "The Allocation of Energy Resources," *Brookings Papers on Economic Activity,* No. 3, 1973, pp. 529–576.

in the upper end of that range. Only coal, although it has several times the resource cost of imported oil, provides a sufficient resource base to be competitive over the long term with pre-embargo oil prices. As a result of the monopoly power being exerted by the Organization of Petroleum Exporting Countries (OPEC), however, import oil prices now make most domestic alternatives economic. The problems for most new domestic sources are the long lead times needed for development and the high investment costs required. Substantial uncertainty exists regarding OPEC price intentions. OPEC is not only capable of substantially lowering world market prices but, after a period of time, it may be in the interest of the member states to do so in order to eliminate market competitors and preserve their own market shares. Their known reserves virtually guarantee their ability to continue as the least-cost alternative source of supply for many years. As if to add to this uncertainty, public officials periodically speak of breaking up the cartel by international policies aimed at substantially reducing consumption. The net result would be a lowering of oil prices, placing investments in higher cost alternatives in jeopardy.

In addition, potentially profitable investments, even at substantially lower world energy prices, may not be undertaken because of price regulations or environmental uncertainty. An example of the former is OCS natural gas, which may not be economic to develop in some areas (i.e., the North Atlantic) [21] because of price ceilings established by the Federal Power Commission.[22] An example of the latter is western coal resources. As Richard Gordon points out elsewhere in this volume, unless current air quality standards are relaxed or sulfur removal technology is developed which allows coal to be competitive with potential alternatives, coal may not increase its share of the domestic energy market. Even though western coal has a relatively lower sulfur content than that from traditional sources, it is also generally lower in heat value. Therefore the net effect, in terms of air quality, changes very little without removal of sulfur pollutants.

As a result of these market uncertainties, the private sector has tended to postpone new investments in alternative energy sources with long payoff periods. Witness the shelving of plans for oil shale development on private lands and the slow development of leased public lands contain-

21. Kalter et al., "Atlantic Outer Continental Shelf Energy Resources," p. 70.

22. Stephen G. Breyer and Paul W. MacAvoy, *Energy Regulation by the Federal Power Commission* (Washington: Brookings, 1974), ch. 3.

ing coal resources. Changes in the current ground rules, however, will require congressional action. Relaxation of environmental standards affecting coal usage has been proposed, along with wellhead price deregulation for natural gas and price floors for shale oil. Resolution of the former issue will depend on congressional perception of the interplay between time, the development of "workable" stack scrubbers, coal desulfurization technology, and the environmental hazards involved. The natural gas price question has become embroiled in a controversy over windfall and monopoly profits, and consumer protection. Even though economists are almost unanimously in favor of some form of deregulation,[23] it is unlikely to occur in the current atmosphere. Price guarantees may be no less controversial, although the need for them could be substantially lessened if a high tariff barrier were erected on imported fuels, assuming that the private sector perceived that barrier as being permanent. Other alternatives include the possibility of government investment guarantees, government participation in the investment, or public development. However, it is often difficult to distinguish between the amount of risk that the private sector is willing to assume over the long run and its short-run attempts to influence the share of risk to be accepted by government. Whatever approach(es) is (are) finally chosen, it appears that some reduction in market uncertainty will be required before sufficient supplies of energy from alternative domestic sources will be made available. The final decisions will be based more on the perception of risk by the various parties involved and the accompanying national security considerations than on free trade economics.

Resource Information Acquisition. Acquisition, by the government, of resource information relative to public lands is closely connected with leasing strategy and the limitations imposed on the development process. For example, determination of where to lease and at what rate could be done with much greater accuracy if better data on the reserves available in given areas were obtainable. Estimates of fair market value, used in deciding whether to accept private sector bids, would also be more accurate, and the potential environmental impacts of development could be more readily forecast. Thus it has been suggested that, rather than immediately leasing potential resource areas off the Atlantic coast, the government undertake an exploration program to determine the location and ex-

23. Patricia E. Starrott and Robert M. Spann, "Alternative Strategies for Dealing with the Natural Gas Shortage in the United States," in *The Energy Question,* E. Erickson and L. Waverman, eds. (Toronto: University of Toronto Press, 1974), pp. 42–43.

tent of probable petroleum resources. Similar suggestions have been advanced in regard to coal in the West, where most unknown resource areas have traditionally been explored under prospecting permits granted to the private sector with an exclusive right to lease after making a discovery. Obviously, fair market value is not captured in situations where discoveries are made, since the economic rents produced will normally far exceed the total exploration costs involved. Of course, under competitive bidding, rents, based upon the best available resource information, would be captured. At the least, it would seem that competitive bidding should be required, regardless of the information base.

Advocates of government exploration maintain that development time would not be lost because exploration must be conducted in any case and the government would stand to gain from higher revenues resulting from reduced uncertainty. In fact, the acquisition of resource information, seen in this light, becomes yet another method of risk sharing, like contingency lease systems. In other words, improved resource information should reduce the private risk premiums in bonus bidding just as contingency lease systems may result in increased risk sharing by the government and the private sector. With cash bonus bidding and improved information, the present value of government revenue should over the long run at least equal that derived under the current system, and planning activities (environmental and economic) should be enhanced.

On the other side, it is argued that government exploration might be less efficient, subject to increased political manipulation, and result in longer development time lags. Government revenue might also be unchanged if a contingency lease system (royalty or profit share) were in place or if risk were an unimportant element in the determination of winning bids. The costs and potential benefits of additional resource information obtained by the government need to be carefully explored before further commitments are made. However, if public leasing programs are not to be subjected to continued charges of giveaways to the private sector, this question must be satisfactorily resolved.

Regional Impacts. Energy resources are not equally spread throughout the country, and development in any one location may cause regional disruptions and inequities. On the one hand, it has been argued that leasing imposes a net fiscal burden on the local jurisdictions surrounding or adjacent to leased acreage. Requirements for schools, hospitals, transportation systems, and other infrastructure necessary to service the development activity occurring in leasing areas, along with the increased work force and associated population, may require public revenues in excess of those raised by additional taxes. Furthermore, adverse environmental impacts may result in regional disbenefits to such industries as recreation and fisheries, and to the public as a whole.

The Department of the Interior has long argued that, for the average state, no net fiscal burden was generated by activities such as offshore leasing. The claim is that the increase in economic activity resulting from leasing also increases revenue through the tax system.[24] However, because of the distribution of economic activity across the nation and the different socioeconomic characteristics of specific labor forces involved, the net impacts are likely to vary widely. More important, the structure of state and local tax systems will be critical in determining the government revenue collected. Gulf Coast states, for example, may achieve substantial benefits from Atlantic coast drilling because most of the support industry is already located in that region, but the tax structure may not be as well developed as for east coast states. Congress apparently recognized this possibility when it passed the 1920 Mineral Leasing Act. That legislation allocated 37.5 percent of the federal revenues collected from oil shale, coal, and onshore petroleum development back to the affected states for use in financing schools, hospitals, and highways. An additional 52.5 percent was credited to the Reclamation Fund used for constructing water resource projects in the West.

Demands are now building for some type of revenue sharing from all leasing activity in the public domain. The problem, however, is twofold. First, it is the "public" domain so that those areas not adjacent to leased areas may also have a legitimate claim on any shared revenue. Second, the derivation of an equitable formula for compensating affected states is complex and often difficult to implement. Ideally, those suffering a net fiscal burden should be compensated; but, conversely, those benefiting should be willing to aid in this compensation. Then any across-the-board revenue sharing (to all states) could be done equitably. The measurement problems involved, however, are severe and intertwined with jurisdiction questions. And now that leasing activity has begun to generate substantial amounts of public revenue on a sustained basis, these problems will become major political issues. In the end, a satisfactory formula will have to be found for revenue sharing. Society does not appear ready to accept the equity implications of our current approach to this problem. Coupled

24. U.S. Congress, Senate, Committee on Interior and Insular Affairs, *Federal Leasing and Disposal Policies*, 92d Cong., 2d sess., June 19, 1972, pp. 77–79.

with proper environmental safeguards, a satisfactory solution to the regional issues now being raised may be the single most important political factor in establishing a long-term comprehensive leasing policy.

Summary

It is clear from this discussion that the issues involved in national energy leasing policy are wide ranging and complex. We have reviewed existing leasing procedures for the various resources and some proposed changes in these procedures. The effects of alternative leasing procedures were examined, and the important policy implications highlighted. We concluded that bonus bidding is an efficient system if competition is adequate and risk is unimportant. Since these conditions are infrequently met, contingency lease systems offer some advantages which should be evaluated further. To this end, it is important that existing laws be changed to allow experimentation with profit share systems.

In the area of tax policy, we examined the effects of the special tax provisions granted to oil and gas production, and in different ways to other resource industries. The depletion allowance and the provision for expensing intangible investment have led to sectoral distortions in the national economy, and to misallocation of resources within the energy sector. Elimination of special tax treatment for energy industries is in the best interests of the nation because resources would be better allocated.

The effects of tract size limitations, ownership restrictions, and lease term were also evaluated. The current rules should be changed to allow tract size to be determined partly on the basis of resource content rather than on geographic area alone. Ownership restrictions currently imposed on some resources may not permit achievement of "learning" economies in the development of new resources. Hence the resource cost may be higher with a low fixed tract size. Lease terms are meaningless if lease provisions are not enforced. It appears that a fairly short lease term with provisions for renewal and amendment would best serve the public interest.

In addition to these issues directly related to leasing systems and policy, four other broader issues were also examined: (1) market uncertainty and public policy; (2) environmental standards relating to energy production; (3) resource information acquisition by the government; and (4) regional impacts of energy resource development. It appears that some form of public risk sharing for market uncertainty may be imperative if oil shale resources are to be developed. Investment participation or guarantee, price supports or purchase guarantee, or permanent tariff or quota systems could be used. It is important that the impacts of these alternatives be closely examined before a public policy is selected.

In addition to market price uncertainty, uncertainties stemming from regulation and environmental costs tend to discourage investment. Within the framework of a national energy policy and considering all relevant social objectives, these uncertainties should be resolved so that appropriate resource development may proceed.

Resource information could be acquired by the government before areas are offered for lease. Improving public information may be viewed as another method of sharing geological risk between public and private sectors. With better information, private risk premiums should be reduced and bids increased. However, the government may not be as efficient or timely as the private sector in collecting information. This is a very important, and often overlooked, issue that must be considered along with questions on leasing systems.

National energy development policy must also consider the regional impacts of resource development. Methods of compensating regions for regional inequities and dislocations caused by the development activity should be evaluated in the context of overall leasing policy decisions.

Energy resource development for the United States in the next decade is one of the most significant areas in which policy is now being formulated. It is important that policy makers give some attention to the whole package rather than just proceeding on a piecemeal basis. Inevitably, there will be lobbies for each region and for each resource, but these influences will be less likely to prevail if energy policy is viewed as an entire package. Within that package, the implications of various leasing systems, leasing schedules, risk analysis, resource information acquisition, and other issues must be carefully examined.

4

Energy Policy from an Environmental Perspective

John V. Krutilla and R. Talbot Page

Until recently we have taken energy for granted as a cheap, ubiquitous ingredient of our material welfare. Now we are learning differently. Gradually, over the past decade, we have become increasingly aware that energy is not quite so cheap when the environmental costs are included. The Clean Air Act of 1967, largely a recognition of the health costs associated with the emissions from coal-burning electric utilities, led to a massive shift from coal to oil. Then, in the face of our dependence on oil, we were more vulnerable to the 1973–1974 oil embargo—and that embargo seemed to draw the attention of the whole world to what was previously the domain of a few environmentalists and resource economists (and the energy industries). In consequence, for a year we had sobering thoughts on energy supply, energy dependence, and energy policy in general. Concern over the energy crisis caused by the embargo will no doubt pass away, crowded out by other crises, but we are still left with the task of formulating an energy policy suitable for the next decade and even the next century. And with the problems remaining unsolved, the crisis may reemerge at any time.

Our energy problems have been developing for many years, deepened by our own past actions. National policy has long followed the assumption that the more we extract and use our natural resources, the faster we build up the economy. The larger the volume of materials we process, the richer and more secure we become—and coal, oil, and gas are the largest material flows, in terms of value. By extracting "dormant" resources today, so the idea goes, we can turn them into productive assets, promis-

Originally published under the title "Towards a Responsible Energy Policy." Copyright © 1975 by the Regents of the University of California. Reprinted from *Policy Analysis,* Vol. 1, No. 1, pp. 77–100, by permission of The Regents.

ing future generations a higher level of well-being than they would enjoy if we were to let the resources lie fallow in the ground. This idea was applied not only to energy materials but to all our natural resources. For two centuries we favored mineral extraction on our national lands, codifying the practice in the 1872 Mining Law. We lowered the price of energy by subsidizing it with depletion deductions and other tax preferences; we further encouraged energy consumption by establishing a promotional price system with volume discounts for larger consumption. We reduced the ostensible cost of energy and materials by ignoring the environmental costs associated with extracting and processing them.

This exploitative policy toward natural resources does not appear to have been entirely intentional. Nor has it been completely uniform. Large areas of land have been preserved from development. The control of gas prices by federal regulation has discouraged exploration and development. Yet the bias in policy toward development and exploitation is pronounced. In the past this policy may have made sense: resources appeared limitless; pollution and other environmental costs associated with their extraction were relatively small and localized; and our comparative advantage vis-à-vis other countries lay in our abundance of natural resources.

Over the years our pro-exploitation policy has had an effect on the economy. As energy became cheaper in this country than in many others, we came to use it more and more intensively, ultimately becoming dependent upon large energy flows. Now that conditions are changing, we are caught in a pattern of our own making. Whatever our stated policy, we will be forced to rely on new domestic sources and to pay higher prices for energy in the years to come. And as we adjust to a less energy-intensive economy implied by the higher prices, the amount and pain of adjustment will be increased by our previous policy encouraging exploitation.

In our shift from coal to oil and gas, we moved from an abundant energy resource—but one with health costs—to two relatively scarce ones. Concurrently, nuclear energy was confidently expected to become a major source of supply. But the predictions about nuclear power turned out to be overoptimistic. Thus, with the switch from coal to oil and with the shortfall in nuclear power, we became increasingly dependent on imported oil—on the same sources sought by most other industrial countries to serve their own growing needs. And now, compounding this tightness in supply, people—and not just those associated with environmental organizations—are increasingly resistant to having a coal or a nuclear electric plant built in their locality.

We cannot fall back on the once comforting assertions that we have hundreds of years' supply of coal and shale oil: in many cases the environmental costs of developing these resources are so high that much of the material may best be left in place. Suddenly we find ourselves in short supply of energy commodities.

For the short run, at least, we are "locked in" from both sides. Short-term adjustments in demand for energy will be painful, and many of the supply options will take years to develop. At first, as the embargo experience demonstrated, it is demand that will have to give way the most. As we look farther ahead, energy conservation would appear to be a more fundamental and far-reaching response, and at the same time, it can be hoped, more supply options will open up. But balanced against these possibilities is the juggernaut of geometric growth. Pushed by a rise in both population and GNP, the growth in energy demand has and will continue to have considerable momentum. While mathematically this growth cannot continue indefinitely or even for many more doubling periods, how and when best to mitigate it is a very open question.

In the following pages we discuss some of the options and considerations which we believe should go into the formulation of a new energy policy. This policy should be a balance of more conservation and new supplies; it should be chosen with the proper concern for associated environmental and private costs, and for the timing and uncertainty of the various options; and it should demonstrate a proper regard for intergenerational equity.[1]

1. This article draws heavily on, among other sources, discussions with many individuals—indeed, too many to mention separately. We have benefited greatly from discussions with present and former colleagues at Resources for the Future and with members of the staffs of the Ford Energy Policy Project, the Center for Advanced Computation at the University of Illinois, the Department of the Interior, and the Federal Energy Administration. Helpful also have been the reviews and comments from members of the Enrivonmental Defense Fund, the Natural Resources Defense Council, the Sierra Club, and the Wilderness Society. While there is doubtless something in the paper with which all of these contributors will agree, it is unlikely that any will subscribe to all of our viewpoints and conclusions. Accordingly, while the assistance we have received from others is great indeed, we alone assume responsibility for the positions taken and for any inadvertent errors of analysis or fact that may remain.

Criteria

How are we to decide on the amount and type of conservation to pursue, and how are we to decide on which new sources to develop under what timing and on what scale? So far, many of these decisions have been left to the marketplace. The desirability of the market decision in the case of energy development and consumption depends upon three conditions: (1) the competitiveness of the energy industries, (2) the nature and size of environmental costs, and (3) the degree to which those affected by today's market decisions are fairly represented in today's market.

A discussion of the nature of competition and its imperfections in the energy industries would lead us far afield and, perhaps irretrievably, into bogs of controversy. Suffice it for us to mention that conventional economic theory predicts that monopolistic industries will restrict output compared with the competitive norm. But, on the other side, electric and gas utilities, being natural monopolies, have the incentive to discriminate between more and less elastic customers, and in fact there does exist a declining block rate structure which promotes the consumption of energy through volume discounts to larger (more elastic) customers; the oil and gas industry has been remarkably successful in achieving low effective income tax rates, often in the neighborhood of 2 or 3 percent; and it has sometimes been alleged that, through joint ventures, the rather small number of major oil companies have colluded to pick up lease contracts at bargain prices. To the extent that there are imperfections in the competitiveness of the energy industries, these are grounds to believe that promotion and consumption of energy will be favored over conservation.

While the nature and implications of market imperfections in the energy industries appear to be perennial and unanswered questions in economics, at the present time—when policy is being formulated in response to potential shortages and dislocations—we can sidestep most of the controversial questions to pose in a practical way a criterion for energy conservation: we should work for more conservation up to the point where the costs of pushing further exceed the benefits. In the short run, the costs of conservation are the costs associated with adjusting to a lower rate of energy consumption. For example, we will conserve more energy by moving toward an inverted electric rate structure, but the amount of energy conserved in the short term should be balanced against the dislocations and adjustment costs associated with the shift. Such costs of conserving a million BTUs are not worth bearing if new supplies of the same amount of energy can be obtained at less cost. This comparison is a useful rule of thumb in a shortage or short-term crisis. In the long run, the conventional rule of thumb is that if energy is priced "correctly," the right amount of conservation will follow automatically. As is mentioned below, complications arise because of environmental costs, uncertainty, and questions concerning the intertemporal distribution of welfare, but here, as in the short run, the general idea is that energy saved through conservation should be balanced against energy obtained through new sources.

When the decision of which new supplies to develop and under what schedule is left to the marketplace, it is made upon the test of profitability. It is sometimes thought that if these decisions are left to the market, economic efficiency will automatically be achieved. But in the market, the only costs and benefits considered are private ones, those borne by the firms making the decisions. Environmental costs are excluded from the analysis except as the firms are forced to bear them by rules of liability, government regulation, or pollution taxes. (It is important to point out that the failure to include environmental costs is not unique to decision making by the marketplace: in choosing and developing new sources of supply, government agencies, too, have often neglected environmental costs.) By the test of private market profitability, new sources will be scheduled in order of their private costs, from lowest to highest. Because of the neglect of environmental costs, as we shall affirm in a moment, not only will the order of introduction probably be wrong, but too much energy will be developed at any given time.

Largely in reaction to this neglect, environmentalists have stressed the importance of considering the environmental costs in choosing and developing new sources of supply. Occasionally they go so far as to advocate the selection of new sources on the basis of environmental costs alone. By this criterion, new sources would be scheduled from those lowest to highest in environmental costs, regardless of the private costs.

Ever since the time of A. C. Pigou, in the early twentieth century, economists have pointed out that such decisions should be made on the basis of both private and environmental costs. Certainly both types of costs should be taken into account, but while this position has made fine reading in textbooks, it has not prevailed in practice. The environmentalists' criterion—which is conceptually just as inefficient as the private market solution and symmetrically opposite to it—does serve a useful purpose in this regard: it nudges us away from the prevailing concentration on private costs and toward a consideration of total social costs.

All this may seem simple and obvious, but there are pitfalls for the unwary practitioner. For example, it is sometimes suggested that environmental costs should be considered along with private costs in deciding upon a set of admissible projects, but that once this set is chosen, environmental costs need play no further role, leaving the selection and scheduling of projects from the admissible set to be made on the basis of private costs alone. Such a procedure would be efficient only if the ratio of private to environmental costs were constant over all the projects in the admissible set.

A deeper problem surfaces when we consider how to count costs and benefits (whether private or environmental) which are distributed over time. By standard practice, future costs and benefits are discounted, but discounted at what rate? Here again we run into an unresolved controversy. It has been argued that when a proposed project carries with it the risk of irreversible costs, or when a project's stream of net costs is growing, the project should be discounted at a higher than normal rate. And in response to the Atomic Energy Commission's cost-benefit study of the breeder reactor, the National Resources Defense Council goes further to argue that for projects imposing the risk of very large future costs, one necessary, *but by no means sufficient,* test should be that the project have a favorable cost-benefit ratio under a wide range of discount rates, including the highest (before tax) rates found in the private economy. A project like the breeder, with potentially catastrophic future costs, should be "an investment at least as productive as the industries it draws resources away from." [2] Another test is one of fairness.

However, when there are uncertainties, irreversibilities, and potentially castastrophic consequences, the matter is both more fundamental and broader than somehow choosing a discount rate. Basically, the problem is one of intergenerational equity. In the example of the breeder reactor, the present generation receives the electricity while future generations are burdened with perpetual care of plutonium, which is both extremely toxic and a prime weapon material. Generally, markets are considered fair only if all those affected by the outcomes are present in the market (without externalities) and the distribution of market power is considered fair. In

2. Thomas B. Cochran and Arthur R. Tamplin, "Comments" on WASH 1536 (The AEC Draft Environmental Statement, Liquid Metal Fast Breeder Reactor Program), xeroxed (Washington: Natural Resources Defense Council, 1974), pp. 4–7.

the case of deciding which new supplies to develop, the distribution of market power is indeed uneven: the present generation controls the total stock of resources, leaving future generations with no voice in today's decisions. Another way of describing the situation is to say that the present generation may undertake projects to its own benefit, yet at the same time regard these projects as leading to an unfair redistribution of welfare. One can be a beneficiary of an outcome and still feel that others are victimized by one's own good fortune—and so it may be between generations.

So far decision-making institutions have not systematically resolved the question of intergenerational equity. Yet as our means of transferring costs from the present to the future increase—for example, by generating long-lived pollutants—the need to bring intergenerational fairness into the decision-making process becomes more compelling. This is especially the case with projects carrying small and largely unknown probabilities of future catastrophes.

How should institutions for this type of decision making function, and what form should they take? These questions are difficult to answer, but it seems clear at least that since the future cannot represent itself, there should be broad opportunity for different groups to bring the charge of unfairness. The decision of what is fair intertemporally is too important to be left to small elite groups of decision makers, especially when there are vested interests at stake. The institutions should function in such a way that the larger the potential adverse effect and the more uncertain the probability of its occurrence, the more cautious and thorough the decision-making procedure should be and the more information should be generated by the procedure itself. Projects with greater risk of future catastrophe should pass stricter tests. There should be some way of setting up barriers against possible redistributions of welfare.

One such barrier would be to subject a potentially risky project to a "penalty" charge at its inception. Presumably, the charge would increase with the size and uncertainty of risk and would be determined by a decision-making process involving opponents and advocates. For a once-only charge, this scheme appears equivalent to subjecting the more risky project to a higher effective discount rate. But if the charge were to be more flexible—levied over several years, from the beginning of the project, in response to what is learned about the project's consequences—the scheme is no longer equivalent to a single adjustment in the discount rate.

Beyond this conceptual difference, a charge explicitly levied and collected would have an important practical effect. We commonly, and often appropriately, subsidize projects with large risks of not attaining good outcomes. Frequently, however, these projects are mixed affairs involving some risk of very *bad* outcomes, so that the government inadvertently finds itself underwriting programs with potentially catastrophic effects. A charge scheme would tend to reverse this, making it possible to discriminate between risks of adverse as constrated with beneficial outcomes.

In the following sections we mention some of the important costs and benefits associated with various options, along with some of the redistributional possibilities. The latter can be safely ignored in the case of projects with little distributional impact, applying standard cost-benefit analysis and scheduling such projects in the order of their total (private plus environmental) costs. One beneficial result is that less promising projects may be avoided entirely and ones with high environmental costs may be delayed sufficiently until such time as technological advances provide us with acceptable defensive strategies for their use. But the greater the distributional potential, the more these projects should be subjected to explicit social choice concerning their intergenerational fairness. We wish to stress that the equity considerations cannot be resolved by a mechanical cost-benefit analysis. The question of intertemporal fairness logically precedes the typical efficiency questions posed by economists. A full and open debate must attend projects in proportion to the potential size and relative uncertainty of their redistributional effects. Only in this way will sufficient knowledge be generated to make sensible decisions, ones we can live with. Setting up institutions whereby this can be done is of primary importance.

Options for Energy Conservation: Prospects and Limitations

If the environmental standards mandated by the Clean Air Act are to be substantially honored, and the limited supplies of oil and gas are to be husbanded so as to ensure that the basic functions of the economy will not be disrupted, there appears to be no alternative in the short run to widespread, makeshift, energy conservation measures. The combination of such conservation measures with one of the mildest winters on record was enough to enable the country to survive the critical period caused by the embargo without economic dislocations. We need to recognize, however, how crucial the bonus of good weather was. Limited refinery capacity will still affect the supply of gasoline, and gasoline stringencies may occur during the more extensive summer driving season for a number of

years. But as enough time elapses to permit normal economic adjustments—e.g., improved commuter facilities promoting the use of more
energy-efficient mass transportation and a shift in our stock of automobiles toward smaller, more energy-efficient, vehicles—substantially
more significant economies in the energy budget may be achieved. In the
longer run, commuters faced with higher travel costs are likely to move
closer to their work, and this relocation can decrease the amount of cross-
commuting.

Estimates of the energy savings that can be achieved through conservation have been made by a number of sources. The Office of Emergency
Preparedness, for example, estimated that anywhere from 15 to 17 quadrillion BTUs—more than 20 percent of expected consumption—might
be saved through conservation practices implemented over the period
from 1972 through 1975. Over a longer period (say, 1980 and beyond),
still an intermediate time frame but one which would permit some of the
adjustments to take place, possible annual savings were set as high as 36
quadrillion BTUs—something like 30 percent of the consumption expected in the absence of conservation measures.[3]

An economic study of the adjustments that would be indicated in response to rising relative prices of energy commodities was undertaken
recently by members of the staff of the Environmental Protection Agency
(EPA).[4] The estimate of relative reduction in annual demand, resulting
largely through substituting capital for energy in response to a 25 percent
rise in the relative price of energy commodities, was put at 41 quadrillion
BTUs by the end of a twenty-year adjustment period, 1970–1990. This
represents an annual saving of about 30 percent of the energy that would
have been consumed in the absence of the change in the relative price of
energy commodities. The EPA study provides a systematic review of the
several sectors accounting for the consumption of energy and an evaluation of the substitutions and reductions based on price elasticities, given
sufficient time to allow economic adjustment processes to work themselves out.

While the study reflects the extent to which demands for energy may
presently be excessive because of the inefficient pricing policies pursued

3. Office of Emergency Preparedness, *Energy Conservation: A Staff Study Prepared for
the Energy Subcommittee of the Domestic Council* (Washington, July 1972).
4. Marquis R. Seidel, Steven E. Plotkin, and Robert O. Reck, *Energy Conservation
Strategies* (Washington: Office of Research and Monitoring, U.S. Environmental Protection
Agency, July 1973).

heretofore, a number of observations seem warranted. It is likely that the relative rise of fuel prices will exceed the 25 percent postulated, but it is not clear that increasing relative costs and prices will be accompanied by an equivalent additional relative reduction in the demand for energy. It will depend in part on what additional areas will permit capital substitution for energy as the relative prices of energy commodities rise. Since the substitution implicit in this economic adjustment process is largely (but not entirely) capital for energy, substantial demands are going to be made for investment funds to develop supply options as well as to finance the massive conversion implicit in the substitution of new plant and equipment in response to the rise in energy prices. Thus, the change in relative prices of energy and capital, rather than of energy and of commodities in general, is relevant. Unless there is also an increase in the propensity to save, capital as well as energy may be in short supply, and the possibilites for substitution may not be as extensive as suggested.

There are nonpricing policies that can be pursued in addition to eliminating preferential tax treatment for oil and gas and subsidizing federal hydroelectric plants (and transmission facilities). For example, we might consider the appropriate taxation of commodities whose prices do not otherwise reflect the external or environmental costs of their production, distribution, and consumption; we might undertake initial public assistance to reduce risk in establishing enterprises requiring a minimum scale of operation for the competitive provision of energy-conserving facilities, e.g., solar residential heating (reporting to be economically competitive provided units are made and distributed in sufficient volume to achieve scale economies); and, of course, we could mount a discriminating and adequately programmed research and development effort to advance the technology of energy conservation and production over the long run.

Despite the prospects for energy conservation, *none of the studies we have cited lead to the conclusion that energy demands will not continue to grow.* A reduction in the rate of growth of about 50 percent over a twenty-year adjustment period, implicit in the EPA study, would still require an annual provision of additional energy in an amount roughly equivalent to the projected savings. But even if it were possible to achieve a negligible-to-zero growth in energy demand, an unrealistic prospect for the time frame relevant to our present concerns, additional sources of energy would be required to replace current sources which would be depleted with time. The important consideration is that while energy conservation is an indispensable objective for both the short and long run, it will not by itself suffice to solve either the short- or long-run energy problem facing the country. *In addition to pursuing the energy-conservation strategy, we must give attention to various energy supply options relevant to each time period.*

A Promised Nonfossil Fuel Option

Part of the present short-term problem relates to the incrimination of coal as a source of unacceptable air pollution when used for the production of electrical energy in steam electric power stations. The substitution of gas and oil for coal and the limitations on the supplies of these energy commodities following the embargo resulted in concern about sufficient fuel for transportation and industrial processes, electric power production, and commercial and home heating, and the concern may continue to be warranted for a number of years. Granted that we appear to require petroleum products for transportation purposes, is there an alternative to low sulfur oil and natural gas for electric power production that does not involve coal?

At one time there was considerable hope that nuclear power would displace fossil fuel as the source of energy in thermal electric power production. The at-site environmental effects of nuclear power plant operation, assuming present light water reactor (LWR) technology, are alleged to be less damaging than the products of fossil fuel combustion. There appear to be two serious difficulties with the nuclear energy option, however. The first is that for a number of reasons—and these are largely unrelated to opposition to nuclear power on other environmental grounds—the development of nuclear plants has been substantially retarded. Technical, personnel, and other factors have intervened to such an extent that actual nuclear power capacity in 1985 is expected to fall short by some 100,000 to 250,000 megawatts of previously projected capacity.[5] There is no way, in the short run, in which nuclear capacity can substitute for fossil fuel burning plants to meet the indicated demand for electrical energy so as to permit our diverting liquid and gaseous hydrocarbon supplies to transportation and residential heating uses while remaining free from dependence on coal.

The second difficulty with nuclear energy concerns its ultimate desirability in any event. While the at-site environmental effects may be less

5. National Petroleum Council, *U.S. Energy Outlook: Nuclear Energy Availability* (Washington, 1973); cf. "Industry Report 1973–74," *Nuclear News,* mid-February 1974.

from nuclear reaction than from fossil fuel combustion, nuclear energy poses a very serious long-run problem of waste disposal. The radioactive products of fission are highly toxic and have half-lives extending to thousands of years—which means that they must be contained safely for tens of thousands of years before decay ultimately dissipates their toxicity. At present we have no satisfactory (i.e., fail-safe) method of storage. Radioactive waste generation imposes at least two burdens on society: first, to provide a fail-safe method of storage in perpetuity, which requires methods not yet known; and second, to develop a social discipline and stability never attained by previous societies. It also raises critical implications about the kind of society that would emerge in response to the need to deal with such a serious and growing safety problem. This poses the moral question of whether the present generation should saddle future generations forever with the burden of safeguarding our toxic nuclear wastes.

This ethical question has already been largely decided by default: there are nuclear plants already on line, and with those on order, nearly 200,000 megawatts are scheduled to be operating within ten years or so. And, as Allen Kneese has said, if such plants operate for only a decade or two, they will have imposed a burden on society in perpetuity.[6] Once the toxic materials are introduced and are susceptible of being released into the environment, the burden is virtually irreversible in terms of a time frame relevant to human societies.

Nevertheless, for years to come we will still be faced with making decisions about the scale and character of the burden. Far-reaching choices are yet to be made regarding the second-generation nuclear technologies involving the so-called breeder reactors. While we have several possible breeder-reactor designs as potential contenders, the liquid metal-cooled fast breeder reactor (LMFBR) is receiving the bulk of the research and development effort, both in the United States and abroad.[7] The breeder technology is more complex than that of the LWR and may pose somewhat higher probabilities of accidental failure. Liquid sodium, used as a coolant in the favored design, is highly reactive with air and water and, becoming radioactive, must be kept extremely free from impurities that would cause it to become corrosive and possibly lead to leaks in the

6. Allen V. Kneese, "The Faustian Bargain," *Resources* (Washington: Resources for the Furture, Inc., September 1973).
7. The United Kingdom, France, and the Soviet Union all have LMFBRs in operation.

intricate plumbing. Using plutonium as the fuel, which is extremely toxic [8] and has a half-life of 24,400 years, a major accident could result in virtually permanent contamination of an area. Consequently, much effort has been expended to develop reliable components for handling the highly reactive sodium—but with reliability, costs mount to the extent that some critics of the LMFBR consider the design to be ultimately uneconomical.[9]

In addition to the non-zero probability of accidental failures, some of major proportions, the vulnerability of power and processing plants to sabotage poses a serious problem. Moreover, the value of plutonium will make it a target for diversion to unauthorized purposes, whether for pecuniary or more malicious reasons.[10] If the LMFBR were to be widely deployed, substantial quantities of plutonium would be in transit, and while conceivably the problem of fail-safe security could be solved within the United States (and this is by no means a certainty), that might not be the case elsewhere. For this reason, we would be wise to undertake a more careful investigation of alternatives to the LMFBR.

One such alternative, which would involve a longer developmental horizon, involves a thermal breeder fueled with molten uranium salts. Because the fuel is molten, continuous on-line reprocessing would be possible.[11] While the technology is not as far advanced as that of the LMFBR, and at present is not receiving much official attention, its capability of confining power generation and fuel reprocessing to one location has substantial security and environmental advantages.

Given our own and other countries' past commitment to one or another of the fission technologies, and given the existing stock of nuclear weapons, it may be that we have lost the option of keeping the environment permanently uncontaminated with highly toxic products of fission. And with the continuing pursuit of fission technology in other countries, it may be that our own persistence in that direction will not add significantly to the problem of developing viable security measures for containing virulent substances in perpetuity. On the other hand, if alternative

8. The toxicity of plutonium has been likened to that of botulism. See Peter H. Metzger, *The Atomic Establishment* (New York: Simon and Schuster, 1972), p. 145, n. 225.

9. Allen L. Hammond, William D. Metz, and Thomas H. Maugh II, *Energy and the Future* (Washington: American Association for the Advancement of Science, 1973).

10. See U.S. Senate, "The Threat of Nuclear Theft and Sabotage," 93d Cong., 2d sess., *Congressional Record* 120, no. 59, 30 April 1974.

11. Hammond, Metz, and Maugh, *Energy and the Future*.

strategies offer some possibility of releasing fewer such materials into the environment and appreciably reducing their impact, we have an obligation to review them conscientiously.

For example, given other countries' attention to the breeder reactor, the availability of energy from this source would not be affected by the failure of the United States to develop its own breeder technology. The industrial world's potential dependence on breeder technology to meet its energy needs after fossil fuel sources have been exhausted does not depend in any essential respect on the U.S. breeder development program. Moreover, if the resources devoted to the development of the breeder in the United States were redirected toward alternative, environmentally more acceptable, energy supply options, it is conceivable that the development of the "ultimate" source of clean, inexhaustible, energy could be advanced sufficiently to reduce appreciably the problem associated with the storage of highly toxic products of fission. It should be noted that the problem concerns not merely the mounting of solar, fusion, and perhaps geothermal research and development efforts but also the decision to support larger, more aggressive, research and development programs in these areas by diverting the resources currently allocated to the breeder reactor program. These are significant policy issues on which the public generally, as well as the technical experts, must be heard. The outcomes are sufficiently important to require testing through public debate and evaluation.

To summarize briefly, one advantage of using nuclear reaction as a source of energy for the production of electricity is that the environmental problems arising from routine operation of the light water reactor are somewhat less severe than those associated with the combustion of fossil fuels, especially the higher sulfur fuels. Moreover, the additional supplies of fissionable materials, particularly if the breeder technology is developed and deployed, would greatly lessen our dependence on fossil fuels in the long run. This latter advantage, of course, could be achieved alternatively by a fusion technology not involving plutonium.[12] The disadvantages are, first, the short-run impossibility of attaining sufficient nuclear reactor production to displace fossil fuel widely enough to solve current needs and, second, the critical long-term hazards of transporting and storing extremely long-lived and toxic products of fission.

12. Lawrence Lessing, "Lasers Blast Shortcut to the Ultimate Energy Solution," *Fortune*, May 1974.

Fossil Fuel Options

If, as appears likely, we cannot rely solely on conservation strategies to meet our short-term and intermediate-term energy needs, and we choose to defer a heavy dependence on nuclear fission on basic ethical, if not other, grounds, where does this leave us? Several possibilities are considered below.

Just as the rise in price is expected to have an impact on the quantity demanded, so it is likely to stimulate some response in fossil fuel supplies. A doubling of the price of crude oil, which has taken place for new sources, will make some deposits that were marginal to uneconomic at the earlier price now economically recoverable. The amount of this crude oil that would be available from onshore sources bears investigation. Since most of the new production has been offshore in recent times, it is likely that the offshore sources will remain the most attractive from the standpoint of private resource costs. As the environmental impacts of these offshore operations are still under investigation, we do not yet have a means of determining whether the total (environmental as well as resource) costs affect the relative attractiveness of the offshore compared with onshore sources—nor the extent to which the environmental costs are likely to differ, say, between Atlantic and Gulf outer continental shelf operations.[13] These important matters must be studied so that discriminating attention may be given to the scheduling of expanded production in order to minimize the total social costs of such oil extraction and transportation. *Information on these questions should be obtained before any further leasing of public lands for oil exploitation.*

Rising prices of petroleum products have implications also for the commercial feasibility of extracting oil from shale. A rough estimate has put shale oil reserves at 168 trillion barrels,[14] with reserves in the richest zones of the Green River Formation of Colorado, Utah, and Wyoming, yielding upwards of 25 gallons per ton, set at nearly 600 billion barrels.[15]

---

13. A beginning in this direction has been made by the Council on Environmental Quality. See the Council's *OCS Oil and Gas—An Environmental Assessment,* a report to the president (Washington, April 1974).

14. Donald Duncan and Vernon Swanson, *Organic-Rich Shale of the United States and World Land Areas,* U.S. Geological Survey Circular 523 (Washington: Government Printing Office, 1965), p. 9.

15. U.S. Department of the Interior, *Prospects for Oil Shale Development—Colorado, Utah, Wyoming* (Washington, May 1968), pp. 11–12. For comparison, the consumption of oil in the United States in 1974 was approximately 6 billion barrels.

If only private resource costs of extraction and transportation are considered, these higher-grade oil shale occurrences are commercially attractive at current high prices.

The environmental costs of exploiting these deposits, however, are formidable. The deer herd and related wildlife in the Piceance Creek Basin in Colorado are unusually valuable—yet their destruction probably represents the least significant of the environmental impacts that extraction would have on the region. The mind-boggling volume of spoils,[16] the attendant risk of disposal-pile failure, the environmental implications of dewatering the mines, and related water-quality problems raise very serious questions at this stage regarding the total social costs associated with using these shale oil reserves.[17] Conceivably, environmentally nondegrading processes might be developed that would eliminate a large share of the expected social cost.[18] Work currently in progress may eventually make it possible to evaluate carefully the social costs of environmental degradation inherent in the extraction of oil from shale. At the moment, however, because of the expected environmental component of total cost, shale oil does not appear to be a strong candidate for the lowest total cost position among the energy supply options.

An alternative option for obtaining petroleum for transportation, and possibly for residential heating, would be to return to coal to generate electricity. In 1973, approximately 1.5 million barrels of petroleum were used daily by the electric utility industry. The amount projected for 1985 runs to 2.67 million barrels a day. The 1973 consumption for electric generating plants is roughly equivalent to 120 million tons of coal, and this volume will almost double to 226 million tons by 1985.

If a nonfission energy option is chosen, however, the amount of coal required for electric generating plants will increase very substantially. If only half of the 300,000 to 400,000 megawatts of nuclear power projected for 1985 were required under a low-growth energy conservation regime, an additional 400 million to 550 million tons of coal would still

16. At 25 gallons to the ton, about 10 billion tons of spoil materials would be generated annually to produce oil at the rate of the 1974 U.S. consumption.

17. Cf. U.S. Department of the Interior, *Final Environmental Statement for the Prototype Oil Shale Leasing Program,* Vol. 1, *Regional Impacts of Oil Shale* (Washington: Government Printing Office, 1973).

18. For an interesting possibility in this connection, see, for example, Ben Weichman, "Energy and Environmental Impact from the Development of Oil Shale and Associated Minerals" (Paper presented at the 65th Annual Meeting of the American Institute of Chemical Engineers, November 1972, revised 1974).

be needed annually to fuel the electric utility industry. Combined electric utility requirements alone would indicate a need for coal production to more than double between the present and 1985.

Initially, coal from low sulfur deposits could be substituted for low sulfur petroleum. Given time and a vigorous research and development program to produce an effective sulfur and particulate emission control technology, more extensive sources of coal could be drawn upon to provide the needed fuel. But the environmental impact of returning to coal will be felt at the extraction stage as well as during conversion. The deep mining of coal may be the most hazardous occupation in America—it averages 100 fatalities and 10,000 nonfatal casualties annually, quite apart from damage done to the miners' health from long exposure to airborne particulates. Advances in underground mining technology and their more widespread deployment, of course, could reduce the number of miners exposed for any given volume of coal mined. Surface mining is not as hazardous, but it has long-run landscape and related aesthetic costs. Where seams are thin and in areas of steep slopes, contour mining is particularly damaging to the landscape. In certain regions of the West—the northern Great Plains, for example—where coal seams are exceptionally thick and the amount of surface area disturbed per unit of coal extracted is small (eleven acres per million tons of coal, assuming an average fifty-foot seam), the relation between volume of coal taken and surface disturbance is much smaller. Where annual precipitation is favorable, it appears feasible to restore the strip-mined areas if this is done with appropriate safeguards and attention to rehabilitation.[19]

The sources of the required coal are a matter of interest. Unpublished preliminary estimates (not for attribution) suggest that deep-mined western coal is available at prices equivalent to those of strip-mined eastern coal, and that deep-mined western coal, while involving higher transportation costs, imposes no rehabilitation costs. The costs of western surface-mined coal, including estimated costs for rehabilitation,[20] appear to be lower than those of deep-mined coal. Unfortunately, the estimates are highly aggregated and no distinction is made regarding the sulfur content of the coal at each location.

Nonfission sources of fuel are abundant and therefore very attractive if

19. National Academy of Sciences, *Rehabilitation Potential of Western Coal Lands,* a report to the Energy Policy Project of the Ford Foundation (Cambridge, Mass.: Ballinger, 1974).

20. *Ibid.*

environmental costs are ignored. But even when these costs are taken into account, their environmental implications appear to be less awesome than those posed by the nuclear fission technology. Yet since the fossil fuel options are likely to vary in total social costs, it is urgent that we evaluate the environmental implications of each to ensure that we do not draw on those of higher social cost while not exploiting others to their fullest capacity.

Possible Nonfossil Fuel, Non-nuclear Options

Most of the serious attention given to the displacement of petroleum in nontransportation energy demands has focused on coal and nuclear materials as substitutes. Yet solar sources of energy appear to be worth considering for our residential heating needs over the intermediate term, and geothermal sources seem capable of meeting part of our electrical generating requirements, even over the short run.

A distinction should be made between the uses of solar energy at lower and higher temperatures. Solar energy is basically a diffuse source of heat. The technology for its application in low-temperature uses such as space heating is simple and proven. In much of the country, it has been competitive with other sources of energy for supplementary residential heating for some time, even at the former lower fuel prices. With the rising cost of fossil fuel, substantial displacement by solar energy could be accomplished with known technology in residential heating and possibly cooling. Of course, there would have to be a redesigning or replacement of existing residential structures that were built without features essential to the efficient interception and utilization of the sun's rays. Replacement of the present housing stock would undoubtedly take a long time, and it is not clear how much of it could be retrofitted to use solar energy.

Because of the high capital cost of setting up a supplementary solar collector, it would take a decade or two for the lower operating cost to result in a saving on the total cost of production. The reluctance of builders to substitute higher capital costs (more visible to buyers) for lower operating costs appears to be one of the main obstacles to the introduction of solar collectors for space heating and cooling.

The use of solar energy directly in high-temperature applications, on the other hand, does not appear to be immediately so promising. Because solar energy is so diffuse a heat source, the investment in collectors to concentrate heat sufficiently to produce temperatures required in conventional steam-cycle central-station electrical generating plants will be some multiple of the investment for fossil fuel and nuclear stations. Accordingly, it seems doubtful that either land or capital will be used extensively for the higher-temperature applications using direct insolation as an energy source.

More sophisticated technologies such as the photovoltaic cell, capable of directly converting solar to electrical energy, are still further from commercial feasibility. While the technology of the photovoltaic cell is known, present economic efficiencies are so low that this energy source is used only for space exploration and similar highly specialized purposes where the cost per unit of electricity is an incidental consideration. Advances that would permit us to produce moderately economical electricity from solar radiation cannot realistically be expected within the near future.

Another possible partial substitute for nuclear or fossil fuel in the production of electricity is geothermal energy. Heat sources in the earth's crust exist in the form of dry steam, hot water, and hot dry rock. The Geysers field in northern California, one of the country's large dry steam fields, has been regarded with interest by the Pacific Gas and Electric Company. The steam it produces is of low pressure and temperature when compared with pressures and temperatures in modern steam electric plants, but there are indications that, with appropriate plant design, energy can be generated economically depending upon various factors, the life of the field being one. The potential of dry steam sources in the United States has been estimated at 100,000 megawatts over a twenty-year-production cycle.[21]

Dry steam wells produce steam unaccompanied by liquid water, which makes power generation both more simple and more economical. Geothermal wells more commonly produce a mixture of steam and water, and in the conventional process the water must be separated from the steam before the latter can be used in power production. Where the water has a high salinity content, disposal can create difficulties if the saline water cannot be reinjected into the system after the steam has been extracted. Alternatively, the hot water itself can be used in power production, serving as a heat-exchange medium to transfer heat to a secondary fluid having a lower boiling point, and this secondary fluid, in turn, can be used to drive turbines. There is some loss of heat in the transfer, but less so than in extracting the usable steam from the hot water. At present we do not

21. U.S. Senate, Committee on Interior and Insular Affairs, "Geothermal Energy in the United States," in Committee Print, 92d Cong., 2d sess., May 1972, pp. 112–116.

have enough experience with the secondary fluid technology to evaluate its commercial feasibility, yet under favorable conditions it is expected to produce electricity at prices comparable to those of fossil fuel plants.[22]

Until now, geothermal technology has concentrated on dry steam and hot water systems. But the preponderant source of geothermal heat in the earth's interior is contained in dry rock. While the thermal content of dry rock is much greater than that of dry steam and hot water systems, it is more difficult to exploit for the production of electricity. Plans to tap this source of energy involve the creation of artificial fractures in the rock occurring below the surface at substantial depth and circulation of water through the area to extract the heat from the rock. Research in this area is being conducted by a group at the Los Alamos Scientific Laboratories, but there is still little empirical, as contrasted with theoretical, information on which to base judgments regarding the comparative economics of the technology. Were it to be found economical, the dry rock sources would represent a reservoir of heat substantially greater than the dry steam and hot water sources combined.

Although geothermal energy is now considered a significant potential source, it is clear that much research and development will be needed for its efficient exploitation. Moreover, the by-products of geothermal technology pose potential environmental problems. Because of their mineralized nature, the water and even residues in the dry steam will require disposal. Where they can be reinjected into the reservoirs conveniently, they may present no environmental difficulties and indeed may serve to prevent the problem of land subsidence that can occur with the withdrawal of steam and water. Reinjection will be difficult in some cases, however, and these will demand attention.

Air pollution can also be a threat. Noxious gases are often a by-product of geothermal reservoirs, and while some gases can readily be separated from the steam, hydrogen sulfide cannot. It has been suggested that the amount of sulfur that escapes into the atmosphere from the Geysers operation is comparable to that emitted from the burning of low sulfur oil in conventional fossil fuel plants.[23]

Like solar energy, geothermal energy merits far more intensive investigation than the meager efforts accorded it so far. The possibilities for exploiting geothermal energy can be realized only by mounting a considerable developmental effort to verify the most likely sources for the short

22. Hammond, Metz, and Maugh, *Energy and the Future,* p. 57.
23. *Ibid.,* p. 60.

run and to provide the defensive strategies essential for dealing with the noxious substances associated with some of the sources. While geothermal energy, like solar energy, is not likely to displace other sources entirely, it holds promise of becoming a significant supplement, whether or not the deployment of fission technology is deferred indefinitely. It could be relatively inexpensive as well when the total cost, including environmental cost, is considered. More important, neither the solar nor geothermal technologies involve the problem of intertemporal equity that plagues the nuclear fission option.

Summary and Conclusions

We have attempted to identify a few of the more important issues and options that need to be considered in providing energy for the American economy. The short-run ''crisis'' may well have been simply the first act of a longer serial that will involve working through fundamental adjustments to our way of thinking and the way we organize our lives over the next several decades. We have argued for energy conservation. Not only would this be part of a program to develop a larger measure of independence from unstable foreign sources of supply, but it might prove necessary in order to bring the consumption of energy into alignment with its total real (resource and environmental) costs.

However, conservation alone will not be able to deal with the problem entirely over the next quarter of a century. One reason, of course, is that in the long run the maintenance of our industrial society will depend on advances in technology that will release us from dependence upon the finite sources of conventional energy. To increase the probability of success in this regard, we shall need a well-functioning industrial economy capable of supporting the kind of research and development effort required. This will doubtless call for some growth in energy consumption. Thus, if we can only partially achieve our objectives through the more efficient use of energy, new sources will be required over the next five, ten, and twenty-five years, and we need to be apprised of the relative total costs of these new supply options.

The problem of determining the optimal schedule of supply is complicated both by the environmental costs suffered currently and by those which will have their greatest cumulative impact in the future, causing intertemporal equity problems. This aspect of the energy supply problem has grown enormously in the past few decades for several reasons: (1) we are beginning to experience a diminishing environmental assimilative capacity as we overload our pollutable reservoirs; (2) we are generating new types of wastes, ones which the environment seems less able, or unable, to assimilate; and (3) geometric growth in the demand for energy and materials generally, along with leaner deposits, promises to result in disturbances of land surfaces of magnitudes far beyond our previous experience. These factors lead to large-scale environmental costs affecting people in the present and spilling over into the future—and as our technological ability advances, so, it appears, does our power to impose even greater burdens and hazards upon generations to come. The enormity of the potential costs demands that they be dealt with in the decision-making process. It carries the matter beyond the point where it can be handled by conventional admonitions for benefit-cost analysis to include externalities or by pleas for generalized "effluent" taxes to perfect the market. The potential redistributions of economic well-being are so great that the problem has become fundamentally an ethical one.

The possibility of shifting increased costs associated with some technological resource options lends importance to the matter of scheduling and timing. Those options that carry the highest risks of serious long-run adverse welfare effects might well receive explicit consideration for deferral in the hope that more benign alternatives can be developed in the interim or at least that defensive strategies can be worked out to cope more adequately with the adverse side effects of their deployment.

So far the decision-making process has lagged in this respect. The satisfactory integration of economic and ethical considerations has not been adequately achieved. It appears, however, that changes are beginning to occur in response to the growing gravity of the problem. The decision-making process is becoming somewhat more broadly based through public hearings and the mechanism of adversary proceedings, so that decisions that have been reached on narrow technical grounds are becoming more open to challenge. But these avenues of public participation need to be increased and the process accelerated.

What if the issues surrounding energy supply (and conservation) do in fact become more susceptible to public participation and there is more responsiveness to considerations of environmental costs and intertemporal equity? In what direction are things likely to go? A more critical view of such options as the fission technologies might emerge, and more interest might be shown in potentially less hazardous sources such as the solar, geothermal, and fusion technologies. Conservation programs might appear more attractive than before, when only private resource costs were considered. In the process, more explicit consideration would be given to intertemporal welfare distribution than has been true in the past.

5

The Public Role
in Energy Research
and Development

John E. Tilton

Signs of energy supply trouble began to appear before the Yom Kippur War and the Arab oil embargo of 1973. The inability of new homeowners to obtain natural gas connections, the occasional failure of electric utilities to meet peak loads during the hot summer months, the intermittent threats of a gasoline or home heating oil shortage, the quotas on domestic production of crude oil equal to 100 percent of capacity, the closing of aluminum potlines in the Northwest—all pointed to possible shortages. But it was the war and the embargo, followed by the large price increases unilaterally imposed by oil exporting countries, that made most Americans abruptly aware of their energy problems.

Little of the blame for these problems can be attributed to the exhaustion of energy resources. Proved reserves throughout the world for all major sources of energy are as large today as ever,[1] and could last for decades if not centuries. Even within the United States, exhaustion is not the problem. Foreign energy sources have penetrated the domestic market in recent years because they are cheaper or environmentally cleaner than domestic alternatives, not because the latter are gone.

Instead, our recent problems are caused largely by shortages in the plant and equipment, and in some instances manpower, needed to produce and transform energy. The country has not built new oil refining and electric generating capacity fast enough, nor has it maintained sufficient capability to mine and process coal. The adverse effects of these short-

This chapter is revised and abridged with permission from the working paper, U.S. Energy R&D Policy: The Role of Economics, copyrighted 1974 by Resources for the Future. The full paper is available from the Johns Hopkins University Press.

1. Reported reserves of coal have fallen, but the reason for this appears to be the use of more conservative estimation procedures, rather than a failure to find new reserves sufficient to offset consumption. In any case, present coal reserves are abundant.

ages are accentuated by government regulation restraining increases in the price of natural gas and more recently in those of other forms of energy, and by interruptions in supply and collusive pricing by the foreign oil producers upon which the country has come to depend.

This diagnosis is in some respects reassuring, for it suggests that our current problems could be resolved within the next decade or two. However, the combined impact of the many decision and policies that produced the present situation was largely unforeseen, or at least greatly underestimated, leaving the market little time to adjust. Since energy supply and demand are relatively unresponsive to price changes in the short run, dislocation and turmoil have been severe and a sense of emergency or crisis has arisen.

Responding to this trauma, the American government has taken action in a number of important ways, including a rapid acceleration in federal financing of energy research and development (R&D). Over the ten years preceding 1973, as Table 1 shows, government support for energy R&D, after adjusting for inflation, grew at a leisurely 4 percent a year. Between 1973 and 1975 the increases averaged about 50 percent a year, more than a tenfold jump. While such rapid growth will not continue in the future, the high levels of spending realized by 1975 are projected to continue for at least several years. The administration has proposed spending $10 billion over the next five years, while Senator Henry Jackson and other members of Congress are pressing for $20 billion over the next ten years.

One consequence of the jump in public support, as Table 1 indicates, is that the government now finances over half the energy R&D carried out in this country. This is more than double the proportion it funds for all R&D outside the defense and space fields. Even in energy, the government has until recently supported only between a third and two-fifths of the R&D.

This change in policy raises several important questions. Why should the government in a private enterprise economy such as the United States support energy R&D at all? How much should it spend? How should it allocate its funds? And at a more fundamental level, what are the appropriate criteria or procedures for making such decisions?

This chapter addresses these issues. In the process, it raises certain questions or reservations about present energy R&D policy in the United States and the way it is evolving. The first section examines the reasons why the private marketplace by itself will not produce an optimal energy R&D effort, and so substantiates the need for some form of government

Table 1. Public expenditures on energy R&D in the United States

Sector	FY 1963 Millions of dollars *	FY 1963 Percent of total	FY 1973 Millions of dollars *	FY 1973 Percent of total	FY 1975 Millions of dollars *	FY 1975 Percent of total	Average annual rate of growth in percent between FY 1963–73	Average annual rate of growth in percent between FY 1973–75
Coal	15	3	85	13	367	24	19	108
Petroleum and natural gas	56	12	19	3	36	2	–10	38
Nuclear fission	293	64	406	60	623	40	3	24
Nuclear fusion	36	8	75	11	145	9	8	39
Conservation and environmental control	†		71	11	253	16	‡	89
Other	60	13	16	2	133	9	‡	188
Total public expenditures	460	100	672	100	1557	100	4	52
Public expenditures as percent of total expenditures	35		40		56			

Sources: Office of the White House Press Secretary, "The President's Energy Message: Fact Sheet," January 23, 1974; U.S. Office of Science and Technology, Energy R&D and National Progress, prepared under the direction of Ali Bulent Cambel for the Interdepartmental Energy Study (1964), Table 1–25; John E. Tilton, U.S. Energy R&D Policy: The Role of Economics (Washington: Resources for the Future, 1974), Table 3.

* All expenditures are in constant 1973 dollars. The implicit price deflator for the gross national product was used to inflate the 1963 data and to deflate the 1975 data.

† Included under other.

‡ Not available.

intervention, though not necessarily government funding of energy R&D. The following section argues that, before the appropriate means of government intervention can be determined, public goals and priorities must be established for energy policy as a whole, as well as energy R&D policy. This section also considers the major shortcomings of government funded R&D and identifies possible alternatives to such funding. On the basis of the preceding analysis, the final section then assesses funding policy for energy R&D in the United States.

The Need for Government Intervention

Most economists start with the presumption that the government should not as a general rule interfere directly in the marketplace. What products should be made, how they should be produced, and what factors of production should be employed are decisions best left to businessmen and resource owners. Economists do, however, recognize that certain activities and certain markets suffer from imperfections that may necessitate government intervention.

One such activity is energy R&D. For a number of reasons, the private sector by itself will not carry out an adequate R&D effort in the energy field.[2]

Incomplete Appropriability of Benefits

The output of energy R&D, as of all R&D, is new knowledge and technology. Unlike the output of a steel furnace, an automobile assembly line, or most other production processes, new knowledge and technology can be sold or given away and still used by the transmitting organization.

2. It should be noted that some of these reasons, such as those based on the incomplete appropriability of benefits and imperfect knowledge, probably apply as much to R&D activity in general as to energy R&D. Other reasons, such as those associated with public goods and regulation, are particularly relevant for energy R&D, but even these are not unique to it. In addition to those discussed in this section, a number of other reasons are often cited for government intervention in the energy R&D area. Among them are the following. Private firms do not have the funds available to support an adequate number of energy R&D projects, particularly the more expensive projects. Firms tend to have a greater aversion to high risk activities such as energy R&D than does society. Moreover, they cannot pool projects and reduce their overall risk to the same extent that society can. They also tend to discount future benefits more than society does, which dampens their interest in energy R&D because of its typically long gestation period. The government cannot expect the private sector adequately to fund the R&D needed to develop the new products and processes that the government itself needs. The practical significance of these and other arguments for government intervention not considered in this section can be disputed. They may be important, but until more evidence is available, we cannot be certain. See Tilton, *U.S. Energy R&D Policy,* Appendix I.

Indeed, because of imperfections in the market for new knowledge and technology stemming in large part from their nature, firms can rarely prevent some dissemination of their R&D results, even if they try through secrecy or patents. Consequently, the benefits that society as a whole reaps from R&D often appreciably exceed the private benefits, and the private sector as a result tends to spend less on this activity than is in the best interest of society.

This is particularly so early in the technological development cycle, at the basic research stage. Here generally there is little pretense of commercial applicability. The objective is understanding, not profits, and results are generally published in technical journals and widely diffused around the world. But even at the development end of the cycle, though the proportion of benefits captured by the firm rises appreciably, substantial benefits often accrue to outsiders.

Some technologies are used across a broad spectrum of industries both within and outside the energy sector. Earth moving, catalysis, combustion, and construction technologies are examples. No single firm or industry can hope to internalize all the benefits arising from new developments in such basic fields.[3] But even the benefits of new technologies specific to a particular industry are rarely captured entirely by the innovating firm. For example, the first American atomic power plant, which began operating at Shippingport, Pennsylvania, in 1957, has never been much of a commercial success, but its operating experience has greatly helped to improve the design and performance of subsequent plants.

There is another possible reason why the social benefits exceed the private benefits late in the technological development cycle. Firms commit some of their R&D resources to stimulating the reduction in costs and improvement in production techniques that occur as production takes place and experience is acquired. The studies now available on this phenomenon, generally referred to as learning by doing, indicate that learning is important, particularly in industries with rapidly changing technology.[4] Presumably some of the benefits are appropriated by other firms through labor mobility and other avenues of interfirm communication.

3. For more on this point, see J. H. Hollomon et al., *Energy R&D Policy Proposals,* Report submitted by the Center for Policy Alternatives to the Energy Policy Project, October 1973, pp. IV-3–7.

4. See Boston Consulting Group, *Perspective on Experience* (Boston, 1970); Harold Asher, *Cost-Quality Relationships in the Airframe Industry* (Santa Monica: Rand Corpora-

Because the proportion of total R&D benefits captured by the sponsoring firm tends to increase later in the technological development cycle, without government support development would in percentage terms more closely approach the optimal level than would applied or basic research. However, because R&D expenditures on new products and processes tend to be relatively low at the basic and applied research stages and then increase sharply at the development stage,[5] in the absence of government intervention the underallocation of resources to development measured in dollars would be greater than the underallocation to basic and applied research. This suggests that the bulk of public funds used to correct the distortion caused by nonappropriability should be allocated to development projects even though the ratio of public to private funds should presumably be higher in basic and applied research.

Public Goods

The benefits from public goods, such as a clean environment and national defense, are enjoyed by nearly everyone. As a result, producers cannot capture a significant share of their benefits, and the government usually assumes the responsibility of providing these goods.

To the extent that energy R&D does promote certain public goods, government intervention is needed to assure an optimal amount of energy R&D. This argument is conceptually the same as that just discussed under nonappropriability: intervention is justified because the social benefits of energy R&D exceed the private benefits. However, the source of the external benefits is different. They arise not from the commercial exploitation of R&D results by others, but rather from improvements in environmental quality, national defense, economic prosperity, and balance of payments and trade.

Environmental Quality. When particulate matter is discharged into the

---

tion, 1956); and William Fellner, "Specific Interpretations of Learning by Doing," *Journal of Economic Theory,* 1 (August 1969), pp. 119–40.

5. For example, a pilot plant for coal liquefaction or gasification is estimated to cost between $20 and $40 million to construct and operate. A demonstration plant runs from two to five times this amount, and a full-scale commercial plant, excluding operating costs, from seven to ten times as much. See *Report of the Cornell Workshops on the Major Issues of a National Energy Research and Development Program,* Cornell University, College of Engineering, December 1973, p. 109; and U.S. Congress, Senate Committee on Interior and Insular Affairs, *Energy Research and Development: Problems and Prospects,* 93d Cong., 1st sess., 1973, p. 46. Hereafter this last source is cited as *The Perry Study,* after its author, Harry Perry.

air, when tailings are left to despoil the countryside, or when other violations of the environment occur for which the users of final products are not charged, the incentives are reduced for both energy producers and consumers to conduct R&D designed to ameliorate environmental damage. Those who bear the costs—for example, residents of a city affected by air pollution—have an incentive to conduct such R&D, but they are so dispersed and the problems of collective action so great that rarely do these incentives produce any nongovernmental R&D activity.

The solution most economists advocate for this problem involves government charges or taxes on polluters equivalent to the pollution costs of their activities. Internalizing pollution costs would correct the distortion in private incentives against environmental R&D. The U.S. government, however, has not adopted this procedure, but has opted instead for a system of regulations that allows firms to pollute up to a point without any charge and then enjoins further pollution at any price. Among the inefficiencies it entails, this procedure distorts R&D incentives. Firms whose activities are not constrained by the regulations will carry out too little environmental R&D, while those seriously affected may carry out too much (or shut down altogether).

Consequently, under the present environmental program, additional governmental intervention is necessary to assure that energy R&D includes an optimal effort on environmental problems. In addition, the present system requires some government R&D effort to counter the claims that invariably arise that environmental standards simply cannot be met because present technology is inadequate. Failure to refute such claims, under our political system, greatly increases the pressures to relax standards below whatever levels are set down as optimal.

National Defense. For a number of years the United States has been increasing its energy imports. Moreover, a growing proportion of these imports has been coming from Middle East countries. The distant location of these countries plus their demonstrated willingness to cut off oil exports for political purposes makes them a particularly insecure source of supply. Although the United States has alternative sources of energy to Middle Eastern oil, they could take a decade or longer to develop. So in the event of an interruption, the economy would for some time be severely disrupted. This, in turn, could undermine the country's defense posture and reduce foreign policy options. Given the public good nature of national defense, the private marketplace will not consider the defense benefits of decreasing the vulnerability of energy supplies to interruptions. Some government intervention is, thus, appropriate to correct this deficiency.

Economic Prosperity. Interruptions in energy supplies, or even large unexpected increases in prices, can play havoc with the economy. Some may argue that the private sector can deal adequately with such risks through stockpiling, long-run contracts, future markets, substitution, and other mechanisms that mitigate the effects of shortages. Still, there are reasons for questioning this presumption. A firm that stockpiles oil in anticipation of war is unlikely to have free rein over the use of that strategic resource should its dire prediction come to pass. Indeed, it knows this to begin with, which reduces the incentive to stockpile. Moreover, severe disruptions in the automobile industry or others tend to percolate throughout the economy. For these and other reasons, the social benefits of increasing the security of energy supplies associated with economic stability exceed the private benefits, requiring some government intervention to assure an optimal energy R&D program.

Balance of Payments and International Trade. The steep rise in foreign oil prices over the last several years has created concern over where the foreign exchange earnings will come from to pay for future energy imports. As a result, some have advocated greater government funding for the development of the breeder reactor, oil shale, coal gasification, and other promising potential domestic sources of energy.

For good reasons, economists have generally questioned this argument. First, it is not clear why energy R&D should be subsidized rather than R&D in some other field. Supporting R&D on agricultural commodities or research-intensive products such as computers may, dollar for dollar, have a greater beneficial effect on the balance of payments than energy R&D support. Indeed, it may be more efficient to subsidize the production or marketing efforts of the private sector rather than its R&D activity. Moreover, most economists would caution against the use of any subsidies as long as the demand for imports and exports is sufficiently sensitive to changes in the exchange rate that moderate adjustments in the latter can rectify a deficit in the balance of payments. Subsidies tend to distort world trade and reduce the worldwide efficiency of resource allocation.

Even assuming that the price of foreign oil remains at its present high level, the net effect on the U.S. balance of payments should be much less than many presume. The oil exporting countries will want to spend at least part of their foreign exchange earnings on American products. And their expenditures for Western European, Japanese, and other foreign goods should indirectly stimulate American exports. Those earnings that the exporting states do not spend for foreign goods and services, they presumably will want to invest in profitable projects abroad. The United States with the world's largest and best developed capital market should receive a substantial portion of these funds.

Still, the heavy dependence of the industrialized world on Middle Eastern oil and rising oil prices have disquieting implications for the balance of payments, the international monetary system, and trade. The vast sums of money being spent for foreign oil need to be recycled. For some countries, such as Italy, this may be difficult because their credit is in question. Yet chaos could follow with adverse political consequences for the United States should the financial system of Italy or any other important industrialized country collapse. To prevent this, the United States may have to extend credit to such troubled countries while allowing the oil exporting states to make safe investments in its own domestic economy.

In addition, since the United States is far less dependent on foreign oil than most other industrialized countries and since much of the earnings of the oil producing countries that are not spent on imports may find their way to the American capital market, the value of the dollar may rise substantially relative to the currencies of other industrial countries. Should this happen, many American industries would find their competitive position in world and even domestic markets impaired. This would slow the growth of many industries and produce stagnation in some. The deficit in the American balance of trade caused by this realignment of exchange rates and imports of foreign oil would be covered by the inflow of capital from oil producing countries. So while domestic production capacity stands underutilized or grows lethargically, Americans could find that they are consuming more than they are producing, paying for the difference by selling to foreigners their investment in American production facilities.

Any significant trend along these lines is very likely to be opposed by restrictions on imports of both foreign goods and capital, thereby threatening the postwar trend toward freer trade. Nor is this the only danger to free trade. Other industrial nations facing serious balance of payments difficulties may resort to import restrictions and bilateral trade deals. Some movement in this direction is already apparent. Both Britain and France, for example, are trying to swap arms and other goods for Middle

Eastern oil. Although free multilateral trade is not usually thought of as a public good, it is in the sense that its benefits are widely dispersed and largely unappropriable. Consequently, some government intervention may be needed to assure that energy R&D adequately emphasizes solutions to the energy problems threatening trade and the international monetary system.

Imperfect Knowledge

The private sector may fail to carry out an optimal energy R&D effort because of imperfect knowledge. For example, if the typical new home buyer is unaware of the importance of insulation, or simply unable to judge the benefits it produces in lower fuel costs, this reduces the incentives for installing the proper amount of insulation as well as for developing better and cheaper means of insulating.

Since generating and disseminating information has a cost, too much as well as too little of this activity can be undertaken in relation to the resulting benefits. Deriving and publicizing the life cycle costs of the various makes of electric carving knives, for example, may simply not be worthwhile. Thus the mere existence of imperfect knowledge does not by itself justify government intervention. Still, there are reasons to suspect that the social benefits of compiling and distributing information exceed the private benefits, even allowing for Consumers Union and other similar private organizations. Also the cost of collecting information is probably less if carried out by the government, for it can require the cooperation of firms. And finally, the government may be able to duplicate the results that widespread knowledge would produce without incurring the dissemination costs. It could set insulation standards that must be met to obtain Federal Housing or Veterans Administration mortgages, or it could provide public funds for insulation R&D, in order to reduce or eliminate the distortions imperfect knowledge creates for private R&D incentives.

Regulation

Almost all firms operating in the energy sector are subject to government regulations of one type or another. Natural gas prices, domestic oil production, oil imports, uranium imports, electricity rates, allowed costs of electric utilities, and safety standards for coal mining have all been regulated for some time. More recently, the allowed sulfur content of the coal and crude oil burned, the prices of coal and petroleum products, and the composition of refinery output have come under government controls.

Regulation distorts the private incentives for conducting energy R&D. For example, it is likely that keeping the price of natural gas below the market clearing level has discouraged R&D on new techniques for finding and producing natural gas and on means for conserving this fuel.

Interest in the impact of regulation on the rate and direction of technological change is growing, but understanding in this area is still far from complete.[6] Since the impact depends greatly on the nature and degree of regulation, assessing its effects is extremely difficult except on an ad hoc basis. Even this approach is plagued by the complex interrelationships among various forms of regulation and between regulation and other market imperfections. The net impact of regulation on the amount and direction of energy R&D, however, is probably substantial.

Market Power

In the energy sector certain firms and governments possess the power to influence prices and in other ways interfere with the free operation of the market. Since these distortions affect the incentives for conducting R&D, some form of intervention by the American government is needed to assure that the country's energy R&D program best serves the interests of its people.

Monopoly Power of Firms. Some industries in the energy sector are natural monopolies, and nearly all are at least moderately concentrated. In many, economies of scale, large capital requirements, lack of good mineral deposits, or other barriers inhibit the entry of new firms. While economists generally agree that monopoly power reduces production and allocative efficiency, they are far less certain about its impact on the creation of new technology and other aspects of dynamic efficiency.[7] One school, fathered by Joseph Schumpeter, argues that only firms with monopoly power have the funds needed for R&D and the ability to internalize the benefits. Other economists have taken issue with this position. The existing empirical evidence, although inconsistent in some respects, does suggest that atomistic industries seldom support much innovative activity. But at the other extreme, dominant firms, though often fast imitators, also tend to be slow innovators. Thus, some market power seems desirable, but just how much is not known. This uncertainty plus

6. One of the few works in this area is William M. Capron, ed., *Technological Change in Regulated Industries* (Washington: Brookings, 1971).

7. For a review of the literature in this area, see Frederic M. Scherer, *Industrial Market Structure and Economic Performance* (Chicago: Rand McNally, 1970), ch. 15.

the diverse structures found among the energy industries raises doubts that the present organization of the energy sector would, without some government intervention, produce an optimal R&D program.

Monopoly Power of Government. For the United States the major threat of monopoly power at the government level comes from the Organization of Petroleum Exporting Countries (OPEC). This cartel was established in 1960, but only recently has it successfully exercised its monopoly power to raise world oil prices. Before 1971 the tax imposed by the major oil exporting countries was under a dollar a barrel. By 1974 it had jumped to seven dollars, far more than the 1971 landed price of Middle Eastern oil in the United States.

The exploitation of monopoly power by governments introduces another imperfection in the energy market. Although its effects on energy R&D, like those of the monopoly power of firms, are far from clear, it raises doubts that the private sector if left alone would carry out an optimal R&D effort. One way the government might try to protect domestic consumers from the abuses of monopoly power is to stimulate the development of an alternative domestic source of energy.

The foregoing considerations not only indicate that the private sector by itself will fail to produce an optimal R&D effort in the energy field, but also suggest that government intervention on an ad hoc basis to offset specific shortcomings of the private market is not likely to be very successful. How would the private sector allocate resources to energy R&D if the benefits produced by new domestic energy sources for defense, economic prosperity, and free trade were completely appropriable? We simply do not know, and have no way to find out. Add in the direct and interactive effects of government regulations, monopoly power, imperfect knowledge, and other nonappropriable benefits, and the question becomes hopelessly complex. Consequently, to improve upon the imperfect energy R&D program that a laissez-faire policy would produce, some government planning, including the setting of public goals for the energy sector, seems necessary.

Means of Government Intervention

Energy R&D is not an end in itself, but a means of increasing the net benefits society realizes from the energy sector. Thus the first step in formulating an appropriate energy R&D policy entails identifying societal goals for the energy sector as a whole. Informed judgments regarding the costs and benefits can contribute to the debate, but ultimately energy goals must be set through the political process. How much the country is willing to pay for environmentally cleaner or more secure energy must be resolved in the same fashion as questions relating to expenditures on natural defense and public health. The second step in formulating an energy R&D policy is identifying the options or instruments the government has at its disposal for realizing energy goals. For our purpose, these can be separated into three classes: government funding of energy R&D, measures that stimulate private expenditures on energy R&D, and all other options. The third and final step involves comparing the advantages and disadvantages of the various options and selecting the most appropriate alternative or set of alternatives.

Energy R&D versus Other Measures

Whether the government should rely upon energy R&D, either publicly or privately funded, or other measures, such as gasoline rationing or greater leasing of public lands for exploration, to achieve a particular energy goal depends on which alternative has the lowest expected cost to society. This, of course, will vary depending on the nature of the goal. Generally, energy R&D is most useful in achieving long-range goals, such as reducing or reversing the trend toward rising real costs of energy arising from the depletion of conventional energy sources. Similarly, R&D should be helpful in reducing the country's dependence on foreign energy supplies and assisting environmental management in the long run.

Conversely, because of the time required for the development and widespread adoption of most energy innovations, R&D will rarely be the appropriate policy instrument for achieving short-run objectives. For example, a new, more efficient, automobile engine, even in the later stages of development, would require several years for retooling and other changes in the production process before it could be introduced commercially. Then, at the rate new cars have replaced old cars in the recent past, it would take about ten years before 90 percent of the automobiles in use would have the new engine.[8] Similarly, if the construction of coal gasification plants were to begin immediately, it would be four years before these plants produced any gas. And, unless this construction had special priority, it is unlikely that more than twelve to fifteen plants with

8. *1972 Automobile Facts and Figures,* Motor Vehicle Manufacturers Association of the U.S., Inc., Detroit, pp. 30–31.

a combined output equal to only 4 to 5 percent of the projected demand for natural gas could be in operation by 1985.[9] Moreover, this assumes that the technology to be employed is now ready for commercial use. If instead of the proven Lurgi process a more advanced and unproven technology is desired, four to nine years may be needed to build pilot and demonstration plants before construction on the first commercial facility can even begin.

While not all energy innovations are so heavily dependent on new and expensive capital equipment, there is little that energy R&D can do to change the performance of the energy sector greatly during the coming decade. Measures that reduce the uncertainties surrounding the future of crude oil import policy and the delays associated with environmental regulations may be able to alleviate the bottlenecks in petroleum refining, electric power generation, and coal mining within five years, but more R&D cannot. Similarly, if the country is serious about being independent of foreign energy supplies by 1980, high excise taxes on energy consumption and greater subsidies for the exploration and development of domestic oil and gas may succeed, but more energy R&D cannot accomplish this goal.[10]

Limitations of Government R&D Funding

For the long-run goals where energy R&D is appropriate, the government can intervene by either increasing public R&D funding or taking a variety of measures designed to stimulate private R&D expenditures. This subsection, which focuses on the first approach, examines the major limitations of government funded R&D, limitations that need to be taken into account if energy R&D policy is to achieve the proper mix of public and private funding.

Distortions in Motivation. The overriding objective of most privately funded R&D is the development of new products and processes that can

9. *The Perry Study,* p. 91.

10. One exception to the conclusion that R&D can have little effect in the short run involves social science research. Studies on OPEC and public policies for dealing with the monopoly power of cartels need not take more than several years, and their recommendations could conceivably be implemented within a year. The same is true for research on various aspects of supply and demand for energy, including the impact on supply and demand of different fiscal policies, environmental regulations, price controls, import restrictions, and other existing and potential public policies. Outside of social science research, however, where the focus of R&D is on developing new energy sources, new methods for exploiting present energy sources, and techniques for improving energy utilization, the gestation period is generally much longer.

be exploited profitably in the marketplace. This objective provides strong incentives to complete projects as quickly and economically as possible. With government funded R&D, the reward structure changes. The ability to get R&D contracts and to please government sponsors becomes important. This tends to shift the emphasis from achieving commercially useful and profitable results to producing difficult and impressive technical advances that may or may not be of great use to society. Even more important, the incentives to produce any results are diminished because a large part of the cost of failure is borne by the government. In addition, a large portion of the benefits of success are inappropriable since the right to patent or withhold information on new developments produced under government contracts is limited.

Even when government funding does produce useful new technology, its commercial utilization may proceed more slowly than in the case of privately funded innovations. This is because the first objective in conducting government funded R&D is fulfilling the requirements of the contract. Demonstrating that the results are commercially useful may even have less priority than identifying further areas of promising research that the government should consider funding.

The problem of getting R&D results out of the laboratory and into use is further complicated if the R&D is carried out in a government laboratory or any facility other than the firm that must in the end use the new technology. This greatly increases the communications problems between those who have developed the technology and those expected to use it. In addition, some firms may eschew new products and processes that they did not invent or develop. This suggests that some of the adverse effects of government R&D funding can be reduced by contracting with private firms for most of the applied research and development the government wants to sponsor. At the basic research end of the R&D spectrum where direct commercial usefulness is not the objective, government laboratories, private research organizations, and universities should assume a more important role.

The joint government-industry venture goes one step further in reducing the distortions in incentives. Here the government shares the costs and the benefits of an R&D project with private firms. If the firms involved are those that will eventually use the new technology, the communications problems, the "not-invented-here" bias, and other barriers to its rapid introduction are reduced. At the same time, the costs of failure and the benefits of success to the firm are increased. Indeed, if the government participation in the project is small, the incentive structure approximates that found with private R&D efforts.

Inflexibility. The development of new technologies typically follows an unpredictable path. Approaches that initially seem most promising often fail. Others thought less promising or not considered at all at the outset eventually prove the best alternatives. As a result, R&D programs must be flexible if they are to be productive and efficient.

For various reasons government funded R&D is usually less flexible than private. First, government R&D, aside from that conducted in government laboratories, involves a formal contract between the government and the organization carrying out the research. This contract generally specifies the nature of the work to be done and often is quite specific about the procedures and steps to be followed. While contracts can be modified, the time and effort involved plus the need to obtain the agreement of all participating parties reduces the ease with which projects can be redirected.

Second, with private R&D where the objective is to develop profitable new products and processes, the market punishes those who are slow to abandon unpromising schemes. Good new ideas must be pursued in order to avoid the unpleasant prospect of creating a new technology that is obsolete at its inception. Government funding, by reducing the discipline of the market, dilutes this strong incentive to maintain an open mind in conducting R&D.

Government agencies and public officials once they commit themselves to a particular R&D program tend to maintain that commitment in the face of increasing evidence that it needs to be abandoned or modified longer than do private firms and businessmen. The emphasis of the Atomic Energy Commission (AEC) on the liquid metal fast breeder reactor (LMFBR) is often cited as an illustration of this point, though certainly other examples abound in the defense field. In part this difference in behavior arises because the day of reckoning that the marketplace provides for private R&D efforts can more easily be delayed and even avoided with government R&D. The greater publicity focused on government R&D decisions and the need for public accountability plays an important role as well. For the government to abandon or greatly modify its commitment to the LMFBR at this point would imply in the eyes of many that billions of taxpayers' dollars have been wasted. Better to continue support for the program than risk such criticism. Moreover, with continued support the LMFBR may eventually be widely used to generate electric power, making it more difficult for the critics to demonstrate that the program was a mistake.

Centralization of Decision Making. The expected costs and benefits of various energy research projects must be compared to determine how best to allocate government R&D funds. Such comparisons require a high degree of concentration of decision making. But this has its dangers, for a promising project that for one reason or another is rejected has no other possible sponsor. Some have argued that the gas cooled fast breeder reactor has suffered this unkind fate at the hands of the AEC.[11] The pluralism and diversity that characterize private R&D activity avoid this problem.[12]

Biases in Project Selection. In allocating funds public officials are likely to have preferences that arise from their own self-interest and biases. Big glamorous projects attract attention and focus publicity on their sponsors. A few large projects are easier to administer than many small ones. Individuals and groups with whom the officials have worked in the past may in some cases get special treatment, while in others they are discriminated against to avoid the appearance of impropriety.

Another source of bias arises from the pressures of special interest groups. Public officials quite naturally try to protect themselves and their agencies from criticism. Often minimizing criticism requires that in making decisions the positions of special interests be taken into account in accordance with the political pressures they can bring to bear. The emphasis shifts from promoting the interests of society in general to mediating among the conflicting objectives of the more powerful special interests.[13] With energy R&D, this raises the possibility that too small a portion of public funding will be spent on energy conservation and in other areas that do not have well organized groups pushing their development.

Instability of Government R&D Funding. Private R&D expenditures expressed in constant dollars grew at an average annual rate of 7.8 per-

11. See, for example, Paul W. MacAvoy, *Economic Strategy for Developing Nuclear Breeder Reactors* (Cambridge: MIT Press, 1969).

12. For an interesting discussion of how the diversity of private R&D helps to make for smooth progress despite the high risk associated with individual projects, see Burton H. Klein, "The Menu of Technology," in Resources for the Future, *Energy and the Social Sciences: A Compendium of Research Needs,* Report to the National Science Foundation, October 15, 1973, pp. IV-385–412.

13. A more extensive presentation of this hypothesized behavior of public officials in the context of regulatory agencies appears in Roger G. Noll, *Reforming Regulation* (Washington: Brookings, 1971), pp. 39–46.

cent between 1953 and 1961, 7.5 percent between 1961 and 1966, and 5.2 percent between 1966 and 1971.[14] The corresponding figures for publicly funded R&D are 13.9 percent, 6.8 percent, and −3.0 percent. Public funding categorized by function is even more volatile as illustrated by the well-known buildups and cutbacks in defense and space R&D.[15]

The reasons for the greater instability of public R&D funding are not entirely clear. Part of the explanation lies in the greater centralization of decision making in the allocation of government funds. But part is probably inherent in the way the American political system operates. As the R&D efforts associated with defense, space, environment, and now energy illustrate, new programs are often slow in getting started because of the inertia in the system, but once the momentum develops to overcome the inertia the buildup tends to take place rapidly. More will be said on this characteristic of the American political system in the next section.

Whatever its causes, the instability of government R&D funding diminishes its efficiency. During major expansions, scientists and engineers as well as other specialists are in short supply. This bids up their salaries faster than would otherwise be the case, and necessitates the use of underqualified people in many positions. Thus, part of the rise in government funding does not increase the real R&D effort, but rather is reaped in the form of higher salaries by those who just happen to be in the right fields at the right time. This manpower problem is aggravated by shortages in research equipment and other facilities. Even the qualified may find their facilities inadequate. When public funds are cut back, these shortages are no longer a problem, but waste now occurs because highly trained people are unemployed and expensive facilities underutilized.

Reduction of Private R&D. For several reasons government R&D funding is likely to reduce the R&D expenditures of the private sector. First, firms may receive government support for some projects they would otherwise undertake by themselves. Second, the R&D capability of firms is limited in the short run, so if they accept government funded projects the R&D they finance may have to be cut back. Trying to avoid this by relying on underqualified personnel and inadequate facilities implies a reduction in real R&D, if not in its monetary costs. In the long run

14. These and the following figures for public funding are from U.S. National Science Foundation, *National Patterns of R&D Resources, 1953–71,* December 1970, p. 2.

15. Although their impact on total public funding is smaller, R&D expenditures on education and manpower, natural resources and environment, and in other areas display as much or more instability as those for defense and space. See U.S. National Science Foundation, *Fiscal Years 1963–1973: An Analysis of Federal R&D Funding by Function,* 1972.

firms can increase their R&D capabilities, but certain inputs are probably subject to increasing costs. Certainly this seems likely for the salaries of scientists and engineers, given the uneven distribution of natural aptitudes for these professions. Thus, greater government funding may drive up the cost of conducting R&D even in the long run, and make private funding for projects that would be marginally profitable in the absence of government funding no longer attractive.

The government might try to prevent its R&D effort from reducing that of the private sector by making its contribution contingent upon private participation. Again, the joint venture arises as a possibility. The government agrees to support a project only if private industry does also. Now projects firms would not have supported may receive some private R&D funding. But this is no guarantee that the net private effort will increase. Joint projects may merely cause firms to shift resources from projects they consider more promising to those they consider worthwhile only because the government is willing to assume a substantial share of the burden. In addition, joint ventures may sponsor projects that the private sector would carry out by itself.

Public Policy and Private R&D Funding

The shortcomings of government R&D funding suggest that public policies stimulating private R&D expenditures deserve serious consideration. Since the measures the government could employ to encourage private R&D are numerous, we make no attempt to review them all here. Instead, we look at six areas—antitrust, patents, taxes, public utility regulation, trade, and government procurement—where changes in public policies are frequently suggested to influence private R&D expenditures.

Antitrust Policy. One reason the private sector fails to carry out enough energy R&D is that only a portion of the benefits from such activity can be captured by the firm conducting the R&D. If most of the benefits from R&D are specific to an industry but not to an individual firm, one possible solution is an industry-wide research effort carried out under the auspices of a trade association or other organization and supported by contributions from firms in the industry. This reduces the financial burden imposed on each firm, and increases the likelihood that the benefits realized by each will cover its costs.

This potential avenue for increasing private R&D expenditures, it is widely believed, is discouraged by American antitrust policy. Yet the one case often cited to support this position is open to a different interpretation. In 1953 the automobile companies set up a joint committee under the Automobile Manufacturers Association to study air pollution problems created by the automobile. Later, they also agreed to cross-license patents in the pollution field royalty free to introduce new pollution control devices simultaneously. The Justice Department sued, claiming the companies were restraining competition, and the case was settled out of court in September 1969. Whether the Justice Department would have objected to an industry-wide research effort in the absence of an agreement not to compete in introducing new technology is unclear. And even if they had, the courts might not have concurred.

There is also the concern that getting together with respresentatives of competing companies, however legitimate the purpose, raises suspicion of collusion. Since this increases the possibility of an antitrust suit, such meetings are, in the opinion of some, best avoided. The significance of this viewpoint for industry-wide cooperative research is hard to assess, but it could be important.

Even if antitrust policy does inhibit cooperative research efforts, the desirability of relaxing the antitrust laws can be questioned. If it were done without greatly weakening competition or rivalry, not much cooperative R&D would be undertaken, particularly at the development end of the cycle, since new technological developments can vitally affect the competitive positions of firms. On the other hand, if changes in antitrust policy greatly reduced competition, the increased production inefficiency and other costs to society could be substantial. This seems particularly likely if government regulation of prices and other aspects of business behavior increases as a countervailing force to the increased market power of firms.

Patent Policy. One way to increase the proportion of benefits realized by firms conducting R&D is to change the patent laws. The present laws restrict the potential profits of patent holders in a number of ways. For example, tying clauses that require the purchaser of a patented good to buy other goods or services as well are illegal. So too are patent pools that eliminate competition. And, over time the cost of defending patents has increased along with the probability of their being overturned in litigation.

While changes in the present patent system are unquestionably needed, whether such changes could provide an appropriate means of stimulating energy R&D seems doubtful. To stimulate more R&D the changes would have to increase the monopoly power of the patent holder. As in the case of antitrust policy, the cost in terms of reduced competition and rivalry may not be worth the benefits. Also, stronger patent rights are likely to restrict the rapid and widespread dissemination of new technology. Finally, for many firms patents apparently are not of great importance in determining the level of their investment in R&D,[16] and consequently changes in patent policy would not increase their research effort significantly.

Taxation. Changes in tax policy have also been advocated to increase the amount that firms spend on energy R&D. Special deductions, such as accelerated depreciation of R&D equipment, have been proposed and undoubtedly would encourage private spending. But R&D expenditures already can be completely deducted as operating costs, unlike investments in plant and equipment that must be depreciated over a number of years or much of the expenditure on education, which is not tax deductible at all.[17] Greater preferential treatment for R&D would bias the allocation of investment funds away from education and physical facilities. Moreover, tax concessions may not be an efficient means of stimulating energy R&D, if the private sector would undertake most projects without this incentive. Still, until more is known about the advantages and disadvantages of this possible alternative it deserves consideration.

Public Utility Regulation. The amount of R&D that public utilities fund is greatly influenced by regulation. If all the costs can be passed on to the consumer, the incentives to support R&D are greatly enhanced. Moreover, since most regulated firms are not restrained by antitrust policy and the fear of competition from other firms, much of their support is likely to be channeled into industry-wide efforts. The major example of such an effort is the Electric Power Research Institute, which plans to spend over $130 million in 1975 on energy R&D.[18]

Such cooperative endeavors can be considered as an alternative to more direct public intervention where the government collects the tax and allocates the funds. This raises the question of whether the government should abdicate responsibility in this area. An affirmative answer seems reasonable on the grounds that firms are closer to the technologies and the needs of both the industry and its customers, and so are in a better posi-

16. Clair Wilcox, *Public Policies toward Business,* 4th ed. (Homewood, Ill.: Irwin, 1971), p. 166.

17. Training expenses incurred by firms as well as contributions to educational institutions are not taxed, however.

18. See Electric Power Research Institute, *A Summary of Program Emphasis for 1975* (Palo Alto, Calif.), p. 26.

tion to allocate R&D funds efficiently. But the question of accountability also needs to be addressed. An unregulated firm has an incentive to carry out only those R&D projects whose technical and commercial potential is high enough that the firm expects them to increase profits, but a regulated firm that can pass on all R&D costs to the customer is not so disciplined. Moreover, if the interests of the industry and society diverge in the development of new technologies, such as those that conserve energy, and if the government has yielded its authority to intervene in the allocation process, how are the interests of society to be served? Regulatory agencies can review R&D contributions, but neither their past performance nor their present expertise suggests that they are particularly well suited to evaluate the effectiveness of R&D activity.

Trade Policy. One major impediment to the development of new domestic energy sources by private interests is the availability of huge reserves of very low cost oil in the Middle East and possibly elsewhere. Estimates of the price at which oil could be extracted profitably from shale with present technology range from just under $4 to $12 a barrel.[19] With Saudi Arabian oil estimated to cost between 10 and 12 cents a barrel to bring out of the ground and around one dollar to ship to the United States, no firm is going to spend much on developing oil shale unless assured of future protection from such low-cost competition. Nor will the high prices now being charged by oil exporting states overcome this reluctance. For potential developers of new energy sources know that once they have a product competitive at today's prices, the low-cost foreign producers may drop prices as necessary to assure that their market share is not seriously eroded. This leaves the oil shale producer with millions of dollars invested in equipment and R&D on which it may not recover the principal, let alone earn a reasonable rate of return.

The government can protect potential developers of new sources of energy from low-cost foreign oil by tariffs, quotas, or other restrictions on imports.[20] This means of supporting energy R&D has several advantages. First, compared to changes in patent policy and some of the other measures discussed, import restrictions can be more discriminating so

19. Most estimates are between $4.50 and $6 a barrel in 1972 dollars. See *The Perry Study,* p. 92.

20. While he was chairman of the Council of Economic Advisers, Herbert Stein suggested this policy. See "All Roads Are Steep in U.S. Drive to Achieve Energy Independence," *Wall Street Journal,* March 7, 1974, p. 1.

that energy R&D, even certain types of energy R&D, can be encouraged without simultaneously stimulating R&D in other fields. Second, compared with direct government funding of R&D, import restrictions leave the decision as to which new energy sources should be developed to the private sector, which should be more knowledgeable about the technical and commercial potential of the various possibilities. This increases the likelihood that the most promising new sources, and only the most promising new sources, will be developed. Indeed, if conventional domestic sources of energy can be expanded more cheaply than new sources can be developed, there is no incentive for private interests to invest in new sources of energy and thereby burden the country with unnecessarily high energy costs.

Protection, however, has several disadvantages. Probably most important is the possibility that a strongly insulated domestic market could be locked into paying substantially higher prices for energy, particularly oil, than the rest of the world. As we have already pointed out, the cost of Middle Eastern crude, even after transportation expenses are added, is very low. Should the solidarity of OPEC eventually collapse, not an inconceivable possibility, the United States could be burdened with energy costs substantially above those of its industrial competitors. Second, the cost of stimulating R&D by restricting imports is borne by the public in the form of higher consumer prices. This cost is not included in the federal budget, and therefore not reviewed annually to assure there are no higher priority needs for the funds. Third, new barriers to trade tend to undermine the movement toward freer trade and the benefits associated with this development. Fourth, the firm that undertakes a demonstration plant or other R&D project because of the protection provided by the government and paid for by the public is still free to restrict the use of the new knowledge and know-how arising from the project. Where the rapid dissemination of R&D results is essential to the realization of energy goals, other alternatives such as government R&D funding that force firms to divulge results may be preferable.

Government Procurement. An alternative means of stimulating energy R&D by the private sector that possesses many of the advantages of protection without some of its shortcomings is based on government procurement activity. Through long-term contracts, the government can guarantee domestic energy producers a market of any size that it wants. If the government's objective is to promote oil shale production, it can contract with one or more firms for the purchase over time of specified quantities of oil produced from shale.[21] This approach has been used in the past to expand the supply of uranium and to stimulate the development of the transistor and other new technologies. If the government's objective is broader, such as assuring a certain degree of self-sufficiency in energy supply, it could simply guarantee domestic producers the price needed to elicit the desired amount of domestic supply. Under this program the government might be forced to buy more energy than it needs for its own operations. Once the desired level of government stocks was reached, the surplus could be sold back to the civilian market. Or if the government preferred not to serve as a middleman, it could simply pay energy producers the difference between the guaranteed price and the lower market price. If imports are allowed to enter the country freely, domestic prices of energy would closely correspond to world prices. And the major impact of either cash payments to domestic energy producers or of government sales of energy back to the civilian market would be a reduction in imports, rather than a decline in domestic energy prices.[22]

Government procurement has several advantages over protection as a means for stimulating R&D. The costs are included in the government budget, so the commitment to such a program can be reviewed annually. In addition, government procurement should have a smaller adverse effect on the trend toward freer trade. And finally, the domestic price of energy would be closer to the international price, reducing the possibility that American producers of energy-intensive products, such as aluminum, would be unable to compete with foreign manufacturers. This does not mean that increased reliance on domestic sources would not have a cost. It would and the cost could be high, but it would be borne by the public qua taxpayers rather than as energy users.

However, there is some merit to having energy users pay the full cost of the energy they consume including costs incurred to reduce insecurity of supplies. To the extent that the benefits of security to individuals and

21. Secretary of Commerce Frederick B. Dent is reported to have advocated that the government agree to purchase or guarantee the price of designated quantities of synthetic fuel produced from shale or by coal liquefaction or gasification. The Dent proposal recommends that the government contract for 625,000 barrels of synthetic fuel a day in 1978 and then raise that figure to 4,100,000 barrels a day by 1982. It foresees the development of 68 synthetic fuel plants by 1982 at a cost to the government possibly as high as $98.1 billion. This figure, which is believed to be an upper limit, assumes the market price is $5 a barrel below the guaranteed price. See *ibid.*, pp. 1, 24.

22. This assumes that the supply of imports is highly elastic. As long as there is substantial excess capacity in the Middle East or elsewhere, this assumption seems reasonable whether oil is sold by a strong cartel or under competitive conditions.

organizations vary in accordance with the amounts of energy they consume, this is equitable. In addition, it restricts demand by discouraging consumers unwilling to pay the actual costs of producing energy from more expensive domestic sources. Given the constraint imposed on imports, this improves the efficiency of resource allocation.

Government procurement also has a drawback compared with government R&D funding. Like protection, it in no way obliges a firm to make public the results of its R&D effort even though that effort is indirectly supported by government funds. Indeed, in order to appropriate a large share of the benefits, the firm is motivated to restrict the dissemination through secrecy and patents.

Some have also argued, within the context of private R&D in general, that attempts by firms to restrict the dissemination of the R&D results lead to wasteful duplication of effort. This criticism, however, should be heavily discounted. The only way to avoid some duplication is through the centralized direction of all R&D, and the problems this would create have already been discussed under the limitations of government funded R&D. Moreover, some duplication is desirable. No two projects, however similar their objectives, will be conducted in exactly the same manner, and where many have failed one may succeed. Even after a project has achieved its initial objectives, other efforts may improve upon the results. So duplication not only increases the likelihood of success, but accelerates the pace of progress. The static inefficiency of duplication may be the essence of dynamic efficiency.

The preceding indicates that the government can promote energy R&D in a number of ways besides directly funding it. Some of the alternatives, such as relaxing the antitrust laws or modifying the patent system, are encumbered with rather serious problems. Others involving changes in regulation, protection, and procurement policies appear more promising. The important point, however, is that alternatives to government R&D funding do exist and that for many objectives they are likely to be preferable to more government sponsored R&D.

U.S. Funding Policy For Energy R&D

As was pointed out at the start of this chapter, energy R&D policy in the United States is undergoing a number of changes. Of particular importance is the increase in government funding, which has more than doubled over the last two years. This section, drawing on the preceding analysis, assesses this change and suggests that a definitive answer regarding its desirability is much more difficult to give than many have assumed.

The last section argued that the formulation of a rational energy R&D policy entails three steps. First, societal goals for the energy sector as a whole should be determined. Then, the various options available to the government for realizing these goals—government R&D funding, measures to influence private R&D expenditures, and other alternatives—should be identified. Finally, the options should be compared, and that combination that minimizes the social cost of obtaining the stated objectives implemented.

In contrast with this procedure, the administration decided first how much it should spend on energy R&D. In his energy message of June 1973, President Nixon recommended that the country spend $10 billion on energy R&D over a five-year period beginning in 1975. At that time he also directed the chairman of the Atomic Energy Commission, Dixy Lee Ray, to undertake a study that would recommend an integrated energy R&D program for the country. In a later message, he proposed "Project Independence," which calls for achieving national self-sufficiency in energy supplies by 1980.[23] Goals for energy R&D policy and for the energy sector in general were more fully specified in Dr. Ray's report, which appeared at the end of 1973.[24] Here self-sufficiency was also given top priority, though the importance of environmental considerations and energy costs was also recognized.

But even this study leaves the impression that societal goals for the energy sector have not received careful consideration. The emphasis on self-sufficiency, in particular, seems somewhat misplaced for a number of reasons. First, the ultimate objective presumably is to increase the security of energy supplies since it is the interruption of supplies that creates hardship and turmoil, not dependence on foreign energy per se. Self-sufficiency would eliminate some sources of instability, but certainly not all, as the strikes by coal miners and truckers in Britain and the United States over the last several years have clearly illustrated. Moreover, there may be cheaper ways to increase security, such as diversifying the sources of imports or stockpiling. And the benefits from total self-sufficiency may not exceed the costs. Greater security than now exists may

23. See the President's energy message of November 7, 1973, which is reproduced in U.S. Senate, Committee on Interior and Insular Affairs, *Presidential Energy Statements,* 93d Cong., 1st sess., 1973, pp. 81–87.

24. See Dixy Lee Ray, *The Nation's Energy Future,* Report to Richard M. Nixon, December 1973, esp. pp. 53–54.

be desirable, but it is far from clear, given the cost (including the environmental costs) of complete self-sufficiency, that the latter is in the best interest of the country. Finally, self-sufficiency for the United States without a sizable reduction in the dependency of Western Europe and Japan on vulnerable energy sources is of dubious value if it accentuates the diversity of interests and so strains the relations between the United States and its allies. Early manifestations of such tensions are already apparent, as Japan's abrupt change in foreign policy in the Middle East illustrates, and if the strain is allowed to continue, it could undermine the political options and defense posture of the United States.

Moreover, regardless of how carefully public goals for the energy sector have been set, they were determined after the decision to spend $10 billion in public funds on energy R&D, rather than before. In addition, there is little indication that the government seriously compared public R&D funding with other possible means of achieving desired objectives before deciding how much to spend.

These deficiencies in approach raise, for several reasons, the possibility that too much government funding has been committed to energy R&D. First, there are no well organized interest groups opposed to such government funding. This is not the case for many of the possible alternative measures for realizing public goals, such as the deregulation of natural gas prices or an increase in the number of outer continental shelf leases. Unless possible options are explicitly identified and compared, political expediency is likely to dictate that public policy follow the course of least resistance.

Second, the primary cause of the present energy shortages in the United States, as we pointed out at the beginning of this chapter, is not inadequate reserves of conventional energy sources, but rather bottlenecks in plant, equipment, and trained manpower. Yet for well over a century the fear of natural resource exhaustion has worried many, even though predictions of calamity have yet to materialize. Indeed, at least until the last twenty years, the real cost of mineral commodities has fallen.[25] If goals are not set carefully and objectively, this prevalent, though basically unsubstantiated, concern may unduly influence the results, shifting attention away from relieving the bottlenecks and toward

25. Harold J. Barnett and Chandler Morse, *Scarcity and Growth: The Economics of Natural Resource Availability* (Baltimore: Johns Hopkins for Resources for the Future, 1963), chs. 8–9. For more on various groups concerned about the exhaustion of resources, see Thomas M. Humphrey, "The Dismal Science Revisited," *Federal Reserve Bank of Richmond Monthly Review,* 59 (March 1973), pp. 2–13.

developing new sources of energy. Since R&D is a more appropriate policy instrument for realizing new energy sources than for relieving bottlenecks in plant, equipment, and manpower, this shift in emphasis tends to promote a higher level of energy R&D funding than is desirable.

Third, even where more energy R&D is appropriate, the present policy may rely too heavily on government funding and too little on measures to stimulate private R&D expenditures. For, as was just pointed out, despite the numerous and important sources of inefficiency associated with government R&D funding, the administration in deciding how much it should spend on energy R&D did not seriously consider the relative advantages of the various alternatives for stimulating energy R&D by the private sector.

The likelihood that the proposed jump in energy R&D spending exceeds the optimum is further increased by two other biases in the political decision-making process. Because of the checks and balances between branches of government and the bottlenecks within each branch, such as the congressional committee system, there is considerable inertia in the American political system. As a result, when problems such as those associated with the environment or energy arise, the tendency is to delay too long in dealing with them. Once a critical level of public concern is manifest, however, the system does respond. Indeed, it then often becomes politically advantageous, partly because of the favorable publicity, for public officials to deal boldly with such problems. This creates a tendency toward overreaction.

That tendency is reinforced by the penchant of experts consulted by public officials to overstate and exaggerate the seriousness of the problems. To some extent this may be a conscious attempt to counter some of the initial inertia of the political system. One may recommend that the government spend $2 billion a year on energy R&D in the hope that this will help provide the necessary impetus for $1 billion. Exaggerations aimed, consciously or unconsciously, to promote government activities that serve the special interests of the experts are also possible. Many of those advocating greater public support for energy R&D are businessmen, consultants, academicians, administrators, and others likely to benefit from increased government funding. Finally, overstatements arise because of the natural tendency to magnify, often unconsciously, the importance of one's field. This occurs not only because an individual has to rationalize to himself the time and effort he has spent in a particular field, but also because he is less aware of the potential of other fields. The Energy experts may overstate the desirability of increasing energy R&D simply because they have little knowledge of the potential benefits of R&D on desalination, disarmament, geriatrics, and other possible projects outside the energy field. In short, they tend to underestimate the opportunity costs associated with increasing energy R&D expenditures.

Even if a doubling of government spending on energy R&D is considered appropriate, the speed with which this increase is being realized should be questioned. While greater funding can accelerate the pace at which new technology is developed, there are increasing costs associated with such efforts.[26] Even more serious are the shortages in trained manpower and facilities that such an acceleration creates. These factors add appreciably to the waste and reduce the efficiency of R&D expenditures.

Another potential problem that deserves more attention is that of the costs and hardships incurred when a major R&D effort is cut back. As the space program has demonstrated, the economic costs to society in terms of unused highly trained personnel and the psychological costs to the individuals involved can be substantial. The seriousness of this problem for a large R&D program in energy will depend on several factors. Any tendency to overshoot the optimal level of R&D effort will aggravate it, for as the excesses of the program become apparent and other problems attract public attention, funds for energy R&D will be cut sooner and by greater amounts than would otherwise be the case. The longevity of public interest in energy will also affect the problem. If the bottlenecks in plant, equipment, and trained manpower primarily responsible for the present energy shortages can be largely eliminated in five to ten years, the level of government R&D spending politically sustainable could decline substantially within a decade. A technological breakthrough, such as *in situ* extraction of shale oil, could have a similar effect.

The consequences of too rapid a buildup of energy R&D and of overshooting the optimal level are serious. Overreaction is in no one's interest. Society as a whole suffers from the waste and misallocation of scarce

26. For more on this phenomenon, referred to as the time-cost trade-off function, see Scherer, *Industrial Market Structure,* pp. 367–76; Edwin Mansfield et al., *Research and Innovation in the Modern Corporation* (New York: Norton, 1971), pp. 126–33; and F. M. Scherer, "Government Research and Development Program," in *Measuring Benefits of Government Investments,* Robert Dorfman, ed. (Washington: Brookings, 1965), pp. 34–56.

R&D resources, and the scientific and industrial communities that have the greatest vested interests in more energy R&D will suffer severely if inappropriate policies attract too many firms and too many highly trained individuals into the energy R&D business.

The conclusion should not be drawn from the preceding discussion that the recent increases in government sponsored energy R&D are necessarily wrong. Given the complexity of the problem, there is no way of knowing for certain what the optimal amount of government funding is. At most, a more modest conclusion seems justified: namely, that it is not nearly as certain as many believe that these increases are right.

But more significantly, this chapter has tried to demonstrate the importance of making energy R&D decisions in conjunction with, indeed as a part of, energy policy in general. The complicated and interactive effects of regulation, inappropriable benefits, and other deviations from the competitive market make government planning essential for the energy sector. Public funding for energy R&D should be treated as one means or policy instrument available to the government for realizing its energy goals. Moreover, because of the serious inefficiencies associated with government R&D funding, for many objectives more effective instruments for public intervention can be found. But this requires that the alternatives be identified and their advantages and disadvantages compared to those of public R&D funding before energy R&D decisions are made.

Finally, the study has tried to caution against an overreaction of public policy in the energy R&D field. Much of the present public concern about energy arises from the monopolistic prices being charged by the major oil exporting countries, and from shortages induced by inadequate petroleum refinery capacity, electric power generating facilities, and coal mining equipment and manpower. These problems have been compounded by price controls on natural gas and other energy sources, environmental restrictions, and the fear of a renewed Arab oil embargo. Just how long these concerns will continue to trouble the American public is far from certain. To a large extent this will depend on how deft the government is in dealing with them. However, the nature of these problems does not dictate that they persist for decades, as would be the case if the exhaustion of energy resources were the problem.

The possibility of overreaction, coupled with the biases toward too much government funding that arise from the process used in determining government expenditures on energy R&D, raises concern that the nation is embarking on too grandiose an energy R&D program. Two billion dollars is more than a third of all government expenditures in 1973 for nondefense and nonspace R&D. How likely is it that the American people will continue to support such a heavy emphasis on energy R&D over an extended period? Moreover, the consequences of overreaction could be serious. During the buildup, resources are wasted and diverted from higher priority uses. And after the cutback, highly trained and experienced manpower and other R&D resources lie idle, or are shunted off to other uses where their capabilities are less appropriate. Ironically, many of those now arguing most forcefully for more government support are among those ultimately likely to suffer the most from inappropriate policies that overallocate resources to energy R&D.

6

Petroleum: An Unregulated Industry?

Walter J. Mead

The oil man and the farmer envision themselves as the last vestiges of rugged free enterprise and individualism, yet both have been favored with protective legislation, at least since the 1930s. For the oil industry, legislation has consisted of special tax treatment described elsewhere in this book by Stephen McDonald, and of a mass of regulations governing petroleum supply usually rationalized in the name of conservation or national security.

Petroleum supply regulations may be classified into four types:

(1) Regulations to benefit the petroleum industry. These include market-demand prorationing, which limits output of oil and thereby causes its price to be higher than free market conditions would permit. Import quotas are also included in this category. The import quota system limited competition from foreign sources, again causing the domestic price to be higher than free market conditions would allow.

(2) Regulations to benefit society, including the petroleum industry. This class includes prorationing regulations of the Maximum Efficient Rate (MER) type designed to avoid physical waste of oil resources. Unitization regulations (requiring that an oil reservoir be managed as a unit) also aim to avoid resource waste.

(3) Regulations designed to protect society's interest, which may also benefit the industry. These include environmental protection and worker safety laws and regulations.

(4) Regulations intended to benefit consumers at the expense of the oil industry. The principal regulatory tool in this class is price control on crude oil and its products. (Natural gas price control also fits into this category but is discussed in another chapter by Stephen Breyer and Paul MacAvoy.) The imposition of federal price controls has created a two-tier pricing system for crude oil, leading to additional regulations establishing

a system of compulsory allocations and an entitlements program. The former requires a transfer of crude oil at below market prices, the latter a transfer of money between firms in the oil industry.

What Are the Economic Justifications for Government Regulation of Any Industry?

First, government action is occasionally desirable when the market system fails to give correct signals to decision makers. Most economic activity in a free enterprise system is self-regulating through competition among producers. In effect, the system of competitive free market prices forces producers to operate efficiently, producing and selling the best possible products at the lowest possible prices. Consumers who are free to allocate their scarce income direct resources in ways that are satisfactory to consumers in total. Inefficient producers, in the long run, are forced out of business, while efficient producers offering new and better products desired by consumers are rewarded with temporary high profits.

This is the way a free market system is supposed to operate. However, the market occasionally fails to allocate resources in a way that is of maximum benefit to society. In some areas there are what economists call "externalities," which lead to market failure. An externality exists wherever some of the costs resulting from production or use of a commodity spill over on to society, rather than being borne directly by the enterprise that generates them. The classic illustration is air or water pollution. The effluent from a smoke stack pollutes the air of everyone in its vicinity. But the individual or organization causing the air pollution bears only his proportionate share of this social cost.

An externality may include a benefit as well as a cost. For example, in the nineteenth century, development of the western area of the United States was of interest to the entire nation. The railroads were important in opening up the West and in the process incurred costs of development but were able to collect benefits only from passenger and freight charges. They could not fully collect the spillover benefits in the form of regional improvement for which they were responsible. In fact, Congress made large land grants available to the western railroads in order to compensate them for the external benefits that they created.

Where externalities are present, we have a justification for government interference, which may take one of four forms. (1) Where there is an external cost such as air or water pollution, the government may regulate the offending industry in order to reduce or prevent pollution. (2) The government may levy a tax on the offender in order to make the act of pollution expensive and lead him to take corrective measures. (3) Where there is an external benefit, the government may seek to compensate the enterprise responsible for creating it by means of a tax or cash subsidy. (4) Where externalities are large, the government may perform the function in question through an organization of its own, as in the case of the Post Office.

Second, government intervention may be necessary to maintain effective competition or, where natural monopolies exist, to regulate such monopolies in the public interest. The essence of private monopoly power is the ability to restrict output in order to obtain higher product prices and monopoly profits. Where competition is effective, collusion to restrict output and earn monopoly profit is impossible. In a few instances, economies of large-scale production are so great that monopoly is the natural condition. This situation appears to prevail in such industries as electric power production, municipal transportation, water supply, and telephone communication. These industries have all been subject to public utility-type rate regulations that attempt to protect the public interest.

Third, a final reason for government interference in a free market system is to promote income redistribution. This is a matter about which economic theory has relatively little to say. Government effort to redistribute income is an appropriate matter to be decided in the political process. As we will see below, income redistribution has, in some cases, been given as a justification for government interference in the petroleum industry and has frequently been a result of government regulation whether intended or not.

In the sections to follow we will first identify and then evaluate major types of federal and state controls over the oil industry. These will include prorationing and other controls over production, import quotas, and price controls with their accompaniment of allocations and entitlements.

Prorationing and Other Controls over the Petroleum Industry [1]

Control over production through state prorationing regulations originated out of chaotic conditions in the past. Three important physical and

---

1. In this section we will draw heavily on a recent and thorough study of petroleum production controls by Stephen L. McDonald, *Petroleum Conservation in the United States* (Baltimore: Johns Hopkins, 1971). Readers interested in a more thorough analysis of pro-

economic characteristics of oil led naturally to prorationing. First, divided ownership of the land surface above any large oil reservoir is a prevailing fact of economic life. Second, the existing system of property rights concerning oil is governed by the "law of capture," which states that petroleum belongs to the landowner or lessee who captures it through wells located on his land regardless of its original location. Third, oil is a migratory resource. Oil in any reservoir behaves as a fluid and will move through the permeable stratum of the reservoir toward an area of lower relative pressure. In most reservoirs oil is pressed upward by water and downward by a gas cap. As oil is produced through a well, an area of low pressure is created within the reservoir. Pressure then forces oil through the permeable stratum in an attempt to establish a new equilibrium throughout the reservoir. Given divided ownership of the surface land and the law of capture, the landowner who gets into a reservoir first with the most wells will get more than his share of the oil.

Each landowner, in order to protect his own interest, will attempt to establish wells as quickly as possible and get them into production and the oil onto a pipeline for delivery to a market. But as each operator attempts not only to get his share of the oil but also to capture shares which might be taken by others, large-scale waste will occur. Waste results from rapid depletion of reservoir pressure, causing a loss of ultimate oil recovery. In addition, there is a waste of capital resources as too many wells are drilled and developed and unnecessary storage tanks are constructed on the surface. Further, there may be waste of oil owing to evaporation from open air storage facilities and to occasional spillage from such facilities. An oil well commonly also produces associated gas. If gas pipelines are not available, rapid exploitation may result in gas flaring and not only in waste of this valuable resource but in air pollution as well. Oil production also commonly yields water, which may include salt water or other brines. Historically, rapid exploitation has involved water pollution as these contaminants are dumped into streams or spilled out onto the surface. Efforts to maintain wellhead pressure by reinjecting gas and water into a reservoir are discouraged by the three basic characteristics described above. If any small property owner reinjects either gas or water into his well, he may drive oil away from it, benefiting adjacent property owners. Even where reinjection is carefully managed, it involves costs

---

duction controls are encouraged to refer to that study, or to Wallace F. Lovejoy and Paul T. Homan, *Economic Aspects of Oil Conservation Regulation* (Baltimore: Johns Hopkins, 1967).

which benefit other property owners; hence there may be underinvestment in reinjection.

Where these three characteristics lead to rapid rates of production from any reservoir, the ratio of ultimate recovery to total oil in place will be relatively low. Under present conditions, about 31 percent of the oil originally present is recovered from reservoirs in the United States.[2] Where reservoir pressure is depleted too rapidly, ultimate recovery will be relatively low. Where reservoir pressure maintenance programs are carried out and where secondary recovery operations by water injection, gas injection, steam injection, burning *in situ,* or other methods of stimulation are followed, some of the benefits will be external to the operator who carries them out. Although such operations may result in substantial increases in ultimate recovery above the rate available without them, the market fails to reward the individual responsible for such benefits.

The optimum solution to these problems appears to be management of a reservoir as if it were under a single ownership. One system by which this is accomplished is unitization, wherein management of a reservoir is delegated to a single operator, usually the largest in the field, who then invests in field development and produces in a manner that maximizes the present value of the oil resource. This procedure serves the interest not only of the owners but of society as well. But while unitization laws exist in some states, the historical trend has been in another direction, that of prorationing controls which have been exercised by states over well spacing, production per well, and other characteristics tending to reduce physical waste.

The results of unrestrained oil production as each owner seeks to maximize his own profits can be seen in the history of oil production and price movements. Table 1 shows oil production in the United States and in the state of Texas, together with crude oil prices for select years from 1920 through 1933. Unconstrained, crude oil production varies with and follows discovery. In the 1920s and early 1930s prolific new fields were discovered, largely in Texas. Table 1 shows a threefold increase in Texas oil production from 1920 through 1929. This is more than the increase that demand could absorb at prevailing prices, and the per-barrel price declined by more than half. Then from 1929 through 1933, during the Great Depression, crude oil production in Texas expanded another 36 percent in the face of a sharp decline in consumption. As a conse-

---

2. Federal Energy Administration, *Project Independence, A Summary* (Washington: U.S. Government Printing Office, November 1974), p. 5.

Table 1. Crude oil prices and production, the State of Texas and the United States, 1920–1933

| | Production | | Price per bbl. at wellhead ($) |
	Texas (thousand bbl. per day)	U.S.	
1920	96.9	442	3.07
1925	144.6	763	1.68
1929	296.9	1,007	1.27
1933	402.6	905	0.67

Source: American Petroleum Institute, *Petroleum Facts and Figures,* 1971 ed., p. 70.

quence, the annual average of U.S. crude oil prices declined again by about half to 67 cents per barrel. The average figures obscure the fact that sales were recorded in the range of 5 to 10 cents per barrel. A crude oil producer from a reservoir subject to divided ownership had no incentive to conserve oil for a better market. To do so would have meant that his inventory would be captured by his neighbor. Any selling price above the variable lifting cost was preferable to no income at all.

These conditions overcame the reluctance of operators to surrender a share of their individual control over output, and led to a political climate which facilitated legislation at both federal and state levels, ultimately resulting in production controls.

Prorationing is of two kinds. First, what is called MER-type prorationing is related to state control over production in order to approximate, in a vague way, the Maximum Efficient Rate of recovery of oil from a given reservoir. This type of prorationing is intended to reduce overinvestment in oil wells and overproduction from any given reservoir. Second, market-demand prorationing is a second step beyond MER-type prorationing and further limits production to an amount equal to the estimated market demand at the prevailing price. Market-demand prorationing appears to be a standard monopoly device whereby production is constrained in order to attain a selling price higher than competition would permit.

Regulation of oil production prior to 1933 was almost entirely done by states and was concerned primarily with controls over well casings and the plugging of wells to prevent flows of fluids between strata and avoid pollution of fresh water and damage to coal mines. Some states also passed laws outlawing discrimination by oil and gas purchasers, including pipeline companies. Increasingly, legislation attacked various kinds of physical waste in oil production.

In 1933 the federal government led the way into production control to attain economic objectives desired by producers and at the expense of consumers. The National Recovery Act (NRA), which passed Congress late in 1933, included a petroleum code that provided for import restrictions, minimum prices for crude oil, limitations on domestic production to total demand less imports, allocation of allowed domestic production among states, reservoirs, and wells, and administrative approval of new reservoir development plans. The NRA represented the first attempt in the United States to legislate a comprehensive system of economic controls on oil production for the benefit of the oil industry. The petroleum code of the NRA introduced monopoly powers enforced by the federal government. The act was short-lived, however. The Supreme Court invalidated it in 1935.

Meanwhile, governors of oil producing states, apparently in anticipation of the death of the NRA, were at work in 1934 to assert additional state control over oil production. The Oil States Advisory Committee produced a draft of a compact to establish an Interstate Oil Compact Commission. The compact was approved by the committee on February 15, 1935. Congress, in turn, consented to the Interstate Oil Compact in August 1935, and the Interstate Oil Compact Commission was created.

Article II of the compact concisely states its aim: "The purpose of this Compact is to conserve oil and gas by the prevention of physical waste thereof from any cause." Article V specifically denies any attempt at price conspiracy: "It is not the purpose of this Compact to authorize the states joining herein to limit the production of oil or gas for the purpose of stabilizing or fixing the price thereof, or create or perpetuate monopoly, or to promote regimentation, but is limited to the purpose of conserving oil and gas and preventing the avoidable waste thereof within reasonable limitations." This statement was designed to avoid conflict with federal and state antitrust laws.

Article VI relates the commission's activities to the enforcement powers to be wielded by member states. It states, "The Commission shall have power to recommend the coordination of the exercise of the police power of the several states within their several jurisdictions, to promote the maximum ultimate recovery from the petroleum reserves of said states, and to recommend measures for the maximum ultimate recovery of oil and gas." Thus, individual states rather than the federal government were charged under the compact with the duties of regulation, but were not required to legislate such programs.

The federal government not only approved the Interstate Oil Compact, but went beyond it and enacted the Connally Hot Oil Act in 1935. In essence, this act enforces state market-demand prorationing restrictions by declaring that oil produced in violation of state laws may not be shipped in interstate commerce. Thus the Connally Hot Oil Act provides the teeth for enforcing market-demand output restrictions.

Prorationing of the MER type limits output by various devices. First, nine states [3] limit output from each reservoir to an estimate of its Maximum Efficient Rate of recovery. This is the level of output consistent with no significant loss of ultimate recovery. The MER is determined for each reservoir and then allocated among the individual producers within it. Even as a concept, the calculation of an efficient rate of production is haphazard. Regulation aims at curbing physical waste whereas the relevant concept is economic waste. Moreover, even physical waste is rarely defined except in terms of itself. Lovejoy and Homan point out that "the regulatory authorities have no working concept of 'waste,' so that it becomes whatever they find themselves engaged in 'preventing.' " [4] Even the Interstate Oil Compact Commission "model statute" fails to define waste rigorously. It reads as follows: " 'Waste' means and includes: (1) physical waste, as that term is generally understood in the oil and gas industry; (2) the inefficient, excessive, or improper use, or the unnecessary dissipation of, reservoir energy. . . ." The Kansas statute similarly states that "the term 'waste' as used herein, in addition to its ordinary meaning, shall include economic waste, service waste, waste of reservoir energy. . . ."

Second, an even more primitive system is applied by six states,[5] which limit production by control over well spacing. By limiting the number of wells which may tap any given reservoir, spacing regulations may be used to restrict the rate of production. While limited well density is clearly preferable to uncontrolled spacing, any other relationship that well spacing regulations may bear to a maximum efficient rate of production is purely coincidental.

Third, some of the leading oil producing states, including Texas, Loui-

3. Arkansas, Mississippi, Alaska, Utah, Colorado, Wyoming, Montana, Nebraska, and California (voluntarily).

4. Lovejoy and Homan, *Economic Aspects of Oil Conservation Regulation,* p. 133.

5. Illinois, Indiana, Ohio, Pennsylvania, Kentucky, and West Virginia.

siana, Oklahoma, New Mexico, and Kansas, limit output on the basis of depth acreage schedules which specify the number of barrels of oil which may be produced per day dependent upon the number of acres per well and the depth of the well. These allowable "yardsticks" permit greater production per well as acreage per well increases, and also greater production per well for greater depth. For example, Texas permits maximum daily production as illustrated in Table 2 for select spacing and depth. The depth acreage approach to MER-type prorationing logically reduces the permissible output per well for smaller acreages drained per well. For example, on a forty-acre spacing basis at 2,000 to 3,000 feet depths, seventy-eight barrels per day may be produced according to the Texas yardstick. However, if ten acres are drained by a single well (this is equivalent to four wells on forty acres) then the permissible output per well is reduced by about one-fourth. This rule avoids the historical excesses of overinvestments in well development, but otherwise approaches an optimum only by chance.

Table 2. Texas allowable yardstick (depth-acreage schedule) in barrels per day

	Acres per well				
Depth (thousand ft.)	10	20	40	80	160
2.0–3.0	22	41	78	135	249
5.0–6.0	26	52	102	171	310
10.0–10.5	48	96	192	300	515

Source: Texas Railroad Commission.

The increased permissible production with depth bears even less relationship to a hypothetical Maximum Efficient Rate of production. Only if lean reservoirs were shallow and rich reservoirs deep would the depth schedule make sense. Instead, the rationale for the depth factor appears to be a political one, that of providing higher allowables for wells that have incurred higher drilling costs. Drilling costs increase geometrically as depth increases. However, this rationale is totally unrelated to the concept of conservation, which is supposed to be the prime concern of production controls. The higher allowables for deep wells are often useless. Many such wells cannot lift their maximum allowable. If they are not subject to unitized management, then the favorable allowables are likely to result in excessive production and a rapid decline in reservoir pressures, in turn sacrificing ultimate reservoir productivity. This is precisely the situation of the 1920s and early 1930s that production controls were designed to avoid.

None of the three methods listed above for determining maximum reservoir allowables appears to be an efficient means of determining the Maximum Efficient Rate of production. Nevertheless, they have served to avoid the waste resulting from vast overinvestment in reservoir development and excessive rates of production that was common in the past. This type of control has, therefore, benefited both oil producers and society at large.

Unitization of reservoirs would eliminate a need for much of the MER-type prorationing regulation. Under unitization, control of production for a given reservoir would be turned over to a designated operator who would further define and develop the reservoir, and then produce from it, distributing its output in accordance with an agreed-upon schedule. The unit operator would have a private incentive to operate the reservoir at a Maximum Efficient Rate of production, and there would be no need for regulations concerning pressure maintenance and gas-oil ratios (the ratio of gas production to oil production). Similarly the costs of overinvestment in well development would have to be fully borne (internalized) by the owners and hence would be avoided. The benefits of secondary recovery would be fully realized by the operator, and so we could expect an optimum level of investment in secondary recovery in the absence of any government regulations. The only remaining externalities resulting from oil production and requiring governmental regulations would be those caused by environmental pollution, including such factors as waste water disposal.

Unitization is currently largely a voluntary matter. However, twenty-one states have statutes that exercise some degree of compulsion leading owners toward it. In view of the benefits of reservoir unitization one may ask why states have not enacted laws to make it mandatory. Unitization involves compulsion, but as McDonald points out, this is a strange reason for objecting to it, given the context of pervasive regulation already existing in the oil industry. "All regulation involves compulsion, and regulation *per se* is no longer an issue. The question is, 'What will be compelled?' In the prevailing system of regulation, compulsion centers on well spacing, rate of production, gas flaring, and similar matters. . . . Free operations under unitization would substitute for specific, detailed kinds of regulations." [6] McDonald further argues that unitization would be "a net grant of freedom—a step back toward free enterprise in petroleum production, which unitization makes compatible with conservation." [7]

Individual operators also fear that they may come out second best in a conflict of interest among owners, some of whom would be limited to crude oil production while others are vertically integrated oil companies. However, current regulations allocate production among the owners of reservoirs in a largely arbitrary manner, frequently on a rule of thumb basis. There is very little in the present system that safeguards individual interest.

Some opponents of unitization point out that there will be great difficulties in arriving at unitization agreements. It is true that this process would be time-consuming, but it would be so because of the need to protect individual interests. The bargaining process, together with supervision by a conservation commission, would offer protection. The benefits would appear to be greater than the cost.

Market-demand prorationing is, in effect, appended to the basic state allowables. Under market-demand prorationing, state authorities limit supplies to the amount of oil that buyers indicate they intend to purchase in the following month. In order to arrive at this determination, the state regulatory commissions have until recently had available to them a monthly forecast of demand provided by the U.S. Bureau of Mines. [8] In addition, they commonly request "nominations" from buyers of oil. The buyers are also the principal producers and sellers of oil in the same state. For example, Exxon is both the largest buyer and the largest producer of crude oil in Texas. Other companies that nominate quantities demanded and are also producers include Texaco, Standard Oil of Indiana, Atlantic-Richfield, Phillips Petroleum, Shell Oil, Mobil Oil and Standard Oil of California. Through their nominations, companies can indirectly control the amount of oil to be produced within a state. By summing the nominations, the state regulatory agency determines the quantity demanded for the ensuing month. When this quantity is divided by the basic allowable for the state, a decimal fraction is determined which indicates the market-demand factor for the month to follow. Thus a 0.7 market-demand factor indicates that a producer may produce 70 percent of his basic allowable for a specific well during a one-month period. An annual average of

6. McDonald, *Petroleum Conservation*, p. 250.   7. *Ibid.*
8. The Bureau of Mines has discontinued estimation of crude oil demand.

monthly demand factors for Texas and Louisiana covering the period 1948–1974 is shown in Table 3. We find that for the state of Texas market-demand factors declined from 100 percent in 1948 to a low of 27 percent in 1962 and rose to 100 percent again in recent years. The Texas Railroad Commission established a 100 percent market-demand factor for Texas for the month of April 1972 and has maintained that level to the present (March 1976). The system of market-demand controls is still fully in effect. State regulatory commissions continue to review market demand and supply each month and to issue the market-demand factors. In

Table 3. Market demand factors, annual average, Texas and Louisiana, 1948–1975 (in percent)

Year	Texas	Louisiana
1948	100	–
1949	65	–
1950	63	–
1951	76	–
1952	71	–
1953	65	90
1954	53	61
1955	53	48
1956	52	42
1957	47	43
1958	33	33
1959	34	34
1960	28	34
1961	28	32
1962	27	32
1963	28	32
1964	28	32
1965	29	33
1966	34	35
1967	41	38
1968	45	42
1969	52	44
1970	72	56
1971	73	73
1972	94	91
1973	100	100
1974	100	100
1975	100	100

Sources: Texas Railroad Commission and Department of Conservation, State of Louisiana.

the event that state commissions in the future find free market prices to be unacceptably low, market-demand factors will probably be issued which direct production below 100 percent of basic allowables, and market-demand prorationing will again become an effective restraint.

Price has never been mentioned, either by the Bureau of Mines when it estimated crude oil demand, or by the state commissions when they solicit nominations and determine the market-demand factor. The implicit and naive assumption is that the demand for crude oil in the respective states has an elasticity of zero. This means that the quantity demanded is the same regardless of price. In the real world of markets, however, the law of demand applies, asserting that at lower prices greater quantities will be demanded. This is borne out if one looks at the demand for crude oil in any particular state.

If the market demand as determined by a regulatory commission is greater than the basic allowable for the state, then a 100 percent market-demand factor applies and each producer is free to produce his full basic allowable. This is the condition prevailing at the moment. On the other hand, where the computed market demand is less than the basic allowable, production curtailments are ordered and nonexempt producers must comply with the market-demand factor. If they fail to do so, and produce in excess of state regulation, then the Connally Hot Oil Act precludes the sale of such oil in interstate commerce.

Some producers are exempt from market-demand prorationing controls. In general, there are three classes of exempt wells. First, discovery wells are generally exempt permitting a period of grace. For example, Texas allows an exemption of twenty-four months, or until the eleventh well is drilled in any new field, whichever comes first. Second, wells in a pressure maintenance condition and where secondary recovery operations are in progress generally are exempt. Third, low capacity wells or stripper wells (normally defined as those wells producing less than ten barrels per day) are generally exempt.

The share of total output accounted for by exempt wells differs by state: the exempt share appears to vary from a low of about 20 percent to a high of about 60 percent. Because exempt wells may produce at their full basic allowable (actual production may be less than the basic allowable for certain fields) the burden of production cutbacks must be borne entirely by the nonexempt wells. These are often the most prolific. Thus one effect of market-demand prorationing is to permit full-scale operations on inefficient wells, while imposing wasteful production inefficiency on the most prolific.

Nine states in which crude oil was produced in 1973 had market-demand prorationing. They are listed with their respective daily production rates in Table 4. We find that these states accounted for 65 percent of total U.S. crude oil production in 1973. The principal non-market-demand states are California, Wyoming, Alaska, Mississippi, and Colorado.

Table 4. Crude oil production from market-demand prorationing states having oil production in 1973 (thousand bbl. per day average)

1973 rank	State	Production
1	Texas	3,544 *
2	Louisiana	1,233 *
4	Oklahoma	524
6	New Mexico	276
8	Kansas	181
12	Florida	90
15	North Dakota	54
17	Michigan	40
18	Alabama	33
Total market demand		5,975
Total U.S. production		9,187

Source: American Petroleum Institute, *Annual Statistics Review*, 1964–1973, p. 9.
* Includes state offshore production, but excludes federal OCS.

The market-demand prorationing states bear the traditional burden of the incomplete monopolist. Given market weakness, these states must reduce output in order to maintain their desired price. The non-market-demand states reap the benefits of prices above competitive levels without bearing the burden of output reductions.

As indicated earlier, the essence of monopoly power is the ability to hold prices above their competitive levels by reducing output below competitive levels. The record of crude oil prices by year and annual average market-demand factors for the state of Texas for 1948 through 1974 is shown in Figure 1. The Texas Railroad Commission reduced market-demand factors from 100 percent in 1948 to 63 percent in 1950. This sharp reduction in output permitted prices to remain approximately constant. Production cutbacks in the mid-1950s were again severe and actually permitted price increases. Further production cutbacks as shown in

Figure 1. Relationship between crude oil price and market-demand factor

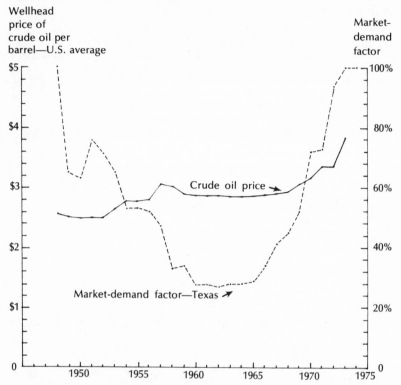

Source: Crude oil prices from American Petroleum Institute, *Petroleum Facts and Figures,* 1971, and *Annual Statistical Review,* 1964–1973; market-demand factor, Texas, from Texas Railroad Commission.

the market-demand factors were ordered in the early 1960s, enabling crude oil prices to remain approximately constant. Then as the period of the energy crisis approached, crude oil prices rose sharply and market-demand factors were steadily increased to 100 percent effective in April 1972. The presence of excess capacity in the 1960s avoided what would have been even higher crude price levels in the early 1970s. Thus, Figure 1 shows evidence to support the monopoly pricing contention as well as a price stabilization function of market-demand prorationing.

Production controls of the MER type are clearly imperfect devices for attaining their intended goals. At the same time they represent a substantial improvement over the uncontrolled conditions which led to the Interstate Oil Compact and to state conservation regulations. The past excesses of overinvestment in well density and output per well are no longer considered to be serious difficulties. These problems of externalities have been partially overcome.

The depth acreage allowable schedules, as well as the well spacing controls, bear little relation to Maximum Efficient Rates of production. Nevertheless, they have the merit of being an inexpensive substitute for a somewhat more efficient MER calculation.

Market-demand prorationing controls have solved some of the early problems of discrimination against firms not having equal access to pipelines. Because the market-demand calculation process involves limiting output to quantities nominated by crude oil buyers, all production that is authorized by the state prorationing authority automatically has a market. Discrimination becomes unlikely.

While the foregoing are positive results of the prorationing experience, it has also had negative effects.

Well spacing regulations and depth acreage allowables are largely arbitrary and have very little relation to conservation principles or to the amount of reserves recoverable per acre.

Even the MER approach to basic allowables is an imperfect measure. It is entirely a physical concept, whereas the relevant issue from both a private and a social point of view is economic efficiency.

Both types of prorationing systems involve resource misallocation among states. Prorationing rules differ from state to state. Some states have market-demand regulations and others do not. Capital flows into oil exploration and production in search of maximum yields. Where state regulations are arbitrary and limit profitability, the capital flow into those states will be suboptimal.

Exemptions from market-demand regulations also lead to distortions. The most prolific wells are penalized by market-demand regulations and hence capital is diverted from its most efficient uses into less efficient but favored operations.

From the point of view of economic analysis, market-demand prorationing is clearly a monopolistic device. Whenever market-demand factors are less than 100 percent, crude oil prices will be artificially high. A free market price is not permitted to perform its resource allocation function. Market-demand prorationing produces an income redistribution effect away from consumers and toward owners of crude oil resources.

Even among the latter, there is a further income redistribution impact, from owners in market-demand states to those in non-market-demand states.

Market-demand prorationing creates excess capacity in crude oil production. Excess capacity has been beneficial on two past occasions when, due to Middle Eastern wars, crude oil production in that area was curtailed. However, during the 1973–1974 Arab embargo there was no excess capacity in the United States. The market-demand prorationing system is not designed to produce excess capacity for national security objectives. The amount of excess capacity changes from month to month depending upon demand, supply, and price conditions. It also places the cost of providing excess capacity inequitably on nonexempt wells and on the more prolific fields.

There are better ways of serving a national security interest in reserve capacity. An optimum method would first require an estimation of how much reserve capacity is desired. This amount could then be purchased by paying reservoir owners who have productive capacity in desirable locations to fully develop but shut in their fields. The federal government already owns one such field, Naval Petroleum Reserve No. 1 (Elk Hills). This reserve, at the moment, is not fully developed, hence its potential reserve production capacity is only partially realized. Petroleum reserves may also be established by developing salt domes, abandoned mines, and steel or concrete tank storage facilities. These latter options may have their place in a comprehensive storage system, but involve higher costs than other storage systems.

In summary, MER-type prorationing would be improved by abandoning much of the existing system of production controls in favor of a system of mandatory reservoir unitization. This system would capitalize on the self-interest of reservoir owners and would be self-regulating with respect to reservoir investment and levels of production.

Market-demand prorationing is currently inoperative. It should be abandoned as a monopolistic device enforced by the federal government. Its existence is inconsistent with a long U.S. history of antitrust legislation. Further, market-demand prorationing cannot be justified as externality. And one would be hard pressed to justify a government enforced system of income redistribution from consumers to owners of oil wells, and from one group of oil well owners to another.

In addition to the controls the states have enacted over oil produced from lands under their jurisdiction, the federal government exercises control over both onshore federal and Indian lands and outer continental shelf lands. Federal controls are extensive and detailed. In this paper, the best we can do is briefly sample some of them to give the reader a feeling for their extent and character.

Leasing of federal oil and gas lands is under the control of the Bureau of Land Management within the U.S. Department of the Interior. After leasing, supervision of production is controlled by the U.S. Geological Survey. The Area Oil and Gas Supervisor has extensive powers. The Code of Federal Regulations states that the supervisor "shall inspect and regulate all operations and is authorized to issue OCS Orders and other orders and rules necessary for him to effectively supervise operations and to prevent damage to, or waste of, any natural resource, or injury to life or property." [9]

This broad authorization is detailed in additional federal regulations. A series of orders has been issued covering such items as production rates, testing procedures, well locations, spacing rules, and so on. Following the Santa Barbara oil spill in early 1969, safety regulations were totally reexamined by Geological Survey and a series of new regulations were issued. In addition, the Department of the Army and the Coast Guard (Department of Transportation) issue regulations governing obstructions to navigation, lights, and warning devices related to safety of life and property. The Corps of Engineers requires that a permit be issued by the corps before a lessee may place a structure on a tract which he has leased. The Federal Power Commission and the Interstate Commerce Commission govern common carriers in interstate commerce. The FPC approves design and economic variables in pipelines and the ICC regulates access to pipelines for petroleum liquids. The Federal Maritime Commission determines financial responsibility for oil shippers operating in ocean waters adjacent to the United States. The Environmental Protection Agency regulates the preparation of presale environmental impact statements and enforces discharge level controls and oil spill contingency planning and implementation. The Department of Health, Education and Welfare makes working condition evaluations which the Department of Labor enforces under the Occupational Safety and Health Act of 1970. The Department of Labor also enforces rules providing that all employees have a safe working environment. The Department of Transportation, in addition, is now establishing a new Office of Deepwater Ports to formalize rules and regulations covering licensing and to coordinate the depart-

9. CFR, Sect. 250.12.

ment's activities with those of other agencies involved in licensing, construction, and operation of deep water ports.[10]

The Oil Import Quota System

Effective monopoly power requires complete control of supply. We saw above that when market-demand restrictions caused crude oil prices to rise above their competitive levels, the fact that not all domestic crude oil was subject to control resulted in the nonexempt producers in market-demand states bearing the burden of output restrictions while exempt producers and producers in non-market-demand states shared in the benefits.

The international counterpart to this problem led to oil import quotas. Crude oil prices in the United States were held above their competitive level through market-demand prorationing, thereby bringing about two effects. First, foreign supplies, not being subject to market-demand prorationing, were free to enter the United States and benefit from this price support umbrella. Second, with domestic price supports, U.S. oil became relatively unattractive in foreign markets, contributing to a decline of exports.

The record of U.S. crude oil imports and exports from 1946 through 1973 is shown in Figure 2. During the 1930s the United States was a net exporter of crude oil. Following the end of World War II, imports increased sharply and exports declined to negligible proportions.

If unconstrained imports were permitted, then market-demand prorationing, as a device for supporting domestic crude oil prices, would obviously become impossible. The burdens placed on nonexempt producers in market-demand prorationing states would become intolerable. As a consequence of rising imports, independent crude oil producers in the United States demanded federal limits on them. In hearings held in 1956 independent oil producers were joined by coal producers who objected to competition from imported residual fuel oil, and together they called for import restrictions. The five major U.S. international oil companies testified on behalf of free trade in oil. For example, the president of Standard Oil of California testified, "It is our carefully considered opinion that the contention of injury to the domestic industry is without substance. . . . There is a serious question in my mind that the economic well-being and strength of this country—the bases of our national se-

10. For a concise review of federal regulation of outer continental shelf oil and gas production, see D. E. Kash et al., *Energy Under the Ocean* (Norman: University of Oklahoma Press, 1973), pp. 93–106.

Figure 2. Crude oil imports and exports of the United States, 1946–1973

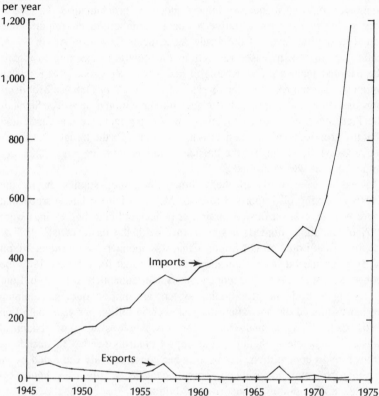

Million barrels
per year

Source: American Petroleum Institute, *Petroleum Facts and Figures,* 1971; *Annual Statistical Review.*

curity—would be promoted by measures of control set up to promote a greater dependence on increasingly costly domestic reserves. . . . I want to reiterate the conviction that the facts demonstrate imports are not injuring the domestic industry in any reasonable sense of the term. Consequently, I submit that on this score the national security has not been impaired.'' [11] Similar free trade sentiments were expressed by spokesmen for other international oil companies.

11. Hearings, Office of Defense Mobilization, In the matter of Petroleum (Oil Import Restrictions), October 24, 1956, pp. 542, 547, 550.

Following the 1956 hearings, President Eisenhower invoked voluntary import restrictions. The voluntary approach failed, and in 1959 Eisenhower imposed mandatory import quotas by proclamation. The statutory authority for administrative action to limit crude oil imports was found in section seven of the Trade Agreements Extension Act of 1955, which authorized increased restrictions on imports threatening to impair the national security. The act established a two-step procedure. First, an opinion was required from the director of the Office of Defense Mobilization asserting that imports did in fact impair national security. Second, the President was required to determine that the facts were accurate and that the proposed action was necessary to counteract the threat. The director of ODM did so certify, the President did so determine, and mandatory import quotas were imposed.

Speaking specifically of the Cabinet Committee studies during the 1950s involving oil imports, Professor M. A. Adelman has charged that there was never a serious discussion or debate and that the hearings were "frivolous, light minded, not concerned with the basic facts." [12] The Cabinet Task Force on Oil Import Control, appointed by President Nixon to examine the oil import question, estimated that for the year 1969 the consumer costs of the oil import quota system amounted to $4.85 billion. Referring to both the prorationing system and import quotas, Adelman earlier estimated the annual cost at just over $4 billion per year, based on 1961 data. "The annual charge for this whole system of organized waste," he wrote, "including the import controls needed to insulate it from foreign competition, has been rather conservatively estimated by an interdepartmental government committee at $3.6 billion. A better estimate, in my opinion, is just over $4 billion." [13]

The control provisions of the import quota system divided the country into two parts. For the region east of the Rocky Mountains, crude oil imports were permitted up to a maximum of 12.2 percent of estimated production within that region. Canadian overland shipments were initially exempt from the quota but were later treated as deductions from the 12.2 percent maximum. For the region west of the Rocky Mountains, the import quota was set at the difference between estimated demand for a calendar year and estimated U.S. plus Canadian supplies produced in or

12. U.S. Senate, Committee on the Judiciary, Subcommittee on Antitrust and Monopoly, Government Intervention in the Market Mechanism, The Petroleum Industry, Part I, 91st Cong., 1st sess., March 11, 1969, pp. 30–31.

13. M. A. Adelman, "Efficiency of Resource Use in Crude Petroleum," *Southern Economic Journal*, 31 (October 1964), 105.

shipped into this region. Thus domestic producers had first claim on the western market at their desired price with imports accounting for whatever was left over.

Because imports were restricted, the right to import lower cost foreign oil became valuable. Under industry pressure, the federal government rejected the idea of selling import tickets at a public auction. Instead the right to import was given away to petroleum refiners on the basis of refinery inputs. A sliding scale was provided to favor small refiners.

For most of the life of the import quota system, import tickets were valued at approximately $1.25 for the right to import one barrel of crude oil. This value resulted from the fact that the cost of crude oil delivered to the east coast from foreign sources was approximately $1.25 less than domestic crude oil production delivered to the same port.[14]

The import quota system represented a major subsidy distributed in various ways. First, those refiners receiving import tickets free of charge received a part of the subsidy. Second, crude oil producers shared in the subsidy because domestic crude oil prices were raised above competitive levels. Royalty owners (owners of crude oil reserves who leased their resources to others who engaged in production) received higher royalties as a result of quotas. Finally, some of the benefits were returned to the federal and state governments through bonus bids submitted for new oil leases and royalty payments on outstanding leases. Most of the costs of these subsidies and transfers were paid by consumers in the form of prices substantially above those which competition would have determined.

President Nixon's task force filed its report on February 2, 1970. The majority of the task force called for import quotas to be removed and replaced by a specified tariff. The majority recommended that "the President proclaim in early 1970 a phased transition to a tariff system for controlling imports, to take initial effect no later than January 1, 1971, with the following principal features: (1) initial imposition of an increased tariff on non-preferred crude oil at a level $1.35 per barrel above existing tariffs; (2) phase-out of special quota privileges over a three-year transition period by means of a 'tariff-free' quota; (3) deferment of decision on further tariff liberalization until January 1972, at which time the program managers may continue the process of liberalization if they are then per-

14. See testimony by W. J. Mead, U.S. Senate, Committee on the Judiciary, Subcommittee on Antitrust and Monopoly, Government Intervention in the Market Mechanism, The Petroleum Industry, Part I, 91st Cong., 1st sess., March 11, 1969, p. 78.

suaded on the basis of the best available evidence that indicated reserves in North American frontier areas will be sufficient to meet the aggregate 1980 production estimates set forth herein. . . . (4) a comprehensive review of the program no later than 1975, including an in-depth study of the post-1980 situation, to determine whether it then appears consistent with the national security to continue—or, if need be, arrest or reverse—the process of tariff liberalization." [15] Inasmuch as there was already a 10.5 cent per barrel tariff on crude oil, the task force was in effect recommending a tariff of $1.45 per barrel.

President Nixon rejected the task force recommendations in total and continued the import quota system. However, from 1970 through 1973 that system became progressively unworkable. A multitude of exemptions were granted to various firms and industries including petrol chemicals. Further, U.S. domestic production reached a peak in October 1970 and declined thereafter at about a 3.5 percent compound annual rate. But imports into the United States east of the Rocky Mountains were limited to 12.2 percent of domestic production, which was now declining. Therefore, unless the quota system were to be modified, imports also had to be reduced.

Effective in 1966 residual fuel oil (a low-value refined product used for electric power generation and to heat industrial plants, apartments, office buildings, schools, hospitals, and other institutions) was exempted from the quota system for PAD-I (seventeen eastern states bordering on the Atlantic Ocean from Florida to Maine). This led some domestic refiners to minimize residual fuel oil production in favor of higher valued products.

The quota system had the effect of accelerating production of a nonrenewable natural resource in the United States. It has been described as a "drain-America-first policy." By 1970 most of the low-cost petroleum prospects in the lower forty-eight states had been exploited. The high-cost prospects remained. The petroleum industry had been subsidized since the early 1920s by the percentage depletion allowance and oil and gas resources overexploited by the absence of unitization laws. Then in the two decades from 1950 through 1970, some sectors of the industry were constrained in their production by market-demand prorationing. Again in 1959 with the import quota system, imports were restricted and domestic reserves were drained at an artificially high rate. These conflicting and

15. Cabinet Task Force on Oil Import Control, *The Oil Import Question*, February 19, 1970, pp. 136–137.

contradictory regulatory policies contributed to the energy crisis that developed in the early 1970s.

Effective May 1, 1973, President Nixon by proclamation eliminated not only the existing oil import quota restrictions but the 10.5 cent per barrel tariff on crude oil as well. He simultaneously imposed a 10.5 cent per barrel import fee on crude oil but exempted an amount of imports equal to the amount covered by import tickets outstanding at that time. The exemptions from the import fee were to be phased out over a five-year period.

Removal of the quota system then brought to light a shortage of refinery capacity. Under the quota system foreign crude oil supplies in the United States were restricted. Therefore, some refineries which would otherwise have been constructed in this country were in fact constructed abroad, outside of the barriers of the quota system. By August 17, 1973, U.S. refineries were operating at 99.6 percent of capacity, up from 89 percent one year earlier.[16]

President Ford's proposed import fee is similar to the task force proposal. Ford announced his intention to establish a $3 per barrel import fee on crude oil effective April 1, 1975. In fact, a $2 per barrel import fee was instituted. The Supreme Court held it to be illegal, and it was removed late in 1975. The effect of this fee (tariff) was to raise the cost of imported crude oil by $2 per barrel, thus providing an equal measure of protection for the domestic petroleum industry.

Another problem created by the import quota system and its sudden removal arises out of the different sulfur contents of domestic and imported crude oil. Domestic crude is relatively low in sulfur and is called "sweet crude." Imported crude on the other hand has a relatively high sulfur content and is called "sour crude." Many refineries in the United States have been constructed to handle sweet crude, and when sour crude is processed through them, excessive corrosion of pipes and equipment results. With crude imports restricted, there was no incentive to convert refineries to handle sour crude. With the elimination of import quotas on May 1, 1973, foreign crude became freely available. Thus, refinery bottlenecks developed not only from capacity limits but also from the character of refineries.

The U.S. experience with import quotas as a regulatory system must be judged a failure. The system was finally abandoned by the President who had supported it only after it became abundantly apparent that its continu-

16. American Petroleum Institute, *Weekly Statistical Bulletin,* August 17, 1973.

ation would impose unacceptable costs on the country. Supporters of the import quota system point out that in the absence of fourteen years of mandatory quotas the United States would have been even more dependent upon foreign crude sources when the nation was confronted with the Arab oil embargo in October 1973. This may be true. However, in the absence of a quota system which was rationalized in terms of national security, it is quite likely that a system of stored crude oil reserves would have been established. In that event, the nation would have survived the five months embargo with less disturbance than actually occurred.

Price Controls, Allocations, and Entitlements

The purpose of market-demand prorationing controls in the oil industry, and their counterpart oil import restrictions, was to raise crude oil prices above their competitive levels. Precisely the opposite policy is now being followed by the federal government. Crude oil as well as petroleum products are now subject to federal price controls to keep price below world levels.

The current phase of price controls started on August 15, 1971, when President Nixon ordered a price-wage freeze. At that time the federal government was pushing both ways on crude oil prices—market-demand prorationing and import quotas were still in effect, causing prices to be above competitive levels, while the freeze tried to hold prices down.

Through successive phases of price controls under the Nixon administration, crude oil prices were allowed to rise and both market-demand prorationing and import quotas became inoperative. Crude oil prices moved up rather slowly from 1970 until 1973. In mid-October 1973 another Arab-Israeli war broke out, and an embargo was immediately instituted by Arab oil producing countries. An attempt was made completely to cut off Arab oil supplies to the United States and a few select other countries. Oil production from Arab nations was reduced 7.8 percent during the most restrictive period of the embargo. Because non-Arab members of OPEC expanded oil production, the net OPEC curtailment was only 2.3 percent. As a consequence, the landed cost of foreign crude oil, which in 1970 was about $2.25 per barrel, rose to $9.59 per barrel in January 1974 under the full impact of the embargo.[17]

Price stability for crude oil prevailed during the 1950s and 1960s because new oil production annually increased at approximately the same rate as demand increased. The United States was the world's largest oil

17. Federal Energy Administration, *Monthly Energy Review,* December 1974, p. 41.

producer during that period of time, increasing output at a compound rate of about 4.5 percent annually until 1970. In October 1970 U.S. crude oil production peaked out and started to decline at approximately a 3.5 percent compound annual rate. Because the United States was the world's leading crude oil producer, a shift from growth to decline had a major impact on world crude oil supplies.

Under the impact of the 1973–1974 Arab embargo and the consequent increase in crude oil prices, the U.S. government strengthened price controls on domestic crude oil production. Domestic production was divided into two classes: (1) "old oil" (oil produced from a well in an amount equal to or less than the amount produced in the same month of 1972), and (2) uncontrolled oil. In turn uncontrolled oil included "new oil" (production from new wells not operating in 1972 and production from old wells beyond the 1972 level), stripper oil (production from wells producing less than 10 barrels per day) and released oil (oil released from control and used as a bonus to encourage producers to expand output from old wells). Old oil is subject to price control and is currently fixed at $5.25 per barrel of crude. Uncontrolled oil on the other hand may be sold under free market conditions. Controlled oil accounted for 66 percent of domestic production as of August 1974 while the remaining 34 percent was uncontrolled. According to the Federal Energy Administration, the average price at wellhead of uncontrolled domestic oil was $10.03 per barrel as of September 1974.

Thus the federal government has created a two-tier price system for domestic crude oil. Two-tier price systems always create administration problems. In the case of crude oil, refiners who must purchase a large share of their crude requirements will inevitably have different shares of price controlled versus uncontrolled oil. East coast refiners buy a relatively large share of domestic crude input, most of which is purchased at the controlled $5.25 per barrel. Thus some regional inequity is created by the two-tier pricing system.

Similarly, refiners in the same area may have different shares of old oil, creating problems of competition. Further, some refiners are highly self-sufficient in crude supplies while others must buy a relatively large share of their crude requirements. Even though a company utilizes its own crude oil, the price control system requires that its own old oil be charged into its refineries at controlled prices. These low input prices are in turn carried through in relatively low product prices. Companies with a relatively large share of price controlled crude will be able to undersell their competitors in gasoline and other petroleum products. Thus, the two-tier pricing system creates problems for both refinery and product markets. As one FEA official observed, "For every problem you solve, it seems you create two more." [18] Interference with the price system at the crude oil level has necessitated additional interference at the refinery level. In order to compensate for the problems created by crude price control the FEA undertook two additional programs, first a system of crude oil allocations and later an "entitlements program."

A price control system which effectively holds prices below their competitive level has two effects. First, it discourages investments in new production if that production must be sold at artificially low prices. Second, it encourages consumption because the price controlled product becomes a bargain. In an effort to avoid the first problem, the price control system permits new oil to be sold at market prices. However, the lessons of price control are learned quickly by people who allocate financial resources, both investors and corporate managers. If oil reserves and production can be classified as old oil and controlled at prices below equilibrium levels, then new oil reserves may at some future date also be classified as old oil and price controlled. Thus, investments to develop new oil resources may be retarded by the present control system even though new oil is currently exempt from it.

The Crude Oil Allocation Program

The Emergency Petroleum Allocation Act of 1973 became effective on November 27, 1973, and provides for mandatory allocation of crude oil, residual fuel oil, and certain refined petroleum products manufactured in or imported into the United States. While the allocation program covers petroleum products as well as crude, this discussion will be concerned with crude allocation only.

The intended purpose of the allocation program is to provide for "an equitable distribution of crude oil among refiners," although the act nowhere defines an "equitable distribution." The crude oil supply in the United States is allocated by the Federal Energy Administration to refineries on a quarterly basis. As a calendar quarter ends, each refiner is required to report to the FEA the capacity of his refineries, actual crude oil quantities processed in the quarter just ending, and estimated quantities to be processed in the following quarter. The FEA then calculates a supply/capacity ratio for each refiner and also a national average sup-

18. *National Journal Report,* May 25, 1974, p. 778.

ply/capacity ratio for all refiners. It then publishes a "Buy-Sell" list which authorizes all refiners having access to crude oil below the national supply/capacity average to purchase crude oil from those refineries having more than the national average. A fifteen-day period is allowed for buyers and sellers to match their quantities, using normal business procedures. Any unsatisfied refiner may then appeal to the FEA for mandatory sales, and the FEA may direct specific firms to sell to specific buyers.

The price at which crude oil must be sold is specified by the FEA and is calculated on the basis of average crude oil costs to the selling company. This average appears to be in the $7 to $9 per barrel range at a time when the landed cost of foreign crude is about $12 per barrel. The selling firm must then replace its crude supply by buying from the only sources available, either foreign crude or free market crude in the United States, both of which are about $4 in excess of his selling price. Thus the allocation system requires a cash transfer from one company to another. In the process it penalizes those companies that, through their own foresight, have provided for their refinery needs in the past. Other effects of the system will be discussed below in connection with the entitlements program.

The Entitlements Program

With the crude oil allocation program still in effect, an entitlements program was added, effective in November 1974. Again we will discuss only the crude oil application of the program, although other petroleum products are covered.

The purpose of the entitlements program is to equalize crude oil costs among refiners with varying amounts of price controlled crude oil available to them. The cost disparities to be eliminated are those created by the two-tier price control system.

As in the allocation program, the entitlements program requires that the FEA calculate for each refinery and company a ratio of the number of barrels of price controlled old oil processed by a refinery to its total refinery throughput. A similar ratio is calculated for the nation as a whole. For the first month of the entitlements program, the national average was 41.05 percent. The FEA then gives to all refiners having less than the national average entitlements equal to the difference between the refiner's ratio and the national average.

Refiners having crude oil in excess of the national average are then required to buy entitlements from those having less than the average, at a price specified by the FEA. For the first two months of operations under the entitlements program the FEA specified a $5 entitlement price. Thus, under the entitlements program, money rather than crude oil is transferred between refiners.

In the first month, the FEA identified twenty-nine refiners as buyers of crude. An additional thirty-eight refiners that might have been designated as buyers received a small refiner exemption. The FEA listed ninety-five refiners as sellers of entitlements. For the first month, the FEA required that specifed refiners purchase entitlements covering 13,825,979 barrels of crude oil and that a like amount be sold by other named refiners.[19] At $5 per barrel this required a transfer of $69,129,895 between refiners. An additional $21 million would have changed hands except for the small refiner exemption. Thus, the exemption was worth $21 million to the small refiners.

According to an FEA news release, the entitlements program "is designed to equalize costs of crude oil for U.S. refiners, creating a more competitive climate in the petroleum industry." Further, the FEA specified that "the program will mainly benefit small and independent refiners who as a class have not had as much access to lower priced 'old' oil as have major refiners." [20] The monetary transfers required under the first month of the entitlements program, however, were contrary to these stated objectives. Among the big five international oil companies, Exxon and Gulf were required to buy entitlements. On the other hand, Standard Oil of California, Texaco, and Mobil were listed as sellers of entitlements. Sales by these three firms exceed purchases by the other two by a net amount of 1,693,865 barrels. At $5 per barrel, this required a net transfer of $8,469,325 in favor of the largest firms at the expense of smaller firms in the refining industry.

The results of the allocation and entitlements programs are not in yet, and may require years before the effects are known. On the basis of present information, the following effects appear likely.

(1) The entitlements program dictates a massive transfer of wealth between companies in the oil industry and between regions in the United States. Between companies, the transfer appears to be capricious. The three largest beneficiaries in receiving cash transfers from their competitors are Amerada Hess, Standard Oil of California, and Mobil, in that order, receiving a gift in excess of $29.5 million in a single month. The

---

19. Federal Energy Administration, Mandatory Petroleum Allocation, Old Oil Entitlement Notice, *Federal Register,* Part V, January 13, 1975.
20. November 8, 1974.

principal losers are Shell, Union, and Exxon, being required to pay more than $31 million to their competitors.

Between regions of the United States, the FEA estimated that during the first month alone the residents of the New England area would gain $29 million, those in the Middle Atlantic states $5 million and those of the South Atlantic states $8 million. These benefits would come at the expense of residents of the Middle West, who would lose $14 million, those in the lower Middle West ($10 million), people in the Rocky Mountain region ($2 million), and residents of the West Coast ($16 million). Subsidies tend to be addictive. The conditions which gave rise to them have long since disappeared.

(2) Both the allocation and entitlements programs tend to be disruptive and create uncertainty within the oil industry. In his energy message in January 1975 President Ford announced that he intended to eliminate both programs on April 1, 1975. This was not done. These programs were still in effect as of March 1976. The uncertainties created by the introduction of such programs, their administration, and their eventual termination all make business investment decision making difficult.

(3) The cost of administering these programs must be borne by the citizens of the nation. The 1975 budget for the FEA amounted to $127 million, and the agency employed 3,125 people. The 1977 budget requests $440 million, and the FEA staff is to be increased to 4,100 people. In addition, companies must assign people and budgets, not only to comply with the program and administer it, but also to find ways to legally circumvent it.

The effect of these regulatory programs on the future is only speculative at this point. It appears that uncertainty is clearly increased for the refining industry. It is also clear that for some refiners the rate of return on an investment in refining is reduced. Both factors should lead to a reduction in investment in refining in the United States. But crude oil must be refined. If refinery investments in the United States are reduced, they must be increased elsewhere.

Both programs involve a small-refinery bias. If it is true, as evidence suggests, that the optimum size of a petroleum refinery is large (about 300,000 barrels per day of capacity) then the regulations which favor small refineries will distort the flow of capital and lead to inefficient refinery investments.

Exploration for new crude oil reserve may also be retarded as a result of both programs. The government in effect is saying that there are penalties involved in finding more crude oil reserves than the national average of crude ownership to refinery capacity. If business decision makers believe that in the future the government will repeat its present pattern, then they may opt for the rewards of being a crude deficit company.

Our experience to date with price controls and their companion allocation and entitlements programs does not enable us to draw firm conclusions about whether or not consumers have in fact benefited from these programs. Consumers and taxpayers must ultimately pay the bill for the bureaucratic costs (both in the government and in the complying industry) necessary to administer the control programs. If capital flows are distorted as a result of the programs, then the nation as a whole will suffer reduced productivity and lower living standards. There are clearly income redistribution effects, but it is not clear that the nation as a whole has benefited from the income redistribution patterns.

Conclusion

It is obvious from the foregoing that the petroleum industry is anything but an uncontrolled industry. Controls were initially introduced to correct for some externalities resulting from divided ownership of oil reservoirs, the law of capture, and the migratory nature of crude oil in place. These regulations were introduced genuinely to benefit both the industry and the public and to avoid physical waste. However, the industry quickly embraced additional controls which were exclusively for its own benefit, including market-demand prorationing as a monopoly pricing device and import quotas to eliminate competition from foreign oil.

As of the early 1970s the oil industry had clearly lost its political clout and new regulations covering price control, allocations, and entitlements are of no benefit to the industry in total, while price controls are specifically designed to reduce oil industry profits. The industry that embraced regulation for its own benefit is now plagued with punitive regulations which it no longer controls.

7

Regulating Natural Gas Producers

Stephen G. Breyer and Paul W. MacAvoy

In recent years the Federal Power Commission has devoted consider-able effort and about 30 percent of its budget to regulating the prices at which producers sell natural gas. Most producers search for gas by drill-ing wells on leased land; they bring gas to the surface, gather it in central locations, and sometimes refine it in the sense of removing liquids that they can sell separately. They sell most of their gas to interstate pipeline companies which transport it from the field and resell it, either to indus-trial users or to distributing companies that in turn resell to industry or to home consumers. Thus regulation of producers has in practice consisted of putting an FPC ceiling on prices in this first sale, given existing ceilings on second sales.

Before World War II, natural gas was mainly a by-product of the search for oil, and as such it was sold at prices that merely covered production costs. However, the growth of pipelines capable of bringing gas from fields in Texas, Oklahoma, and Louisiana to distant markets increased demand to the point where higher prices stimulated greatly ex-tended supplies. By 1970, one-third of national energy consumption was from natural gas. Less than 25 percent of the gas comes from oil wells; most comes from wells that produce only gas, found in the search for gas itself. Naturally the pipeline industry has also expanded. Before 1955 many fields were worked by hundreds of producers but served by only one pipeline; at the beginning of the 1970s at least two or three pipelines were competing to buy gas in nearly every producing area.

This chapter is reprinted in abridged form, with slight revisions, from Stephen G. Breyer and Paul W. MacAvoy, *Energy Regulation by the Federal Power Commission* (Washington: Brookings, 1974), by permission of the Brookings Institution. Copyright © 1974 by the Brookings Institution, Washington, D.C.

Since the early 1960s, commission regulation has been remarkably effective in holding down producer selling prices. Whether this regulation benefited the nation or even the consumers it was designed to help is another matter. Low prices have led to heavy buying and consequently to a substantial shortage of natural gas; they have also led producers to sell to unregulated industrial or intrastate customers instead of regulated interstate pipelines. To explain how this state of affairs arose and what should be done about it, this chapter explores the objectives of producer price regulation and the methods used by the commission to achieve them.

Regulating Producer Sales

In 1954, somewhat to the Federal Power Commission's surprise, the Supreme Court held in *Phillips Petroleum Company* v. *Wisconsin* that the commission was responsible for regulating sales by the gas field producers to the interstate pipelines.[1] The court held that, although certain language in the Natural Gas Act appears to grant producers an exemption, the act does in reality provide for regulation of producers. Somewhat ambiguously, the act states that "the provisions of this chapter shall apply . . . to the sale in interstate commerce of natural gas for resale . . . but shall not apply . . . to the production or gathering of natural gas." [2] If a field producer's sale to an interstate pipeline is "a sale in interstate commerce for resale," how is it possible to exempt "production or gathering" of natural gas from regulation? Possibly the physical production and gathering operations themselves can be held distinct from sales and other operations, but no guidelines are offered.

Although the legislative history of the Natural Gas Act has little to say about producer regulation, what is said seems to support the Supreme Court's decision. A House of Representatives committee report states that the words "production or gathering" are "not actually necessary, as the matters specified therein could not be said fairly to be covered by the language affirmatively stating the jurisdiction of the Commission." [3] This statement, if it accurately indicates intention, suggests that Congress did not mean to exempt from regulation sales by producers to pipelines at the wellhead, for such sales surely could be said "to be covered by the lan-

---

1. 347 U.S. 672 (1954).   2. 15 USC 717(b) (1970).

3. *Interstate Transportation and Sale of Natural Gas,* H. Rept. 709, 75th Cong., 1st sess. (1937), p. 3. See also "Legislative History of the Natural Gas Act," *Georgetown Law Journal,* 44 (June 1956), 695.

guage affirmatively stating the jurisdiction of the Commission'' over sales for resale in interstate commerce. The producers perhaps anticipated this reading of the law. Although the Federal Power Commission consistently refused to regulate producers, at the urging of the gas companies Congress passed a bill in 1949 granting a clear producer exemption—a bill that President Truman vetoed. The producers, the Congress, and the President all acted as if without a new law the producers might be regulated.[4]

Despite the logic of the court's position, it can still be criticized. The court did not examine, more than superficially, the economic purposes that producer regulation might serve. Without such an examination, the court could not tell whether producer regulation was a consistent application of economic policy, in the sense of being consistent with regulation of "monopoly" distribution companies in the gas industry. If producer regulation did not further economic policy, then to assume a congressional intent to regulate in the face of ambiguous language and an uncertain legislative history was not warranted.

After the decision in *Phillips Petroleum Company* v. *Wisconsin,* Congress passed a bill exempting field sales of natural gas from regulation. President Eisenhower vetoed the bill, not because he favored regulation but because he disapproved of the fact that lobbyists had overtly offered campaign contributions from the industry in return for congressional votes for the bill.[5] At that point, once it became clear that Congress was not going to force through exemption for producers, the Federal Power Commission began to struggle with the problem of how to regulate. The first approach was to treat producers as individual public utilities and set prices on the basis of individual costs of service. After this approach proved unwieldy, the commission set regional ceiling prices, allowing all individual producers within each gas production region to charge less than, but no more than, the regional ceiling. To accomplish this, the FPC in 1960 divided the Southwest into five geographical areas, set interim ceiling prices at the 1959–1960 levels for new contracts, and began hearings to determine the final, legally binding ceiling prices for each area. Over the 1960s, hearings, agency decisions, and court reviews took place

4. This argument is advanced by Edmund W. Kitch, "Regulation of the Field Market for Natural Gas by the Federal Power Commission," *Journal of Law and Economics,* 11 (October 1968), 243–80.

5. *Ibid.,* p. 256; *New York Times,* February 18, 1956.

in formal array for prices in the Permian Basin of west Texas and New Mexico and in southern Louisiana. At the close of the decade the process had not yet been completed for the other areas.

Because of statutory limitations on commission authority, the area rate proceedings could set limits on prices only *prospectively,* that is, from the time an area rate proceeding was completed. To control producer prices during the many years that the proceedings were in progress, the commission worked out a legally complex, though operationally simple, procedure. Price increases for existing contracts presented little problem, for any such increases took effect subject to an obligation to refund any excess above the ''reasonable rate'' which the area rate proceeding was to find. Prices for new supply contracts were controlled by the certificate-issuing procedure. The commission, with the help of the courts, developed the practice of withholding certificates allowing producers to sell newly produced gas in interstate commerce if the producer intended to sell the gas at more than the interim ceiling prices. Although some certificates were issued to producers proposing higher prices, the commission adopted the practice frequently enough so that new gas prices generally were priced roughly at the interim ceilings.

Because the area rate proceedings lasted through the decade, the provisional prices held all new contract agreements near the 1960 unregulated average. The first complete area rate proceeding in 1968 set prices for the Permian Basin only slightly higher than the provisional (or 1960) prices. The second proceeding set ceiling prices for southern Louisiana at about the 1960 level, but the reopening of the case raised the ceiling by about 25 percent. Since the remaining area rate cases were not complete and thus the 1959–1960 interim ceilings remained in effect, contracts for new reserves throughout the decade were written as if economic conditions had not changed since the late 1950s.

By mid-1974, a worsening natural gas shortage, possible curtailments in other energy sources, and the long regulatory lags that had developed forced the FPC to alter its approach to rate setting. In a June 21, 1974, opinion, the FPC abandoned the area rate proceedings and set a single uniform national rate for interstate gas producer sales.[6] That rate, 42 cents per thousand cubic feet for sales made on or after January 1, 1973, was itself quickly abandoned. A December 4, 1974 FPC opinion in-

6. See *National Gas Rate,* FPC Opinion 699, June 21, 1974.

creased the national rate to 50 cents.[7] Both opinions permitted a one cent per year escalation beginning with January 1, 1975.

The Objectives of Producer Price Regulation

The area rate proceedings had moved very slowly and had been expensive. Whether they, or the new uniform national rates, represent "good regulation" depends on the reasons for wanting to regulate gas producers and on the results achieved in pursuit of this rationale. Upon close inspection, two conceptually distinct purposes for these regulations emerge. That neither the agency nor the courts took pains to distinguish between them makes the task of evaluating regulation more difficult.

Control of Market Power

Restraint of market power is a traditional economic rationale for regulation. Stated in highly simplified and direct terms, where one firm or a very small number of firms produces the entire output for a market, it is usually expected that output is going to be less than the amount that would be provided by competitive suppliers. Monopoly or oligopoly firms restrict market output in order to increase the market price, assuming the higher price is more profitable to them. In many cases prices would presumably be quite high. Monopolistic tendencies can in theory be controverted by public agencies, such as antitrust and regulatory commissions. If it is costly to introduce competition into an industry via antitrust policies—because economies of scale make production by a greater number of firms less efficient—the government is moved toward trying to restrain prices directly.

It is often claimed that state regulation of gas distributors and federal regulation of interstate pipelines have been needed to curtail market power and to eliminate arbitrary price behavior. Supporters of producer regulation have advanced similar reasons for field price controls. Some of them have asserted that gas production has been concentrated in a few petroleum companies—so few that the largest have controlled the supply of gas to the interstate pipelines.[8] Unless market power at the wellhead is

7. See *National Gas Rate,* FPC Opinion 699-H, December 4, 1974.

8. See, for example, Paul H. Douglas, "The Case for the Consumer of Natural Gas," *Georgetown Law Journal,* 44 (June 1956), esp. p. 589, where he goes so far as to claim: "Competition in the field is limited by the domination of supply and reserves by a very few companies."

checked, so the argument runs, pipeline regulation will not be effective. Monopoly prices paid for gas at the wellhead by pipelines and retail distributors will be passed through as costs to final consumers. According to this rationale, the Federal Power Commission should determine the price at which gas would be sold under competitive conditions and should then forbid sales at higher prices.

The question of producer market power played an important role in the debate in the 1950s over the need for regulation of producers, but this concern has diminished during the more recent controversy on *how* to regulate the producers. The "market structure" evidence accumulated in the 1960s—on number of sources of new production and reserves of gas—has not supported the assertion that gas producers possess unbridled market power. Rather, decentralization of ownership is as prevalent in gas production as it is in many workably competitive American industries.

The principal indicator of market structure is the degree of ownership concentration in the production of gas or in reserve holdings for future production. Federal Power Commission statistics show that in the early 1960s the four largest gas producers accounted for less than 10 percent, and the fifteen largest for less than 50 percent, of national production.[9] Shares in particular geographical markets were not highly concentrated either, even when the market definition was narrow. For example, in the Permian Basin of western Texas and eastern New Mexico, the five largest producers accounted for somewhat less than 50 percent of production.[10] Commenting on similar dispersion for county-sized production districts, M. A. Adelman has characterized even this degree of production concentration as "low," in fact "lower than 75–85 percent of [industries in] manufactured products"; and James McKie has shown that entry into the industry is so unimpeded that, even if concentration were higher here than elsewhere, the largest producers would not be able systematically to charge higher than competitive prices.[11]

The rejoinder to indicators of wide ownership of *production* is that the

9. Clark A. Hawkins, *The Field Price Regulation of Natural Gas* (Tallahassee: Florida State University Press, 1969), p. 248.

10. 34 FPC 159 (1956) at 182, n. 17; *Skelly Oil Co.* v. *FPC,* 375 F. 2d 6 (10th Cir. 1967); 390 U.S. 747 (1968).

11. Testimony of Professor Adelman before the Federal Power Commission, *Champlin Oil and Refining Co.,* Docket G-9277, p. 458 L.C., quoted in Paul W. MacAvoy, *The Crisis of the Regulatory Commissions* (New York: Norton, 1970), p. 156; James W. McKie, "Market Structure and Uncertainty in Oil and Gas Exploration," *Quarterly Journal of Economics,* 74 (1960), 543.

relevant market is in sales of rights to produce from new *reserves* and that no doubt ownership of uncommitted reserves must be highly concentrated. Petroleum companies sell gas by committing new reserves for production in ten- to twenty-year contracts. The contracts specify initial-year prices and procedures for making price changes. Once the contract has been signed, production has been "locked in," so that the critical price effects on supply have accrued at the dedication of new reserves. Proponents of regulation have argued that this new reserves market is so concentrated that a few producers have been able to raise prices and that the higher prices have been passed through by the device of "favored nations" clauses calling for the same prices in old as in new contracts.[12]

This argument, however, has little basis in fact. The four largest petroleum companies provided at most from 37 to 44 percent of new reserve sales in west Texas and New Mexico and a maximum of 26 to 28 percent in the Texas Gulf region—all in the 1950–1954 period just before the *Phillips* decision. These levels of concentration in supply of new reserves were all less than half the concentration in the demand for these reserves by the four largest pipeline buyers in each of these regions. Power to control new contract prices probably did not exist on either side of the market, but if there was "a balance," then it lay with the pipelines rather than the producers.

Of course, one can still argue that, despite its apparently competitive structure, the producing segment of the industry has behaved noncompetitively. Certain proponents of regulation, such as some of the gas distributing companies in the early 1960s, asserted that the rapid rise in the field price of natural gas between 1950 and 1958 was evidence of noncompetitive performance (prices rose from 9 cents per thousand cubic feet to a peak of 24 cents in the Gulf Coast region). Economic studies of the markets for new contracts suggest, however, that anticompetitive producer behavior did not cause the price increase. Rather, during the early 1950s the presence of only one pipeline in many gas fields resulted in a monopoly buyer's (monopsony) price for new gas contracts. Thus the field price for natural gas was often depressed below the competitive level because of the lack of effective competition among buyers. During the next few years, several pipelines sought new reserves in old field regions where previously there had been a single buyer, and this new entry raised the field prices to a competitive level from the previously depressed

12. As an example of this argument, see the testimony of Alfred E. Kahn in the Champlin Oil and Refining Company case, FPC Docket G-9277, p. 489.

monopsonistic level. New competition among entering pipelines, not concentrated market power, accounted for much of the price spiral that was later said to prove "the need" for regulation.

Proponents of regulation also argued that competition among producers was bound to be negligible because their customers (the pipelines) had no incentive to bargain for low prices. Since the final sales made by the pipeline companies were regulated on the basis of costs plus a fixed profit on capital, the pipelines, instead of resisting price increases, would simply pass any purchase-price increase on as costs to be paid by the consumer. This argument is theoretically suspicious, for strict regulatory supervision would force the pipelines to worry about whether they would be able to pass along a price increase, whereas weak regulatory supervision would allow them to keep any extra profits they earned through hard bargaining with producers—at least until "regulatory lag" caught up. More important, the "passing on" argument applies to capital costs too. Given limits on price increases set by some combination of consumer demand and regulatory awareness, the regulated firm would prefer to hold down fuel prices (on which no "gain" was earned) in favor of enhancement of capital prices (on which a rate of return was allowed).[13] Moreover, the slim empirical evidence available suggests that pipelines did in fact bargain for minimum prices. In the 1950s, pipelines pushed field prices below competitive levels wherever possible, and, when the low price threatened to drive producers out of exploration and development, rather than raise prices for all producers the pipeline firms themselves went into the exploration business. They selectively produced higher cost gas themselves, paying monopsony prices for the low-cost gas from petroleum companies, so as to reduce payments of producers' "windfall" rents to the minimum.[14]

In addition to conjectures about "ineffective competition," supporters of regulation point to producer profits as possible evidence that field price controls were necessary. And, in fact, profits did appear high in comparison with some other industries. Economic experts appearing for the dis-

13. On this point, most of the economic theories of the regulated firm agree. The Averch-Johnson theory of the profit-maximizing firm subject to a constraint on rate of return implies no enchantment of the price paid for a noncapital input factor. See Harvey Averch and Leland L. Johnson, "Behavior of the Firm under Regulatory Constraint," *American Economic Review,* 52 (December 1962), 1052–1069; William J. Baumol and Alvin K. Klevorick, "Input Choices and Rate-of-Return Regulation: An Overview of the Discussion," *Bell Journal of Economics and Management Science,* 1 (Autumn 1970), 162–190.

14. See Paul W. MacAvoy, *Price Formation in Natural Gas Fields: A Study of Competition, Monopsony, and Regulation* (New Haven: Yale University Press, 1962) esp. ch. 5.

tributing companies in the Permian Basin area proceedings reported average returns on capital between 12 and 18 percent for oil and gas companies at a time when the average return in manufacturing was less than 8 percent. This profit comparison, however, is not enough to establish the presence of monopoly pricing, for three special features of returns in the gas producing industry must be recognized. First, lucky discoveries in a world of uncertainty might earn unusually efficient or fortunate producers a high economic rent in natural gas because of the importance of the discovery process. Second, the Permian Basin figures reflect profits only of firms still in business, not of those that failed. The uncertainty in exploring and developing gas—seven out of eight exploratory wells have been dry in most years—suggests that risks of failure are unusually high; measuring the industry returns on the basis of companies that survive results in an upward bias. Third, the profit figures in the Permian Basin proceedings overstate the true return to capital because of the accounting procedures used. The rate-of-return estimates were calculated simply by dividing total profits that producers reported they had received by the total capital that they reported they had invested. This does not account for the extensive time lag in this industry before an investment begins to earn a return. The accounting return on a dollar invested here must be far lower in real terms than elsewhere if payment begins five years, rather than one year, after the investment is made; the simple bookkeeping profit rate must be adjusted to take the long lag between exploration and production into account. Producer witnesses in the Permian Basin case estimated that an "apparent yield" of 16 to 18 percent was equivalent, because of the lag in production, to a "true yield" of about 10 percent.

In brief, arguments to the effect that competition does not exist in the gas production industry are unconvincing. If the firms involved do not have the market power imputed to them, regulating them as though they have can cause nothing but trouble. The following chain of events becomes possible. The Federal Power Commission, believing in the monopoly rationale, pushes prices below the competitive level. Since lower than competitive price stimulates demand, some of the buyers able to get gas use this fuel even though the economy could provide for their needs with other fuels at lower real costs. Simultaneously the lower price reduces incentives to supply new reserves and production, for it cannot provide sufficient returns to the producers now at the margin. By increasing the quantity demanded and decreasing the quantity supplied, regulation causes a shortage.

Regulation To Reduce Rents and Windfalls

Even in a competitive market, the distribution of gains from production might be so unacceptable as to justify the regulation of prices. Price in a competitive market is equal to the cost of producing the marginal units that can be sold. Some producers can sell—at that market price—intramarginal units that are far less costly to produce, perhaps because they have special skill or expertise or because they control a resource that cannot easily be duplicated. Such producers realize economic rents, or returns in excess of those required to being forth production. It has been claimed that these rents are exceptionally high in the oil and gas industries and therefore that price control systems should be devised that would deprive producers of such incomes and give them to consumers in the form of lower prices.

Although no one has measured the amount of rent that gas producers would have earned without regulation during the 1960s, there are reasons to believe that rents would be large compared to those earned in other industries. For one thing, gas is a wasting resource, and knowledge of its presence in the ground in commercial quantities is uncertain until exploration and development are complete. At that point, the price of the gas is set by the cost of marginal additional exploration and development (when demand is increasing sharply). The difference between this price and the production costs of fully explored reserves could constitute an appreciable windfall divided between producers and landowners. Meanwhile, the cost of finding and developing gas reserves has increased since 1950. Thus gas found and sold to pipelines fifteen years previously in reserve commitments, but still not tapped, would entail lower costs than new reserves. If this ''old gas'' were to be priced at new long-term marginal exploration and development costs, the windfalls or rents might constitute as much as one-half the payment.

Proponents of regulation wish to eliminate such windfalls and rents without interfering with the market-clearing mechanism. To do so, regulation would have to hold down the price of intramarginal volumes of gas while allowing marginal units to be sold at a price that equaled long-term exploration and development costs. In effect, regulation would have to set separate prices for each source of supply. Of course, such regulation would result in excess demands for the lower-priced intramarginal units. To ''clear'' the excess demand created by the lower intramarginal prices by auctioning off these volumes would be to give the windfall rents to the pipelines taking the highest bids; to "clear" through rationing would provide the windfall to the retail distributor.

This type of regulation would be somewhat unusual but not unheard of. Differential regulated prices are most commonly found in housing, where rent control laws may hold the price of existing housing at previous levels, while allowing the price of new housing units to rise so as to clear the market of demands for new rental units. But this policy requires extraordinary sensitivity to changes in supply so as to react with marginal price changes, and, even in the best conditions, it also requires a complicated rationing procedure.

Where the primary aim is to bring about the redistribution of income away from windfall gains to producers toward higher real income for consumers, the problem is to do so *without* affecting output. This requires knowledge of the location and shape of the supply curve for both established and additional supply. Moreover, when reduced intramarginal prices bring about the increase in quantity demanded, the excess demand has to be limited by recourse to such rationing devices as classifying users and designating one or more classes as "low priority" so that they experience shortage. Finding the low-priority consumer—on some grounds other than willingness to pay—turns out to be a never-ending search.

Neither the Federal Power Commission nor the Supreme Court has clearly distinguished the two separate regulatory objectives of controlling market power and transferring rents to consumers. The commission often issues statements as though it were trying to achieve both of them at once. In recent years, there has been some shift toward the second objective. For one thing, the commission has expressed the belief or fear that efforts to limit prices have reduced the supply of new reserves and the actual level of gas production. Lowering prices from "monopoly" to "competitive" levels should have had the exact opposite effect of increasing both reserves and production by moving along the demand function, at least down to the point of equality of average price with long-run average costs. The commission's continued efforts to regulate, in the face of this result, suggest that it no longer sees itself as basically trying to control monopoly power. For another thing, the commission set two price levels in the area rate proceedings—higher prices on "new" gas and lower prices on "old" gas.

The agency and the courts have not completely abandoned the notion that producers hold price-raising power. Still, in view of the lack of empirical support for the notion that producers are "monopolists," we shall assume that regulating producers' market power is not a sensible regulatory goal. It seems more reasonable—because it corresponds more closely to the facts in the gas industry—to try to limit producer rents and windfalls. It is almost necessary to hypothesize that this is what the commission has been trying to do.

Regulating Prices through Individual Rate Cases

The Federal Power Commission first tried to regulate gas producers as if they were public utilities allowed to earn "fair return on fair value." The procedure was the same as for setting gas pipeline prices, with the agency judging the "costs of service" and allowing prices sufficient for a company to recover these costs but no more.

Although this method allowed producers with different costs to sell at different prices, it did not provide ways to determine who should get the cheaper gas. Also, this method took for granted that substantive information was available on elements of cost in great detail. The agency expected that costs for new additions to reserves could be determined in the same way as the historical costs from the accounting records of gas transporters and electricity generating companies. But, as the examiners found out, determining the cost of gas production is an especially difficult undertaking.

Since gas is often produced in conjunction with oil, finding the separate costs of natural gas posed several extraordinary difficulties. Joint expenditures on *exploration* may yield joint production of petroleum and natural gas, separate production, or no production—some gas from oil wells, some from gas wells, in addition to many dry holes. Expenditures on *separate development* of gas fields yield gas with liquids of a number of types, and expenditures on *gas refining* yield both "dry" gas and salable liquid. Outlays to produce two products jointly complicate the regulatory process because there is no direct way to decide whether or to what extent a specific dollar should be considered to be the "cost of gas production" or the "cost of liquid production."

The problem is distinctly a regulatory problem. Without price controls, under competitive conditions, producers would recover marginal joint costs from the sale of gas and oil, but the relative amounts recouped from each would vary from firm to firm. With price controls over both oil and gas, the regulator might try to reproduce competitive market results sim-

combined revenues from the sale of th
he company could propose any combi
r total costs. (In fact, this procedure has
egulation of jointly produced industrial and
well as peak versus off-peak long-distance tele
istinct regulatory problem for gas has been that oil
.gulated by the Federal Power Commission. Therefore the
mission had to find the exact costs of one of the joint products or els
to try for indirect regulation of the earnings on the unregulated sal
liquids.

The commission's efforts at exactitude were not successful. Atte
were made to apply various accounting techniques for allocating
costs so as to find precise gas costs. One method allocated joint cost
cording to the ratio of separable costs of oil production to separable (
of gas production. A second method allocated joint costs in accordance
with the number of thermal units (BTUs) contained respectively in the oil
and gas produced. A third method, recognizing that BTUs of oil and gas
might not be of equal value, multiplied the BTUs by a factor representing
relative value (a circular procedure, since value determined cost, cost determined price, and price determined value). None of these procedures
had much to do with the price that gas would command under competitive conditions. An economic analyst could not find long-term marginal
costs of a single product by using them; nor could he produce with them
an estimate of the historical average costs for that product. On the contrary, these accounting methods created the illusion of separable costs
when in truth the costs were intermingled and could not be separated.[15]

The commission struggled with a number of further, extremely serious
difficulties in finding costs for each company. Judging whether historical
returns were comparable to those earned by firms in other industries
where ''risks are comparable'' was especially difficult since the ''comparable'' industries were not readily identifiable. Though it could be ac-

---

15. To be fair to the commission, joint production was not preponderant in the industry.
After the mid-1950s, the number of joint wells diminished to the point where gas output
from them accounted for less than 25 percent of total gas production. And it has been
strongly argued that exploration is ''directional''—that gas and oil can be searched for separately, and usually one is not found as a result of a search for the other. Insofar as producers
acted on this belief, exploration expenditures might have been more easily allocated to one
or the other product. Nonetheless, joint expenditures were still sufficiently important to
warp the pricing system.

knowledged that gas production was more risky than providing telephone service, it could not be agreed that gas extraction was more subject to cost-and-demand changes than copper mining or steel production.

Even if a method had been found for choosing comparable industries, it was not then possible to compare costs of capital. Gas producers had insignificant debt holdings. Equity returns were not directly comparable: few of the smaller gas companies sold shares in organized trading markets providing price information, and the larger companies—though providing information on returns—produced both gas and petroleum.

The very numbers of producers of natural gas created overwhelming difficulties in rate-of-return regulation. In 1954 there were more than 5,000 producers, and by 1960 more than 2,900 applications for increased rates were awaiting FPC action. By the end of that year the Federal Power Commission had completed only 10 of these cases. The remaining backlog led the Landis Commission, appointed by President Kennedy to study the regulatory agencies, to conclude that "without question," the Federal Power Commission represents the outstanding example of "breakdown of the administrative process." [16] Sheer glut caused the abandonment of the procedure of finding individual costs of service.

Area Rate Proceedings

In the early 1960s the Federal Power Commission embarked on a policy of setting producer prices in batches, dividing the country into five producing areas and determining price ceilings separately for "new" gas and for "old" gas in each area. This tier pricing system was designed to provide a fairly simple way of transferring rents from producers to consumers without seriously discouraging gas production. It was assumed that gas found in conjunction with oil and gas found several years before a hearing cost less to produce than new gas. More pragmatically, the agency assumed that low prices for such gas would not discourage production, given that its supply was relatively fixed. Both of these assumptions are plausible. Low prices presumably deprive the producer of possible rents, to the benefit of the consumer, while higher prices for new gas ought to encourage enough additional gas production to satisfy total consumer demands. [17]

16. James M. Landis, *Report on Regulatory Agencies to the President-Elect* (1960), p. 54.

17. Some supporters of regulation argued that the supply of new gas is also fixed (or relatively inelastic). In their view a new gas price set below the level attainable in a free market would not cause much harm. Although the "low" price would cause a gas shortage,

Despite its apparent simplicity, however, the tier pricing system also exhibited a number of serious flaws. For one, it provided no way to ration the low-price gas. For another, there was no assurance that the two prices (for old and new gas) were equal to the long-term marginal costs of production. Any gas shortage resulting from these two flaws was bound to be compounded by the fact that the commission could regulate producers' interstate sales but could not regulate the price at which they sold gas intrastate in Texas, Oklahoma, and Louisiana. Thus, in times of shortage, producers were able to sell gas intrastate, where prices were allowed to rise, particularly to industrial purchasers on the margin of choice between petroleum, natural gas, and the other sources of hydrocarbons. The gas that these industries purchased was likely to be diverted from retail distributors willing to pay a much higher price but unable under regulation to do so.

How likely is it that the commission in fact induced a significant shortage by setting new gas prices below the long-term costs of exploration and development? An examination of the methods used by the agency to set area prices suggests that the answer must be "highly likely." The first method used by the commission was to set the new gas price equal to the *average historical costs* of developing recent reserves. Thus, in the Permian Basin case, the commission staff surveyed both major and minor producers in order to find the annual total costs for the base year of 1960. Experts employed by the producers, and some employed by retail distributors, made similar surveys, and the results from the three sources produced a range of estimates of historical average exploration and development costs.

The similarity of final ceiling prices to the provisional prices is not at all surprising, given the method. This is because the provisional price ceilings themselves probably biased the effort to ascertain the cost of new production. If producers surmised that they were unlikely to be able to sell gas at more than these 1960 prices, they would have developed only those reserves having marginal costs lower than such prices. This would have resulted in the average costs of new reserves being slightly below the interim ceilings. Thus using the historical average costs to set future prices was to use historical prices to set future prices. In principle, if the Federal Power Commission had set provisional prices at 1 cent per thou-

---

only a few potential customers would suffer, while all actual customers would benefit from lower prices. This view is enticing; yet all the problems that developed with the simpler arguments for tier pricing in fact apply to this rationale a fortiori.

sand cubic feet, it would have discovered in retrospect that the historical average costs of gas production were slightly less than 1 cent, for no gas that had higher marginal development costs would have been offered for new reserve contracts. If the commission had then used historical average costs in its standard way, they would have "confirmed" that the interim price was the correct future price.

The commission further increased the bias by using average costs rather then marginal costs. If the aim was to encourage new production, the ceiling prices should have been set as high as prospective marginal development and extraction costs. Given a wasting resource from a fixed stock of uncertain size, it is probable that the marginal costs were greater than the average costs of finding and developing new reserves. The category of higher cost producers included not only the unlucky or less skillful operators but also those forced to search farther afield or deeper underground after having exhausted their more promising leaseholds. Averaging their costs in with the new gas costs of fortunate or unusually skillful producers concealed the costs of some further new gas production. Setting ceiling prices on the basis of average costs would guarantee that the exploration and development of the marginal reserves would not take place.

The examiners tried to take account of "the margin" by adding an "allowance for growth" to the average historical costs of finding new gas. In the Permian Basin proceedings, for example, the commission added 1.11 cents per thousand cubic feet to the ceiling price in recognition that producing enough new gas in the future to meet growing demands would probably require the exploitation of more expensive reserve sources. But it did not determine the size of this premium by analyzing producers' probable marginal costs. Rather, an expert appearing for the distributing companies stated that in his judgment this was the proper amount, and experts for the producing companies in turn testified that in their judgment the proper figure was 2.15 cents per thousand cubic feet. The commission chose between the two without stating any guidelines of its own on (1) reduced probability of finding gas, (2) higher drilling costs, (3) the rate of return required to attract speculative capital into gas production, or (4) the long-term output of this industry. Thus the commission's use of historical average costs, along with its acceptance of the distributors' estimate of the premium required to encourage exploitation of marginal reserves, made it likely that the new gas prices would bring about a gas shortage.

Negotiated Prices

Facing continued difficulties, in the late 1960s the commission turned to a process of direct negotiation to set prices. In the southern Louisiana case, representatives of the producers, distributors, and other customers bargained out a settlement which most of them then presented to the commission for approval. The agency and the courts took the negotiation under advisement, along with a great deal of information on historical costs, and decided to set price ceilings slightly below the settlement figures. When a deepening gas shortage led the commission to reopen the southern Louisiana proceedings, once again the parties negotiated a settlement. This time the FPC adopted the settlement figures on its own, holding that they constituted reasonable ceiling prices.[18]

To set ceiling prices by negotiation comes close to abandoning both goals of regulation. Negotiation among interested parties to "settle" a Federal Power Commission proceeding does not constitute much of an effort to control monopoly power, since the process bears no resemblance to haggling among buyers and sellers in a competitive market. Rather than competing for purchases or sales, the parties bargain in blocs—the buyers together in one bloc, dealing with producers in the other bloc. The price may end up higher than, lower than, or equal to that set in a competitive market; it depends on the skill and power of particular blocs. Nor is this form of regulation likely to provide two-tier prices that will eliminate producer rents. The new gas price is unlikely to induce enough new reserves to clear excess demand—for the reason just given and for the additional reason that the parties are constrained in their bargaining by their knowledge that the agency and the courts have the power to approve or disapprove the result.

The one undeniable advantage of setting prices through negotiation is administrative simplicity. Whether the prices set by this method could possibly alleviate the gas shortage that developed in the late 1960s, and at the same time reduce producers' rents, is the next major subject we want to investigate.

Uniform National Rates

In turning to a uniform national rate during 1974, the FPC recognized the effect of regulatory lags and the need for a partial restoration of

18. *Southern Louisiana Area Rate Proceeding* (*Southern Louisiana Area*) 46 FPC 86, Opinion 598.

market forces to bring supply and demand into better balance. However, the method for determining price was similar to that used in the area rate proceedings, and the distinction between old and new gas was not abandoned. Cost recovery plus a 15 percent rate of return was set as the regulatory target. Although the demise of the area rate proceedings gives the appearance of regulatory streamlining, similar economic problems still remain with the procedures ostensibly used to set a national rate. Moreover, FPC objectives have become increasingly clouded as regulatory opinions began to emphasize restoration of market forces.

The Shortage of Natural Gas

The economic problem with field price regulation was the lack of a way to set ceiling prices without causing excess demand. We have addressed reasons why FPC policy might bring about a shortage. We have hinted that a shortage did occur. Now is the time to address two questions in detail. How serious was the shortage? Could the commission reasonably justify the shortage as "worth it," in terms of the gains for the consumer in income transfer?

Initially, the shortage of natural gas took the form of a deficiency of reserves in the 1960s. The lack of large new *reserves* early in the decade curtailed *production* at the end of the decade. This was not generally recognized at the time. Whereas the current production shortage was widely noted and decried by 1971, only a few industry spokesmen had noted the diminishing reserve findings in the middle 1960s. Even buyers of gas at the wellhead eventually agreed that regulation created excess demand for production and that ceiling prices under new contracts were too low.

In 1971 and 1972, retail distributors had to announce restrictions on deliveries of gas to new customers in Illinois, New Jersey, and Pennsylvania. One of the pipelines serving the New York metropolitan region had to *reduce* winter deliveries by 8 percent—just when demands were increasing not only because of the season and increased population but also because of local pollution regulations that called for substitution of gas for dirtier fuels. There were frequent further instances of inability of pipelines and their buyers to obtain as much gas production as they wanted at regulated prices. In fact, pipeline firms reported to the commission substantial shortfalls on the quantities they were under contract to deliver. A subsequent FPC study estimated that shortfalls as a percent of total sales were even greater: 3.6 percent in 1971, 5.1 percent in 1972, and an expected 12.1 percent by 1975.[19] The Ford administration forecast a 15 percent deficiency during the winter months of 1975–1976.

The commission not only acknowledged the existence of a substantial shortage but also suspected that regulated prices might be at fault. Neither these expressions of opinion nor measurements of production shortfalls reveal the full extent of the gas shortage, however. What is more, the sources of excess demand are as important as the magnitude, because consumers doing without might be subject to very high costs resulting from the technical disadvantages of using substitute fuels. The nature, extent, and incidence of excess demand are estimated here by recourse to an inventory analysis, in which attention is paid to both production and reserve *backing* that ensures more production.

The concept of production shortfalls is not altogether satisfactory for analyzing the extent of the gas shortage, inasmuch as gas is not purchased at the time of production. Both industrial gas customers and retail distributors enter into long-term gas contracts because they wish to buy not only gas for immediate consumption but also security of supply. In present-day markets, producers commit or dedicate reserves for future production only if buyers are willing to pay a premium for a long-term commitment. The FPC insisted upon certain reserve commitments but at the same time undercut the market mechanism that promoted reserves. Perhaps the agency acted on the theory that it was protecting residential buyers who were unable to bargain for the "desirable" reserve backup, but all parties to gas production sought reserve security anyway. The extent of the shortage in the 1960s lay in the gap between the reserves needed to secure existing demand and the actual reserve requirements established by the commission.

An Inventory Approach to Reserves

Inventory needs obviously exceed a few years' production. Pipeline companies would not make connections for only two or three years of deliveries; in fact, they traditionally have sought ten to twenty years of reserve backing for contracts to retailers. Optimal backing is a question of

19. U.S. Federal Power Commission, Bureau of Natural Gas, *Natural Gas Supply and Demand, 1971–1990*, Staff Report 2 (1972), Table 16, p. 123. The critical element in this estimate and forecast is the judgment of the industry's Future Requirements Committee as regards demand.

balance between the greater security that reserves provide a pipeline against default on its promised deliveries and the greater initial pipeline outlay necessary to have such reserves on tap.[20]

The FPC has considered the proper amount of reserves to be twenty times initial production, so that (regulated) demands for new reserves have been based on "the assumption that each new market commitment is backed by a twenty-year supply." [21] Long before the commission had much influence on demand for reserves, however, both pipeline and nonpipeline buyers manifested a preference for reserve backing. In 1947 new reserves secured by both pipeline and nonpipeline buyers provided backing equal to 14.5 times new production, and in subsequent years additional reserves to support additional production rose until by 1957 new reserves equaled 24.5 times new production.

A simple, rough estimate of demands for reserve inventory under ceiling prices in the late 1960s might be obtained by multiplying total new production—for all new contracts plus any renewals of expiring contracts—by either the FPC ratio for reserve backing or the "market" ratio that prevailed from 1947 to 1957. To do this, it is necessary to reckon, for each year of the "study" period, the extent of additional demand and the extent of replacement demand for production to be delivered to final home and industrial consumers.

To estimate total new production, we have assumed that in a given year gas was supplied from reserves that had been committed evenly over time to buyers who wanted roughly fourteen years' backup (the national rate of depletion of new reserves in 1947). Thus 1/14 of the production was for contracts that would expire in any one year. The total new production demanded, then, would equal the increase in production over the previous year, plus 1/14 of that year's production.[22] (The latter amount is for renewal or replacement of expiring contracts.) To estimate new reserve demands in each year, the total new production figure can be multiplied either by 20 (the FPC's recommended backup figure) or, to be

20. In theory at least, a longer waiting period for production imposes higher costs on the supplier, necessitating higher contract prices to the pipelines. This cost increase was not reflected in significantly higher prices on long-term contracts, however, during the period just before area rate regulation. See MacAvoy, *Price Formation in Natural Gas Fields,* pp. 262–265.

21. Federal Power Commission, Bureau of Natural Gas, *National Gas Supply and Demand* (1969), p. 18.

22. The market analyzed here is delimited by the territory in which the pipelines taking gas for resale along the east coast made their purchases. The area roughly comprises Texas Railroad Commission Districts 1–7 and 10; also Louisiana, Kansas, and Oklahoma.

very conservative, by 14.5 (the smallest backup demanded by buyers before regulation, in 1947).

The total demands for reserves for 1964–1968 under these conditions are set forth in Table 1. Total new production each year ranged from 0.9 trillion cubic feet to more than 1.6 trillion cubic feet. If companies wanted to back that new production with 14.5 years of reserves, they would have demanded each year amounts that ranged from 13.2 to 23.6 trillion cubic feet of reserves, depending on the year. If they had wanted twenty years of backing, they would have demanded each year amounts that ranged, depending on the year, between 18.4 and 32.8 trillion cubic feet of reserves. The real supply of new reserves, as shown by the total commitments actually made to the pipelines under new contracts, was far less, ranging from 9.4 to 15.7 trillion cubic feet per year. For the five-year period as a whole, if pipelines' would-be "demand" for reserves is measured by 14.5 times new production, then that would-be demand amounted to 156 percent of the new reserves actually committed under contract. If measured by the commission's standards (20 times new production), would-be demand amounted to 219 percent of the new reserves actually committed. In other words, in the late 1960s, demand for new reserves ranged somewhere between 1.5 and 2.2 times the reserves supplied.

Of course, this inventory analysis depends upon restrictive assumptions. The increased demand for reserves is calculated on the assumption that the preference of pipelines for security in reserve backings is constant—that no change occurs in the conditions that translate security needs into reserve demands. If this assumption holds up, it is fair to conclude that a "shortage" of reserves developed that injured buyers by

Table 1. Estimated demand by companies for natural gas reserves, before and after FPC regulation, and actual additions to reserves, 1964–1968 (in trillions of cu. ft.)

Year	Reserves demanded to back new production		Actual additions to reserves
	14.5-year backing	20-year backing	
1964	19.8	27.4	10.7
1965	13.2	18.4	12.8
1966	22.1	30.7	14.9
1967	21.4	29.8	15.7
1968	23.6	32.8	9.4

Source: From or derived from Federal Power Commission, *The Gas Supplies of Interstate Natural Gas Pipeline Companies, 1968* (1970), p. 92.

reducing their security. One cannot really determine the extent to which higher prices would have ended this shortage (perhaps by eliciting more supply or by drying up demand for more reserves) without trying to determine how market-clearing prices would have affected supply and demand for reserves.

A Supply and Demand Analysis

In the absence of price ceilings, higher prices would have been specified in new gas contracts, and significantly greater new reserve commitments might have been made. General increases in demands for energy, during a period in which the supply responses in coal and oil markets were a little sluggish, should have led to short-term price increases for new gas reserves. The gas supply response might have been substantial—enough to fill in part of the excess demand shown in the inventory analysis of reserve commitments. Without price ceilings, the demand response should also have been substantial; by rationing the new volumes available, the price increases would eliminate the rest of the excess demand.

To test these hypotheses, the first steps are to construct supply and demand schedules pertaining to the 1950s and to use these schedules to find the market-clearing prices in that period. Here supply and demand relations are fitted to data for the 1950s and used to find ΔR_{tj} (new reserves added in year t in producing district j) and P_{tj} (the average of the initial base prices on new contracts signed in year t in producing district j). Southwestern fields where gas was produced for resale along the east coast are the ones scrutinized.[23] The values for ΔR_{tj} and P_{tj} that clear the supply and demand system in the 1950s appear to be close to the actual values of new reserves and prices for those years. As a result, it can be concluded that markets operated in the 1950s so as to satisfy demands as they arose. The model is then applied to the 1960s by inserting 1961–1967 data into the supply and demand equations and then solving the system for market-clearing values ΔR_{tj}, P_{tj}^* characteristic of the 1960s. Differences between model values and actual reserves and prices are attributable to the rigidity imposed through regulatory ceiling prices.

The amount of new reserves found ("supplied") in a year depends on geological, technical, and economic factors. Over time, the density of de-

23. The data used in the regressions and simulations were all obtained from publicly available sources. These consisted of the official publications of various federal agencies and the publications of professional associations related to the petroleum industry.

posits in a given region will become more or less evident. Drilling inputs further affect the amount of available reserves. (The only data on such inputs show number of gas development wells in the 1950s and 1960s by drilling district. These are not indicative of all inputs, because of great differences in depth and strata conditions, and wells themselves are joint factor inputs both of capital and of knowledge of surrounding geological conditions.) Finally, the supply of newly discovered reserves also depends in part upon the prices producers can expect to get for new gas.

On the demand side of gas field markets, prices are affected by the pipelines' costs of transport from each district. The volume of discoveries is important in setting these costs—large discoveries provide the opportunity to put in large-scale gathering lines which reduce the costs of transporting each additional thousand cubic feet of gas. Distance also is important—the greater the distance of the reserves from the final industrial and home gas users, the greater the costs to the pipelines.

As for the final consumer, in years in which prices of substitutes are rising and incomes or other determinants of personal consumption are increasing, demand is increasing, and so bid prices should be higher. An indicator of final consumer demand increase is an increase in the price of substitutes, as shown by the index of all fuel prices at retail.

Having listed the principal components, we are now in a position to prepare a model of the supply and demand relationships. Gas markets without price ceiling regulation are expected to clear gas reserves ΔR_{tj}, gas production ΔQ_{tj}, and the number of development wells W_{tj} at initial contract prices P_{tj}. The market-clearing solutions depend on the outside or "exogenous" variables: district characteristics j; reserves demanded $\Sigma \Delta R_{tj}$; capital stock of gas-burning furnances in the country K_t; index of all fuel prices at retail fp_t; distance M_j; rate of interest i_t; and oil price op_t (more gas drilling occurs where there are prospects of profitable oil discoveries).

Data series for each of these variables have been constructed for the preregulatory period 1955–1960 in eleven drilling regions that provided gas on contracts to pipelines serving the east coast and the Midwest.[24]

---

24. The "hat" variables $\hat{W}_{tj}$, $\hat{P}_{tj}$ use values fitted from the first-stage regressions of the four endogenous variables on the purely exogenous variables, to reduce the effect of simultaneous determination of (a) both independent and dependent endogenous variations by (b) the exogenous variables. The simultaneity effect produces inconsistent estimates; two-stage least squares eliminated this inconsistency.

Compare with Phoebus J. Dhrymes, *Econometrics: Statistical Foundations and Applications* (New York: Harper and Row, 1970), pp. 167–174.

These data are used to fit the supply and demand relations by two-stage least squares, with the four endogenous variables, ΔR_{tj}, ΔQ_{tj}, W_{tj}, P_{tj}, simultaneously determined. The procedure is to find "reduced form" equations for ΔR_{tj}, ΔQ_{tj}, W_{tj}, and P_{tj} separately, given the exogenous variables, and then use the fitted values $\Delta \hat{R}_{tj}$, $\Delta \hat{Q}_{tj}$, $\hat{W}_{tj}$, and $\hat{P}_{tj}$ to find the supply and demand equations.[25]

The fitted supply and demand equations are thus four least-squares regressions: one for the supply of new reserves, the second for the supply of wells, the third for new production, the last for the demand for new reserves. The number of wells and the supply of reserves for the 1955–1960 period are given by the following equations:

$$W_{tj} = -648.60 + 11.46\,\hat{P}_{tj} + 175.52\,op_t + \sum_1^{10} a_i J_i$$
$$\quad\quad\quad (1.73) \quad\quad\quad (1.73)$$

$$R^2 = 0.734$$

$$\Delta R_{tj} = -5.41 + 2.45\,\hat{W}_{tj} + \sum_1^{10} b_i J_i$$
$$\quad\quad (0.98)$$

$$R^2 = 0.831.$$

Note the positive cumulative effects from well drilling, new gas contract prices, and the all-fuels price index. The elasticity of reserve supply with respect to new contract gas price is estimated to be equal to 0.51 at average 1956 price and 1956 new reserves, so that a 10 percent price increase theoretically leads to a 5.1 percent increase in discovery of new reserves.

The production equation is as follows:

$$\Delta Q_{tj} = -34.33 + 0.015\,\Delta R_{tj} - 27.49\,i_t + 11.37\,fp_t$$
$$\quad\quad\quad (2.89) \quad\quad (-2.27) \quad\quad (2.75)$$

$$R^2 = 0.693,$$

which shows a positive production–reserve relation, a negative production–interest rate relation, and a positive production–fuel price relation. The elasticity of production with respect to reserves was approximately

25. The sets of variables $\Sigma a_i J_i$ and $\Sigma b_i J_i$ are district dummy variables taking the value one for observations from that district J and zero otherwise. This method of treatment of the geological differences between districts follows from Franklin M. Fisher, *Supply and Costs in the U.S. Petroleum Industry: Two Econometric Studies* (Baltimore: Johns Hopkins Press for Resources for the Future, 1964).

0.40 and was "statistically quasi-significant." The elasticity with respect to interest rates was negative and with respect to the fuel price index was positive. Both coefficients were quasi-significant and had the expected effect on production: the higher the capital cost (i_t), the lower the production rate; the higher the price of alternative fuels, the higher the gas production rate.

The demand equation has also been estimated in the second stage of two-stage least squares as follows:

$$P_{tj} = 12.22 + 0.0012\ \Delta\hat{R}_{tj} - 0.000094\ \Sigma\Delta R_{tj} - 0.0013\ M_j$$
$$\quad\quad (8.93) \quad\quad (-1.12) \quad\quad\quad\quad (-1.95)$$
$$+ 0.088\ fp_t + 0.00083\ K_t$$
$$\ (0.99) \quad\quad (5.02)$$

$$R^2 = 0.616.$$

The elasticity of gas prices with respect to total reserves $\Delta\Sigma R_{tj}$ at 1956 average values (the reciprocal of the usual elasticity of demand) was -0.06, while the elasticity of gas prices with respect to the fuels price index was $+0.02$ and with respect to the stock of gas-burning furnaces (an index of the size of the resale market) was $+0.05$. These values are low, indicating small responsiveness of bid prices to changes in the values of these variables. The elasticity of demand is substantial—a small change in prices P_{tj} brings forth large changes in total new reserves demanded $\Sigma\Delta R_{tj}$. This elasticity equals $(-1/0.00009)\ (P_{tj}/\Delta R_{tj})$. The other elasticities—for variables ΔR_{tj} and M_j, differentiating the drilling regions—are as expected from the economics of pipeline costs and demand.

This four-equation formulation indicates that the supply of newly discovered reserves and of new production depends upon new contract prices. These prices in turn depend on the size of total discoveries, on pipeline costs, and on conditions of demand in final gas resale markets. The four equations together make up an equilibrium system that describes well the actual prices and discoveries in the late 1950s. An indication of the closeness of description is the accuracy with which equilibrium in the four-equation system reproduces the actual values of new reserves, prices, and production in the 1955–1960 period. The simulated prices and the actual annual average prices from the eleven-region sample (in cents per thousand cubic feet) compare rather closely, as can be seen when they are listed side by side.

Year	Average actual price	Simulated price
1956	17.0	17.9
1957	18.1	18.4
1958	19.3	18.8
1959	19.1	19.7
1960	18.4	20.0

The two sets of prices are quite similar, and the difference between average actual reserves and simulated reserves comes to less than a trillion cubic feet of gas for the five-year period analyzed here. These similarities make it likely that market clearing was accomplished by price changes within the year, in the years 1955–1960, before price controls.

The question is whether markets cleared in the 1960s or whether the ceilings on prices in the early 1960s had such a substantial effect on gas reserve discovery and disposition that the shortage developed from the price controls alone. In order to formulate a judgment on these possibilities, the four equations have been used, along with 1961–1968 values of the exogenous variables, to find the values ΔR_{tj}^*, ΔQ_{tj}^*, W_{tj}^*, and P_{tj}^* which solve the equations or, in other words, "clear" the gas market as if there were no price ceilings. These "unregulated" values are compared with actual values in Table 2.

Table 2. Actual prices and simulated unregulated prices, production, and changes in reserves of natural gas, east coast and Midwest, 1961–1968

Year	Price P_{tj} (cents per MCF)		Production ΔQ_{tj} (billions cu. ft.)		Changes in reserves ΔR_{tj} (billions cu. ft.)	
	Actual av.	Simulated *	Actual	Simulated *	Actual	Simulated *
1961	17.7	20.0	292	817	5,567	12,480
1962	19.0	21.1	230	755	5,805	12,858
1963	16.5	22.4	447	688	4,884	13,077
1964	16.7	22.9	200	814	5,512	13,221
1965	17.4	24.1	348	750	6,015	13,621
1966	17.2	25.5	347	627	4,204	14,147
1967	17.4	26.7	575	520	3,693	15,026
1968	18.0	27.8	434	548	951	15,572

Sources: American Gas Association (AGA), *Reserves of Crude Oil* (1969), pp. 175–219, Tables XVII-1 to XVII-45; AGA, American Petroleum Institute, and Canadian Petroleum Association, *Summary of Estimated Annual Discoveries of Natural Gas Reserves*, various issues.

* The simulations are estimates of what the values would have been without FPC regulation.

The simulated or unregulated prices that would have cleared the reserve market were on the average 6 cents per thousand cubic feet higher than ceiling prices for the entire period and over 7 cents higher for the period following 1962. On the supply side, the higher prices—if they had been allowed—would have provided considerable incentive to add to the volume of new reserves. The simulated reserves are more than twice as high as the actual reserves over this period. On the demand side, the market-clearing price would have significantly reduced the amounts of reserves sought. The amounts demanded are not known, since all that have been registered are those reserves both demanded *and* supplied. That excess reserve demands would have been reduced is indicated by the rate of change in the total reserve demand function with respect to field price (the reciprocal of the coefficient -0.00009): demand would have decreased approximately 10 trillion cubic feet for each cent of price increase.

Another indication of the potential impact of clearing prices appears in the difference between the actual and simulated production series. Actual production falls short of simulated production by approximately 52 percent over the eight-year period. It appears that unregulated prices would have brought forth much greater output.

The overall impression is that new reserve supplies might have been three times greater, and immediate production twice as great, if there had been no field price regulation.[26] The higher market-clearing prices would have brought forth additional discovered reserves more than twice the entire amount of additions to the interstate inventory over the 1961–1968 period. The buyers' response to higher prices observed in our sample suggests that higher prices would have eliminated the remaining supply-

26. This conclusion is based on the premise that supply conditions—as in the equations pertaining to wells and reserves—stayed the same in the 1960s as they had been in the 1950s. To the contrary, however, supply equations may have changed so that less new reserves would have been forthcoming at prices ranging from 20 cents to 28 cents. (If so, then prices would have been higher under market clearing—unless regulation itself had caused the supply functions to change.) An initial test for functional changes is to compare the actual reserves in 1961–1968 with simulated reserves which are calculated on the basis of simulation values obtained at *actual* prices. These simulated reserves are 61.4 trillion cubic feet greater than the actual 36.6 trillion cubic feet shown in Table 2 (and 12.0 trillion less than the 110.0 for "market-clearing" prices). Thus it might be concluded that the supply functions changed over the 1960s. This could have occurred because of attrition of in-ground deposits (or other geological conditions), or it could have happened because of dampened supplier incentives under price controls. The first possibility implies that the conclusions of the following section on the shortage experience by consumers is overstated. But the second possibility implies that these conclusions are if anything understated.

demand gap observed in the inventory analysis. The shortage of natural gas can be attributed to Federal Power Commission field price regulation, in the sense that continuation of 1955–1960 market processes rather than regulatory ceiling prices would have prevented excess demands for reserves.

As it was, a serious reserve shortage developed in the 1960s, invisible on the surface. It revealed itself in the pipelines' reduction of their reserve-to-production ratio, a change that reduced the security of service that many old customers with twenty-year contracts desired and that many new customers sought. This "security loss," shared by all those connected to interstate pipelines, was soon translated into a more tangible actual production shortage. In 1971 and 1972, many pipelines had to curtail deliveries because they could not take gas from their reserves fast enough to fulfill their contracts. The reserve base was too thin to support full demand for production during the winter heating season. Thus the shortage became plainly visible, following directly from the reserve shortage which in turn was a creature of FPC regulatory policy.

The Impact of the Shortage

Before attempting to assess the results of gas field price regulation, we should try to determine who felt the shortage. Although the gains and losses are hard to pin down, and any conclusion is highly speculative, those who felt the shortage most were probably the interstate residential buyers—exactly the group regulation was designed to benefit.

Evidence supporting this view shows that, during the 1960s, home consumer reserves were reduced in the course of meeting the demands of unregulated customers. Three observed changes constitute especially strong evidence.

(1) The regulated pipelines—those selling gas interstate for resale—obtained somewhat less than their proportionate share of new reserves in the late 1960s as compared with earlier years. In 1965 these pipelines held contracts for 68 percent of the nation's 284.5 trillion cubic feet of reserves. Between 1965 and 1971, additional gas totaling 92.9 trillion cubic feet was found, of which the interstate pipelines obtained 62 percent (only 57.9 trillion cubic feet), and their share of all reserves, to be used primarily to supply home comsumers, fell to 67 percent.

(2) As distinct from reserves, in the division of total annual gas production between residential and industrial users proportionately more went to industrial users over the decade. The percentage of gas sold to

residential users declined about 2 percent between 1962 and 1968. The decline was caused by a large increase in unregulated industrial sales.

(3) Sales to industrial users by intrastate pipelines and by producers themselves expanded far more rapidly than sales by regulated interstate pipelines. Between 1962 and 1968 the regulated pipelines increased their direct industrial sales by 24 percent; intrastate pipelines and distributors did so by 62 percent; producers themselves expanded their direct sales to industry by 39 percent.

That the reserve shortage hit the residential buyer—supplied by a regulated pipeline—most seriously is still more evident when certain particular gas supply regions are examined. The Permian Basin, for example, held about 2.5 percent of total U.S. gas reserves in the early 1960s. In the late 1960s, additional discoveries raised this figure to about 10.5 percent. Six large interstate pipelines, two intrastate pipelines, and many direct industrial buyers bid for the new reserves. From 1966 onward, the intrastate lines and the direct industrial buyers obtained almost all of them. In fact, interstate pipelines, which absorbed 84 percent of production from new reserves in 1966, absorbed only 9 percent in the first half of 1970. Prices for new gas offered by intrastate buyers rose from 17 cents per thousand cubic feet in 1966 to 20.3 cents in 1970. Toward the end of 1970, the intrastate pipelines bought more than 200 billion cubic feet of reserves at initial delivery prices of 26.5 cents per thousand cubic feet. During the same period, interstate prices remained between 16 and 17 cents per thousand cubic feet—near the regulatory ceiling. The interstate pipelines were simply outbid.

The gains of the consumers who, because of the regulation-induced shortage, received gas production at 6 cents less than market-clearing prices did not offset the losses of those consumers who had to go without. The losses from excess demands for new reserves are not observable, since they took place in the form of reduced backing on continued production; but gas pipelines were willing to pay an "insurance premium" of 6 cents to obtain *more than twice as much* reserve backing. If this willingness to pay indicates the value of guaranteed deliveries to the final consumer, then the losses exceeded the gains.[27] Those persons "de-

27. For the kind of loss referred to here, economists use the term "consumers' surplus." Consumers' surplus is defined as the excess over the price charged which consumers are willing to pay for a given amount of a product rather than do without it. (See George Stigler, *The Theory of Price*, 3d ed., [New York: Macmillan, 1966], p. 78.) When a market is at equilibrium, the market-clearing price equals what consumers are willing to pay for the last or marginal unit of output. Since consumers would normally be willing to pay more for

prived'' of reserves were, for the most part, residential gas consumers who wished to buy them. On very conservative assumptions, these buyers wanted 14.5 years of reserves—an "insurance" that they bought before regulation in the 1950s. They would have been willing to pay 6 cents per thousand cubic feet, or $500 million per year, more for that reserve backup.

The losses from excess demands for production are observable; buyers willing to pay the 6-cent "premium" to obtain production curtailed by regulated prices lost more than was gained by others getting their deliveries at the lower prices, because they lost deliveries as large as the total production. That is, the shortage was larger than the actual deliveries going to retail distributors, as shown in Table 2.

These losses are not the end of the matter, of course. The economic costs of litigation and delay from the area price proceedings have been substantial. A further cost resulted from displacement of industry by price ceilings—even if this loss is not directly measurable. Industrial firms for whom energy costs were a large part of total costs moved to the producing states solely to obtain natural gas that in effect was kept off the interstate market through the interstate price ceiling. The extra costs from such a move are appropriately part of the cost of regulation. (There are no statistical estimates suggesting the amount of such costs at the present time, but it should be possible to trace relative industrial development in Texas, Oklahoma, and Louisiana over ten years to assess these costs.)

Finally, the worsening gas shortage results in increasing shifts by consumers to other energy sources, many of which are also in declining domestic supply. Thus, it has added to U.S. energy dependency problems. It has also lead to suggestions and proposed government incentives to develop synthetic natural gas from coal. Unfortunately, the cost of such ventures have been forecast at three to four dollars per million BTUs produced. This is substantially above forecasts for free market natural gas prices and exceeds current intrastate gas prices by over 100 percent.

In total, the roughly measurable costs of producer price regulation seem high. Regulation induced a gas shortage of considerable dimensions, forced lengthy and expensive administrative proceedings on a highly complex, decentralized, and previously unregulated sector of the

---

intramarginal units of output, the equilibrium price affords them a savings or "surplus" on these intramarginal units. The savings of this kind which gas consumers who in fact experienced a shortage could have realized under unregulated conditions is a measure of the cost to them of FPC policy.

industry. And its major objective—benefiting the home consumer—was not achieved. The lower prices produced benefits with one hand that were taken away with the other. Excess demand generated from the reduced prices took away the benefits—regulation denied consumers gas reserves for which they would have been willing to pay.

Alternatives

The arguments against continued efforts to control the exact price of natural gas are strong. Regulation is not necessary to check the market power of producers. Moreover, there is no practical way to calculate and capture rents in competitive gas markets: setting the prices for producers individually is not feasible; setting area rates is administratively complex and of necessity produces a gas shortage.

Some consumer groups have argued that the Federal Power Commission should deal with the problems that arise from its regulatory efforts by introducing still more regulation. The FPC might, for example, seek to expand its jurisdiction over intrastate sales to end the "leakage of supply." It might then establish end-use controls, specifically allocating gas to particular individuals or classes of customers. Such an approach, however, would not solve the problems raised here. More intense regulation would reduce even further the incentives to increase reserves or improve gas production technology. It would simply impose the additional burden upon the commission of determining which end uses were "superior" and which "inferior." Such a task is difficult, to say the least. In the 1960s, for example, to burn gas under an industrial boiler or in a power plant was considered an "inferior" use. Today, the "pollution-free" quality of natural gas makes such a judgment less certain. Once prices are abandoned as a measure of value, the number of claimants, citing a variety of economic and social imperatives, becomes impossibly large. There is no reason to believe that the commission—which was unable to determine the marginal cost of gas production—would find a proper solution to this still more complex problem. In all probability, it would simply arrange for a series of compromises among such claimants, as in the case of gas prices. Such compromises would lead to continued excess demand for gas and shortages in which, as likely as not, those who were supposed to benefit from gas regulation would still be left without.

The alternative is deregulation. Our analysis strongly indicates that less, not more, regulation is required. The commission could obtain, through economic analysis, a rough idea of whether competitive conditions exist in each producing region. Unless the evidence strongly suggests that producers possess monopoly power, the commission should allow new gas prices to approach market-clearing levels. At the same time, by using prices in the competitive areas as benchmarks, the commission could set prices in those few producer regions where monopoly power existed.

A gradual return to market-clearing prices after an investigation and finding of competitive market conditions would be consistent with the commission's legal obligations as determined in the *Phillips* case. Nothing in that decision *requires* the commission to set prices; the decision simply gives the commission jurisdiction to do so. Moveover, if the commission maintains continuous supervision over market conditions, accepting as "just and reasonable" only prices set by workably competitive regional markets, it will carry out the statute's mandate (as interpreted in *Phillips*) that it regulate producers. *Permian Basin, Hope Natural Gas,* and many other cases provide an agency with very broad discretion over the methods used to achieve a statute's regulatory objectives. And, in this instance, there is no other way to carry out the statute's twofold purpose: gas sales "at the lowest possible reasonable rate consistent with the maintenance of adequate service in the public interest." (See *Atlantic Refining* v. *Public Service Commission,* 360 U.S. 378, 388.) In a workably competitive context, the market-set price will satisfy both objectives; any other price will be either too high, unreasonably taxing consumers, or too low, preventing adequate service. The legal attitude that best harmonizes the statute, legal principles of administrative discretion, and the economics of gas production is that reflected in a recent observation by the Fifth Circuit Court of Appeals. "The Commission," reasoned the court, "does not have to employ the area rate method, or for that matter regulate price directly at all, but it has chosen to fulfill its duty in that manner here." [28]

28. *Southern Louisiana Area Rate Cases,* 428 F 2d 407 (1970) at 416, n.9.

8

Coal—The Swing Fuel

Richard L. Gordon

For many years coal has occupied a paradoxical place in the American energy economy. The apparently enormous quantities of measured coal reserves have appeared to offer great potential for meeting the future energy needs of the nation. Yet, in practice, coal has become decreasingly important, at least in relative terms, over most of the twentieth century. As of 1975, the future of coal remains as ambiguous as it has ever been. Many believe that we are on the threshold of an era in which new techniques for the transformation of coal into synthetic fuels will lead to a great increase in its use. Yet at the same time, environmental considerations make it increasingly difficult to continue the present uses of coal.

This article attempts to review both these aspects of the future of coal. The analysis begins with a discussion of the problems of evaluating the much used figures on coal resources. Then questions relating to coal use in present markets are treated, and the prospects for major new markets for coal as the source of synthetic fuels are discussed. Finally, the crucial role of public policy is considered.

At the outset, it is critical to note that the fate of coal depends to a large extent on forces far outside the control of the coal industry. Government policy, not only in this country but elsewhere in the world, will have a great deal of effect upon what role coal can in fact play. For example, it is shown below that a severe conflict exists between the desire to use domestic coal resources immediately to fill our energy needs and our desire rapidly to attain vigorous environmental control standards. Similarly, important questions exist about whether the present higher prices of oil will persist for an extended period. This article cannot pre-

This study is based on research supported by Resources for the Future and the National Science Foundation.

tend to resolve these political questions; what it does attempt to do is lay out the logical possibilities and provide some basis on which the reader may appraise prospective developments.

The Question of Coal Resources

A chronic problem in appraising the long-term potential of coal is that methods for measuring coal resources in the United States differ drastically from those employed for other fuels and indeed for most other minerals. Traditionally, so-called reserve estimates for other fuels and for most other minerals are based on what are known as proved reserves. Such proved reserves consist of the estimated mineral contents of already discovered, developed, and operating mineral properties. Moreover, for a variety of reasons, these content estimates are deliberately conservative. The natural unwillingness of geologists to commit themselves to the existence of greater resources than can be easily proved is itself an inhibiting force. This conservatism is further stimulated by securities regulations. The Securities and Exchange Commission clearly looks askance upon exaggerated figures on reserves. Taxes on reserves create further pressures to limit the amounts proved. Thus typical proved reserve figures have been well characterized, particularly in the writings of M. A. Adelman, as working inventories.[1] They include only the amount of minerals that have been discovered and made ready for exploitation in quantities sufficient to support current production. The amounts that may be uncovered by future exploration activities, and also substantial amounts of fuel known to exist but simply considered uneconomic at present prices, are excluded from proved reserve figures.

In contrast, coal reserves are estimated on the basis of inferences from surface geological exploration. Coal has a tendency to outcrop on the surface and on the basis of observing these outcrops and making guesses of what lies between them, geologists throughout the world have made estimates of how much *in toto* exists in the way of coal resources. These figures then do not measure only developed coal resources but also represent an effort to estimate those that might be developed in the future. For example, while possible coal resources in the United States have been estimated to exceed 3.2 trillion tons, a 1973 National Petroleum Council

---

1. The fullest statement of his position appears in "Economics of Exploration for Petroleum and Other Minerals," *Geoexplorations*, 8 (1970), 131–150. However, all his writings on oil, such as *The World Petroleum Market* (Baltimore: Johns Hopkins for Resources for the Future, 1972), contain material suggesting the proposition.

study indicated that readily available reserves amounted to only 149 billion tons. This disparity arises from elimination of coal whose existence has not been adequately verified, which lies in deep seams, lies in seams too thin to mine economically, will not be recovered because present mining techniques cause significant amounts of coal to be left behind, or is located where other land uses preclude mining.[2] Because of this great difference in conceptual framework, it is extremely difficult to make accurate comparisons between coal estimates and the estimates of the future availability of other fuels.

In addition, there are fossil fuels, such as oil from shales, which are not yet used but are potential competitors for coal. More criticially the age of fossil fuels may end long before all the fossil fuels are depleted. Virtually inexhaustible alternatives such as fueling nuclear fusion with deuterium from sea water or direct conversion of solar energy could be developed. Indeed a great deal of effort is already being devoted to such alternatives. Should the efforts pay off soon enough and produce sufficiently low-cost technologies, much of our fossil fuel could be left in the ground. Just which fuels would be used would, of course, depend upon their comparative economics. Conceivably, enough lower cost reserves of fuels other than coal might exist to meet a sizable proportion of our needs until a low-cost way of utilizing inexhaustible resources emerges. In this case, the often predicted massive shift to coal would not occur. To be sure, this is but one of many possible outcomes. The present argument only shows we lack the information to prove or disprove conclusively that reliance on coal will increase greatly and, therefore, should be more cautious in our forecasts than often has been the case.

It should be noted that the suggestion that a long-run shift to coal is not inevitable is quite different from an assertion that a shift to nonfossil fuel alternatives is imminent. All too many advocates of such alternatives as fusion, solar energy, or geothermal steam grossly exaggerate the speed with which such techniques can be developed. The stress on speed is based on the same fears that cause simplistic calls for greater coal use— underestimation of the prospects for other fossil fuel alternatives. It is conceivable that these oil and gas alternatives exist in sufficient quantities so that they can, without the aid of coal, cover energy needs over the

2. See National Petroleum Council, *U.S. Energy Outlook, Coal Availability,* Washington, 1973. This is by no means the only possible basis for adjustment. The U.S. Department of the Interior has a somewhat different adjustment of the figures in its *Final Task Force Report on Coal, Project Independence* (Washington, 1974).

long period until nonfossil alternatives become viable. In short, the swing
to coal is by no means a guaranteed physical necessity. The actual development will depend upon the comparative economics of the fuels and the
technologies for their use. It is to these forces that the remainder of this
article turns.

It may be useful to comment parenthetically before proceeding about
the role of "conservation" in the process of future fuel use. For reasons
that are rarely explicitly articulated, calls for conservation inspire a great
deal of controversy. It is by no means clear whether the dispute is over
facts or value judgments. No one would deny the basic economic principle that higher energy prices such as the 1973–1974 quadrupling of oil
prices will inspire lower energy use. It is similarly recognized that consumer ignorance about the energy usage of appliances and certain public
policies such as outmoded building codes may encourage excessive energy use. The conservation debate may be over only such factual issues
as how big a reduction in energy consumption will be produced by higher
prices and improved knowledge and public policy. (Other important
issues include expectations about foreign oil costs and how much expenditure on environmental controls is desirable.)

However, some advocates of conservation hint without explicitly stating their premises that further considerations are involved. Apparently
what this means is a belief that American society is too materialistic and
unconcerned with the needs of other countries and future generations.[3]
Conservation, it is thought, should include sacrifices to remedy these
defects. Questions can be raised about this proposition on at least three
grounds. First, the damages to others may be illusory; the shift to inexhaustible energy resources, for example, may be effected painlessly if the
requisite technology proves sufficiently inexpensive. Second, a call for
energy conservation seems a halfhearted response to the alleged shortcomings; so profound a defect in our attitudes surely leads to more sins
than excessive energy consumption. This conclusion should be made explicit and the call for changes in the energy sector should be presented as
part of a program for a broader transformation of American society. This
immediately suggests the third objection—that these views will prove politically unacceptable.

All too many advocates of a change in attitudes, moreover, seem to be

3. A good example of proposals for conservation that suggest without actually proposing
explicitly a change in values is the Energy Policy Project of the Ford Foundation, *A Time to
Choose: America's Energy Future*, Final Report (Cambridge, Mass.: Ballinger, 1974).

attempting to avoid the difficult battles that will inevitably rage over expanding energy output. This hope seems a vain one. The change in attitudes needed to eliminate disputes over energy developments seems quite unlikely to emerge. Indeed, the only way to avoid such fights is to eliminate energy use. Existing deposits will in time be depleted, and their mere replacement will open disputes over new energy developments.

Along these lines, many advocates of coal development heavily stress that it would probably be much easier to secure its acceptance than that of, say, deregulation of natural gas prices or increased offshore drilling for oil and gas. This belief presumably is based on the severe present opposition to these noncoal alternatives. (Moreover, coal development would generate vast pork-barrel projects that might seem politically attractive. Most proposals for increased coal use have centered around multimillion dollar programs to develop technologies for producing synthetic fuels from coal.) This belief may be doubly erroneous. Coal development may in time produce as much opposition as the alternatives. Moreover, objectively, limiting spills from offshore oil platforms may be a far simpler task than reclaiming strip-mined coal lands.

The Nature of Coal

Hamlet cried "O, that this too too solid flesh would melt, thaw and resolve itself into a dew." Such is the problem with coal. Throughout its history coal's solid state has been problematic in its mining, processing, and utilization. In our present day of environmental concern, the difficulties have been aggravated by the tendency of many coals to accumulate impurities, particularly sulfur, that make environmentally safe burning difficult (see below). The solid state of coal means first that it is much more difficult to extract than oil or gas; second, that a larger proportion of the coal is waste material; third, that it is more difficult to transport than liquids or gases. In some sense energy is transported at every step that takes place from its extraction until its final use so that the transportation problem hinders coal at every stage of the process. Were this not bad enough, solid waste material is left behind in coal combustion and waste disposal has been a persistent problem. In short, coal in its natural state is a far less attractive fuel than oil or natural gas. It is for this reason that the many existing and proposed processes for transforming coal into a synthetic oil or gas have been considered so attractive as alternatives for its long-term future.

The Use of Coal: History and Prospects

As recently as the middle 1940s coal was still supplying the United States with more energy than any other fuel and had uses broadly distributed throughout the economy. It propelled our railroads, it was the major fuel for industry, a substantial amount was used in home heating and for commercial purposes, and of course it was then as now the principal fuel for the generation of electricity. Since that time, the nature of coal use has altered radically. Today the market for coal in the United States is essentially in the generation of electricity and in the manufacture of pig iron. There are to be sure residual markets in other parts of the manufacturing sector, but these are much smaller in absolute terms than they have been at any time in the recent past and the trend over the years has been the steady decrease of use outside of the electric power and iron making sectors.

This can be seen in two different fashions. First, we can note that the proportion of British thermal units supplied by coal has fallen from 44 percent in 1947 to 18 percent in 1974.[4] Secondly, we can observe in Table 1 the radical shifts in markets. General retail sales have almost vanished; sales to manufacturing have diminished. The railroads are no longer a market large enough to record.

The iron making sector can be ignored here. Technical progress that has reduced the coal input per ton of iron produced has almost exactly offset the impact of growing iron output. Coal use in iron making has shown no long-term growth, and all indicators suggest that no substantial future growth is likely in this market.

However, coal use for electric generation has shown substantial growth, and the future of coal heavily depends upon its ability to maintain its position in this market. Moveover, rising oil prices and the continuation of controls on natural gas prices have produced interest in reconversion of manufacturing to coal. The prospects, however, are difficult to predict.

Coal in the Electric Utility Market

Historically coal was the predominant fossil fuel employed to generate electricity east of the Mississippi (its markets elsewhere were quite lim-

4. These and other coal and energy data come from U.S. Bureau of Mines reports; the BTU content of fuel is a widely used common denominator but by no means the only property affecting choice. Indeed, much of coal's loss of markets was to fuel with significantly higher costs per million BTUs. These rival fuels had properties that made consumers willing to pay the premium.

Table 1. U.S. consumption and exports of bituminous coal in selected years (thousand tons)

Year	Electric power utilities	Railroads	Coking	Steel and rolling mills	Other mining and manufacturing	Retail deliveries	Total U.S. consumption	Exports
1946	68,743	110,166	83,288	12,151	127,354	98,684	500,386	41,197
1950	88,262	60,969	103,845	10,877	105,827	84,422	454,202	25,468
1955	140,550	15,473	107,377	7,353	99,639	53,020	423,412	51,277
1960	173,882	2,102	81,015	7,378	85,648	30,405	380,429	36,541
1965	242,729	*	94,779	7,466	95,142	19,048	459,164	50,181
1970	318,921	*	96,009	5,410	83,207	12,072	515,619	70,944
1972	348,612	*	87,272	4,850	67,294	11,748	519,776	55,960
1974	390,068	*	89,747	6,155	57,899	8,840	552,709	59,926

Source: U.S. Bureau of Mines data.
* No longer reported separately but included in other mining and manufacturing.

ited). In recent years this pattern has altered drastically. Much of the east coast market from Maine to Virginia has been lost to oil. New markets have developed in the West. Both these historical developments and future trends are the result of the interaction of numerous forces. The shift on the east coast was initiated by a 1966 U.S. government decision to effectively eliminate controls on the imports of residual fuel oil into the east coast. (Residual fuel oil is a heavy tarlike oil made up by adding small amounts of lighter oil to the heavy residuum left at the bottom of distillation columns used in refining. Residual oil is difficult to handle, but its low price has made it an attractive fuel to large users such as electric utilities for which it is the standard form in which oil is burned.)

The lower price of this oil compared to coal triggered a switch to oil. The rise of environmental concerns, to be discussed shortly, accelerated the shift. Thus, New England, which secured the majority of its electric power fuel from coal in 1966, had only one major plant still using coal by 1972. Coal use ended in New York City. Regions such as Virginia, Maryland, and the District of Columbia, once almost totally dependent on coal, drastically reduced their use of it (see Table 2). Oil use even began far inland (e.g., Chicago) as a means to meet environmental standards, and plans to build large oil burning plants to serve Chicago and Detroit were announced. The Federal Energy Administration is trying to reverse this movement, but considerable problems may arise in doing so. The lead times in plant development and conversion and in coal procurement may make it difficult to secure a rapid major drop in oil use.

In contrast, in the West coal use expanded considerably. The most impressive development along these lines was the formation of the West group of utilities—a collection of companies from west Texas to southern California. The group was established in the wake of environmental objections to building additional dams in the Colorado River. It was suggested that instead coal in Arizona, Nevada, New Mexico, and Utah be used to fire power plants for the West group. A series of plants, several of which are already in operation, was proposed (each a joint venture of a different subgroup of the overall West group).

These developments and the future of the electric power industry have become entangled in the overall debates over the future of U.S. energy. A complex combination of present technical possibilities and economic realities, the prospects for changes, the environmental impacts, and their evaluation affects the choices.

We cannot hope to deal adequately with all these issues. A full analysis

Table 2. Coal consumption by electric utilities in the eastern United States, 1966 and 1972

Region	1966		1972	
	Thousand tons	% of BTUs consumed in region's steam plants	Thousand tons	% of BTUs consumed in region's steam plants
New Hampshire	311	45	1,099	68
Massachusetts	3,725	43	68	1
Rhode Island	375	62	–	–
Connecticut	4,429	84	76	1
New York City	5,087	35	146	1
Other New York	7,992	99	5,951	57
New Jersey	6,836	61	1,109	10
Philadelphia	4,759	76	2,166	28
Other Pennsylvania	19,365	100	33,093	99
Delaware	1,174	87	903	45
Maryland	6,678	99	4,436	46
District of Columbia	494	98	176	14
Virginia	8,322	99	4,868	44
North Carolina	11,467	99	18,737	95
South Carolina	2,969	79	5,582	84
Georgia	6,094	100	10,625	80
Florida	3,012	20	5,464	18

Source: National Coal Association, *Steam Electric Plant Factors,* 1966 and 1973 eds. (Washington, 1967 and 1973).

should encompass long-run oil and gas developments. The possibility exists that the prevailing cartel of oil producing countries may collapse or at least be undermined by discovery of large amounts of oil outside its control. Whether gas will ever be cheap enough to remain a fuel for electric power generation is so doubtful that the question is ignored here.

This discussion will consider coal and nuclear power the relevant long-run alternatives for the generation of electricity, with oil serving perhaps as a temporary fill-in device. Moreover, stress is placed upon the choice of fuel for "base loaded" electric power plants. Electric power demands fluctuate radically over the course of the year, different days of the week and even different hours of the day. Thus it is customary to distinguish different types of plants used to meet different portions of the demand. The base load is that which occurs steadily, and base loaded plants then are those that operate most of the time they are available. (No electric power plant is ever available all the time; repairs of breakdowns, routine preventive maintenance, and, in the case of nuclear plants, refueling, all put plants out of service. Just how much reliability can be maintained by different plant types is a subject of considerable controversy.) At the other extreme, some units, called peaking plants, operate only at periods of very high demand. Clearly in practice the utilization of different plants will range between these two extremes.

Base loaded units are both the major consumers of fuel in the electric utility sector and considered the main battleground in coal-nuclear competition. Most nuclear plants will be base loaded because they are likely to have much lower cash operating costs than fossil fuel plants. More critically, at least for some decades, intermediately loaded plants are likely to be older fossil fired plants. The discussion below of problems of conversion among fuels provides the critical information on intermediate loaded plants that are older fossil fired plants (and the basis for estimating, if it became necessary to build new plants for intermediate loads, whether and under what conditions nuclear plants might be competitive).

At the outset we should recognize that considerable debate exists about whether either coal or nuclear energy is an environmentally acceptable source of electric power—with concerns more often raised about nuclear energy. The critics of nuclear sources are primarily concerned with the hazards of radioactive material. Malfunction of a power plant or supporting facility could lead to release of such material. The wastes from nuclear processes remain potentially lethal for many centuries, and many doubt our ability to store the wastes safely. Some fear the diversion of nuclear materials into the hands of terrorists or countries seeking to become nuclear powers.

The long-run case against coal is usually limited to the argument that the degradation of the landscape by that portion of coal mining conducted on the surface is intolerable. However, it can be argued that it is even more intolerable to expose men to the rigors of underground mining, and further, that the hazards of burning coal can never be reduced to satisfactory levels. Sulfur oxides, nitrogen oxide, and particulate emissions may be greatly reduced, but the residual might remain a severe health hazard.

The present facts do not support either extreme position. It is doubtful whether the control of environmental effects of nuclear power and coal is so difficult as to justify reliance on oil at the high 1975 price (but incidentally less clear that at its 1970 price, oil would not have been the preferable fuel). There are no other alternatives likely to be viable at least until early in the twenty-first century so the choices for the rest of the century are limited to coal, oil (including that from shales and tar sands), and nuclear.

In viewing the choices, we must recognize the considerable amount of inertia in the energy field. All major industrial activities take time, and the range differs widely from case to case. Similar variation occurs in the cost of change. At one extreme, conversion of a coal fired power plant to oil involves perhaps eighteen months of installing pipes and tankage. The actual connection can take place during the annual shutdown for preventive maintenance so that no operating time is lost. At the other extreme, it appears that only great good fortune would make a fast breeder nuclear reactor available for routine commercial use before the 1990s.

In between we can note that a standard fossil fuel plant takes about five years to build and nuclear plants may take up to ten years to build. It appears that the processes discussed below to develop a clean fuel from coal will not be commercially available at best until the early 1980s. Our policy choices clearly then are constrained by these lead times.

We may limit our consideration of the nuclear option to recalling the lead times and noting that at least most published observations indicate nuclear plants have lower fuel costs but higher capital costs than an environmentally acceptable coal fired plant. (Some estimates suggest, however, that an environmentally acceptable coal plant may cost more than a nuclear plant.) Like all new technologies, nuclear power has been plagued with problems of attaining its goals on schedule, and there is some debate about how long it will take to resolve these problems.

Fossil plants have only limited ability to shift among fuels. A basic barrier is set by boiler size—a larger boiler is needed for coal than for oil, a larger one for oil than for gas. However, even if the boiler is of proper size, conversion may be difficult. Coal burning requires vast storage areas and complex coal receipt and moving equipment. The required land may be prohibitively expensive to acquire. Further problems arise with differences among coals; a given coal may be difficult to burn in boilers designed for other types of coal.

In any case, the heart of the coal burnability issue has become the ability to meet sulfur oxide standards. This is the most critical of the pollutants associated with coal burning. Particulate control technology is well developed, and nitrogen oxide pollution resulting from coal combustion is not now an issue of overriding importance. (While all forms of combustion produce nitrogen oxides, automobiles generate more than stationary sources. Moreover, both the absence of large-scale concern about impacts and the lack of satisfactory control techniques have limited the pressures to reduce nitrogen oxide emissions from coal burning. Some observers fear that this leniency eventually will end, and that coal use will be hindered by the need to meet nitrogen oxide control regulations.)

Sulfur is by no means exclusively a coal problem. Oil and natural gas can also contain unacceptably high levels of sulfur. But since the sulfur corrodes gas pipelines, the gas industry long ago perfected sulfur removal techniques so that consumers receive a low sulfur product. Many residual fuel oils are high in sulfur content, but fairly inexpensive desulfurization processes quickly emerged, and the only problem was to build the required desulfurization units as quickly as necessary.

For coal, alas, no such simple cure existed, and for nearly a decade the industry has suffered from failure to find a viable solution. There are coals naturally low enough in sulfur content to meet environmental standards. Unfortunately, such coals did not seem readily accessible to eastern coal users. A concentration of low sulfur coal exists in eastern Kentucky and southern West Virginia, but mining conditions supposedly are such that the coal would be far more costly than that previously used. Moreover, the coal has attractive properties for manufacture of metallurgical coke, and doubts have existed about the utilities' ability to outbid the steel industry. (The coal also often has properties that make it hard to burn in existing boilers.)

An even vaster stock of low sulfur fuel exists in the West—particularly in Montana, Wyoming, and North Dakota. Much of the coal could be very cheaply strip-mined, although the situation is perhaps not as favorable as is often suggested. Just how much of the coal is strip-mineable is unclear. Moreover, it is generally lower in BTU content than eastern coals. As Michael Rieber has pointed out, this means that the sulfur contents of much of the coal is less acceptable than it would at first appear. It is generally considered that a sulfur content of 0.7 percent or less by weight meets environmental standards. However, air pollution standards for specific sources are set in terms of content per million BTUs; those for new plants amount to allowing 0.6 pounds of sulfur per million BTUs. For a typical eastern coal with 12,000 BTUs per pound, 83.3 pounds constitute a million BTUs and 0.6 divided by 83.3 gives the 0.7 percent figure. However, a western lignite might only have 8,000 BTUs per pound so that 125 pounds of coal would be required to constitute a million BTUs and 0.6 divided by 125 is a sulfur content of only 0.48 percent. Published data tell only how much coal meets the 0.7 percent standard applicable to eastern coal, not how much western coal meets the more rigorous standards applicable to it.[5] The use of this coal, moreover, was initially dismissed as being too expensive because of the high cost of transporting it much further east than Wisconsin. (However, our review below of alternative approaches to sulfur control indicates that a drastic revision of this appraisal has emerged.)

Sulfur content can be reduced by washing the coal to remove that portion of the sulfur that is chemically separate from the coal, but little evidence exists that much could be accomplished by this route. Few coals appear cleanable at reasonable cost to acceptable sulfur levels. Some discussions have suggested that improved cleaning techniques could contribute significantly to meeting sulfur emission standards.

Still another possibility is that coal could be chemically converted into a clean fuel. One could develop simplified processes of converting coal to, say, a low BTU gas, a heavy fuel oil, or a special product known as solvent refined coal.[6] In all cases, the transformation would create a low-grade fuel unsuited for the specialized uses of oil and gas, and in the case of the gas so low in heat content that it would be prohibitively expensive to transport long distances. These drawbacks are irrelevant for production of such fuel at power plants to provide the means to generate power. At power plants, the cheapest environmentally acceptable, usable source of heat is what is wanted.

Interest in the new fuels has been heightened by the fact that existing methods of generating electricity from fossil fuels appeared to have come to an economic dead end. By the middle 1960s, improved technical performance appeared prohibitively expensive to attain. New methods of generation were considered necessary to provide technical improvements. Many such have been proposed, but the most fully developed to date is what is called the combined cycle. Here we start with a gas turbine (a stationary adaptation of a jet engine) and use the still quite hot exhaust gases in a conventional steam turbine boiler. Such combined cycles are already in operation (using natural gas or light fuel oil), and prospective improvements in their technology are such that a thermal efficiency of 50 percent

5. See Michael Rieber, Shao Lee Soo, and James Stukel, *Low Sulfur Coal: A Revision of Reserve and Supply Estimates,* Final Report, CAC 163, Appendix C (Urbana, Champaign: Center for Advanced Computation, University of Illinois), May 1975.

6. Solvent refined coal emerges from processing as a liquid and could be used in that form. However, it solidifies if allowed to cool.

(compared to the 40 percent rates of the few best current conventional plants) can be expected. It is clear that low BTU gas from coal and perhaps other synthetics could fuel the combined cycle. The main problems are the need to perfect the technology both for the substitute fuels and improved combined cycles.[7]

With all the apparent drawbacks of these alternatives, numerous observers, particularly the Environmental Protection Agency and its predecessors, argued that stress should be placed on processes for cleaning the sulfur from the stack gases of the power plants.

The technique has been known for many years, and in the late 1960s the U.S. government, the National Coal Association, and some electric utilities argued that scrubbers would soon be available and cost only 5 cents or so per million BTUs treated. In 1975, however, the technical status of scrubbers remains highly controversial. A few small units have operated, including one in Japan with over two years' experience. A unit burning low-sulfur coal has been in reliable operation in Arizona for over a year. However, many other units have suffered severe difficulties and failed to perform reliably.[8]

In any case, the costs promise to be appreciably higher than was previously expected. A U.S. government study of 1973 suggested costs of around 15 cents per million BTUs treated.[9] A leading utility contended that actual costs would be closer to 50–60 cents, as did estimates made for a process developed by General Motors.[10] Thus, scrubbers involve several serious questions—when will they be reliable, once reliability is established how long will it take to install them in the plants needing them, and what will they cost?

As if these complications were not serious enough, major difficulties arose on the coal supply side. Between 1969 and 1973 eastern underground mining costs doubled. Underground mines are the most likely eastern source of coal for new power plants since local supplies of low-

7. A report by the Tennessee Valley Authority, D. A. Waitzman et al., *Evaluation of Fixed-Bed Low-Btu Coal Gasification Systems for Retrofitting Power Plants* (Palo Alto, Cal.: Electric Power Research Institute, 1975), indicates present low BTU gasification processes are far more expensive than stack gas scrubbing.

8. Pedco-Environmental prepares reports (monthly until mid-1975, bimonthly since then) to the Environmental Protection Agency on scrubbers. Various reports from June 1975 to January 1976 were consulted for this study.

9. U.S. Sulfur Oxide Control Assessment Panel, *Final Report on Projected Utilization of Stack Gas Cleaning Systems by Steam Electric Plants,* 1973.

10. Commonwealth Edison Company, *Memorandum Regarding SO$_2$ Removal and Cost Estimates* (Chicago, 1973).

cost strippable reserves apparently have already been fully committed. The cost increase was widely attributed to the passage of a stringent new coal mine health and safety act. However, discussions with people in the industry make clear that this is a gross oversimplification. Unrest among miners reflecting such factors as an influx of young workers and the turmoil in the United Mine Workers also made for lower productivity. Labor attitudes and the need to attract new workers made for sharply rising wages. Some of these problems are transitory, but others threaten to create persistent cost pressures. As the 1974 mine labor contract made clear, the demand for rising wages will persist. It was apparent before these recent developments that new methods of conveying coal to the surface were needed; existing methods cannot move the coal as fast as it can be cut by modern continuing mining machinery. It is not clear when the requisite technology to remove this bottleneck and produce other advances in output per worker will emerge. Sharply rising coal prices, therefore, may be a persistent feature of the energy market.

The initial main response of the utilities to this situation was to base their long-term plans on nuclear power and employ a combination of conversion to oil, delaying tactics, and modest use of western coal to meet immediate needs. However, more and more eastern utilities are reconsidering their initial positions. Given the sharp rises in eastern coal prices, high scrubber costs, and questions about scrubber reliability, conversion to western coals is now receiving greatly increased attention. American Electric Power and Detroit Edison, for example, have already made commitments to burn substantial amounts of western coal.

In short, we have two coal problems in the electric utility industry. The first is how we are to make do in the next few years with the technical options available. Second, the question of the optimal long-run solution must be resolved. The answer to the second question appears somewhat clearer. High stack gas scrubbing costs and rising coal prices make it difficult for eastern coal to compete against nuclear power. The prospects for the use of western coal in the East are better, although far from assured. Indeed these prospects may be better than in the West. In the East, western coal represents a marked improvement over eastern coal and its use might obviate the need for scrubbers. In contrast, western coal would degrade the air quality in most western regions in which it was used. Pressures have already arisen to force the use of scrubbers in western plants, and this may ultimately lead to a shift to nuclear power. As discussed below, the ultimate development of federal policy affecting western coal could also have a profound effect on fuel choice. The best hope for coal lies in developing a modified fuel probably for use in a new technology such as a combined cycle.

The question of how to react until these new plants can be installed is harder to resolve. Not only are difficult value judgments involved, but the critical facts are themselves in dispute. The Environmental Protection Agency seems to feel that the technology and productive capacity is available to permit installation of all the necessary scrubbers by 1980. Many utilities, most notably American Electric Power, insist that this is extremely unsound advice. The basic case is that scrubbers are not yet perfected and create a solid waste that may cause problems almost as bad as those being eliminated. While the industry attack may be overstated, EPA's extremely bad forecasting record in the scrubber realm makes one skeptical that the scrubber solution is really that easy to implement. If it is not, lessening the pressure to rapidly meet sulfur emission standards may be desirable. The choice of an optimal policy here will require considerable skill on the part of policy makers. The decisions will be heavily influenced by the desire to reduce dependence on imported oil. This article can do no more than point out that the optimal choice of policy will differ markedly from site to site. Emissions are clearly more tolerable in plants in isolated rural regions than in a New York City plant downwind from a major hospital complex.

What should be kept in mind is that a pressure to attain sulfur control rapidly may create intolerable temporary strains that we could avoid by a more gradual transition. For example, it is more than likely that scrubbers cannot be installed as quickly as expected and crash programs to develop western coal and possibly even facilities to import oil will become necessary. The physical strains on capacity and costs that each expedient will produce may prove intolerable. Clearly efforts to ease environmental pressures on electric utilities that have been introduced since the 1973 Arab embargo may be helpful. However, these measures may be grossly inadequate. In particular, the policies seem to perpetuate the belief that scrubbers can be installed to insure that coal use can continue without compromising environmental standards. (The idea of obtaining relief by accelerating nuclear plant construction, moreover, appears to have proved a great fiasco. Uncertainties about future demand and, more critically, pressures by self-styled consumer advocates to prevent electric power rates rising to reflect recent inflation have led to a massive setback for nuclear power; numerous plants have been delayed and some even canceled. Some observers fear that these trends will create power shortages or the very increase in oil use that supposedly public policy is seeking to prevent.)

Thus, an enormous amount of ignorance beclouds our ability to predict the best electric power fuel pattern. Much of the ignorance can be resolved only by time. Just how new technologies will evolve and what their costs will be cannot, of course, be determined in advance (although some hardheaded estimates of what is reasonable in terms of timing and cost are feasible and desirable). However, our ignorance is far greater than necessary. The data on coal, oil, and uranium resources are woefully incomplete. Given the importance of transportation, we are badly in need of extensive analyses of the present fuel-carrying capacity of our transportation network and the cost of its expansion. This leaves us with a need for policies that simultaneously reduce our ignorance and permit us enough flexibility to adapt to different developments.

In sum, coal appears presently to play an indispensable but by no means rapidly augmentable role in electric power generation. It remains to be seen whether in the long run the role will alter, and none of the logical possibilities can be ruled out. Success at improved technology for mining and using coal might lead to a greatly augmented role. Conversely, failure in these areas could lead to greatly reduced coal use.

The available data indicate, in particular, that prospective prices for coal and plants to burn it in an environmentally acceptable fashion will be more expensive than nuclear plants. Unless the costs of coal and coal firing plants are drastically reduced, we are headed toward an electric power economy dominated by nuclear power. Ironically here once again, failure to anticipate the trends in this direction may cause the same failures to develop the needed facilities in a timely fashion that we have seen in the past.

A Note on Coal as an Industrial Fuel

Another possible use of coal would be its revival as a fuel for manufacturing. The simple synthetic fuels proposed for electric power plants might also be usable for large industrial plants. The chief drawbacks to such a development are the basic problems in developing a satisfactory synthetic and the limited number of plants large enough to accommodate optimally sized synthetic fuel plants.

High Grade Synthetic Fuels from Coal

As we noted, the great hope for massive new markets for coal is in the synthesis of close substitutes for gasoline, light fuel oils, and methane. The sums involved are staggering. Conversion efficiency would run at perhaps two-thirds—i.e., 1.5 million BTUs of coal would be required for each million BTUs of synthetic fuel. Thus to produce a trillion cubic feet of gas per year requires 1.5 quadrillion BTUs of coal. At 17 million BTUs per ton of coal, that would require some 88 million tons of coal per year. Over the thirty-year life of the requisite plants, the coal used would amount to 2.6 billion tons. Similarly, a million barrel per day synthetic fuel oil industry would require 161 million tons of coal per year or 4.8 billion over its thirty-year life time.

No one has expressed a firm vision of what would constitute a reasonable level of synthetic fuel production, but assuming that 10 trillion cubic feet of gas per year and 10 million barrels of oil per day were produced (i.e., amounts well below current use of oil and gas), some 2.5 billion tons of coal would be required annually. Over thirty years 75 billion tons would be absorbed. These figures make clear both why the coal industry is so anxious to see the market develop and why the residents of the West fear the development. The figures also warn that the apparent ready availability of coal is not so clear when a synthetic fuel industry is visualized. The demands are easily covered by the 1.6 trillion tons of coal reserves reported by the U.S. Geological Survey. However, as was noted above, the National Petroleum Council has issued a more conservative estimate that only 104 billion tons of underground and 45 billion tons of strippable coal resources are available in thick, well-explored seams. These figures suggest that known strippable reserves are inadequate for a substantial synthetic fuel industry and substantial amounts of underground mining might be required. We can employ the prior arguments to point out that all this really establishes is that the availability of coal for synthetic fuel is less clear than is conventionally argued. We might be forced to turn to underground coal mining, raising costs above those of alternatives.

More fundamentally, we are back to the argument that the physical presence of large amounts of coal is no guarantee of the inevitability of a massive return to coal as the basis of synthetic fuels or anything else.

Moreover the barriers are more formidable in the synthetic fuel realm than elsewhere. As we have already suggested, more complex—i.e., more expensive—methods must be used to secure replacements for methane, light fuel oils, and gasoline than are necessary to develop an industrial fuel.

Coal faces an enormous amount of competition, including its own, in this realm. The rise of coal synthesis in any case is possible only so long as the cartel of oil producing countries remains effective. A collapse of the cartel would make imported oil the cheapest energy source. Moreover, it remains far from clear what supplies of oil from noncartel sources will prove to be. The rise of the cartel has greatly increased interest in oil and gas exploration elsewhere. Europeans now expect substantial oil and gas from the North Sea. A major new find has been announced in Mexico. Good prospects exist on Alaska's North Slope and offshore on both U.S. coasts. Sufficient success in these and other areas could exert severe downward pressures on fuel prices, particularly as they would substantially heighten the problems the OPEC countries are likely to face in agreeing on an appropriate price and the appropriate share of production cutbacks each country should assume to maintain prices at the desired level.

Still further competition is provided by oil from shales in the Rocky Mountain states. Study after study has indicated that such oil from shale would be cheaper than oil from coal. Moreover, the shale oil technology is further advanced, and this headstart may be difficult to overcome.

Finally, low BTU coal gas and other simple fuels from coal also create competition for high-grade synthetics. The simpler fuels release oil and gas to other uses and lessen the need for high-grade synthetics.

Inflation and other concerns have caused substantial reconsideration of synthetic fuels from coals (and a bewildering collection of revised cost estimates that are quite difficult to interpret). The Project Independence Blueprint volume on synthetic fuels from coal (p. 8) indicated that the cost per million BTUs of gas from $4-per-ton western coal would range from $1.30 to $3.11, depending on the interest rate assumption used. The range for gas from $12-per-ton eastern coal was $1.75 to $3.56. The coal costs may be much too low. Deregulated natural gas prices in this range might produce enormous amounts from conventional sources now priced around 40 cents per million BTUs. Moreover, $3 gas might well force reconsideration of energy independence based on synthetic fuels (and the fears of such high priced synthetic gas clearly will preclude extensive private action without strong government guarantees).

Coal and Future Public Policy Developments

For many years coal was the fuel least affected by the mass of public policies that have long had profound impacts on world energy markets. As the prior discussion indicates, this situation no longer exists. A broad assortment of new policies have had major impacts on coal. Those of controls on the environmental effects of coal use and on practices affecting coal miner health and safety have been noted above because they have already had a significant influence.

This section is concerned with other policies that might affect coal— namely, new regulations on strip mining and on federal leasing of coal lands. The discussion is limited to a broad description of the problems. The issues are simultaneously too complex and too inadequately studied to permit a full consideration here. Since the policies have not yet been fully defined, a vast number of alternative approaches might be adopted. Their impacts would differ markedly from site to site, and we do not have satisfactory information about what those impacts might be.

Strip mining and leasing are not completely independent issues because so much of the coal on federal lands is suitable for strip mining. As a result, the Department of the Interior's efforts to formulate a leasing policy involve formulation of regulations of strip mining applicable to the leases. Conversely, congressional efforts to legislate controls on strip mining have included specific provisions for altering the power of the Interior Department to lease coal lands.

Coal leasing policy became an important issue because of the widespread interest in developing the coal resources west of the Mississippi. As Table 3 shows, a significant fraction of this coal is federally owned. At least four questions arise about coal leasing practices. First, there is the question of strip-mining control already noted. The second problem relates to what are known as reserved mineral rights. Significant portions of the transfers of the ownership of public land to other parties for purposes other than mining reserved the mineral rights to the federal government. Therefore, leasing of the coal held under these reserved rights must consider the interests of the owner of the surface. Another issue is that of the proper charges for the use of federal land. The fourth problem is to insure that the ownership of the coal will not be concentrated in so few hands that monopolistic conditions will develop in the coal industry.

The details of existing laws need be only briefly mentioned here. Basically, the Interior Department can both seek competitive bids on mining

Table 3. Estimated federally owned coal resources in selected western states

State	Federally owned (million tons)	Total (million tons)	Federal as % of total
	Surface mining reserves		
Colorado	265	500	53
Montana	1,700	6,897	25
New Mexico	1,450	2,457	59
North Dakota	519	2,075	25
Utah	123	150	82
Wyoming	6,706	13,971	48
	Underground mining reserves		
Colorado	21,111	39,829	53
New Mexico	16,661	28,239	59
North Dakota	43,310	173,240	25
Utah	9,605	11,714	82
Wyoming	22,251	46,357	48

Source: U.S. Bureau of Land Management, *Draft Environmental Statement—Proposed Federal Coal Leasing Program,* 1974, p. I–209.

rights to lands known to contain coal and allow people to prospect for coal. Should the prospecting prove successful, the holder of the permit can be granted a lease (requiring him to pay specified royalties on the coal). In early 1973 a moratorium was declared on both leasing and issue of prospecting permits until new guidelines could be established. A Draft Environmental Impact Statement outlining such a policy was issued in 1974, but it took until late 1975 for a final report to emerge, and that report inspired numerous objections from environmentalists. A prior independent suit by the Sierra Club has also restricted leasing activity.

The suspension of leasing and of the issue of prospecting permits seems to have reflected concern over both environmental problems and the fact that in 1972 only 10 million tons of coal were produced on federal lands although 15 billion tons of reserves had been leased. This large accumulation of reserve holdings that were not being exploited created suspicions both that efforts were being made to buy the coal at bargain rates before the federal government came to realize its true value and that a few companies might be proceeding to lay the basis of a monopoly by taking over the best lands. The National Environmental Protection Act requirement that major federal actions be justified by a statement that showed what steps were being taken to limit the environmental impacts of the action was another influence on leasing. Environmental groups had won a court case accepting the argument that leasing of oil and gas land offshore was a major action requiring environmental impact statements, and presumably the argument was applicable to coal leasing.

The proposed leasing program would involve developing estimates of the amount of coal required to meet national energy needs. Then the required amount of coal land would be leased. The lands selected would be the economically most attractive of those that could be reclaimed to the degree the Interior Department deemed satisfactory. Part of the program would be efforts to improve the government's knowledge of the nature of its coal holdings so that a determination of the best resources and their proper valuation could be made.

Strip mining has numerous environmental impacts. A similarly wide range of views exists about what should be done to correct the environmental damage. It is frequently pointed out that strip-mining impacts are somewhat different at every location, but certain gross generalizations are possible. In particular, three basic situations can be distinguished: Appalachia (except Ohio) where much of the strip mining is done on hilly lands; the Midwest, including Ohio, where the land is flat and fertile; and the Rocky Mountain states, where the land is flat and arid. Thus, reclamation is somewhat less of a problem in the Midwest than elsewhere. Once a hill is cut up, it is difficult to patch back together. The main problem in the West is the difficulty of restoring vegetation.

The possible impacts of strip mining include the aesthetic insult caused by disruption, the removal of land from other uses, the imposition of barriers to free movement within a region, possible safety hazards, and creation of conditions that may cause landslides and resulting siltage of rivers.

A neat description of present and proposed regulation is not feasible here. The present system consists of state regulations together with the reclamation rules imposed in recent federal leases. A federal law has been debated for several years, and in late 1974 a bill did pass both houses of Congress but was pocket vetoed by President Ford. A similar bill passed in 1975 and Congress failed to override its veto. The variation among existing standards is considerable, and an even broader range of approaches has been proposed.

Every imaginable form of control up to and including total elimination of strip mining has been proposed. One important alternative is banning strip mining on particular types of land—because of difficulties in reclaiming them to the desired standard or because the present uses are deemed superior to mining. The standards of reclamation advocated also range widely from patching up the most serious damage to virtually full restoration.

Evaluation here involves perhaps more than the normal amount of uncertainties that hinder the appraisal of the costs and benefits of public policy. It is quite likely that a sizable portion of the objection to strip mining is on aesthetic and cultural grounds. The unsightliness of the mines and their intrusion into regions where traditional ways of life will be disrupted seem to weigh heavily in the attacks. Thus, the strip-mining issue can be taken as a graphic example of the presently unresolved issues, raised above in the discussion of conservation, of what basic national goals should be.

Summary and Conclusions

This article has argued that coal's best prospects lie in the realm of fuel for electric power and other large industrial uses. Even here the outcome is unclear. On one side, there are the enormous unresolved questions about the relative environmental attractiveness of coal and nuclear power. Assuming that both fuels prove acceptable, the critical problem is to develop systems for extracting, transforming, and using coal at costs competitive with nuclear power. This is a formidable task on which much work is required and on which success is not guaranteed. High-grade synthetics look much less promising. Further problems arise about whether public policy affecting mining will provide a favorable climate for coal.

9

Electric Power: Regulation of a Natural Monopoly

Alvin Kaufman

In the recent past, electric utilities lived in the best of all possible worlds. Costs steadily declined, consumption and revenues steadily rose, earnings tended to increase year by year, and investors were delighted to pump the needed capital into utility enterprises at reasonable cost. Utility stocks and bonds were regarded as the bluest of the blue chips.

Investors were happy with the steady growth of earnings, customers were pleased with the declining rates, and regulators were glad to preside over an occasional case of appeal for lower rates. On top of all this, planning problems were relatively few—load grew at a steady, predictable rate; generation siting was easy; and regulation tended to be minimal.

Then, in the mid 1960s, the utility world started to turn sour. There were delays in planning, building, and securing approval for new facilities due to technical and design problems with nuclear plants and with environmental control systems, as well as because of intervention by environmental and other citizen groups. These difficulties contributed to cost increases that were aggravated by delays in obtaining rate relief, lower than expected sales and a consequent decline in revenue, and sharply increased costs for major items such as fuels. The resulting reduced earning power eroded investor confidence. This erosion, together with inflation and tight money, resulted in increased costs of capital financing. All these difficulties caused utilities to reduce their expansion plans, and so we come full circle.

A variety of cures have been suggested for the ills of the electric utilities. These have primarily dealt with minimizing regulatory lag, restruc-

All opinions expressed in this paper are those of the author, and do not necessarily represent those of the New York Public Service Commission

turing rates, and reducing the cost of capital. This paper will consider some of these issues.

Regulatory Lag

Regulatory lag is the time period between the filing of a rate case and the resolution of that request. It can take from a few months to several years to reach a decision, depending on the complexity of the case and the energy level of the regulatory body. As a consequence, when costs are declining utilities will earn more than the allowed rate of return pending completion of rate cases, and thus have an incentive to reduce costs further. When costs are rising, the rate of return earned by the utility will be below that allowed by the regulatory body. Utilities, therefore, will be under pressure during periods of rising costs to become more efficient in order to improve their earnings. A certain amount of heat is good for the economic soul.

It has been suggested by some students of the industry that this heat be cooled by reducing the time it takes to resolve a case or through greater use of automatic adjustment clauses. Reduction of regulatory lag by faster resolution of cases would increase the cash flow of the utility companies, under current conditions, by raising rates at a faster clip. At the same time, it would tend to rob the utilities of their incentive to reduce costs.

There is no doubt that some commissions have in the past proceeded at a rather leisurely pace in completing rate cases. The urgency of the current utility situation, coupled with increases in regulatory staff, has helped to reduce lags. Some further speedup may be needed, but the number and the complexity of the issues will vary from case to case. A hard-and-fast time limit might defeat the purpose by robbing the regulator of sufficient time to assess these issues properly. On the other hand, some kind of reasonable limit, such as one year, would force a decision, which, if necessary, could be corrected or modified in the next rate case.

Of greater importance are the suggestions to expand the use of automatic adjustment clauses (AAC) to reduce lags. The AAC is a provision in a company tariff permitting rates to be increased or decreased automatically in phase with changes in a selected cost item.[1] The adjustment clause is not a bonus to the utility. It permits the recovery of already incurred costs at a reduced rate of lag—say, sixty days—instead of the

---

1. Subcommittee of Staff Experts on Economics, "Automatic Adjustment Clauses Revisited," National Association of Regulatory Commissioners Economic Paper 1R, July 1974.

usual twelve months required for a rate proceeding. The most common form of adjustment clauses are those based on fuel costs, although automatic adjustment clauses may also be used for wages, taxes, and other such easily identifiable cost items. As a general rule automatic adjustment clauses are used where the change in cost can be easily determined, and where these changes can be easily audited.

Automatic adjustment clauses are advantageous to the company in that they protect its rate of return during a period of inflation from the impact of a rapidly changing cost item by reducing the time lag between the change in cost and the collection of compensating revenues. During a period of declining cost the automatic adjustment clause helps to prevent the company from earning more than the commission permitted. These clauses also ease the administrative burden on the regulatory body by eliminating repetitive tariff petition filings over short periods. On the other hand, these clauses tend to give undue weight to a single cost item while ignoring others. For example, a fuel adjustment clause tends to put great emphasis on changes in fuel cost while minimizing the importance of possibly compensating changes. The clauses thus tend to pass on increased costs to the consumer without allowing for compensating economies that may accrue from economies of scale, improved technology, or other sources of higher operating efficiency. In the case of fuel adjustments, fuel costs may rise but may be more than balanced by operating economies accruing from greater combustion efficiency. This tendency can be eliminated by careful design of the adjustment clause.

The use of automatic adjustment clauses also tends to dampen the company's incentive to seek lower prices from its suppliers, or to bargain for better wage settlements, and so on, since these cost increases can be passed on to the consumer quickly and easily. As a consequence, the clauses tend to serve as a negative factor in the use of regulatory lag. It might be appropriate to limit recovery to a portion of the increased cost, say 85 percent.

A profusion of automatic adjustment clauses will also tend to make the utility into a "cost plus" business, thus robbing it of its incentive to operate efficiently. One of the great dangers of AAC is the possibility of such clauses becoming a subsidy for inefficiency. Further, during a period of rapidly rising costs the automatic adjustment clause may bias the selection of production methods, or of fuels, in favor of those whose costs are covered by the clauses rather than those permitting optimal system efficiency.

The major current use of automatic clauses is for the flow-through of fuel charges. All such clauses should take account of fuel heat content, the trend of the company heat rate, the proportion of purchased power, the generating mix, and various other operating conditions affecting the company's use of fuel. As a general rule, they do not take account of these factors.

Whenever such clauses are introduced they should be weighted to reflect the relative importance of the item in the company's cost structure and should include provisions to compensate for economies that might accrue from improved managerial efficiency, technological innovation, or economies of scale.

Regulatory bodies often think of automatic adjustment clauses as useful only during periods of rising costs. If used, such clauses should be operable in both directions. They should be permitted to track increases during periods of rising costs and to track decreases during periods of declining costs. The consumer should be permitted to benefit from cost reductions as quickly as he is penalized for rising costs.

Restructuring Rates

In recent years, there has been considerable agitation over rates and rate structure on the part of consumers, environmentalists, regulators, and those they regulate. This agitation has been based on opposition to rising rates, a desire for a clean environment coupled with the feeling that energy conservation is vital to the successful achievement of that goal, and opposition to continued unbridled economic growth, as well as a general dissatisfaction with the regulatory process.

This dissatisfaction may stem from the fact that commissions are supposed to answer two basic questions in rate proceedings. First, how much revenue is required, and second, who will pay how much. In actual practice, regulatory groups have dealt almost exclusively with the revenue question in the past, leaving rate structure to the utility except for obvious cases of discrimination. As a consequence of the agitation, rate structure has become a major concern of the regulator.

In its effort to establish rates, a commission holds a rate hearing based on the application for increased revenues from the company. A rate hearing is a quasi-judicial proceeding conducted in courtroom style. The process is lengthy, expensive, and cumbersome, with a great devotion to a legalistic adversary system. The latter precludes the use of information not tied to the case record in some way. Further, the adversary system tends to put a premium on good courtroom technique and good witnesses rather than on competent professional advice. This legalistic system hardly seems suited to the determination of highly technical issues involving the exercise of professional judgment. It seems to the author to be a poor system, but it is all we have.

Current Rate Design

Electric utilities, like most companies, have both fixed and variable expenses. The latter vary with the quantity of electric energy produced. As a consequence, the utilities establish rates for each customer class for blocks of kilowatt hours consumed by the customers. These use blocks, more or less, match the changes in cost that occur as usage changes. In other words, the use blocks are supposed to account for the economies of scale.

The traditional approach in the design of residential rates is to recoup most of the fixed costs in the first one or two use blocks, charging primarily variable costs in the later blocks. This approach results in the declining block structure (higher price per kilowatt hour in the early blocks, lower unit price in the later blocks). Industrial-commercial customers, on the other hand, usually pay a two-part rate. The first part, or demand charge, is designed to cover fixed costs. The demand charge is determined by the highest use in some unit of time during the billing period, usually use over fifteen minutes in one month. The energy charge, by and large, recovers variable costs. The latter also tends to have a declining block structure.

Most commissions currently base rates on the concept of fully distributed cost. This procedure is often modified by a value-of-service concept.

Fully distributed cost is a method of allocating revenue requirements among customer classes. Both fixed investment and operating costs are measured for a test year. These costs, including an allowance for a suitable rate of return, are then distributed among customer classes and use blocks within those classes, by various complex methods. Based on these allocations, rates are designed, usually with the aim of equalizing the rate of return earned from each customer class.

The test year referred to above is a reference point from which to proceed. In order to provide a base from which to compute costs, companies file cost data for some particular period, usually the year preceding the case. These cost-of-service studies are then adjusted so that they approximate the anticipated costs during the period in which the new rates will be operative. In some jurisdictions, most notably in that of the Federal Power Commission and in California, a future test year is used. In the case of a future test year, the utility files estimates and projections of its costs and revenues for the year in which the new rates will apply. Other commissions use a past test year coupled with adjustments for known changes, such as taxes or wage increases, occurring during the period that the rate case has been pending. In any case, the goal is to have revenues equal the overall cost of service in the year during which the rates will be collected.

The quality of the cost-of-service studies, indicating fully distributed costs, varies from jurisdiction to jurisdiction. In some instances, these studies are little more than gross estimates of the cost of service by class of customer. In other cases, they are detailed and up-to-date, and indicate the rate of return earned from each class of customer, and from each use block within the class.

Even the best of these studies are estimates, and by definition exhibit a heavy dependence on historical data. These sunk costs are not necessarily reliable measures of future costs, given the current inflationary climate, the march of technology, and the shift in demand with a consequent change in new plant requirements. Fully allocated cost studies also require a heavy judgmental factor. Although the costs for the various services are presumably known with accounting precision, these costs must be allocated, on the basis of judgment, to the various use categories. As a consequence, the studies lack the precision of original data. Further, there is always the possibility that the judgment used in assigning costs might be influenced by the outcome desired.

Fully distributed cost studies, as noted above, are often modified in the rate-setting procedure to reflect the value of service. Value of service can be interpreted as a method of rate setting that recognizes, at least in part, differences in the relative price elasticities of demand for electric utility services. Thus in highly competitive markets the price derived from the fully distributed cost study will be modified to represent the cost of alternatives to the customer. Value-of-service pricing is often justified on the grounds that the customers who can obtain substitutes for electric power generally contribute high load factors to the system so that the costs for all users are reduced. The value-of-service concept provides price flexibility for the fully distributed cost system.

Fully allocated cost studies, as a basis for rate making, worked reasonably well in the past when price levels in the economy increased at a moderate rate. In any case, inflationary impacts were more than offset by new technology and economies of scale. At present, however, rates based on these cost studies do not appear to be serving the purpose of economic efficiency.

The point of a price system is to regulate supply and demand. Thus rate structure must "induce consumers to behave in such a way that, as a group, they derive the maximum satisfaction from the limited total resources that society has available to serve them." [2]

Marginal Cost Rates

Optimal resource allocation, according to economic theory, is obtained at the point where marginal cost equals price. Marginal cost is the cost of producing one more item. Marginal cost theory holds that prices should be set at short-run marginal cost (SRMC) which would exclude sunk costs; short-run is defined as the period in which plant capacity does not change. Long-run marginal cost (LRMC), on the other hand, covers a flexible, open-ended time period. Since all costs are variable over the long term, long-run marginal cost includes future capacity costs; sunk costs again are not counted. Only future capacity costs needed for additional production would be involved in the calculations. Thus, there is a closer relationship between LRMC and accounting cost than exists in the case of SRMC, and long-run marginal costing may be a better route to follow.

The theory holds that if utility services were marginally priced to customers having substitutes available, existing capacity would be more fully utilized in the short run, with the optimal size of the system being determined over the long run for the benefit of all customers. Customers responsible for load growth would be charged the correct cost for that growth, and could decide whether the price was worth the benefits. Therefore, a misallocation of economic resources would be avoided.

Paul Joskow defines short-run marginal cost at the peak as the energy cost (less fixed charges) of supplying additional demand plus shortage costs that result if demand is greater than available capacity. [3] Off peak, SRMC is the incremental energy cost. Long-run marginal cost, on the other hand, is defined as the total costs incurred to meet a sustained

2. A. E. Kahn, "Electricity Costs, Pricing and Use: A Regulatory Evaluation," paper delivered at Edison Electric Institute Convention, Denver, June 3, 1975, p. 8.

3. Paul L. Joskow, "Marginal Cost Pricing of Electricity," Testimony in NYPSC Case 26806, June 30, 1975, pp. 10–13.

increment in demand during the year allowing for economic adjustments in plant and equipment. From these definitions flows the presumption that short- and long-run marginal cost are equal if capacity is perfectly and economically adjusted to demand. This, of course, happens only occasionally.

If LRMC is a suitable proxy for SRMC, its use is difficult because of measurement problems involving investment decisions, forecasts of demand, and so forth. As a consequence, a concept called long-range incremental cost (LRIC) has developed. This attempts to develop costs for relatively large increments of capacity. In a sense, LRIC is closer to real life since most capacity additions or subtractions occur in relatively large increments in order to capture economies of scale. Another reason for moving to LRIC is to avoid the revenue instability that would result from application of short-run marginal cost as plant and fuel mixes changed. Such instability would not only pose problems for the utility, but could provide confusing price signals to the consumer. Since prices would be constantly changing, the consumer would find it difficult to make buying decisions.

Paul Joskow has suggested that long-run incremental cost can be developed by costing for three consumption periods. He would assign the capital and energy costs of peaking equipment for all consumption at the system peak, but only the marginal energy costs during the off-peak period. The shoulder peak would be charged marginal energy costs plus a proportionate share of capacity costs. He contends that this system will yield sufficient revenue to cover all costs and is equivalent to LRIC.

The adoption of LRIC, or any other marginal cost method, may result in other problems. For example, the optimum allocation of resources may not be achieved if only one sector of the energy industry utilizes marginal cost pricing. Let us assume the electric power industry operated on a marginal cost concept while the oil industry continued to operate on an average cost concept. During a time of increasing cost, energy users might shift to oil because the marginal cost of electricity will be rising faster than the average cost of oil. In periods of declining cost the reverse may occur. Consumers will be receiving an incorrect price signal.

Some people also raise the possibility that when marginal costs are higher than average costs, as at present, the utility might receive too much revenue to meet the regulatory constraint of a fair and just rate of return. On the other hand, when marginal costs are lower than average costs, the utility would not collect sufficient revenues to meet its needs.

Some investigators suggest that it might be necessary for the utility to accumulate revenues during periods of rising average cost to compensate for eventual periods of declining average costs. The administration of such funds could pose a regulatory problem. Another alternative would be a tax during times of surplus, and a subsidy during times of deficit. A far simpler and more logical alternative would be to establish a revenue requirement as at present, then establish rates to raise those revenues on marginal cost principles, modified as necessary to suit rates to revenue requirement. The problem does not appear to be insurmountable.

Storage, Peaking, and Incremental Pricing

In any effort to apply marginal theory to rate setting, one must consider the characteristics of the industry involved and modify theory accordingly. Among the major characteristics affecting the electric power industry are: 1) the tendency for demand to peak; 2) the inability to store the product to meet the peak; 3) the legal requirement that all customers desiring service be served; and 4) high fixed costs.

The existence of high fixed costs may well be one of the most important forces in rate setting in that it requires stability of revenue and optimization of load factor. Revenue stability is necessary to assure adequate funds to pay off the bond holders and to guarantee interest payments. Optimization of load factor is important because the more units produced the lower the cost per unit since fixed costs can be spread across more output. Thus customers whose use tends to improve load factor will reduce costs for all customers. Rate concessions to improve load factor are desirable, even in today's social atmosphere, providing they do not stimulate demand to the point where additional plant must be built, and providing that the improved load characteristics result in lower overall costs for all other users of the service.[4] Perhaps we require a rate structure with a flat rate or declining blocks for energy (Kwh) together with increasing blocks for load (Kw). Such a structure would encourage overall use of energy, but discourage peak usage.

The optimization of load factor is complicated somewhat by the legal requirement that all customers desiring service must receive it. Such a requirement means that the utility is in a limited position to manage demand, and must accept demand in the short term essentially as a given. A utility, therefore, cannot optimize its profits as a monopolist can, in the

4. A. E. Kahn, *The Economics of Regulation*, 2 vols. (New York: John Wiley, 1970).

traditional economic sense, by restricting supply. Rather, it must use other methods, such as convincing its customers to consume less at the right time.

The inability of the utility to store its product to meet the peak generally means that it must build capacity to handle the peak. As a consequence, utilities tend to treat peak load as a problem in supply availability management. They accept the maximum demand as a given without examining its relation to cost. Capacity is adjusted to meet this requirement regardless of the values and costs associated with providing service at the peak.[5] Utility rates are then established without regard to the time of use. Rates might better vary with the time of demand, the contribution to coincident peak, and the consequent changing cost conditions thus imposed on the utility. Even though utility products may be physically the same, variations in supply-demand conditions will cause changes in costs depending on the load curve. The cost of producing utility services at the peak is greater than at other times, since more resources are required, usually of a lesser energy efficient and more expensive nature.

The configuration of a system's generating equipment will vary between peak and off-peak hours, as well as between seasons, and even operating costs will not be constant between those times. At the peak, the utility will often use gas turbines to meet its load. These have a low capital cost and very high operating cost, thus making it advantageous to use this equipment as little as possible. Base load equipment, such as nuclear or coal plants, has a high capital cost and relatively low operating costs. As a consequence, the use of these units will be maximized in order to reduce the capital cost per Kwh. At the peak, say a hot summer day, base load and peaking equipment will both be used to satisfy the demand. The result of this generating mix will be a higher cost per Kwh than during the off-peak hours when base load equipment alone will be used. The time and duration, and even the season, of the peak will vary from utility to utility. The mix of electrical generation will likewise vary.

Fluctuations in demand, however, are not all bad. Reserve generating requirements would be higher if there were no seasonal fluctuations in order to permit capacity to be taken off the line for periodic maintenance.

5. See S. H. Hanke and R. K. Davis, "The Range of Choice in Urban Water Management: Demand Management through Responsive Pricing," *Journal of the American Waterworks Association,* September 1971; and also H. P. Wald, "Electric Rates and Energy Policy," paper delivered at Retail Rate Conference, National Rural Electric Cooperative Association, Dallas, March 26, 1974.

Reserve generation is equipment, usually gas turbines or older units, held for emergency use in the event of a breakdown of regular equipment and to assure reliable service when other euipment is undergoing maintenance.

Insofar as peak responsibility is concerned, if rates were levied in proportion to customer responsibility for the peak, timed meters would be required. At the current level of technology, these are expensive and could pose a substantial financial burden on the utility. There is also a question as to whether the installation of time-of-day meters would save the equivalent cost in new capacity. If not, the costs and benefits of peak-hour pricing may not be acceptable.

Recently, J. Joskow noted that peak-load pricing might not result in sufficient savings in electric demand to permit the utilities to reduce capital requirements.[6] The inference that such pricing would substantially reduce the need for generating capacity is based on the British and French experience. These countries have used peak-load pricing for some years, but their experience may not be transferable to the United States because of differences in the way electricity is supplied and used. Peak pricing was introduced in Europe on a nationwide basis, while in the United States it would be done piecemeal. The United States has a more energy intensive economy than the French and British so off-peak shifts would be somewhat more restricted. Those countries also made the change when alternative sources of energy were more abundant whereas current options are limited. In addition, the English and French had winter peaking systems which permitted the use of heat storage devices. In the United States many systems are summer peaking, thus requiring cooling storage devices which are not currently available.

The savings have taken some twenty years to accrue in Europe, and might take longer in the United States.

It has also been suggested that surcharges be levied for peak-season use. Such an approach has the advantage of administrative simplicity and offers the possibility of dampening seasonal demand. These attributes, however, might be more than balanced by simply reducing off-peak use while leaving the seasonal peak at high levels. In other words, air conditioners would stay off at 80°F but would be turned on at 90°, thus aggravating the needle-peak with a consequent drop in load factor.

6. J. Joskow, Letter to Senator Floyd Haskell (Dem., Colo.), *Electrical Week,* July 28, 1975.

To sum up, economic theory indicates the desirability of using some form of marginal costing. In most cases, this will probably involve, computation of a differential rate between peak and off-peak usage.

External Costs

Part of the controversy over regulation and the method of establishing rates has been the result of the need to compensate for external costs. As a general rule, the effects of an economic transaction between a buyer and a seller are felt only through the marketplace. There are, however, some resource impacts which may affect third parties as a consequence of jointly held property (such as air and water). The market prices do not reflect the value of these jointly held resources, however, nor is the impact of pollution on others often reflected in the market price. Until recently no one worried about these external costs.

An external effect occurs when an economic activity, such as electric power generation, has an impact on the production of or consumer preference for another activity. These externalties can be either positive or negative depending on the value system and viewpoint of the affected party. To eliminate or reduce external costs will often entail other costs, sometimes of rather staggering magnitude. The cost of abatement must be measured against the benefits in order to determine the trade-off point between abatement and suffering. In some instances it may be possible to internalize the externalities by forcing the cost on those who cause the damage. Generally, however, it will not be possible to pinpoint either the identity of those who cause the problem, or the value of the effect sufficiently to determine cost.

In the case of electric utilities the external costs tend to stand out much like a red flag to a bull. There has been a strong movement to force internalization of the various external costs that are caused by the production, transmission, and use of electricity. In most instances there has been little effort to measure either the costs or benefits, or to determine the trade-off point.

For example, there is little question that the generation of electricity causes environmental problems. In the case of fossil fuels these arise from intrusion on the land, the creation of solid and gaseous by-products, and the disposal of waste heat. The seriousness of these problems in the context of overall environmental awareness, however, is very much at issue. In some cases, it is claimed that generating units are major polluters of the air and water. On the other hand, some studies seem to indicate that there is minimal impact. It is not my intent to go deeply into this question here, as it is discussed in detail in another chapter.

Nuclear plants generally do not cause conventional air pollution, but there is a possibility of radioactive contamination either as a consequence of the accidental rupture of the reactor, or through low-level persistent radiation. The latter generally will result from the collection and venting of gases as well as cooling water.

The major discussions involving water pollution from generation plants revolve around the question of waste heat. All steam plants produce such heat; nuclear plants will yield 50 percent more waste heat than fossil fired units. Some people maintain that thermal abnormalities can result in stimulation of unwanted plant growth, death of some organisms, and disruption of food supplies. Hot water discharges, however, can also be beneficial by improving food supplies in some cases and stimulating fish growth. The severity of the impact is mainly dependent on the volume of water, the velocity of flow, and the total heat load of the water body. Studies conducted on the Ohio River, the Connecticut River, and elsewhere tend to indicate that the thermal pollution problem may be grossly overstated. The major generating plant water problem may be improper design of intake tubes and screens. This results in the destruction of fish, fish eggs, larvae, and plankton.

In an effort to mitigate the external costs indicated above, considerable pressure has been brought to bear to prevent the construction of electric generating plants. As a consequence of this resistance to plant siting, it is estimated that the New York consumer paid an additional $117 million in 1972 to cover the operation of older and less efficient plants, for load shedding, and other such detrimental items. Not included in the $117 million figure are items such as the cost of fighting legal actions brought to stop plant construction or operation, or the cost of planning for plants that were never built.[7]

Whether the consumer received $117 million in benefits as a consequence has not been resolved, and the answer is in large measure a function of one's value system. The main point is that, if costs are to be internalized, it should be done in such a way that the consumer receives the right price signal between competing energy sources.

In large measure, the effort to internalize external costs has revolved

7. A. Kaufman, "Beauty and the Beast: The Siting Dilemma in New York State," *Energy Policy,* 1 (December 1973), pp. 243–253.

around the imposition of environmental standards with resulting requirements for abatement equipment. Whether this approach has resulted in
improved economic efficiency is debatable, since we cannot be sure competing sources have been penalized in proportion to the cost they impose
on society.

It seems to the author that the best way to handle external costs is
through effluent taxes. These would penalize the polluter for his damage.
Some people object to this approach on the grounds it provides a license
to pollute. Kahn has noted that ". . . environmental protection, like conservation, is an economic good, and, like all other economic goods, we
cannot have unlimited quantities of it except at unlimited costs." [8]

The imposition of a tax gives the producer a choice of paying all the
tax, installing some abatement equipment and paying some tax, or completely abating the nuisance and escaping payment of the tax. In any
case, the external costs will be reflected in the price of the good, but at
the least cost level as required by economic efficiency. Such a result will
occur, however, only if the tax represents the costs of pollution imposed
on society. Making this calculation may be extremely difficult, but is
probably no more difficult than having a government agency decide the
best way to eliminate the problem—and is likely to be much less disruptive.

Reducing the Cost of Capital

Over the years, electric utilities have been considered "blue chip" investments. In recent years, however, most companies have suffered a
lapse of investor confidence. This lapse has resulted from the interplay of
a variety of factors.

Inflation, reduced earning power, and the failure of new technology to
reduce costs all tended to converge on a single point in time. Federal efforts to restrain inflation caused a tight money situation with highest interest rates resulting in record high capital costs for utilities as well as other
businesses.

At the same time, utility earnings declined as a result of the lag in
regulatory response to rate increase requests coupled with a reluctance to
raise rates because of public pressure. This was compounded by lower
sales with consequently reduced revenues and sharply rising costs, especially for fuel.

8. A. E. Kahn, "The Recognition of Environmental Costs," paper delivered at Iowa
State University Regulatory Conference, Ames, Iowa, May 20, 1975, p. 7.

In response to these factors, the utilities have generally cut back their expansion plans. *Electrical World*'s Annual Electrical Industry Forecast issue (September 15, 1974) indicated that because load growth was lower than expected, capacity reserve margins in 1974 reached 26 percent of peak requirements. As a general rule, 18 to 20 percent is considered normal. Electrical World expected reserves to reach 28 percent in 1975 and to start dropping after 1976. By 1983 capacity reserves should decline to 18.5 percent. Reserves are required to assure the reliability of the electrical system. All machinery requires maintenance and suffers breakdowns, and extra equipment must be kept on standby to replace machines out of service for planned maintenance or unexpected failure.

Planned additions to capacity by 1983 are now estimated at 875,000 megawatts. Assuming no change in load factors and reserve margin requirements (18–20 percent), this indicates the utilities expect a 6 percent annual load growth rate. In the event growth resumed its historic pattern (7–8 per year), the present planned capacity additions would imply a reserve level of only 7 percent by 1983. Thus, depending on the rate of future load growth, electric system reliability could range from satisfactory to completely unsatisfactory. It does not appear to the author that load growth rates will climb back to the historic level. The strong movement to peak pricing, coupled with other innovations designed to encourage off-peak usage, should tend to dampen load growth.

To achieve the desired capacity level will require substantial sums of money. A recent study indicated the cumulative capital needs of the electric utility industry for the years 1971 through 1985 would range between 320 and 400 billion constant 1970 dollars.[9] This substantial capital requirement is based on the assumption of continued growth at the historic rate. It is estimated by National Economic Research Associates that cutbacks in utility construction plans will result in a $21 billion drop in construction through 1979. The Conference Board Quarterly Survey of Utility Appropriations (first quarter, 1975) indicated electric utility capital appropriations were seven percent above the previous year. Project cancellations dropped to $0.39 billion compared with the average of $2 billion over the three preceding quarters. Despite the rise in appropriations, actual expenditures of $3.8 billion represented a lower rate than in any quarter of 1974.

The utilities' need to borrow such vast sums will pose a challenge for

9. J. E. Hass, E. J. Mitchell, and B. K. Stone, *Financing the Energy Industry* (Cambridge, Mass.: Ballinger, 1974), pp. 51–93.

regulation. It is unlikely that new cost-reducing technology will be introduced before 1980. As a consequence, some way of inducing gains in productivity in order to counter the ravages of inflation will have to be found. Failure to do so will make it difficult for the utilities to obtain needed capital because revenues will always be substantially behind costs, in terms of historical rate-making procedures.

A variety of cures have been recommended. These suggestions include reducing the cost of capital through government aid in utility financing. Such help would reduce investment risks, and presumably interest rates on utility borrowings, and thus decrease the upward pressure on consumer rates.[10]

Alternative methods of accomplishing this include an insurance or guarantee system, a direct subsidy, or public ownership. The insurance system requires the state to guarantee the repayment of the utility bonds and has the advantage of eliminating out-of-pocket costs to the state except in the event of a default. The guarantees will not reduce utility bills in themselves, but might improve the salability of utility bonds at an interest rate somewhat below market. A recent study indicated consumers might save 4 percent on their bills after eight years as a consequence of an insurance program.[11] There is an indirect cost to the state in that taxes would have to be forgone on the differential interest payments that would have accrued without guarantees, but this loss would be relatively minor. The major advantage of a financial insurance program might well be the breathing space it would provide the utilities.

Direct subsidies, on the other hand, involve specific governmental action such as the tax exemption of interest on utility bonds or the loan of government funds at low interest rates. As a result of a subsidy, the price of electricity would be lower than it would be if all societal costs were included. Consumers would receive an improper price signal, and electric consumption would be stimulated so that resources were improperly diverted from other uses. Electric utility subsidies should, however, be judged in the light of subsidies granted competing energy sources.

Public ownership is often advocated as a key to lower rates. Many countries throughout the world own their utilities outright. There are also a large number of publicly owned electric systems in the United States, the most notable of which are the Tennessee Valley Authority and the

10. Harry Guttman, ed., *Alternatives for Electric Utility Financing,* New York State Department of Public Service., O.R. 75–6, June 1975.
11. *Ibid.*

Power Authority of the State of New York. In addition, there are a substantial number of municipally and state owned utilities as well as rural
electric cooperatives. The major municipal systems are those in Los
Angeles, Seattle, Sacramento, Springfield (Ill.), and Jacksonville.

Publicly owned utilities are, to say the least, controversial, and considerable effort has gone into attempts to create or to abort them. Those in
favor of creation contend that publicly owned electric utilities are more
efficient, have lower costs, and are more responsive to public needs.
Those against contend rates are lower because the public companies pay
no taxes, have no need to earn a profit, and have the advantage of taxfree
bonds with resulting lower interest rates. Of perhaps greater importance,
however, is the fact that many of the publicly held companies purchase
power from large hydro projects (which have inherently low operating
costs, and often benefit from low-cost federal financing) or buy it at
wholesale rates from regional power grids. These companies thus avoid
the major investments needed to support generation and transmission
plant while gaining the benefits of technology and of economies of scale.

Publicly owned electric utilities do pay lower taxes and interest rates,
as Richard Hellman notes.[12] Such reduced payments, however, are often
offset by higher depreciation rates, contributions to the municipal general
fund, free services for street lighting and water pumping, and other expenses. It is unlikely, however, that the offset is sufficient to balance the
subsidy impact of lower taxes and interest rates coupled with the absence
of the need to earn a profit. In terms of economics it makes little difference whether an electric utility is publicly or privately owned as long
as all costs are included.

Public ownership does not appear to provide an inherent proclivity for
efficiency. In fact the major advantage of public ownership may be that it
provides a spur to the surrounding private companies to improve efficiency and service by establishing a benchmark standard. For example,
Hellman's case studies indicate that major changes in the behavior of
private electric companies occurred when government competition was
introduced nearby. Rates were lowered, some services improved and
others previously refused, were made available. He notes, however, that
the mere fact of public ownership will not bring about the desired result;
performance standards higher than those found in the private companies
must be imposed. In short, government competition is effective only if

12. R. Hellman, *Government Competition in the Electric Utility Industry: A Theoretical
and Empirical Study* (New York: Praeger, 1972).

the publicly owned utility provides a goal toward which the private companies can strive. Otherwise the publicly owned company is just one more utility. Public ownership may be a substitute for regulation, but it works only if the publicly owned utility is forced to stay on its toes.

Other Issues

Aside from the major issues discussed in the foregoing pages a large number of other items, which are beyond the scope of this paper, impinge on the regulator and the electric utility. These include the efficacy and structure of regulation itself, whether or not electric utilities should be regulated, and other questions of this kind.[13]

Conclusions

Most of the proposals discussed above tend to treat the symptoms rather than the disease. The utilities are suffering from the exhaustion of economies of scale, a shift in the demand curve, and high inflation rates. There is very little that regulators or utilities can do in regard to inflation. Insofar as the other items are concerned, regulators need to push for utility research and innovation, as well as to adapt their own procedures to take account of the changes that are occurring, and restructure rates to keep revenues abreast of costs. Revision of regulatory procedures or the more liberal use of automatic adjustment clauses in order to reduce regulatory lag may well be counterproductive. There is little doubt that some speedup in resolution of rate cases may be required, but the elimination of regulatory lag would remove one of the most effective spurs to efficiency.

On the other hand, the financing alternatives discussed above could

13. For details, see H. A. Averch and L. L. Johnson, "Behavior of the Firm under Regulatory Constraint," *American Economic Review,* 52 (December 1962), 1053–1069; W. J. Baumol and A. K. Klevorick, "Input Choices and Rate of Return Regulation: An Overview of the Discussion," *Bell Journal of Economics and Management Science,* 1 (Autumn 1970), 162–189; N. Bernstein, "Utility Rate Regulation: The Little Locomotive that Couldn't," *Washington University Law Quarterly,* Summer 1970, pp. 223–264; P. W. MacAvoy, ed., *The Crisis of the Regulatory Commissions* (New York: Norton, 1970), especially the articles by W. J. Baumol ("Reasonable Rules for Rate Regulation: Plausible Policies for an Imperfect World," pp. 187–206) and G. J. Stigler and C. Friedland ("What Can Regulators Regulate? The Case of Electricity," pp. 39–52); P. Rosoff, *Economics and Regulation,* Annual Report, Public Utility Law Section, American Bar Association, 1971; and W. G. Shepherd and T. G. Gies, eds., *Regulation in Further Perspective; The Little Engine that Might* (Cambridge, Mass.: Ballinger, 1974), especially the articles by H. Demsetz ("Why Regulate Utilities?" pp. 125–136) and H. Trebing ("A Critique of Regulatory Accommodation to Change," pp. 41–65).

contribute to reliable and adequate electric service, but they are accompanied by other social costs which tend, in the opinion of the author, to outweigh the benefits.

Restructuring of rates, however, could be a major contribution to the solution of the utility problem. Marginal cost pricing should result in improved load factor and thus declining costs for the consumer. A major problem, however, is the development of equipment to allow institution of the system at reasonable cost.

It is my feeling that the move to peak pricing may be as important a development as the various technological improvements introduced over the years, which resulted in a declining-cost industry. Time-of-day pricing is not going to resolve all the problems of the utilities; it is simply another way of apportioning the revenue requirement. But in concert with other developments, including new technology, it should result in a more viable electric industry. In the process of implementing this pricing system, impacts and problems not yet understood will be encountered, but it is worth the gamble.

10

Nuclear Energy and Public Policy Issues

John F. O'Leary

Nuclear energy, uniquely among our energy resources, is a product of government policy. From the very beginning of the U.S. government's involvement in nuclear power, its proponents looked beyond the era of its applications in weapons systems to the day when it would, in their words, "liberate mankind" by providing enormous, inexhaustible supplies of low-cost energy.

Again uniquely among our energy resources, nuclear energy is the product of scientific discovery that is surprisingly recent. Fission was first demonstrated to be technically feasible in late 1938; the first sustained chain reaction occurred in 1942; the first nuclear bomb was exploded in the summer of 1945 (followed only a few weeks later by the devastating attacks on Hiroshima and Nagasaki); and the first successful power reactor went on-stream in 1951, followed by full commercialization in the 1960s. Thus, we have witnessed the translation of a startling new scientific phenomenon into a commercial technology of massive proportions in just a little over two decades.

This collapsing of normal development time was accomplished by a linking together of government, industry, and the scientific community in an effort, with almost evangelical overtones, aimed at commercialization of peaceful uses of nuclear energy. During the critical period beginning in late 1946 with the creation of the Atomic Energy Commission (as the successor of the Manhattan Engineering District, the wartime agency charged with the development of the atomic bomb), the commission, the congressional Joint Committee on Atomic Energy, and the Atomic Industrial Forum formed a tripartite coalition that carried out the most successful peacetime technological effort in our history and brought nuclear technology to its current state. The Atomic Energy Commission, because of the enormous prestige it inherited from MED, was able to bring together the cream of U.S. scientific and engineering talent. The Joint Committee saw to it that necessary funding was made available and that progressive changes in the statutory setting for nuclear energy were made in ways that complemented the technology. The Forum provided a focus for efforts of the private sector aimed at creation of a nuclear industry. From the late 1940s until the early 1970s these three organizations worked in fundamental harmony and dominated the development of nuclear energy.

The generation of electrical power from nuclear energy is based upon a controlled ''chain reaction'' in which neutrons enter the nucleus of fissile material, causing the nucleus to split. When the split is accompanied by the release of more neutrons than are absorbed in the process, a chain reaction occurs. Early in the history of nuclear energy, it became evident that a chain reaction would not be sustained if natural uranium alone were used. It was found that only 0.7 percent of the uranium found in nature, that with an atomic weight of 235, was fissile. The production of fuel for a nuclear reactor must, of course, take this into account.

The fuel cycle associated with light water reactors (LWRs), the dominant type of reactor in the United States, consists of the following steps. Uranium ore is mined and milled into highly concentrated form as yellow cake, a uranium oxide. The yellow cake in turn is converted into uranium hexoflouride, a gas which is charged to a gaseous diffusion plant which in the course of hundreds of separation steps is able to increase the proportion of the fissile uranium isotope U-235 from 0.7 percent to the range of 2–3 percent.

This slightly enriched material is converted to the oxide form, cast into small pellets, and assembled into fuel rods approximately one-half inch in diameter and twelve feet long. The fuel rods in turn are assembled into bundles which make up the fuel for the reactor. The fuel bundles, which together represent the core of the reactor, are inserted into a thick-walled pressure vessel and immersed in circulating water. The pressure vessel contains control rods which have the capacity to control the neutron production of the core. When the control rods are withdrawn from the core it becomes ''critical''; that is to say, a chain reaction is initiated. This reaction results in the heating of the fuel rods. The heat in turn is transmitted to the water circulating through the pressure vessel and is drawn off to drive, directly or indirectly, a conventional steam turbine.

About 25 percent of the fuel bundles in a core are changed annually. As a result of this one-to-four-year residence in a highly radioactive environment, much of the uranium in the core is converted to a group of isotopes known as transuranics and fission products, with varying degrees of radioactivity and half-lives. Some of these products emit little if any radioactivity and have half-lives measured in seconds or minutes. Others are capable of strong emissions and plutonium, the extreme case, has a half-life of 24,000 years.

Most of the difficulties currently influencing the development of nuclear power in the United States arises from the hazards associated with the presence of these fission products in the core. These hazards take essentially three forms. First, a nuclear reactor could conceivably suffer a loss of coolant accident in which the decay heat within the reactor arising from the fission products could cause the core to melt, resulting in a potentially catastrophic release of radioactivity into the atmosphere. The possibility of this type of accident forms the basis for the attacks on nuclear power on safety grounds. The annual fuel changeover made in the course of normal operations gives rise to the two other major policy issues relative to nuclear power: the complex of difficulties relating to the safeguarding of special nuclear materials, and the problems associated with disposal of high-level waste.

The spent fuel being discharged from nuclear reactors is now simply being stored, awaiting the development of a reprocessing industry. When reprocessing plants are built, they will chemically separate the elements within the spent fuel rods into low-level wastes, highly radioactive wastes, the remaining uranium, and relatively pure plutonium. The plutonium in turn will become a significant element in the second generation fuels destined for light water reactors. By 1990, or thereabouts, if the mixed oxide (uranium and plutonium oxides) fuel economy comes into being, plutonium will represent 10 percent of the fissionable material used as fuel in light water reactors in the United States. The high-level waste material, which will continue to be hazardous to man for tens of thousands of years, will be disposed of, first in retrievable surface storage facilities but ultimately in a geologic setting—salt domes, granites or shales, or other stable geologic strata.

These three issues, safety, safeguards, and storage, arising from the nuclear fuel cycle and from the nature of nuclear reactors themselves constitute the basis for public concern about the future of nuclear energy. In addition, the mode of development of nuclear energy raises a number of other issues that should be broadly assessed as we begin to apply the lessons learned in the course of the creation of this industry to the development of other new technologies in the energy sphere.

Research Policy

The first of these latter issues is the fundamental question whether, in a society constituted as is our own, the government should make massive research investments aimed at influencing market competition. Until recently, nuclear energy was not seriously regarded as a necessity. A great deal was said in the course of congressional debate over new initiatives in the nuclear field with regard to freeing mankind from a reliance on a disappearing fossil fuel source base, but in fact, during the 1950s when the basis for the current nuclear industry was being laid, no one in authority in government expected fossil fuels to be anything other than abundant during the remainder of this century and well into the next.

The principal justification for promotion of nuclear energy, therefore, was economic.

In the fossil fuel arena the federal government deliberately held its support for research and development efforts at a very low level, despite the fact that reductions in energy costs were clearly attainable through an augmented federally sponsored research effort. It took this course primarily because of a consensus in the executive branch and in Congress that when new technology—for example, for the conversion of coal to synthetic fuels—was necessary, industry was able and willing to make the necessary investment for its development. There was a tacit agreement at the public policy level that direct intervention in the sphere of energy R&D in order to influence interfuel competition was not an appropriate function of government. By the late 1960s, the result of this policy was a total fossil fuel R&D budget of less than $50 million annually, inefficiently administered and subcritical in all respects. In contrast, federal support in the nuclear sphere approached $500 million annually.

The creation in early 1975 of the Energy Research and Development Administration (ERDA) signalled political recognition of the necessity for attaining "balance" between the nuclear and non-nuclear elements of our national energy R&D by significantly augmenting the fossil fuel effort. Thus the underlying question as to the propriety of the government's influencing interfuel competition through its R&D investments is now dormant. But when we emerge from the immediate period of energy crisis (in reality, the period of our adjusting to the new energy realities), it is almost inevitable that this debate will be resumed.

Promotional Activities

A second major policy issue arising from the history of the nuclear field is that of the government's role as an active promoter of a given form of energy. In retrospect, it is clear to any impartial observer that nuclear energy penetrated the market much more rapidly than it would have done had technologic merit alone been the determining factor. From the late 1950s onward, an enormous promotional effort was funded by the government and executed by the Atomic Energy Commission. It took the form of soft-sell campaigns aimed at all levels of our population from school children through the President and in some cases, particularly where direct financial interest was involved, of more or less hard-sell efforts aimed at the utilities industry. In many respects the AEC and the individual members thereof acted as an inside lobby, using a broad range of governmental powers in order to launch a new industry.

It is clear that much of this promotional effort had at its roots the almost evangelical fervor with which the commission sought the commercialization of nuclear power. The AEC was morally convinced that the prospect of beating nuclear swords into plowshares justified extraordinary intervention in market decisions. The result was a one-sided presentation of nuclear energy, publicly highlighting its virtues, and, particularly from 1965 onward, deliberately downplaying its weaknesses. For example, the commission kept from the public for seven years an analysis of the effects of a core meltdown which indicated that a nuclear accident could cause tens of thousands of deaths and billions of dollars of property damage. The study, the Wash-740 update, prepared in 1965 at Brookhaven National Laboratory,[1] was not released until 1972 and then only because of a suit brought by an intervenor group. Similarly, throughout this period, the AEC consistently underfunded safety research and with equal consistency underfunded its regulatory arm. The net result was an attempt by the government to create a public image of nuclear power which stressed its advantages and ignored the dangers inherent in its deployment. The commission during this period treated nuclear energy as an energy source that could be used wherever coal or natural gas or oil could be used, without any public acknowledgment of the potential damage to public

1. U.S. Atomic Energy Commission Press Release, "AEC Releases Final Draft of Reactor Safety Report and Working Papers on 1965 Study," R-252 (Washington, June 25, 1972).

health and safety should a poorly located nuclear plant experience a serious accident.

In a very real sense the government during this period became a part of the nuclear energy business, providing the technology, the prestige, the aura of acceptability that made financing available, and the assurances of safety without which the industry simply could not have developed. We should ask ourselves as we begin to repeat the nuclear experience with other energy sources whether government participation as a full partner with industry in technology transfer is appropriate.

Regulatory Policy

A third and related issue is that of the regulatory dilemma that arose from the AEC's promotional activities. Until 1971 or thereabouts, the resources allocated to the regulation of nuclear power were the minimum necessary to lend credible coloring to the licensing process. As public opposition to nuclear power began to grow, coincident with the widespread deployment of the technology, it became evident to the AEC, particularly during the Schlesinger era of 1971–1973, that the capability of the regulatory staff had to be greatly increased in order to prevent erosion of the entire nuclear structure. Beginning in 1972, therefore, adequate resources were made available to the commission's regulatory staff, who began to utilize them to examine safety issues that had been swept under the rug for a decade. Gradually, as the competence and influence of the safety-oriented staff increased, an era of regulatory conservatism was ushered in.[2]

The pendulum during this period swung from too little regulation to too much. This in turn led to increased construction cost for nuclear plants and, of even more importance, to extended construction schedules. The regulatory staff, caught up in a public process, could not find means to rationally control the application of improvements in the safety features of the plants that it was licensing. If a new safety requirement was found even marginally desirable for a plant about to be built, the staff would try its best to impose the same requirement on as many plants under construction as could be reached. This created major stretch-outs in construction schedules and, in consequence, major inflation in plant costs.

The public policy issue here is how much regulation of a hazardous technology is enough. How much risk should the public be expected to

2. U.S. Atomic Energy Commission, "Commission Memorandum and Opinion, CLI 73-39," *Regulatory Judicial Issues,* 73 (December 1973), pp. 1085–1138.

accept from nuclear technology and how much avoidance of risk should they be expected to pay for?

The phenomenon of overregulation directly influenced the economics of nuclear energy. Nuclear designs being developed throughout the 1960s had a clear economic superiority over competitive fossil fuel plants. Nuclear plants took about the same number of months to construct, cost 20 to 25 percent more than their fossil fuel competitors, and had fuel costs that were sufficiently below the cost of fossil fuels even before the spectacular increases in the prices of oil, gas, and coal of the early 1970s to provide them with an unquestionable advantage. In the past two or three years this superiority has begun to blur, first because plant construction schedules are being extended and, in consequence, costs are rising more rapidly than the costs associated with fossil fuel plants, and second, because of the disappointing performance of the nuclear plants constructed. On the average, nuclear plants in the United States in recent years have operated at 55 to 60 percent of capacity [3] in contrast to the 80 percent that was projected in computing their economics.

The nuclear industry points out correctly that the performance of large new fossil fuel plants has been equally disappointing. However, a nuclear plant with its high capital cost and low fuel costs provides its owner with a much heavier economic penalty when it is not operating than does a fossil fuel plant. Thus, a low availability factor can more than offset the economic advantages of nuclear generation. For example, a recent study [4] shows that a nuclear plant has a ten-mill-per-kilowatt advantage over a coal-fired plant when both are operating at 80 percent capacity, but the advantage is completely lost when both plants operate at 55 percent capacity.

There are two questions of public policy inherent in the foregoing: should the government undertake initiatives to improve the reliability of nuclear plants, and should it develop procedures that can shorten the licensing-construction cycle? Both these lines of action are clearly within the capacity of the government. It could, for example, mount a program aimed at systematically identifying and resolving the technical questions relative to plant reliability. This might involve substantial expenditures

3. U.S. Atomic Energy Commission, Office of Operations Evaluation, Directorate of Regulatory Operations, "Nuclear Power Plant Operating Experience During 1973," (OOE-ES-004) (Washington, December 1974).
4. Robert Cornell, "Prospects for Growth in Electrical Usage and the Requirements for Generating Facilities" (New York: The Coleman Company, July 1974).

and would certainly take the government another step into active partnership with industry in the promotion of a single competing technology. The government could also provide, through changes in regulatory practices or through new legislation,[5] means to shorten the construction cycle: it could soften the impact of technical changes arising from safety reviews conducted by the regulatory agency, and it could reduce the potential for delay in adjudicatory hearings by curtailing intervenor participation. The question is: are these shifts in current licensing practice warranted from the standpoint of public policy?

Financial Aid

In the second half of 1974, a number of U.S. electric utilities, confronted with severe financial problems and with an at least temporary dampening in the demand for electrical energy, canceled or postponed additions to generating capacity. These postponements and cancellations affected about 15 percent of the capacity of fossil fuel plants then planned or under construction and about 68 percent of new nuclear capacity planned or under construction. The net effect of the utility industry's 1974 actions will be to reduce radically the amount of nuclear generating capacity available to the United States in the mid-1980s. In 1973 the Atomic Energy Commission projected 1985 nuclear capacity in the range of 250,000 megawatts. Early 1975 projections, taking into account the utilities' announcements, place the 1985 figure at 120,000 megawatts, a reduction of more than 50 percent from the projections of only two years earlier. The government has the power to intervene directly in utility financing to enable the industry to reach the higher projection. The intervention might take the form of Federal Housing Authority-type guarantees for utility financing or outright government loans or subsidies. From the standpoint of public interest, should the utilities be given this extraordinary assistance?

Price-Anderson

A final policy problem has to do with the future of government insurance applicable to nuclear reactors under the Price-Anderson Act. This legislation, passed in 1957, established a form of "no-fault" insurance under which liability for a nuclear accident is limited to $560 million, of which currently $110 million is covered by private insurance pools paid

5. U.S. Congress, House of Representatives HR-7002, 94th Cong., 1st sess.

for by the nuclear industry and the remainder is provided by the government. Many opponents of nuclear power have cited the Price-Anderson legislation as an extraordinary subsidy for nuclear energy and suggested that the government withdraw entirely from insuring nuclear plants, leaving the burden on the private sector. These critics also object to the limited liability inherent in the Price-Anderson approach, contending that the nuclear industry should bear the full cost of an accident, whatever they might be.

Supporters of the industry point out that, because of its excellent safety record, there has never been a claim under Price-Anderson; that Price-Anderson was an absolute necessity in the early days of nuclear development to provide the actuarial basis for assessment of risks. The nuclear industry now recognizes that the time has arrived for a gradual phase-out of the government's insurance role, as its own size and financial strength increase to the point where it can accept the burden.

The industry is now supporting a phase-down of government support, which should be completed sometime in the mid-to-late 1980s.[6] It still desires to maintain a limit on total liability, however, and this promises to be a major legislative issue. The underlying public policy question again is the degree to which the government should adopt extraordinary means to assist in the commercialization of a new energy technology and particularly the degree to which it should directly subsidize particular aspects of that commercialization.

Safety

The primary safety concerns related to the operations of nuclear reactors are those associated with the possibility of a loss of coolant accident (LOCA). In such an accident, the cooling water essential for removing heat from the reactor and thus to its safe operation is abruptly cut off, and, in the absence of backup systems, in a few seconds the radioactive core of the reactor overheats, melts to the floor of the pressure vessel, and proceeds to melt through the vessel and through the concrete foundations of the reactor building. In the meantime, there is some possibility that the steam pressure generated by the interaction of the melting core and the remaining water in the vessel could overstress the main containment structure surrounding the reactor, permitting radioactive materials to escape into the atmosphere. These materials, depending on their volume

6. U.S. Congress, House of Representatives HR-8631, 94th Cong., 1st sess.

and on wind direction and other meteorological conditions, could be spread over a broad area, resulting in significant property damage and the direct exposure of individuals to radioactivity.

The consequences of this accident sequence have been analyzed by Norman Rasmussen of MIT at the request of the AEC.[7] Rasmussen concluded that in most instances the meltdown sequence would create relatively modest property damage and little if any threat to public health and safety, but in other, much less probable instances it could generate property damage in the billions of dollars and kill thousands of people.

The Atomic Energy Commission over the years developed a "defense in depth strategy" to deal with the possibility of a LOCA. First, extraordinary care was taken with the design, manufacture, and installation of key elements of the reactor, failure of which could precipitate the accident. If, however, a failure were to occur, a series of backup systems are available to bring emergency coolant immediately to the core and prevent a meltdown. These Emergency Core Cooling Systems (ECCS) are engineered with the objective of reducing the probability of a meltdown to less than one accident per million reactor operating years. The commission in establishing this criterion sought a safety standard that would reduce the risk of death or injury to any member of the U.S. population from a nuclear reactor accident to levels below those associated with death or injury by lightning, earthquake, or other natural phenomena.

Critics of nuclear energy question the basis for the estimates of risk and consequences made by the AEC. They point out that the emergency core cooling systems installed in light water reactors in the United States have been developed on the basis of computer codes which may or may not actually reflect the behavior of a reactor under stress, and that until clear proof of effectiveness of the ECCS has been provided there should be a moratorium on construction of future reactors in the United States.[8] The classic response from advocates of nuclear power is that we depend heavily on engineering criteria for the development of safe systems in many other technologies and that we would not regard it as either necessary or

7. U.S. Atomic Energy Commission, "Reactor Safety Study, An Assessment of Accident Risks in U.S. Commercial Nuclear Power Plants," WASH-1400 (Washington, August 1974).

8. H. Kendall, *Nuclear Power: A Declaration by Members of the American Technical Community,* Union of Concerned Scientists, August 1975.

desirable to test, for example, a dam to destruction in order to prove the merit of the original design.

In fact, the industry and the AEC may well have been remiss in addressing the safety hazards associated with reactors. In the mid 1960s, the commission began construction of a Loss of Flow Test facility (LOFT) designed to give additional insight into the LOCA problem. Because of sheer mismanagement, the LOFT facility was some seven years late in entering service, and test results will not be available until 1978 or 1979 at the earliest. This inattention to safety, combined with the commission's unwillingness until recently to adopt conservative ECCS criteria for operating reactors, has tended to add strength to the arguments of critics. Although it has long been recognized that the threat to public health and safety presented by a possible LOCA would be reduced by distancing reactors from population centers, the commission has been unwilling to take a firm stand with respect to the siting of reactors.

Safety remains a serious public policy issue for the future of nuclear power but one that appears to be solvable through future R&D activity at the LOFT facility and through the adoption of siting policy that ensures that nuclear plants are located at sufficient distances from population centers to minimize risk to public health and safety.

The possibility of deliberate sabotage of a nuclear reactor is another facet of the overall safety problem. The concern here is that a terrorist group or perhaps a dissident or demented employee could sabotage key control systems within a plant, thereby provoking a serious accident that would release radioactivity into the environment. The potential for sabotage can probably be minimized by design, by careful screening and rescreening of personnel, and by perimeter security systems. At the moment, the threat is not regarded by the nuclear industry or by the Nuclear Regulatory Commission as sufficiently serious to require any significant investment. Nonetheless, nuclear reactors do in fact represent an attractive target for terrorist groups, particularly when they are sited adjacent to large population centers. It seems reasonable for the government to insist upon strong perimeter security, a continuing screening program for in-plant personnel, and the adoption of designs for critical systems within the nuclear plant that would offer a potential saboteur minimum opportunity for success.

Storage

The second of the classic nuclear issues has to do with the disposition of the high-level wastes that are generated in the course of fuel burn-up in nuclear reactors. These wastes will be separated in plants which will have as their major objective the recovery of the plutonium produced when a portion of the U-238 in the reactor core accepts an additional neutron, becoming U-239, and subsequently decays into Pu-239. As was pointed out earlier, these high-level wastes constitute an extremely long-term disposal problem. Some of the radioactive substances in the wastes have half-lives of 24,000 years. The Atomic Energy Commission's rule of thumb was that radioactivity remains a concern for twenty half-lives; thus the extremely long-lived materials must be in safe keeping for periods approaching half a million years.

There is, of course, no prospect that any human institution can be designed to provide the necessary security over a period of this duration. Consequently, what is required is the development of a storage capability in a stable geological environment that will provide a high level of assurance that radioactive contamination from these wastes is permanently prevented.

A feeling for the magnitude of the problem can be obtained from the following comparisons. A thousand-megawatt reactor generates approximately one cubic meter of high-level waste per operating year. The high-level wastes that would be associated with producing the total electrical energy requirement for the entire lifetime of an average member of the U.S. population would be equivalent in volume to a package of king-size cigarettes.

Two broad options are available to make long-term storage possible. First, and currently the most acceptable, is the development of storage caverns in bedded salt or in salt domes that have been untouched by mining or drilling activities. These structures have typically been stable for hundreds of millions of years. They contain no water strata, and should water somehow penetrate the storage area the mixture would be highly saline, thus providing for rapid precipitation of the radioactive materials and a low likelihood of their accidental introduction into potable water supplies.

Another of the attractive features of salt storage is that techniques could be developed for total recovery of the high-level wastes should applications be discovered for the materials of which they are composed or should a superior disposal technique be found.

A second alternative would be disposition of the waste material in deep-lying granite, shales, or other geologic strata where water is not present and which have a long history of stability. The radioactive material would be permitted to fuse with the native rocks and thus would become permanently beyond reach.

Two other possibilities for the ultimate disposition of wastes have been discussed. James Schlesinger, former chairman of the Atomic Energy Commission, suggested that studies should be made of the potential for firing high-level wastes into the sun in rocket propelled vehicles. This approach has generally been criticized on the grounds that the consequences of an aborted shot are too severe to accept. There have also been proposals that the high-level wastes be subjected to further transformation in a radioactive environment. Some theoretical studies indicate that wastes could be virtually eliminated if they were introduced into modified breeder reactors. Calculations demonstrate that the energy created from burning wastes would be sufficient to compensate for the additional processing required. These same calculations indicate that virtually all the long-lived isotopes present in high-level wastes could be eliminated except for strontium and cesium, materials with a half-life of approximately thirty years. These materials, after 600 to 1000 years of storage, would have residual radioactivity approximately equal to that of pitchblende, and thus would offer no particular hazard to health and safety.

Recently, the policy of the federal government with regard to storage of high-level wastes has favored the establishment of interim surface depositories where the material would be recoverable. This policy evolved after the Atomic Energy Commission retreated in some disarray from an attempt in the early 1970s to establish a permanent storage facility in a salt dome structure in the vicinity of Lyons, Kansas. The AEC study of the geology of the Kansas salt structure was inadequate, and it was found, after the project was well advanced, that the integrity of the structure had been compromised by early oil drilling and mining activities. Crystalization in the salt beds indicated some history of water intrusion.

After the Kansas experience, the commission ceased to deal with the long-term storage problem and began to explore short-term alternatives, including retrievable surface storage. This posture has been seized upon by nuclear critics as a tacit admission that the development of techniques for safe long-term disposition of wastes is questionable. They have called upon Congress to invoke a moratorium on further development of nuclear energy until satisfactory long-term solutions have been demonstrated.[9]

In all likelihood, acceptable solutions to the waste problem can be arrived at within the next few years. Supporters of nuclear energy maintain that there is a 100 percent certainty that an acceptable solution can be found in the near future and that nuclear development should not be side-tracked because of the waste disposal issue.

Safeguards

The most serious of the classic nuclear issues arises from the possibility of theft of special nuclear material and its use as a terroristic psychological device, as a poison, or in a nuclear bomb. There is a consensus within the nuclear community that the impact on public health and safety from even a crude illicit bomb could be much more severe than the results of any accident deemed credible at a nuclear plant.

The radioactive material that is used to fuel light water reactors is not sufficiently enriched to permit its use in the construction of a bomb, nor would it be particularly hazardous to public health and safety if dispersed in the atmosphere or in water. The fuel used in high temperature gas reactors (HTGRs), on the other hand, is highly enriched. The amount of U-235, the easily fissile isotope of uranium, is in the range of 90 percent of the total uranium oxide content of the fuel and, if it could be separated, would be an ideal raw material for bomb construction.

Fuel assemblies for high temperature gas reactors are massive, and together their sheer size and their chemical composition create a difficult chemical processing hurdle to illegal diversion. While the possibility of a well-financed, well-equipped, and well-organized group seizing fuel assemblies and recovering sufficient highly enriched uranium to produce a bomb can not be completely ruled out, it can be regarded as of very low probability.

The fuel cycle of the high temperature gas reactor will, however, offer a much more attractive target for diversion. This possibility will not open up until sometime in the late 1970s or early 1980s, but by that time, several commercial sized high temperature gas reactors may be approaching completion. The exposed portions of the HTGR fuel cycle will be the

9. *Ibid.*

points in the isotope separation process at which uranium is available in highly enriched form suitable for weapons making, the transporation link between the isotope separation plant and the fuel fabrication plant, and storage and early processing steps at the fuel fabrication plant.

The light water reactors safeguards problem, similarly, will not emerge until commercial reprocessing of spent fuel is initiated sometime in the late 1970s or early 1980s and brings with it the emergence of the "mixed oxide" economy. The significance of the reprocessing plants (none of which will be operating before 1978 or 1979 at the earliest) is that in addition to separating the high-level wastes, discussed earlier, they will produce plutonium of a quality that makes an ideal raw material for the construction of fission bombs. A thousand-megawatt reactor, for example, operating steadily for a year, would produce about 250 kilograms of plutonium, an amount that could provide the core material for ten or more fission bombs. The possibility of using this plutonium in light water reactor cores as a supplement to the fissionable U-235 traditionally used in reactors provides the economic motivation for reprocessing plants.

From the standpoint of safeguards, the separation, handling, and storage of plutonium at reprocessing facilities, the transportation of plutonium oxide to fuel fabrication facilities, and handling and storage at fuel fabrication facilities are the points most susceptible to diversion. A successful diversion would place in the hands of the diverting group material that could be either discharged into the atmosphere—for example through the air-conditioning system of a building, with the near certainty of killing all of the building's occupants—or made into a crude bomb.

The fundamental issue here arises from a growing recognition that the construction of a workable atomic bomb, once regarded as a venture that could be engaged in only by governments commanding large technical organizations, can now be accomplished by a handful of well-informed individuals working in a home workshop with (except for the nuclear raw material) easily available equipment and materials. At present, largely as a result of activities in the public sector, there are 400–500 transportation movements of strategic quantities of highly enriched uranium or of plutonium per year. These figures will increase radically by the early 1980s if plans now being developed for the introduction of reprocessing plants and mixed oxide fuels are carried forward. At the moment, it is generally recognized that even a relatively small group would have a more than negligible probability of success in an attempted diversion, because in-plant accounting for nuclear materials and plant security precautions are generally considered inadequate. The Nuclear Regulatory Commission is acutely aware of these deficiencies and is developing plans to institute safeguards systems that will make a theft of trigger quantities of special nuclear material significantly more difficult.

The possibilities now being discussed include the establishment of federally guarded enclaves within which the vulnerable steps in the fuel cycle would take place. These integrated fuel cycle facilities (IFCFs) would receive low enriched uranium and spent fuel from outside the enclave and ship completed fuel assemblies and wastes from within it. The phases of handling and storage after reprocessing, transportation to the fuel fabrication facility, and handling and storage within the fuel fabrication facility would take place within a secure perimeter.[10]

But even assuming that the IFCF approach could be made 100 percent effective, the safeguards problems associated with light water reactors would still exist in that a successful diversion of fuel assemblies could lead to recovery of the plutonium content of the fuel in a form usable for bomb making through relatively simple chemical processing. To meet this problem, the concept of nuclear parks has been advanced. This would involve a federally guarded perimeter within which light water reactors as well as fuel reprocessing and fuel fabrication facilities would be located. It has been further proposed that as breeders are deployed they be sited in generating parks in numbers that from the standpoint of fuel generation and use match the light water reactors within the parks, thus maintaining a closed plutonium system within a single perimeter. This balanced generating and processing park approach provides for the minimum physical exposure of plutonium to the outside world. In this ideal arrangement, nonstrategic raw materials enter the park and nonstrategic wastes leave it, and all activities of the entire breeder/light water reactor fuel cycle that offer a risk take place within the enclave.[11]

The park concept raises serious institutional questions, however. It contemplates, for example, a forced relationship between the generating and processing facilities that has potentially severe anticompetitive overtones. It may result in suboptimization of fuel cycle facilities and thus an increase in costs of power. An optimal reprocessing plant, for example,

10. M. R. Kraiter and A. M. Platt, "The Report of the Ad-Hoc Study Group on Integrated vs. Dispersed Fuel Cycle Facility," Energy Research and Development Administration, BNWL-1906, Draft, April 1975.

11. General Electric Company, Center for Energy Systems, "Assessment of Energy Parks vs. Dispersed Electrical Power Generating Facilities—Interim Report," CFES-PR-74–5, NSF Grant EN-40053-000, October 1974.

would be able to serve eighty 1000-megawatt light water reactors. A park, because of market limitations, security, or environmental constraints, may be limited to fifteen to twenty reactors; thus the reprocessing facility would be suboptimal in that all the economies of scale potentially available could not be realized. The inevitable mixing of the generating capacity of several individual utilities in a single park offers additional institutional problems. The transportation problem arising from the movement of power from a single location rather than a number of locations probably closer to load centers must also be considered. At the same time, there may be some offsetting economies. A stable construction force and the strong incentives for capturing the cost-saving available from plant standardization that would exist within a nuclear park may serve to reduce costs somewhat from those that would otherwise prevail.[12]

Alternative proposals have been put forward to achieve enhanced security without creating the economic and institutional disadvantages associated with the nuclear park concept. The establishment of a federal guard force, which would protect the sensitive points in the fuel cycle without necessitating the artificialities of collocation, has been discussed. Under this concept federal guards would provide security at dispersed fuel reprocessing and fabrication facilities and for the transportation links between them. There is a general consensus, however, that the safeguarding of nuclear enclaves could probably be effected more economically against a given level of threat than could guarding of dispersed locations and their transportation links. Trade-offs are now under analysis by the Nuclear Regulatory Commission.

Another alternative would involve "spiking" all special nuclear material with a highly radioactive source. The theory here is that diversion could be prevented simply by making the hazard to the potential diverter so great that he would be effectively deterred from making the attempt. The counterview is that "spiking" would cause difficulty throughout the fuel cycle by increasing worker exposure and creating additional material handling problems. In addition, given human ingenuity, there is no guarantee that a potential diverter could not find some expedient means of preventing contamination from the "spiked" material, and proceed, regardless of the "spiking," to construct a bomb.

It appears that means can be found to reduce the risk of diversion to

12. J. Just, "Perspective on Energy Center Development," The MITRE Corporation, MTR-6974, July 1975.

levels that society will find acceptable, even though this may involve severe technological and institutional changes for the nuclear industry. Critics of nuclear power contend that further deployment of nuclear energy should be halted pending the development of acceptable solutions. Supporters of nuclear power tend to understate the hazards associated with diversion and have, until recently, traditionally not addressed the subject with the attention that is its due. The public policy question is whether further deployment of nuclear technology should await resolution of the safeguards issue.

A related issue is that of nuclear proliferation. As reactor technology is spread throughout the world, the potential for heretofore non-nuclear powers entering the nuclear ranks increases. The 1974 detonation of a nuclear device by India is an example of the probable course that proliferation will take. The Indian government was able to reprocess nuclear fuel, probably from Canada, obtain plutonium, and manufacture a fission bomb that it subsequently detonated. As nuclear technology spreads and particularly as reprocessing plants follow the spread and are developed on a national basis, we can expect that other nations will join the nuclear club. At the moment only six nations, including India, have demonstrated the capability for producing nuclear weapons. Ten more nations may be able to do so within the next decade unless international means are found to control the arms potential of nuclear reactor and reprocessing facilities.[13]

The Breeder Reactor

The foregoing summarizes the current suite of public policy issues that relate to continued commercialization of nuclear power in the United States. It should be recognized that the national discussion on nuclear power now going forward transcends the individual issues. It is at bottom a debate between interest groups that are dedicated to the expansion of nuclear power and interest groups that have an equally strong dedication to minimizing its spread.

Those who advocate nuclear power do so for economic reasons, because it promises to be cheaper than its alternatives; for environmental reasons, because a nuclear plant when operating properly provokes far less environmental insult than does a fossil fuel plant; or for emotional

13. U.S. Congress, Senate Government Operations Committee, Testimony before the Government Operations Committee on the Export Reorganization Act of 1975, August 1975.

reasons, the swords into plowshares idea. The opposition comes from local interests that could be adversely influenced by a plant; from those who regard nuclear power as potentially damaging to the environment; from the advocates of zero growth; and from individuals and groups who feel that the three classic issues discussed above—safety, safeguards, and storage—create overwhelming problems that are essentially insoluble and that, therefore, government policies that foster the spread of nuclear power are fundamentally immoral.

These issues have all come together in the debate now going forward on the construction of the first large-scale breeder reactor—a plant that would be designed to demonstrate the feasibility of producing power while at the same time converting more nonfissile material into fissile fuel—in this case, plutonium—than is consumed in the process. Proponents of the liquid metal fast breeder reactor (LMFBR) take the view that it is environmentally more advantageous than any other form of energy generation in that it will use tailings from old mining operations and will not directly require new milling or mining activities; that it will enormously expand our fissile fuel resources (increasing the useful energy in our uranium resource base by a factor of 70); and that it will provide safe and economic power. Opponents point to the potentially hazardous nature of the technology, which uses sodium, a highly reactive element, as its coolant; oppose the massive acceleration of the availability of plutonium that would flow from successful introduction of fast breeders; and object to federal participation in financing the development effort.

The breeder issue will be resolved in the course of congressional debate over the next year or two. In the meantime, it is fair to observe that the attitude of the old Atomic Energy Commission contributed to, rather than diminished, the basic attitudinal split in the public perception of the breeder and of other aspects of nuclear energy. The tendency of the AEC to be less than frank in public discussions of critical nuclear issues left an aura of distrust which still permeates public debate. We can hope that the new Energy Research and Development Administration and the new Nuclear Regulatory Commission will be much more open in their treatment of these issues and will operate genuinely to expand public understanding of nuclear power and that, in consequence, decisions relative to nuclear power will be made in ways that advance the public interest.

Central to this understanding is an improved public comprehension of the consequences of denial to the U.S. economy of the nuclear option. As economic growth continues, our need for basic energy, regardless of the success of conservation efforts now being advanced, will continue to expand. On the basis of its brief operating history, the nuclear industry appears to be capable of making a major contribution to meeting these increased demands in ways that are beneficial to the public interest.

On the other hand, it is clear that the development of nuclear energy has proceeded more rapidly than has the development of means to minimize its potential adverse impacts. The major public policy issue raised by the breeder and by the other questions discussed above is the need to be absolutely sure that these adverse aspects of nuclear energy receive timely attention. The most useful outcome of the current debate, therefore, would be to permit the United States to have access to the nuclear option while at the same time assuring acceptable resolution of the basic public policy issues—safety, safeguards, and storage.

11

System Interdependencies and Government Policy

Martin L. Baughman
and Esteban Hnyilicza

The behavioral and technological constituents of the production and consumption processes in the various energy sectors of the U.S. economy differ widely, which means the sectors have separate degrees of responsiveness to the market mechanisms of supply and demand. In addition to the inherent complexities of each sector, the multitude of interrelations among the individual energy sectors and the overall economy make the formation of energy policy an arduous and challenging task.

This set of interdependencies constitutes the focus of the present chapter. We will concentrate on analyzing system interrelations such as substitutability and complementarity between end uses and factor inputs in both the short and the long run, especially as they relate to the underlying objectives of public policy in the energy field.

In a sense, many of the interdependencies stem from the inherent diversity of our national economy. For instance, it is true that in many instances competing sources of energy can substitute for one another. In 1964 the Energy Study Group, in a governmental study headed by Ali Bulent Cambel, wrote, "While there are some markets for which only one energy form is now economical, as much as 95 percent of total U.S. energy is consumed for purposes in which several or all of the primary energy sources are potential substitutes (directly or through conversion)." [1]

Where substitutability is possible, the user must choose one source of energy over another. In some cases this choice may be between different products from the same source, such as kerosene and distillate fuel oil,

---

1. Energy Study Group, *Energy R&D and National Progress* (Washington, June 5, 1964).

both derivatives of crude oil. In other cases the choice may be between fuels derived from completely different raw materials, such as distillate fuel oil and coal. This choice may be influenced by price, and also by other factors such as convenience in handling, cleanliness, and availability. The high degree of substitutability characteristic of competing energy sources means that one cannot discuss the supply, demand, and price of a given basic form of energy without also considering their effects on the alternatives.

As is often the case in economic analysis, there are two aspects to the study of system interdependencies in the energy field. The purely *descriptive* aspect relates to the assessment of empirical relationships that can be observed in the portion of economic reality under study. For instance, an answer to the question: what is the cross-elasticity of supply of coal with respect to the price of natural gas? would entail a purely descriptive assessment. The normative viewpoint, on the other hand, attempts to extract *prescriptive* recommendations valid for policy formation: e.g., how does a particular value of that cross-elasticity affect, for example, the desirability of regulation or deregulation of natural gas?

In this chapter, we will attempt to identify the critical interrelations within the energy sector and to establish the impact that they have—or ought to have—on the process of policy formation. It will be repeatedly emphasized that partial equilibrium analyses and analysis performed under *ceteris paribus* assumptions are useful in gaining initial insights and in offering a first approximation to a solution, but one must rapidly go beyond them if a coherent framework for policy analysis is to be developed.

It is virtually self-evident that the need for an explicit government policy in the energy field arises from the presence of factors which result, in the real world, in departures from the general equilibrium paradigm of perfect competition, which leads in textbooks to an efficient allocation of resources.

Such instances of market failure and departures from effective competition are especially prevalent among natural resource industries such as energy extraction, processing, and distribution, and they include, for example: (1) oligopolistic market structures; (2) negative externalities (such as pollution); (3) existence of natural monopolies (e.g., electricity); (4) nonrenewability of resources; and (5) extra-economic goals (such as independence from foreign supply sources). As we set out to discuss the policy implications of interdependencies in the energy system, these and other examples of ineffective market operation should be kept in mind as the underlying determinants of the need for government energy policy and, indeed—more often than not—as the driving forces behind the interactions that account for many of the system's characteristics.

In the following section we categorize and discuss the types of interdependencies that exist within and among the various energy sectors. Since these are most important in analysis and selection of policy options, in the subsequent section we compare and contrast the results of recent analytical work designed to quantify the strengths of these interdependencies on a relative scale. Finally we discuss the policy implications of the interdependencies, as they affect both the measures of policy performance and the analysis of specific policy instruments.

Characterization of Interdependencies in the Energy Sector

If one were to construct a taxonomy for the study of the interdependencies that arise among the various subsystems of the energy sector, it would have to include the following categories:

temporal interactions, ranging from the adjustment dynamics of the short run to the trends and secular cycles of the long run;

spatial interactions, including the effects of regional disaggregation and locational diversity;

sectoral interactions, reflecting the peculiarities of each individual energy source;

systemic interactions, encompassing global spheres of influence as between components of the economy at large.

In a more fundamental sense, however, system interdependencies can be categorized in terms of whether they take effect through market mechanisms, or alternatively, correspond to forces that propagate through channels *external* to the market. In a general equilibrium model, an adjustment process will lead to a simultaneous determination of prices and quantities consistent with reducing all excess demands to zero. In the resulting equilibrium configuration, prices are the only signals that need be exchanged among the various economic agents in order to achieve globally optimum behavior. This results in *informational decentralization:* each agent need not know the variables of the remaining agents in the economy—and in *behavioral decentralization:* each economic unit need know its own objective only and not the objectives of the other units. This is not to say that interactions among subsystems are eliminated, but they are restricted to those that take effect through the informational properties of the price mechanism.

Superimposed upon this first category of interdependencies within the market, there exists a second category of interactions that relate to problems of externalities and other instances of market failure to which we have referred above. For the purposes of discussion in this section, we categorize them as follows:

(1) economic interdependencies between the energy sector and other sectors of the national economy;

(2) market interdependencies arising from the substitution possibilities between alternative energy forms;

(3) demand-induced interdependencies stemming from the characteristics of end-use sectors;

(4) supply interdependencies that derive from the commonality of factor inputs.

Economic Interdependencies

The oil embargo, initiated in October 1973, and the subsequent price rise in the world oil market brought up a variety of pressing questions for policy makers and members of the academic and industrial communities. Which particular industries are being hurt by the rising prices and which are benefiting? Will there be sharp reductions in productivity? Will capital spending be sharply curtailed? Will the relative worth of labor and capital be reevaluated by the management of the leading industrial firms? How will the real resource costs of delivering energy to final users be affected? What changes, if any, will take place with regard to income distribution? How significant will be the effect on our balance of payments?

Various answers were provided and subsequent action taken. However, the adjustment process is not over, and a lot of these questions are still causing concern. A study conducted by Chase Econometrics lists the following industries as being adversely affected by the rise in oil prices: farm machinery, motor vehicles, household appliances, drugs, cleaning products, petroleum refining, fuel oil, knitted goods, photographic equipment, and airlines. Most of these industries are expected to lose sales due to the energy-intensive nature of their manufacturing processes. Some, like photographic equipment, will suffer reduced consumer demand because of the relatively high income-elasticity of their demand functions. On the opposite side, several industries will benefit from increased consumer spending because of the relatively small amount of energy they require for production; therefore they will effectively have lower prices relative to the remaining goods in the economy. These industries include alcoholic beverages, house trailers, household furniture, dairy products, tobacco products, apparel, batteries, and motorcycles.

An accurate assessment of the energy requirements—and therefore the effects of price changes on a specific industry—cannot be undertaken without a complete interindustry framework of analysis. For instance direct utilization of energy in the fabric industry amounts to only 1.2 cents per sales dollar. But if the energy necessary to produce synthetic fibers used in fabric production is considered, the total energy input comes to about 7 cents rather than 1.2 cents per dollar.

Another aspect which can be usefully analyzed in an input-output framework concerns the substitution possibilities between energy, capital, and labor in industrial production. The effects of higher energy prices depend in this case also on the specific industry under consideration. For instance, an increase in the output of aluminum by $100,000 would require 38 billion BTUs of energy and 5 additional man-years of labor. In contrast, an identical increase in output in the tobacco industry would require only an additional 5 billion BTUs but 32 more man-years.[2] This example shows that an increase in energy prices will change the composition of final demand in the overall economy. In particular, a shift can be expected from goods to services, since the price of the latter will be falling in relation to the price of most goods, which are more energy intensive.

It should be emphasized that these shifts in final demand provide one of the crucial links between short-run and long-run effects. In the short run, the higher level of energy prices will result in a redistribution of income involving large transfers from labor to the owners of capital and natural resources. However, once industrial concerns and individual consumers have had a chance to adjust to higher energy prices by altering their patterns of demand, the money will flow in the opposite direction, and the long-run result will be that labor's share of national income will rise and the share of capital—i.e., bondholders, dividend recipients, and property owners—will fall.

Whereas energy and labor are largely substitutable, the relation be-

2. Robert A. Herendeen, "Use of Input-Output Analysis to Determine the Energy Costs of Goods and Services," *Energy: Demand, Conservation, and Institutional Problems,* Michael Macrakis, ed. (Cambridge: MIT Press, 1974).

tween capital and energy is complementary, at least in the short-to-medium term. It has been estimated that the cross-elasticity of demand between capital and energy is about $+0.15$.[3] However, once again because of interindustry interactions, it would be erroneous to conclude that reduced energy demand will imply a decline in the demand for capital—especially since the estimates are based on data corresponding to a period of declining prices. The compensating effects in the short run will include added demand for drilling and mining equipment, as well as energy-saving capital equipment such as more efficient furnaces, heat exchangers, temperature control devices, and insulating structures.

The importance of the availability of low-cost energy, or the lack thereof, upon the structure and long-run growth potential of the national economies of the United States and other countries is a subject of intense research among strategic analysts and of great concern to energy policy planners. There are numerous important policy questions for which complete analysis is lacking because energy-economy complementarities and substitution possibilities are not fully understood. This large and relatively unexplored area of concern—large because of the inherent complexity of national and international economies, unexplored because of the relatively recent rise of energy issues to preeminence—lies at the heart of much current national debate on energy policy.

Market Interdependencies

Alternative energy forms exhibit varying degrees of substitutability. This means, in particular, that an increase in the price of fuel A will result, *ceteris paribus*, in an increase in the demand for fuel B, i.e., the cross price-elasticities of demand are positive among alternative fuels.

The substitutability of various energy sources determines that there exists a tendency for the corresponding prices to be equal at the margin. At the limit, by disregarding adjustment and conversion costs and by assuming conditions of perfect substitutability, one would obtain a configuration that is often referred to as a "BTU equilibrium." In such a case, the valuation and consumption levels of various fuels would reflect their energy content and would determine that the *user cost* per BTU would be equal for all fuels. It must be emphasized that even the highly idealized situation of a "BTU equilibrium" does not imply equal prices for all fuels, since the user's cost would include, in addition, transportation and

3. R. Halvorsen, "Demand for Electric Power in the United States," Discussion Paper No. 73-13, Institute for Economic Research (Seattle: University of Washington, 1973).

distribution margins, storage costs, capital costs, and the discounted value of operating expenses associated with the use of that particular fuel.

Evidence of adjustment toward a "BTU equilibrium" in response to the recent change in oil prices exists in reality. Since the increase in oil prices, the spot market price for coal has risen from about $9 per ton to about $20 per ton on a national average, reflecting the improved competitive position of this fuel. The Federal Power Commission, in an opinion handed down since the rise in oil prices, has increased the regulated price of natural gas in new contracts from 13–34 cents per thousand cubic feet to a current rate of 52 cents per thousand cubic feet. In addition to the shortages that had arisen purely in response to the existing price regulation, the huge increase in the cost of oil was no doubt a consideration. Further, the reasoning behind the current administration's proposal to place excise taxes on domestic oil and natural gas and impose an import tariff on foreign oil reflects an acceptance of the effects of market forces in altering consumption patterns.

It scarcely needs to be pointed out that the idealized "BTU equilibrium" view of the energy system does not wholly apply—especially if we consider the adjustment lags in the short-to-medium term. There are numerous and varied end uses for energy and several characteristics peculiar to each energy form. Both factors lead to a much more complicated set of forces operating in the energy market than the "BTU equilibrium" view of the world provides for. This is true even if we neglect, for the moment, the complicated structure of regulatory forces that currently exists.

An illustration of the perils of overextending the notion of a "BTU equilibrium" can be found in various hypothesized consequences of an often proposed policy action: the deregulation of the price of interstate sales of natural gas. In Figure 1, S denotes a hypothetical long-run supply curve for natural gas. D_1 represents the demand curve for natural gas under the assumption that it is a preferred good and that it is perfectly substitutable with oil—the assumption implicitly made by the proponents of the "BTU equilibrium" viewpoint. D_2 represents the demand curve for natural gas incorporating the restrictions on substitutability vis-à-vis oil. Point A represents the historical configuration with the price ceiling of about 25 cents per thousand cubic feet. The corresponding quantity consumed is approximately $Q = 20$ quadrillion BTUs. It can be seen from the diagram that the consequences of deregulation can be dramatically different under the two distinct assumptions on oil-gas substitutability.

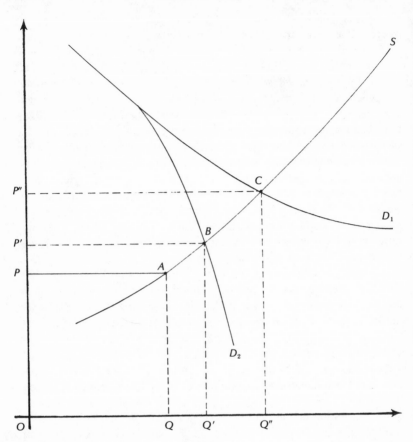

Figure 1. Equilibrium points for the natural gas market under regulation and deregulation showing different substitution possibilities

Under the full substitutability assumption, deregulation results in the new equilibrium point C, with $P'' = \$2.25$ per thousand cubic feet and $Q'' = 43$ quadrillion BTUs. Under the assumption of restricted substitutability—i.e., incorporating the fact that gas can truly substitute for only *part* of the oil demand—deregulation results in the new equilibrium point B, with a price $P' = 65$ cents per thousand cubic feet and $Q' = 27$ quadrillion BTUs. This incorporates the fact that only about 7 quadrillion BTUs of oil demand—corresponding to the residential, industrial, and utility end-use sectors—are genuinely substitutable by gas. Around the value of

$Q' = 27$ quadrillion, the demand curve for gas becomes very inelastic. We emphasize once again that these figures are hypothetical and presented for illustrative purposes only.

Demand Interdependencies

The end uses of energy have been broadly classified into residential, commercial, industrial, and transportation consumption categories. These uses account for, respectively, approximately 20, 15, 40 and 25 percent of the energy consumed in the United States. In 1972 the Stanford Research Institute reported that, although there are over a hundred separate user categories within this broad four-sector breakdown, twelve applications account for all but about 3 percent of the nation's total energy consumption.[4] Table 1 lists these twelve end uses and the percentage of energy consumption accounted for by each in 1968. To derive some notion of the importance of interdependencies among alternative energy sources, it is worthwhile to examine the substitution possibilities in each of the various end-use sectors listed in Table 1. The reader must be cautioned to keep in mind the distinction between choices among forms of the same fuel and choices among different basic energy resources.

In the largest category listed in Table 1, transportation (25 percent of total consumption), petroleum products account for 96 percent of the fuel consumed. Gasoline, for use in the internal combustion engine, makes up over two-thirds of this amount. Jet fuel accounts for another 15 percent. The heavy reliance on petroleum products in this sector constitutes a trend that is long and unvaried. Until alternatives to the internal combustion engine become available, which is not expected to happen in the short run, one must consider this sector's potential substitution possibilities as small and insignificant.

Three of the remaining categories—space heating, process steam, and water heating—account for approximately 40 percent of total energy consumption. In these categories energy alternatives are highly substitutable. Coal is not widely used in the residential-commercial sectors, but this is due to market decisions, not to technical infeasibility. The use of electricity is not prevalent in the process steam category, but this again is not because of technical infeasibility but rather is a natural result of historical trends in market forces.

In the direct heat category (11.5 percent of total energy consumption)

4. Stanford Research Institute, *Patterns of Energy Consumption in the United States* (Palo Alto, Cal., January 1972).

Table 1. Significant end uses of energy

	Percent of total
Transportation (fuel—excludes lubes and greases)	24.9
Space heating (residential, commercial)	17.9
Process steam * (industrial)	16.7
Direct heat * (industrial)	11.5
Electric drive (industrial)	7.9
Feedstocks, raw materials (commercial, industrial, transportation)	5.5
Water heating (residential, commercial)	4.0
Air conditioning (residential, commercial)	2.5
Refrigeration (residential, commercial)	2.2
Lighting (residential, commercial)	1.5
Cooking (residential, commercial)	1.3
Electrolytic processes (industrial)	1.2
Total	97.1

Source: Stanford Research Institute, Patterns of Energy Consumption in the United States, Palo Alto, Cal., January 1972, p. 7.
* Includes some use for space heating, probably enough to bring total space heating to about 20 percent.

where fuel is burned directly in the manufacturing process (e.g., in the manufacture of cement or steel), there are uses for which fuels are substitutable. For the most part, however, processing techniques have evolved as fuel-specific (e.g., the use of coking coals in the manufacture of steel). Thus the direct heating category is probably best characterized as bordering on the non-substitutable.

In the feedstock category (5.5 percent of total energy consumption) fuels are used for the manufacture of various chemicals rather than for their latent heat value. The predominant fuels in this category are oil products and natural gas, together making up 93 percent of the total. Although, with the adoption of coal conversion technologies (coal liquefaction and coal gasification), the primary fuel supply for this category could be shifted from a petroleum base to coal, no such change is expected to occur until well into the 1980s. For the next seven to ten years, therefore, this end use for energy is also best categorized as non-substitutable.

The remaining end uses listed in Table 1—electric drive, air conditioning, refrigeration, lighting, cooking, and electrolytic processing—account for about 17 percent of total energy consumption. Electricity constitutes about 65 percent of the energy consumed in these categories, while basic fuel inputs (mostly natural gas) make up the rest. At first glance, it may seem that these usage categories, given their prevalent use of preferred fuels (especially electricity), could probably not employ lower grade substitutes. However, the fact that electricity is such a large component forces us to come to the opposite conclusion.

Electrical generation currently accounts for over 25 percent of total energy consumption (in Table 1 the losses in electricity generation have been allocated to each end use in proportion to the electricity consumed). The electricity sector is also the only fuel processing sector where, currently, all primary forms of energy can be used as direct substitutes. In 1973 the mix of basic energy inputs used to generate electricity was 44 percent coal, 20 percent natural gas, 17 percent oil, 15 percent hydro power and a little over 4 percent nuclear. This mix existed as a result of management decisions in which the cost and availability of the alternative resources were influential factors. It is anticipated that over the next ten years all these sources will continue to be utilized, with nuclear power expected to show the most dramatic growth. Technologically, all the primary energy resources can be substituted for one another in the long run, and even in the short run some flexibility between fuel inputs can be made to exist by varying the usage of alternative plant types. The utility sector, therefore, offers a classic example of how the impacts of an action taken in one sector of the energy system can be transmitted across sectoral lines to have secondary repercussions elsewhere. Given also that the growth in electricity consumption is expected to exceed that of other fuels in the end-use sectors of Table 1, the outlook is that the interdependencies derived from the substitution possibilities in the generation of electricity will increase in importance in the future.

In summary, we see that at the point of final consumption about 40 percent of energy consumed is currently technologically substitutable (corresponding to consumption in the space heating, water heating, and process steam categories). All the fossil fuels and electricity are used as energy forms to fill these functional needs, and with changes in the price configuration of alternative energy resources, one would expect adjustments in energy use to take place.

An additional 17 percent of the energy consumed in this country is used in electric drive, air conditioning, refrigeration, lighting, cooking, and electrolytic processing. Electricity accounts for about 65 percent of the consumption in these categories. Given the substitution possibilities existent in the electrical generation sector, these end uses also possess high derived substitution possibilities—derived in the sense that several options exist for primary energy sources to generate the electricity. We see, therefore, that even by conservative counting, over 50 percent of the energy consumed in this country is easily substitutable as to basic energy sources, either directly or through electricity. In the longer run—say, to the year 2000—development of new technologies such as coal conversion and advanced motive power units, and changing consumer habits, such as lessened dependence on the private automobile, could result in even greater interdependencies among alternative sources. Nevertheless, there is another 40 percent of total energy consumed where substitution possibilities in the intermediate term are not nearly so apparent. The categories of motive power (for transportation), direct heat, and feedstocks are adapted to the availability of specific energy or chemical forms and therefore are not susceptible to substitution mechanisms.

Supply Interdependencies

Another important form of interdependency occurring in the energy system derives from the common use of factor inputs and basic commodities in alternative energy supply sectors. We refer to these interrelations as supply interdependencies. Examples of such commonalities of input are: (1) flat-plate and tubular steel goods used in the oil fields, gas fields, petroleum refining, and for electrical generating stations; (2) drilling rigs used for petroleum exploration and development as well as for exploration of uranium ore; (3) skilled and unskilled labor employed in the construction of new plant: welders, pipefitters and plumbers, electricians, steel workers, and so forth; (4) the same capital markets utilized for new financial resources. In the long run some of these interdependencies will be likely to have much more significant impacts than others. The financial interdependencies, although they have received much attention in the last couple of years, are not well understood even though their long-term effects could be crucial for the future evolution of the system. Although for the sake of this discussion the supply interdependencies are restricted to effects derived from commonality of factor inputs, it is true that these effects naturally impact on demand and consumption trends through market interdependencies.

The Federal Energy Administration *Project Independence Report,* issued in November 1974, concludes that the estimated availability of drilling platforms, drilling rigs, and steel products may impose potentially severe constraints on production increases in the short term in oil and natural gas. Currently, approximately 30 percent of the natural gas produced is produced in association with oil. The fact that these are joint products, at least to some extent, means that factors affecting the behavior of one fuel naturally overlap into the other. It has been argued that the technology of directional drilling has progressed to the point where much of this interdependency has been removed.[5] Nevertheless, it is important to note that approximately 80 percent of drilling platforms, 60 percent of drilling rigs, and 30 percent of steel pipe and tubing produced in this country are used in the petrol supply sectors.[6] As the country moves along the path toward increased reliance on domestic resources, one would expect demands for these goods to exceed overall economic growth trends. This could imply potential intersectoral allocation problems for these commodities.

A specific illustration of the importance of short-run intersectoral allocation exists in uranium supply. Even though the current stock of uranium reserves is less than the historically maintained average of ten years' advance requirements and the price of uranium concentrates via long-term contracts for delivery in 1980 has recently risen from $8 per pound to around $20 per pound, footage drilled for uranium exhibited only a slight increase in 1974, and was not expected to increase much in 1975. A partial explanation for this lack of growth is that the electricity consumption growth rate has declined, and financial cash-flow problems in the utilities have forced postponement or cancellation of many previously labeled "firm commitments" to nuclear plants. In addition, however, the expertise and equipment required for uranium exploration is similar to that for coal, shale, and oil exploration. The uranium industry is having to compete for these services. High returns and relatively short lead times are available in the fossil fuel sectors, while the uranium industry faces longer lead times. As a consequence, some of the drilling capacity has been bid away from the uranium industry. In the long run this could mean that shortages of nuclear fuel could develop within the utility sector.

The National Academy of Engineering has concluded that, in view of the current trend toward rapid expansion, the manpower requirements of

5. Policy Study Group of the MIT Energy Laboratory, "Energy Self-Sufficiency: An Economic Evaluation," *Technology Review,* 76 (May 1974), p. 36.
6. Federal Energy Administration, *Project Independence, A Summary* (Washington: U.S. Government Printing Office, November 1974), p. 239.

the energy supply industries also represent a potential constraint on growth.[7] In particular, it is estimated that the need for skilled construction workers will more than double over the period 1973–1985. The seriousness of the problem is underscored by the slow increase in the membership of the building trade unions in the AFL-CIO, the major source of skilled craftsmen for the industrial construction trades. The required incentives for people to relocate will undoubtedly increase—with resultant increases in cost. The point is, nonetheless, that excessive demands for these labor inputs have important effects on their short-run costs and, consequently, on their intersectoral allocation.

The final set of interdependencies in supply arises from the common use of capital markets to finance new construction. This is an important factor because the energy supply industries are all quite capital intensive and are responsible for a very large portion of new investment in plant and equipment in this country. The energy industries invested about $24.5 billion, or almost 21 percent of total business capital outlays ($118 billion) for the year 1971. Under optimistic projections of economic growth, this fraction of total outlays is expected to increase to over 26 percent in the period 1980–1985, and possibly to reach as high as 30–35 percent under more conservative growth assumptions.[8] This suggests a definite trend in financial resource allocation, with larger and larger fractions of capital outlays being made in the energy supply sectors. Obviously, to finance such expansion the prices of energy commodities will have to increase to attract capital from other forms of production. To a large extent we see this happening already—oil prices have increased, natural gas prices have been raised from area ceiling rates of around 13–34 cents per thousand cubic feet to 52 cents, and coal prices have also risen. However, in the electric utility sector, prices have not been able to respond because of regulatory pressure.

The sudden increase in fuel prices accompanied by an unexpected decline in electricity consumption has had very unfavorable financial consequences in the electricity supply sector. The direct effect of the rise in fuel prices was to increase the cost of electricity generation significantly, especially for those regions of the country highly dependent on oil. The increase was passed through directly to the consumer in most cases, via

7. National Academy of Engineering, *U.S. Energy Prospects: An Engineering Viewpoint* (Washington, 1974).

8. J. E. Hass, E. J. Mitchell, and B. K. Stone, *Financing the Energy Industry* (Cambridge, Mass.: Ballinger, 1974), p. 104.

the "fuel adjustments" allowed in that sector. However, this higher kilowatt-hour cost, combined with the sudden conservation awareness, has led to a decline in electricity consumption, reduced net revenues, and, ultimately, created cash-flow problems for many utilities. The reluctance of regulatory commissions to increase rates (the internal source of capital) on top of the fuel cost increases has forced many utilities to lower their capital expansion budgets drastically. Nuclear plants, because they possess the longest lead times and the highest unit capital costs, have naturally been the first to be canceled or delayed. These plants will presumably later be replaced with lower capital cost but higher fuel cost fossil fired units. Some have suggested that the more fuel-intensive configuration that results will lead to much higher electricity production costs in the 1980s.

Interdependencies Quantified: Prices, Income, and Energy Use

Because of the long-run importance of market interdependencies in the analysis of energy policy alternatives, it is essential to place in perspective the relative importance of the interactions across various market sectors. Lately, a large body of work revolving around the estimation of own-price and cross-price substitution elasticities in various market sectors has been in progress. Although in some cases the results of the various studies are not comparable owing to differences in data or model specification, it is worthwhile to review and contrast these results.

Historically, most of the econometric work on demand has focused on estimation of functions for specific fuels. Equations relating demand for a specific energy form to the price of that commodity and various other demographic variables have been reported in the literature for years.[9] However, with the increased awareness and deeper analysis which followed the 1973 oil embargo, analysts have come to view fuels not so

9. Examples of such work are F. M. Fisher and C. Kaysen, *A Study in Econometrics: The Demand for Electricity in the United States* (Amsterdam: North Holland Publishing Co., 1962); R. Halvorsen, "Demand for Electric Power in the United States"; J. W. Wilson, "Residential Demand for Electricity," *Quarterly Review of Economics and Business,* 11 (Spring 1971), 7–22; P. W. MacAvoy and R. S. Pindyck, "Alternative Regulatory Policies for Dealing with the Natural Gas Shortage," *Bell Journal of Economics and Management Science,* 4 (Autumn 1973), 454–498; T. D. Mount, L. D. Chapman, and T. J. Tyrrell, "Electricity Demand in the United States: An Econometric Analysis," Oak Ridge National Laboratory (ORNL-NSF-49), (Oak Ridge, Tenn., June 1973); and K. P. Anderson, "Residential Demand for Electricity: Econometric Estimates for California and the United States" (Santa Monica: Rand Corporation [R-905-NSF], January 1972).

much as desirable commodities in themselves, but rather as a means to accomplish various ends: heating, cooking, generation of process steam, and so on. Consistent with this view is the acceptance that fuel choices are made at a second level of the decision process either explicitly or implicitly, as the decision to use or not to use energy is finalized. This leads to a two-level characterization of energy demand. At one level there exist the substitution possibilities between energy and non-energy factor inputs in the performance of various tasks. Examples of such trade-offs are investment in insulation versus fuel costs, or investment in capital equipment which utilizes energy more efficiently versus higher energy costs incurred if the additional investments are not made. At the second level, at least for those energy end-use categories previously delineated as substitutable, there exists another set of substitution possibilities—this time between alternative energy forms. For example, for house heating, electricity, oil, and gas are all technically feasible, and the ultimate choice is left to the consumer; economic factors and personal tastes are the critical decision variables.

Fundamental questions in energy policy formulation are those of relative effects that changes in energy costs have on decisions to use or not to use energy and the effects that changing fuel prices have on the mix of fuels consumed in various market sectors, in both the short and the long run. Much recent econometric work, including some performed by the authors, has been addressed to these questions. To convey the uncertainties involved and also to show the direction of current thinking, we review the results of some of the more recent analyses.

For convenience, we report these results in the form of consumption elasticities, dimensionless measures of responsiveness defined as the ratio of the percentage change in consumption to the percentage change in the independent variable (for the purpose of this discussion, the independent variable will be either price or income). Depending upon the aggregation level of the sample under consideration, these elasticities can be further categorized as: (1) fuel-specific elasticities; (2) sector-specific elasticities (end-use sector); and (3) system elasticities (total energy). Finally, since it takes time for the full effects of a change in price or income to be felt through the system, the elasticities are also conventionally reported as short run, for fixed capital stock, and long run, the total response that can be expected after complete adjustments have taken place.

Table 2 shows a compilation of recently estimated elasticities. The sector and system elasticities appear at the top of the table, and the fuel-specific elasticities (those that relate the response in consumption of a specific fuel form to a change in price of that fuel) are given at the bottom. Note that the fuel price elasticities are higher than the system elasticities. This is so because the response to a price increase of one fuel

Table 2. Summary price and income elasticities

Use	One year	Long run	Income long run	Source
Residential and	−0.08	−0.5	+0.8	(A)
commercial	−0.23	−0.23	+0.64	(B)
Industrial	−0.05	−0.15	+0.65	(C)
	−0.41	−0.7	+0.46	(B)
Transportation	−0.2	−0.8	+0.6	(B)
Total		−0.35		(D)
Total		−0.31		(A, C) excluding transportation

Average U.S. fuel price elasticities (long run)

Residential and commercial	(A)	(E)	(C)
Oil	−0.81	−1.58	−0.64
Natural gas	−0.62	−1.73	−0.37
Electricity	−1.31	−0.84	−0.44

Industrial	(C)		(C)
Coal	−1.14		−0.59
Oil	−1.32		−1.4
Natural gas	−0.81		−1.51
Electricity	−1.29		−1.36

Transportation	(F)	(G)	(B)
Gasoline	−0.32	−0.82	−0.8

Sources: (A) M. L. Baughman and P. L. Joskow, "Energy Consumption and Fuel Choice by Residential and Commercial Consumers in the United States" (Cambridge: MIT Energy Laboratory, July 1974); (B) Federal Energy Administration, Project Independence Report, Washington, November 1974; (C) M. L. Baughman and F. S. Zerhoot, "Energy Consumption and Fuel Choice by Industrial Consumers in the United States" (Cambridge: MIT Laboratory, March 1975); (D) E. A. Hudson and D. W. Jorgenson, "U.S. Energy Policy and Economic Growth, 1975–2000," Bell Journal of Economics and Management Science, 5 (Autumn 1974), 461–514; (E) K. P. Anderson, "Residential Demand for Electricity: Econometric Estimates for California and the United States" (Santa Monica: Rand Corporation [R-905-NSF], January 1972); (F) H. S. Houthakker and P. K. Verleger, "Dynamic Demand Analyses for Gasoline and Residential Electricity," American Journal of Agricultural Economics, 56 (May 1974), 412–418; (G) M. Kennedy, "An Economic Model of the World Oil Market," Bell Journal of Economics and Management Science, 5 (Autumn 1974), 540–577.

form is partly a reduction in demand for that fuel, but also partly a shift of demand to competing energy forms. Thus, the total drop in energy consumption is less than the drop in demand for the specific fuel under consideration. Consequently, via the mechanisms of normal market response, a policy action that affects the price of one form of energy has long-run secondary implications for alternative energy forms.

To relate the magnitude of the effects on alternative fuel forms, we need also to review the cross-price elasticities, i.e., the response in consumption of alternative fuels to a change in price of the fuel under consideration. In Table 3 we present an elasticity cross-elasticity matrix estimated for one sector, in this case the industrial sector, to help illustrate the effects of an increase in price of just one fuel on the consumption of alternative fuels.

The self-elasticities, it can be seen, are the same as those presented in Table 2. The cross-elasticities are all the off diagonal terms in Table 3. The first column, giving the demand responses to a change in natural gas price, shows that a 10 percent increase in price results in an 8 percent decrease in demand for gas, and about a 7.5 percent increase in the demand for each of the other fuel forms in the industrial sector, in the long run. To break down the substitution and net total consumption effects we must know the accompanying market shares of each fuel. These are shown at the bottom of Table 3.

With gas making up 52 percent of the market under consideration, the 8 percent decrease in gas demand corresponds to a gross 4.2 percent decline in total consumption for the sector. But, with the 7.5 percent

Table 3. Long-run elasticity/cross-elasticity matrix for the industrial sector (less feedstocks)

Elasticity of consumption of	In response to a price change at the point of consumption in			
	Gas	Oil	Coal	Electricity
Gas	−0.81	0.14	0.15	0.34
Oil	0.75	−1.32	0.14	0.33
Coal	0.75	0.14	−1.14	0.33
Electricity	0.73	0.13	0.14	−1.29

Source: M. L. Baughman and F. S. Zerhoot, "Energy Consumption and Fuel Choice by Industrial Consumers in the United States," MIT Laboratory, Cambridge, March 1975.

Note: Mean values calculated for the following fuel consumption configuration: 52% natural gas; 19.5% oil; 7.4% coal; 21.1% electricity.

increase in demand for each of the competing fuels (comprising 48 percent of the total market), 3.6 percent of the gas decline is picked up by the other fuels. This leaves a net decline in consumption for the sector as a whole of 0.6 percent. Thus, for this example, 85 percent (3.6/4.2) of the price response is simply a shift to competing fuels in the long run, and 15 percent (0.6/4.2) is a real reduction in total overall consumption in the sector.

Of course, in other energy consuming sectors, one would expect the relative substitution and reduction effects to be different. For example, where we have found 85 percent substitution and 15 percent net total reduction response for the industrial sector, we have estimated 50 percent substitution and 50 percent net total reduction response in the residential and commercial sectors. In the transportation sector, one would expect that the relative effects would be more like 10 percent (or less) substitution and 90 percent total reduction response, because real substitution possibilities will be lacking over the next ten to fifteen years. In the utility sector, on the other hand, the substitution possibilities between fuel inputs far outweigh the energy/non-energy substitution possibilities, assuming constant output requirements. There is the opportunity to use more efficient generating plants in response to higher fuel costs, but this effect is still quite small compared to the fuel substitution possibilities. Consequently, we would quantify the relative responses in this sector as something like 95 percent substitution and 5 percent (or less) reduction in total demand.

However, to fully appreciate the sensitivities of the market interactions, one needs to compare these results with the more aggregated energy-economy interdependencies. In terms of the impact on energy demand, overall economic growth and income effects are far more important than the effects of energy prices. The income elasticity of total energy demand is generally accepted to be in the neighborhood of $+0.65$ to $+0.85$. Thus, a 10 percent error in one's projection for the level of economic activity results in a 6.5 percent to 8.5 percent error in one's demand forecast; whereas, with a total energy price elasticity of -0.3 to -0.4, a 10 percent error in one's aggregate energy price forecast results in only 3 percent to 4 percent error in energy demand. Consequently, for the purposes of deriving point forecasts of energy demand, a reliable estimate of economic activity (in real terms) is twice as important as one's projection of energy price.

The interdependence between the overall economy and the energy sectors is therefore of prime importance in energy analysis. The converse—the effects of energy costs and availability on regional economic growth—is also important. For example, in one study [10] an effort was made to quantify the importance of the availability of low-cost energy on industrial location decisions. This was done utilizing cross-sectional data on historical costs and energy use patterns in the U.S. industrial sector. The result was that the locational energy price elasticity for industrial consumption was estimated to be -2.0 in the long run (with a twenty-five-year adjustment time). The implication is that, if in one region of the country energy costs were to rise 10 percent, then *ceteris paribus,* a full 20 percent of the industrial activity in the region would move to other regions over the long run. This is not at all inconsistent with historical economic development patterns, for one of the fastest growing regions of the country over the last twenty-five years has been the Southwest, a region which historically has enjoyed an almost exclusive supply of low-cost natural gas. The impact of national energy policy on regional industrial development patterns through this effect is one that should be of paramount concern to state and regional planning authorities. One must suspect that the expressions of concern by the administrations of New England states over the federal government's proposal to institute a $3 per barrel tariff on imported oil announced early in 1975 stemmed in part from an understanding of this effect.

Policy Implications

To assess the policy implications of the interrelationships described, we must attempt to relate the latter to the rapidly evolving perceptions of government policy makers as to what the focus of energy policy ought to be.

The turning point in the evolution of U.S. policy in the energy field occurred—as is commonly known—when the embargo on exports was imposed by the oil producing nations of the Persian Gulf in October 1973. The reassessment of U.S. energy policy that followed was a direct response to the high degree of vulnerability of energy supply sources exposed by the embargo. At this point it is fair to ask: to what extent could the weakness of our energy system have been anticipated prior to the boycott by the oil cartel? What does the new emphasis on self-sufficiency imply with regard to our long-term national goals? More important: how

10. M. L. Baughman and F. S. Zerhoot, "Energy Consumption and Fuel Choice by Industrial Consumers in the United States" (Cambridge: MIT Laboratory, March 1975).

much of the misdirection of energy policy prior to the 1973 embargo can be attributed to a neglect of system interdependencies?

Let us briefly review some of the facts and changing perceptions regarding energy policy in recent years.

As early as 1960 the United States was importing 15 percent of its total oil supply, and by 1970 imports had increased to 26 percent (or 3.4 million barrels per day). Over that decade the price of domestically produced oil remained approximately constant, between $2.60 and $3.25 per barrel. In addition, the demand for oil over the period increased at a rate of about 3.4 percent per year, and most forecasts, until recently, held that oil prices would remain roughly constant in real dollar terms, accompanied by a continued growth of over 4 percent per year in the demand for oil until 1985.

A good example of what the future was perceived to hold was given by the National Petroleum Council (NPC) in their 1971 document *The U.S. Energy Outlook: An Initial Appraisal.* This was one of the most widely circulated studies predating the embargo and the subsequent rise of energy into its present preeminent position in the national consciousness. The document projected that oil imports would rise from 26 percent of oil consumption in 1970 to almost 60 percent by 1985, with the same prices and government policies continuing to prevail. Some concern was expressed within government and industry circles about this trend, but the prevailing attitude among policy strategists is best summed up by the following statement: "The relationship between Free World oil reserves as of December 31, 1970, and estimated Free World oil demand through 1985 indicates that total crude oil requirements for this period can be more than covered by proved and expected additional Free World oil reserves." [11] This complacent attitude was sharply reversed after the 1973 embargo. The reassessment that followed led to a drive toward self-sufficiency that has come to be known as Project Independence. Since it was announced, considerable effort has been expended to define the options and lay out the implications of meeting a complex set of interdependent objectives. The big problem in moving ahead with Project Independence has been not only that significant interdependencies exist within the basic operating mechanisms of the system, but also that the concept itself involves the definition, at the policy level, of a set of energy and non-energy objectives and selection among them.

11. National Petroleum Council, *U. S. Energy Outlook: An Initial Appraisal 1971–1985,* Interim Report (Washington, July 1971), 1: 27.

A useful framework for the specification of objectives is to categorize the types of decisions to be made into three levels which can be labeled, rather arbitrarily, (1) *the policy level,* (2) *the strategic level,* and (3) *the planning level.* Decisions on the three levels are obviously interrelated but there are differences in the kinds of underlying issues.

Policy Objectives. The goals of Project Independence must be quantified in terms of three basic dimensions: (a) foreign dependence, (b) economic costs, (c) environmental costs. As it now stands, the overall goal could be stated as "reducing U.S. vulnerability to interruption of foreign sources of energy supply while at the same time keeping the associated economic and environmental costs low." How large the reduction? How low the costs? These are the questions which are, to this point, unanswered and to which the political decision-making apparatus is currently addressing itself. The main point, nevertheless, is that any particular policy that is ultimately adopted will signify, whether explicitly or implicitly, a certain trade-off among *vulnerability, economic costs,* and *environmental costs.* At this level, the relevant decision is precisely the selection of a particular trade-off among the three attributes (regarding institutional difficulties of implementation as a nonquantifiable fourth attribute).

Strategic Targets. Whatever level of independence is selected as desirable will in general be attainable by many different strategies, each combining *supply expansion, demand reduction,* and *stockpiling* in varying degrees. What particular mix should be chosen in any given instance? The decision will obviously depend not only on the policy objectives— e.g., a high weighting of environmental costs will tend to make conservation seem more attractive—but also on the relative ease with which the specific actions required to attain a given mix of strategies can be implemented.

Planning Instruments. Finally, any particular mix of strategies can be achieved by various combinations of specific measures enacted through the legislative processes. The specific measures will at least potentially include all such frequently proposed actions as regulation and/or deregulation of prices, various taxation schemes, modification in licensing, land leasing and outer continental shelf leasing policies, price guarantees, direct subsidies, preferential credits, import quotas, and investment tax credits.

Although it is clearly not possible to talk about decisions on any one of the three levels without regard to the other two, the breakdown provides a useful framework for characterizing the various spheres of decision making. It is in analysis at the strategic and planning levels that the kind of system interdependencies detailed in the previous sections are most relevant. These should not be confused with the various dimensions of the goals to which decision making at the policy level is addressed.

The initial appraisal of the NPC has already been mentioned as illustrating the thinking that prevailed prior to the embargo. The NPC completed a more thorough investigation of the U.S. energy outlook in December 1972. It is interesting that this newer study already showed mounting concern over the growing dependence on foreign sources of energy. The final report stated, "The Nation must face *now* the fundamental issue of how to balance energy and demand most advantageously in the term beyond 1975. The major options involve (a) increased emphasis on development of domestic supplies, (b) much greater reliance on imports from foreign sources and (c) restraints on demand growth." [12] But, although this set of strategic options had been set down, the decision to decrease dependence had not yet been made at the policy level. Consequently, even though the NPC suggested the implementation of numerous planning instruments—e.g., expanded leasing programs, oil import quotas, deregulation of the wellhead price of natural gas—the institutional infrastructure to carry forward a coordinated national program did not exist.

Late in the winter of 1974, the embargo was in full force, the price of oil had quadrupled, and massive shortages of heating fuel and gasoline seemed more than just a potentiality. In this environment the policy decision was made to embark upon Project Independence. The responsibility for formulating and evaluating alternative courses of action aimed at securing energy self-sufficiency was assigned to the Federal Energy Administration (FEA) which undertook an extensive study that culminated in the *Project Independence Report* issued in November 1974.

One of the points of debate that arose as a result of the report was whether it gave too much emphasis to mandatory controls, rather than relying on market mechanisms. This argument tends to overlook the fact that specific measures such as excise taxes, investment tax credits, and tariffs will be effective *only to the extent that they activate the inherent price-responsiveness that is determined by the market forces of supply and demand.* That is to say, market-induced price-responsiveness would

12. National Petroleum Council, *U.S. Energy Outlook* (Washington, December 1972), p. 3.

not only not be disregarded in the enactment of such measures, but would in fact constitute a prerequisite for their successful implementation.

Another point raised by the FEA study is the question of the sensitivity of the various policy scenarios to errors in empirical estimates of, for example, elasticities. An inspection of the FEA results provides an illuminating illustration of how important these sensitivites can be. If one compares the total consumption of oil in 1985 in the FEA analysis at prices of oil equal to $7 and $11 per barrel,[13] the associated levels of oil consumption are 47.9 and 37.8 quadrillion BTUs respectively. Therefore, the implied elasticity of oil demand derived from these results, after adjustments in the prices of other fuels is about −0.39. This value is only about one-half to one-third of the estimates for this quantity listed in the FEA report. The explanation for the difference lies in the adjustments in the prices of the alternative fuels. Whereas if only the oil price had changed we would expect the kind of response indicated by the elasticities of −.8 to −1.0 in Table 2, the effect of the interfuel interactions is further to lower the net demand for oil. In this case we see that the system aggregate response is a reduction of about 40 to 50 percent in the demand for oil while the other 50 to 60 percent represents a shift in consumption to other fuels. Given the configuration of the end-use markets for oil, this is not unreasonable. But, if the ratio of the system's demand reduction to substitution effects were higher, so that the effective elasticity after adjustment were in reality −0.49 (compared to −0.39 used by the FEA), the result would be a reduction in oil consumption as we go from $7 to $11 per barrel of about 13.4 quadrillion BTUs—compared to the FEA's figure of 10.1 billion. This 30 percent change represents enough reduction in the demand forecast of the FEA that we would require only half their projected imports in 1985.

The most striking contrast occurs, however, when the methodology behind the FEA's results is compared to that of the NPC studies. Whereas several studies have reported projections of energy supply and demand and their policy implications, most have made only partial use of analytical models and have relied heavily upon extrapolation and perceptive judgment to maintain internal consistency. The NPC studies are a good example of this approach. The policy level decision to become energy independent, however, required more systematic analysis in order to construct and weigh the alternatives for reaching this goal. It was at this

13. These results are for the Business as Usual cases, and can be found in *Project Independence Report,* p. 46.

point that the perceptions of the system interdependencies began to shape the character of analysis at both the strategic and the planning instrument levels. The FEA's Project Independence analyses are the culmination of this effort to analyze energy policy within a highly systematic and rigorous mathematical framework. This change in the tools of analysis reflects not only the increased awareness of energy in our society, but also a heightened perception of the importance of energy system interdependencies and their implications for future energy planning.

12

Why U.S. Energy Policy Has Failed

William A. Johnson

It has become something of a fad among energy experts to observe that the government has yet to adopt an energy policy. In fact, the government has several energy policies, and they are inconsistent with one another. Not only do policies vary between Congress and the administration, which is to be expected; internal differences exist within the administration. Because federal energy policy making is fragmented and inconsistent, the national objective of greater self-sufficiency in energy is not being achieved.

Several recent events suggest that the government is moving toward a more coherent energy program. The Federal Energy Administration has been established by law. So have the Energy Resources Council, the Nuclear Regulatory Commission, and the Energy Research and Development Administration. The *Project Independence Report* was issued in November 1974, the product of a major effort on the part of the administration that spanned eight months. In January 1975 President Ford announced several important new energy initiatives. Subsequently, he called for the creation of an Energy Independence Authority to help finance high-risk investment in energy production and conservation. Finally, on several occasions he has urged gradual deregulation of oil and natural gas prices as a way of increasing self-sufficiency.

Yet there have been disquieting indications that these efforts are not moving the nation toward this goal. For example, a number of refinery expansion programs have been suspended or canceled since mid-1974.[1]

This study was partially funded by the National Science Foundation, Office of Energy R&D Policy. The conclusions are the sole responsibility of the author.

1. Among the oil companies that have publicly announced cancellation or postponement of plans for expanding refinery capacity in the United States are Gulf, Continental, Mobil, ARCO, Amerada Hess, Murphy, Clark, and Charter. Many other companies have shelved programs for expanding their U.S. refinery capacity but have not made their decisions public.

The total loss in new refining capacity now exceeds over two million barrels per day, the current level of U.S. refined products imports.

U.S. oil companies have several reasons for postponing plans to expand their refinery capacities: rising costs of plant and equipment, worldwide reduction in demand for refined products, and existing capacity that is underutilized. However, another reason often cited is uncertainty about federal energy policy, in particular, the possibility that Congress will enact punitive legislation and the Federal Energy Administration's issuance of inconsistent and poorly conceived regulations.[2] These regulations have, among other things, made refining unprofitable and future planning for the supply and pricing of oil extremely difficult.

Production of oil from shale has been set back by Colony Development's suspension of plans to construct a commercial oil shale plant. Again, one of the reasons given has been uncertainty about federal energy policy.[3] Many electric utilities have also scrapped or postponed expansion plans because of environmental and demand uncertainties.[4] Particularly hard hit have been plans to construct nuclear power plants.

The one bright spot has been exploration and development of crude oil in the United States. New drilling, both onshore and offshore, has been brisk. By January 1976 more than 1700 drilling rigs were operating in the United States, a figure not reached since 1963.[5] The future is less certain, however. In 1975 new drilling contracts reportedly declined partly because of changes in the depletion allowance and congressional attempts to roll back the price of oil. Many oil companies have reduced their budgets for exploration and development for the same reasons.[6] Yet the rig count has remained high. Whether drilling will be affected over the long run remains to be seen.[7]

2. See, for example, *Oil and Gas Journal,* November 11, 1974, p. 130; November 25, 1974, pp. 35–38; December 16, 1974, pp. 26–27; December 30, 1974, pp. 71–76; and April 7, 1975, p. 37. See also *Platt's Oilgram,* November 7, 1974, and November 21, 1974.

3. *Energy Users' Report,* October 17, 1974, p. A-13, and *Oil and Gas Journal,* October 14, 1974, pp. 52–53.

4. See, for example, President Ford's State of the Union Message, January 15, 1975.

5. *Oil and Gas Journal,* January 19, 1976, p. 91.

6. See, for example, *ibid.,* June 9, 1975, pp. 11–15. See also *Wall Street Journal,* June 9, 1975.

7. It will take some time for existing drilling contracts to expire and for a significant reduction in drilling to occur. Some of the pessimism created by changes in the depletion allowance seems to have abated. See, for example, *Oil and Gas Journal,* June 16, 1975, p. 25. However, pessimism was to a certain extent rekindled in December 1975 by the Presi-

Most disturbing of all has been the decision by several petroleum companies to diversify out of the oil and gas industry. Some oil companies are making major investments in other energy activities such as coal mining and processing. Others are planning to enter completely different lines of activity. Mobil's decision to acquire Marcor and, through it, Montgomery Ward has received widespread publicity and censure from oil industry critics. Socal has purchased a 20 percent share of Amax, a metal mining company. Other oil companies are considering or have made substantial investments in such industries as petrochemicals, mining, real estate, and food production and distribution. Again, one reason for diversification has been a growing concern in the industry over possible punitive actions by the government, especially Congress, and the various regulatory policies of the administration.

Several integrated oil companies, including Gulf, Continental, and Sunoco, also announced major reorganizations in 1975. These changes would facilitate diversification into non-oil industry activities. A Sunoco executive was quoted as saying "major roadblocks to long-term investment" in oil production and marketing were the primary reason for the changes in his company's organization.[8]

In short, the United States appears to be moving away from rather than toward energy self-sufficiency. Why is there such a contrast between the stated policy of the administration and what is actually happening?

The Shifting Sands in Washington

The need for the administration to concern itself more directly with energy matters had become apparent by late 1972. At that time the nation was experiencing the first manifestations of an energy crisis—home heating oil shortages brought on by, among other things, the government's price controls.[9] Federal energy policy was the responsibility of a relatively small, specialized group within the administration. The Department of the Interior concerned itself with such traditional matters as leasing federal properties, financing coal research, and administering the oil import program. The Office of Emergency Preparedness was put in charge

---

dent's signing of the Energy Policy and Conservation Act, which extended price and allocation controls and rolled back the average price of crude oil.

8. Cited in the *Petroleum Intelligence Weekly,* August 11, 1975, p. 7. See also *Business Week,* August 18, 1975, pp. 24–25.

9. For further discussion, see William A. Johnson, "The Impact of Price Controls on the Oil Industry: How to Worsen an Energy Crisis," *Energy: The Policy Issues,* Gary Eppen, ed. (Chicago: University of Chicago Press, 1975).

of oil import policy in 1971 and by late 1972 had created a reasonably competent energy staff. The director of the OEP was, along with the secretary of the Interior, co-chairman of the Oil Policy Committee, an interagency body charged with setting oil import policy. Finally, basic energy policy was the overall responsibility of Peter Flanigan of the White House. During 1972 Flanigan used the prestige and power that the White House then possessed to develop a coherent set of federal energy initiatives. Assisting Flanigan was the State Department's James Akins, certainly one of the ablest government officials involved in energy policy in recent years. Flanigan and Akins enlisted the support of over twenty departments and agencies in the preparation of several early drafts of the President's 1973 energy message. These drafts contained many important policy directives that still form the basis of the administration's energy program.

This organization had its deficiencies. Yet, in the relatively low-key atmosphere that then prevailed, it worked reasonably well. Flanigan's precursor to the "Project Independence Blueprint" was a comprehensive and well-researched policy program. Although there was some reason to criticize the OEP's handling of oil import policy, the agency would have been ideally suited to an emergency situation like that created by the Arab oil embargo in October 1973. Early that year, however, the Office of Emergency Preparedness was disbanded and its staff distributed among several different agencies. Some of the OEP's best people left the government. Flanigan was shunted aside by John Ehrlichman, who wanted to become the administration's energy czar. Eventually Flanigan also left government service, and Akins was pushed out because he was too closely associated with Flanigan. Finally, the President's energy message was revised several times, each version emerging more insipid than the one before. The final product said little that was new or needed to be said about how the nation could avoid future energy shortages.

The new energy organization began to take shape by February 1973. Heading up energy policy was the Special Committee on Energy, sometimes called the "Committee of Three" or the "Triad," which consisted of John Ehrlichman, Henry Kissinger, and George Shultz. One news report commented that "by picking three administration 'strongmen,' the President underlined the seriousness of the problem." [10] The Committee on Energy was not formally established by executive order until April 18,

10. U.S. News and World Report, May 5, 1973, p. 55.

1973, the same day the President's energy message was issued to the public. For various reasons, the committee never functioned effectively. Henry Kissinger was much involved in other matters and did not yet consider oil a central foreign policy concern. George Shultz generally delegated authority on energy matters to his deputy secretary, William Simon, and John Ehrlichman was preoccupied with Watergate. He continued in the administration for only a few weeks after his formal designation as a member of the triad.

William Simon, then deputy secretary of the Treasury, was named chairman of the Oil Policy Committee by executive order on February 7, 1973. Simon's most immediate job was to revise the mandatory oil import program which was, by early 1973, in almost total disarray. Treasury seemed the appropriate agency to be in charge of oil import policy because of its traditional concern with foreign trade. In fact, however, the department had few energy experts except for a small staff inherited from the Office of Emergency Preparedness. Most of the OEP personnel involved with energy had been moved to the Interior Department. The director of Interior's Office of Oil and Gas was to administer oil import policy, reporting to the chairman of the Oil Policy Committee even though he was formally responsible to the secretary of the Interior.

Also in February 1973 Charles DiBona was named "special energy consultant" to advise the President through the Special Committee on Energy. On April 18 DiBona was formally appointed director of the National Energy Office, also reporting to the Special Committee on Energy. In theory he was to head up a small staff of energy experts which would give the committee, and especially John Ehrlichman, effective control of federal energy policy. At the same time, the secretary of Agriculture, Earl Butz, was named counsellor for Natural Resources, and the secretary of the Interior, Rogers Morton, was made chairman of the Energy Subcommittee of the Domestic Council.

The *Oil and Gas Journal,* one of the industry's most respected publications, had difficulty trying to describe the new structure of federal energy policy.[11] This is not surprising. There was very little structure. The new organization's primary purpose was to focus energy policy in John Ehrlichman's Domestic Council while giving everyone but Peter Flanigan and James Akins a role of some sort. The disruption the changes created continues to this day.

11. *Oil and Gas Journal,* March 26, 1973, pp. 32–36. For other articles concerning energy policy organization, see *ibid.,* February 5, 1973, p. 19, and March 5, 1973, p. 26.

With the Special Committee on Energy largely inoperative, primary responsibility for federal energy policy actually fell upon two individuals of starkly different temperaments: William Simon and Charles DiBona. At first each man had his own mission to fulfill. Simon focused on long-needed changes in the oil import program, and DiBona concentrated on rewriting the President's energy message. Both the energy message and the new import regulations were issued on April 18, 1973.

Other energy problems had to be resolved, however, and unless the administration acted Congress threatened to take the initiative. Perhaps most important was a growing concern for the "independent" oil companies and the belief that the majors were trying to put the independents out of business. Convinced that something had to be done to allay this concern, Simon supported a voluntary allocation program for crude oil and refined products. However, DiBona objected to the concept of allocation and to Simon's involving himself in energy issues other than oil import policy. DiBona was convinced that a voluntary allocation program would inevitably lead to mandatory controls. The problem was also one of personalities. DiBona tended to be deliberative. Simon, on the other hand, was action-oriented and believed that the administration's delay in responding to congressional demands for help for the independents would jeopardize other important policy initiatives. The controversy was eventually carried to George Shultz. Simon won and on May 10, 1973 announced the administration's voluntary allocation program.[12]

By May it was clear that the reorganization, having been formally decreed only a month earlier, was in shambles. Several new plans were circulated. One put forward by the director of the Office of Management and Budget, Roy Ash, became the basis of a new federal energy structure. Ash had hopes of becoming the administration's next energy czar. According to him, restructuring the government's energy framework would "announce a major organizational move and beginning of action which will signal to the public that the President has taken command of the energy situation." [13] The Energy Policy Office was created by executive order on June 29, 1973. Its director was to be the administration's chief policy officer on energy matters. He was also intended to be an adviser to the President, taking the place of the now defunct Special Com-

12. This was in testimony before the Senate Committee on Banking, Housing and Urban Affairs, chaired by Senator Thomas McIntyre of New Hampshire. A description of the voluntary allocation program appears in Exhibit A of Simon's testimony.
13. Memorandum from Roy Ash to the President, dated May 22, 1973.

mittee on Energy. In addition, the President's Energy Policy Council was formed. This was to include representatives of all federal agencies and departments concerned with energy matters and to replace the Oil Policy Committee headed by William Simon. After a lengthy search, the President appointed Governor John Love of Colorado as director of the Energy Policy Office. Love, in turn, made Charles DiBona his deputy.

From the beginning, Governor Love was frustrated in his efforts to get the attention of a President preoccupied with Watergate and apparently not yet convinced that there was an energy problem. Partly for this reason, Love was never able to launch an effective energy program. Both Love and DiBona also generated distrust on Capitol Hill because of their seeming insensitivity to the problems of the "independents." With the declaration of the Arab oil embargo in October 1973, and the ensuing national crisis, there were demands for still another change in federal energy leadership. Both Love and DiBona became expendable and another reorganization occurred.

The President now turned to William Simon, who had the confidence of Congress and a reputation for being decisive. The Federal Energy Office was created by executive order on December 4, 1973, with Simon as its head. At the same time, the President requested the creation of the Federal Energy Administration by Congress. In anticipation of congressional action, the FEO was forged from some of Governor Love's staff, Simon's Treasury Department energy office, and Office of Management and Budget personnel. In addition, several offices in the Department of the Interior were transferred to the FEO, in effect stripping Interior of its oil and gas policy-making role. Price control authority for oil was transferred from the Cost of Living Council to the Federal Energy Office, as was the newly created office charged with administering petroleum allocation. In the process, a major new federal bureaucracy was created overnight.

The FEO was born in almost total confusion. By December the first effects of the Arab oil embargo were being felt. There were demands from every conceivable interest group for preferential treatment. Congress held hearings daily, and it seemed that every committee or subcommittee wanted William Simon to testify personally. On November 27, 1973, Congress also passed the Emergency Petroleum Allocation Act, which required the administration to draft a mandatory allocation program for crude oil and refined products within thirty days after the bill became law. At the same time, the Defense Department invoked provisions of the

Defense Production Act under which it could in an emergency take possession of refined products destined for civilian uses. This action threatened to ground several domestic airlines. Simon was given the unenviable task of creating an organization out of many different groups within the government, some of which had been feuding over much of the past year. Compounding his difficulties was the fact that the Federal Energy Office was unable to find a home for several months. At one time, the FEO staff was spread around nine separate buildings in Washington, with some officials spending much of their time commuting from one building to another.[14]

Many of these problems were eventually resolved. Although relations with Congress continue to occupy a disproportionate amount of the time of top federal energy officials, the pace has slackened as the glamor of the energy crisis has waned. The Defense Department was bought off with the grant of highest priority under the allocation program. The allocation program itself was drafted and became law only slightly behind schedule. However, the regulations were a mess and created problems which persist to this day.

Despite its charter, the Federal Energy Office was never able to bring together under one director all elements of federal energy policy making. Such agencies as the Environmental Protection Administration and the Federal Trade Commission had to remain outside the FEO umbrella. Yet their actions created disincentives to growth in energy capacity and the achievement of reasonable self-sufficiency. The FEO also developed a split personality. Both it and its successor, the Federal Energy Administration, proved unable to decide whether they were organizations primarily intended to make the United States reasonably self-sufficient in energy, as the President had declared, or regulatory bodies controlling the pricing and distribution of oil, extracting hidden data from the oil industry, and exposing industry misbehavior, as Congress demanded.

In April 1974 William Simon succeeded George Shultz as secretary of the Treasury and, a month later, John Sawhill succeeded Simon as director of the Federal Energy Office. An act establishing the Federal Energy Administration was passed by Congress and signed by the President in May 1974. Sawhill, it would seem, was now undisputed head of the federal energy establishment, and what had been a jerry-built organization

14. For a discussion of some of the problems faced by the FEO, see *Wall Street Journal*, March 8, 1974.

created in confusion, without a legislative base, was now formally established and operating. By all indications, federal energy policy should at last have been on a reasonably stable footing.

Wrong. Sawhill was never able to organize the FEA effectively; nor did he appoint a deputy administrator to tackle organizational problems for him. Also, at the same time, President Nixon created the Committee on Energy with William Simon as its head. The Committee on Energy was, in theory, responsible for coordinating energy policy within the executive branch of the government. The FEA's role was to administer policy set by the committee. This created another situation of conflict, as Sawhill refused to accept Simon's authority. Moreover, Simon never really had a chance to exercise his authority because in August President Nixon resigned and with his resignation the federal energy policy-making establishment underwent yet another reorganization.

Secretary of Interior Rogers Morton, who had had his authority on energy policy chipped away during the previous year and a half, now moved to the front. A close friend of President Ford since they served together in the House of Representatives, Morton became the new administration's chief spokesman on energy matters. The Committee on Energy was dissolved and, in its place, the Energy Resources Council established with Morton as its chairman. Sawhill was fired largely because of, as Morton put it, "a matter of style." Whether intentionally or not, John Sawhill had assumed public positions on a possible gasoline tax and other energy issues independent of the administration. One basic law of survival in any administration is never to upstage the President. Andrew Gibson was appointed the new federal energy administrator, but his nomination was withdrawn when controversy arose over possible conflict of interest arising from previous ties with industry. Finally, Frank Zarb, who had been in and out of the administration's energy policy structure for two years, was named Gibson's replacement.

In 1975 Morton became secretary of Commerce, but retained his post as chairman of the Energy Resources Council. Even so, his role, as well as that of the Energy Resources Council, diminished over time. Partly because of poor health and partly because of temperament, Morton never made full use of his commanding position in the energy policy process. It was Frank Zarb who gained effective control of federal energy policy in 1975. There have been grumblings in the White House, OMB, and various government departments about Zarb's high-handedness and independence. However, he apparently weathered this opposition and in

December 1975 cemented his position by persuading President Ford to sign the Energy Policy and Conservation Act despite the opposition of most other high administration officials. By the year's end Zarb appeared to be undisputed energy czar.

Wrong again. In January 1976 Rogers Morton resigned as secretary of Commerce. His replacement at Commerce, Elliot Richardson, has assumed the chairmanship of the Energy Resources Council and has indicated that he will take an active role in directing federal energy policy. Once again, the stage has been set for a struggle over who will be the country's top energy dog.

The United States has had at least nine energy czars in three years, and many pretenders to the throne. Few in either category have been particularly well qualified to resolve the nation's energy problems.

What does the experience of the last three years suggest? Most Americans probably accept the view that political instability in the Middle East is imperiling the U.S. oil supply. They should be equally concerned about political instability in Washington. The shifting sands of the U.S. energy policy-making establishment are one reason why the United States is failing to meet its goal of greater energy self-sufficiency.

Differences in personalities and jockeying for power have often dominated the administration of federal energy policy. Time has been spent in continuing debate between agencies over what policy should be. As one observer put it, federal energy policy making is like a game of musical chairs. When the music stops, each player must find a position not shared by someone else even if that position might differ from that held by the same player only a few months or weeks earlier. Thus, during 1975 Frank Zarb was for deregulation one month and against it the next.

Jockeying for power is the name of the game in Washington, no matter who the President or what his energy organization, but the game is likely to be played with special vigor in the absence of a clearly designated energy authority with the President's evident blessing. Creating an undisputed and reasonably stable chain of command is certainly not the whole answer, however. An energy czar who is unwilling to do the job or incapable of it is of little use to the nation, and may actually be harmful. Unfortunately, in energy policy making perhaps more so than elsewhere in government, the good seem to die young. The best of the energy policy makers have left the government with varying degrees of disillusion and disgust. And those who are competent and remain seem, as a rule, to have been removed from the center of the stage.

Further, not until the Arab oil embargo did the administration seem to take seriously the energy problem confronting the United States. Throughout most of 1973 the various czars were given minimal budgets and staffs to perform a monumental task. They also had limited access to the President. With the creation of the Federal Energy Office, however, just the opposite became true. A major federal bureaucracy was created overnight. What had been a problem of starvation became, instead, one of indigestion. The government tried to do too much and, as we shall see, much of what it did actually undermined the administration's objective of energy self-sufficiency.

Finally, the nation's experience with repeated reorganizations of the federal energy policy-making apparatus during the past two years exhibits a more general pattern of bureaucratic and political behavior: the way to appear to solve a problem is to reorganize. Governments, it often seems, measure their success in terms of the new organizations they have created. "We tend to meet any new situation by reorganizing; and a wonderful method it can be for creating the illusion of progress while producing confusion, inefficiency, and demoralization." This was said, incidentally, not by William Simon or Rogers Morton or Frank Zarb, but by Gaius Petronius Arbiter, a confidant of Nero during the first century A.D. And, in the spirit of Gaius Petronius one might add: *maxima agendo; minima regendo*. (For those readers not versed in Latin this translates, roughly, "lots of motion, little direction.")

The public should bear this in mind as it weighs Senator Stevenson's Federal Oil and Gas Corporation, Senator Jackson's National Energy Mobilization Board, and President Ford's Energy Independence Authority. When politicians lack substantive policy proposals, more often than not they offer the public new organizations that will, in one way or another, "solve" the problem. And, more often than not, these new organizations will create lots of motion and offer little direction. Unfortunately, they may also cause even greater problems than those they are supposed to correct. As we shall see, the FEA has done just that.

The Schizophrenic Nature of the Federal Energy Administration

Not only has federal energy policy been confused by frequent reorganization; it has also suffered from a severely schizoid personality. This is particularly true of the Federal Energy Administration. Since its inception, the FEA has had three distinct and contradictory personalities. For convenience, I call these the public relations personality, the Project Independence personality, and the regulatory personality.

The Public Relations Personality. The government's top energy policy makers and their immediate staffs have had to allocate much of their time to activities that might properly be called public relations. I mean not only such conventional PR activities as press conferences, television appearances, and speech making, but also testimony before Congress, attention to the special needs of congressional constituents, meetings with interest groups, and many other activities designed primarily to create the impression that the federal energy establishment is responsive to the public's needs and is solving the energy problem.

This emphasis on public relations is not in itself bad. Particularly during the Arab embargo it was necessary to enlist public support for conservation and other measures if the United States was to endure the crisis with minimal damage to its economy. Creating a national awareness of an energy crisis, even though most of the public still believed it to be contrived by the major oil companies, was one of the more important accomplishments of the Federal Energy Office under William Simon.

The problem with the PR focus of the high-level energy policy makers is that it has tended to dominate all else. Public relations has occupied a disproportionate amount of the time of successive energy czars and, for this reason, has diverted their attention from important policy matters.

Particularly time-consuming are relations with Congress. Hearings before congressional committees and meetings with individual or groups of congressmen and their constituents occurred daily during the embargo. Such meetings are, of course, a necessary part of the FEA's job, particularly if it is to have any hope of cooperation from Congress in implementing administration policies. But, even though now less frequent, they still require a disproportionate amount of the time of top administration officials.

Responding to insinuations by Representative John Dingell of Michigan that he had been unresponsive to Congress, William Simon testified in October 1974 that he had personally appeared on Capitol Hill at the request of Congress 213 times since coming to Washington.[15] Nearly half (102) of these appearances were made in his capacity as administrator of the Federal Energy Office, an average of over one appearance on the Hill per working day. Subsequently, the Energy Research and Development

15. Testimony by William E. Simon before the House of Representatives Subcommittee on Activities of Regulatory Agencies Relating to Small Business, October 2, 1974, p. 2.

William A. Johnson

Administration urged Congress to lessen its demands on the time of ERDA's officials. In its first 135 days of life, ERDA witnesses were required to testify for 109 hours of formal hearings before six full congressional committees and twenty-seven subcommittees.[16] Frank Zarb recently noted that he had to testify personally before Congress 86 times during the first ten months of 1975. Zarb went on to observe (correctly, I suspect), "That's got to be some kind of record for hearings that go nowhere." [17]

The waste of the time of high administration officials is, in part, a reflection of how the game of politics is played in Washington. One way for Congress to punish, intimidate, or otherwise harass unfriendly and uncooperative administration officials is to threaten them with prolonged hearings. An example occurred in January 1974. An unnamed FEO official was quoted in the *Boston Globe* as saying that New England had made itself vulnerable to the oil shortages it was then experiencing under the Arab embargo. In the past, the region had demanded and received special exemptions under the mandatory oil import program. For this reason, New England had become dangerously dependent on foreign sources of oil. The official's understanding of New England's position was accurate. Senator Muskie of Maine was outraged, however, and wrote to Simon demanding to know the name of the official. He wanted to call the man as a witness before his committee so that he could explain his actions.[18] Muskie's office telephoned Simon daily to find out whether the unnamed official had been identified. This threat to use the hearings process as a form of harassment was by no means unique.

During the crisis created by the Arab embargo, when energy was front page news, hearings also provided members of Congress with maximum public exposure. The enormous waste of administration time in seemingly useless hearings reflects the disorganization of Congress itself. Representative Barry Goldwater, Jr. (Rep., Cal.) has cited a Commerce Department study that illustrates Congress's "scattershot" approach to energy policy. According to this study, eighteen federal agencies concerned with energy made a total of 344 appearances before eighty-six congressional committees and subcommittees during the first eight months of 1975.

16. Letter from H. Hollister Cantus, Director of the Office of Congressional Relations for ERDA, to Senator Hugh Scott, June 3, 1975. This letter is reproduced in the *Congressional Record,* June 25, 1975.

17. *Washington Post,* October 15, 1975.   18. *Ibid.,* January 15, 1974.

Approximately 732 hours were spent in giving testimony and at least 15,855 man-hours were used in preparing it. Yet, Congress has passed very little constructive legislation as a result of these hearings. Representative Goldwater concluded: "Right now, the score is: Committees: 86, solutions: zero. At least the American people now have an answer as to why we have no comprehensive energy plan—the Congress is pulling in 86 different directions." [19]

Congressional hearings have covered many topics from the effect of the energy crisis on the farmer to its impact on the nutrition of the poor. The issue of greatest concern to a congressman or senator, however, is invariably whether the interests of his constituents are being considered. This is to be expected. The first duty of a congressman is to serve his constituents' needs. But doing so has occupied a disproportionate amount of committee time, and during the embargo, especially, many members of Congress asked and some insisted that high-level federal energy officials also meet with their constituents about various oil problems. For a time, haranguing William Simon or other high-level officials in front of constituents seemed to have become a favorite sport on the Hill. On occasion entire state or regional delegations played it together.

The New England congressional delegation is by far the most vocal and best organized. During the embargo, the New England members of the House and Senate insisted on regular meetings with Simon or Sawhill. These meetings were often attended by New England fuel oil interests seeking preferential treatment under federal regulations. And, partly as a result of them, the New England fuel oil interests got much of what they wanted.

Answering letters is another time-consuming activity. This is especially true of letters from Congress, which are sometimes monograph-length questionnaires requiring book-length replies. Often the same congressional letters are sent to several administration officials simultaneously. One of the functions of these letters, according to one congressional staffer, is "to keep the administration occupied." Another purpose is to find discrepancies in the answers of different officials and, in this way, generate issues with which to embarrass the administration.[20] The letters also serve constituents' needs and help to keep the Hill informed about

19. *Congressional Record,* September 18, 1975.
20. One discrepancy in response to congressional inquiries concerning the administration's position on a gasoline tax contributed to the firing of John Sawhill.

the administration's policies and to express congressional satisfaction or dissatisfaction with these policies, so they have some useful purpose. But, they take time.

Letters from the public are necessarily given lower priority. During the Arab embargo, many of these were lost in the sea of paper which flooded the Federal Energy Office and, for this reason, went unread and unanswered. In some of these instances, the government failed to respond to real problems arising from oil shortages.[21]

The most serious consequence of the public relations focus is that it has diverted attention from more important matters. Relatively little time has been left for the administration's top officials to consider substantive policy issues. For this reason, all the FEA's administrators have found it difficult to supervise effectively what was happening within the organization. This has been a major reason for the agency's schizoid personality.

The Project Independence Personality. In October 1973, shortly after the embargo was declared, President Nixon launched "Project Independence," a program that in its original statement was aimed at making the United States energy self-sufficient by 1980. This goal received widespread support, although there was also widespread skepticism that total independence could be, or needed to be, achieved by the end of the decade. But despite quibbles about the target date, there has been general acceptance, within the administration at least, of the need for a number of policy measures that would enable the United States to achieve greater self-sufficiency, either by increasing domestic supply or reducing demand. Some of these measures, such as deregulation of new natural gas at the wellhead, had already been proposed to Congress, Others, such as accelerated development of the outer continental shelf, had already been implemented by the administration. The need early in 1974 was to determine not what had to be done, but how to do it. Most important was a need for more effective working relations with Congress and communication with the public so that there would be greater acceptance of the administration's energy proposals, for despite the emphasis on public relations, communication with both groups was seriously wanting.

What the administration chose to do, instead, was to study the issue. The Federal Energy Office, and later the Federal Energy Administration,

21. For example, a letter from the president of the Mobil Oil Corporation to William Simon warning of the "double-dip" provision in the allocation regulations went unheeded probably because it was one of the thousands of letters sent to the FEO daily. See *Washington Post,* September 22, 1974.

undertook a massive interagency effort involving complex computer models to prepare a "project independence blueprint" which would, in theory, answer all questions about the appropriate policies necessary to achieve self-sufficiency in energy. This exercise required the efforts of over 500 professionals. The FEA also held public hearings throughout the country, another manifestation of its PR focus. Finally, in November 1974 the "project independence blueprint" was published under the more modest title, *Project Independence Report.*[22] The report has, itself, raised more questions than it has answered. One thing it has not done is to provide the administration with a coherent set of policy guidelines.

There is reason both to praise and to criticize the report. Given the time constraint under which its authors operated, they prepared a quite comprehensive assessment of the nation's energy problems. Qualified observers differ over whether in some of its particulars the report is too ambitious or not ambitious enough. However, to know a restaurant one must look in the kitchen. According to informants within the FEA, the Parameters of the underlying model were manipulated to yield results consistent with predilections of FEA officials as well as with common sense. The report, in effect, assumed its own conclusions. As a result, some of its assumptions about drilling and finding rates, discount rates, and other important parameters have raised eyebrows, particularly among knowledgeable observers in the various energy industries. It takes time, certainly more than eight months, to work out the bugs in any modeling effort of the scope and magnitude involved, no matter how much manpower might be assigned to the job.

However, discussion of the merits and demerits of the *Project Independence Report* is not my purpose here. The primary failing of the report is not what it says or does not say, but the diversion it created. Like public relations, it absorbed enormous amounts of time and talent in the federal energy policy-making establishment. Perhaps worse, throughout 1974 it provided high-level policy makers with a means of reassuring the public and themselves that the goal of self-sufficiency was being advanced when, in fact, it was being studied. Reorganization is one way to create the illusion of progress; studying a matter is another.

Because many policy proposals were deferred until the blueprint was completed, the Project Independence exercise actually helped to neutralize progress toward energy self-sufficiency throughout 1974. What was

22. Federal Energy Administration, *Project Independence, A Summary* (Washington: U.S. Government Printing Office, November 1974).

needed was more effective horse trading with Congress. Despite the extraordinary attention given to congressmen and their constituents, the administration received little return for its efforts. And little return was asked. The Ninety-third Congress voted to create the FEA and ERDA and to speed up construction of the Alaskan pipeline. The administration's bill to deregulate natural gas was ignored, however, and a bill to open up the Elk Hills Naval Petroleum Reserve died in the House. Congress voted for a number of measures opposed by the administration, such as restrictions on strip mining and a rollback in the price of crude oil. Many congressmen also expressed opposition to accelerated offshore leasing and initiated investigations of alleged industry improprieties. In general, the actions of the Ninety-third Congress detracted from rather than contributed to the nation's progress toward the goal of energy independence.

If there ever was an opportunity to accomplish this goal, it was during the embargo. In a period of national crisis, the public and Congress are more likely to make the necessary sacrifices. By the time the *Project Independence Report* was published, the embargo was over and a new Congress elected that was even less likely to support the administration's energy programs.[23]

The diversion created by the *Project Independence Report* continues. In 1975 the FEA decided to update its report. Again it dedicated much of its analytical talents to this effort. And again, according to informants, it has had to fudge some of its results to make them consistent with common sense.

The Regulatory Personality. In the vacuum created by the emphasis top policy makers placed on public relations and the *Project Independence Report,* a third personality, the regulatory personality, has become the dominant and most visible face of federal energy policy, particularly as far as the oil industry is concerned. Congress has devoted much of its time to considering various measures that would punish the major oil companies. Oil price, allocation, and entitlements regulations have been

23. By February 1976 the 94th Congress had done little to alter this rather pessimistic view of its probable accomplishments. A bill to deregulate natural gas floundered in the House. Both Houses of Congress passed bills to develop the U.S. naval petroleum reserves, but are at loggerheads over whether the Defense or Interior Departments will have jurisdiction, a matter of no small importance to the congressmen since it will also determine which committees in Congress will have jurisdiction. The Congress did pass needed legislation authorizing a petroleum storage program. However, the program is itself defective and was part of the Energy Policy and Conservation Act, a bill that, as we shall see, contains other features that will discourage achievement of energy self-sufficiency.

the primary output of the Federal Energy Administration. To many in the oil industry, these regulations have been the administration's only energy policy. Yet they have worked in a direction opposite from the objective of energy self-sufficiency. The expanding web of controls has added to uncertainties over whether crude oil produced by a company would be available to its own refineries and whether products manufactured in a company's refineries would be available to its retail outlets. It has also increased uncertainties about the prices likely to be received for petroleum produced and refined by the oil industry.

Among the punitive measures voted by Congress have been several bills that would roll back the price of crude oil. Congress has also considered legislation that would impose penalties for withholding data and turn the major oil companies into public utilities. In October 1975 the Senate came within a whisker of voting vertical divestiture of the large integrated oil companies. A few days later, it mustered a sizable vote for horizontal divestiture. In addition, Congress has held a number of hearings into alleged abuses by the oil industry and the major oil companies especially. Many punitive bills never got out of committee; several were passed by Congress but vetoed by the President. Some have become law.

Perhaps the worst piece of legislation to emerge from the Ninety-third Congress was the Emergency Petroleum Allocation Act of 1973. This act extended federal controls over oil prices and required the President to allocate crude oil and refined products. It also set in motion the regulatory morass that the FEA has now become. By January 1976 the Federal Energy Administration had over 3200 employees, most of them concerned with administering price and allocation controls. On January 2, 1974, the government first published 27 pages of allocation regulations for comment in the *Federal Register*. By January 1976 it had published over 5000 additional pages to amend, clarify, and otherwise "improve" upon its initial effort. The Commerce Clearing House tabulation of the FEA's regulations—the regulators' Bible—is now a three-volume compendium, seven inches thick, of turgid, legalistic prose unintelligible even to many of the FEA officials who must administer the controls. The Commerce Clearing House has also published two additional volumes containing decisions by the FEA Office of Exceptions and Appeals. Most recent regulations are intended to plug loopholes and modify or otherwise correct errors in earlier regulations. Just as one rule of bureaucracy is to reorganize and another to study issues, a third is that when one regulation doesn't work, establish two more. And if two don't work, establish four.

The administration's price and allocation regulations have become so complex that many oil companies have only an imperfect understanding of them. Reporting requirements have become burdensome. The larger oil companies may be able to hire the staff necessary to meet FEA requirements; most smaller companies cannot and, for this reason, many are actually violating the law.

Some FEA officials have also been unable to keep abreast of the regulations. Interpretation of them varies from one FEA office to another. At least one oil company has had to prepare a briefing book to explain FEA rules to the FEA's resident auditors stationed at the company's headquarters. Increasingly, the drafting of regulations has become an occult art practiced by FEA lawyers. FEA administrators have lost control of the regulatory process.

This failing is rooted in two fundamental mistakes made originally by the FEO and perpetuated by the FEA. The first was the decision to hire as general counsel and legal staff lawyers from the about-to-become defunct Cost of Living Council. These lawyers, for the most part, had a regulator's bias and a vested interest in controlling the oil industry. They also had little if any commitment to policies that would increase domestic production or encourage conservation of energy, that is, to Project Independence. The second mistake was the decision to allow FEA lawyers and regulatory staff to write and rewrite the regulations as they saw fit, without adequate review by other divisions within the FEA or groups within the administration. This has been one of the most serious consequences of the preoccupation of the administration's highest level policy makers with public relations. The many energy czars have not had time to tend the store. While, as a rule, they have urged deregulation to Congress, FEA regulators have extended controls over all segments of the oil industry. They have even threatened to extend controls over other energy industries as well, the most notable example being coal.

The administration has also made an about-face in its commitment to deregulation of oil. Decontrol of oil was one of many proposals made by President Ford in his State of the Union message in January 1975, and during that year he submitted several decontrol programs to Congress. Congress rejected these programs and, instead, passed a number of bills that would extend controls and roll back the price of domestically produced crude oil. President Ford vetoed these bills. By autumn 1975 it appeared that the controls would lapse and, with them, a major source of the uncertainty that had inhibited new investment by the oil companies.

In September, however, the President agreed to another attempt to draft a compromise energy bill. The Energy Policy and Conservation Act was subsequently voted by the Congress and signed by the President in December 1975. It includes several important energy programs sought by the administration. However, it also contains a modified version of a bill, vetoed by President Ford in July, which extends controls and rolls back the average price of domestic crude oil by over one dollar per barrel. The regulated price of crude oil will be allowed to rise by no more then 10 percent per year. Subject to review, controls may end after forty months. Then again, they may not.

The Energy Policy and Conservation Act was opposed by independent as well as integrated segments of the oil industry. Many industry officials now believe that decontrol will never occur, and the hope that had been kindled by the President's successful thwarting of congressional attempts to enact price rollbacks earlier in the year has become despair over a future in which continuing government regulation of all the industry's activities seems certain.

The regulatory personality has dominated federal energy policy. It has been the one area where the government has made substantive policy decisions and, unfortunately for the nation, these decisions have not advanced but have detracted from U.S. progress toward energy self-sufficiency. The dominance of the regulatory personality is a major reason why, despite the intentions of the government, the oil industry and especially the major oil companies have been backing away from previously announced expansion programs.[24]

The Mistrust of Expertise

While federal energy policy has been schizophrenic, the policy makers have also displayed, with some justification, the symptoms of paranoia. These symptoms were evident, for example, in John Sawhill's rule forbidding FEA employees to accept free lunches from industry representatives, presumably on the assumption that an invitation to lunch might influence an employee's judgment. FEA employees are also required to log all meetings and telephone conversations with industry representatives.

Much worse, however, has been the denial to the government, and especially to the Federal Energy Administration, of the talents of people

24. A larger, book-length study of FEA price, allocation, and entitlements regulations is now being completed by the author.

most qualified to participate in policy making because of their experience in various energy industries. There has been particularly sharp and persistent criticism of the administration's hiring of individuals formerly employed in the oil and gas industry. Representative Benjamin Rosenthal (Dem., N.Y.) has condemned the "incestuous game of musical chairs that is played so frequently by industry and government." [25] In the same spirit, former Senator Howard Metzenbaum (Dem., Ohio) has warned against "a takeover of the Federal Energy Administration by former oil industry executives." [26] Martin Lobel, a Washington lawyer and outspoken critic of the oil industry, has also criticized the administration's hiring of former oil and gas company officials. According to Lobel, the administration could "easily find 100 academicians and perfectly competent economists and specialists to fill those jobs, without turning to the very industry that is being regulated." [27] Congressman Robert Drinan (Dem., Mass.), borrowing Lobel's words, asserted at hearings on Project Independence in Boston that "the Administration should easily be able to find perfectly competent economists and specialists to fill these jobs without turning to the very industry that is being regulated." [28] There have also been several congressional investigations of the administration's hiring of former industry employees. In January 1975 Congressman John Moss (Dem., Cal.) announced that his subcommittee would investigate every FEA employee with an industry background and, if necessary, require each employee to testify in person.

There has been no want of objections from Congress, the press, and the public to historical connections between administration officials and the oil and gas industry. The real want has been a lack of expertise in the government, and one of the reasons for it has been an unwillingness to hire experienced personnel because of criticism that it would allow ex-oil industry employees to set high-level energy policy.

Responding to this criticism, in March 1974, the Federal Energy Office surveyed its then more than 2000 employees, turning up 102 who had formerly been employed in the oil industry. Of this group, 50 held "key" jobs. [29] The employees with industry experience included one assistant administrator, two deputy assistant administrators and two division directors. [30] They were in the minority. At the time, there were six assistant ad-

25. *Washington Post,* March 6, 1974.   26. *Ibid.,* December 3, 1974.
27. *Ibid.,* March 1, 1974.   28. *Weekly Energy Report,* September 2, 1974.
29. A key job was defined as a position at the GS–13 level or above.
30. See *Washington Post,* March 6, 1974, and April 1, 1974.

ministrators, over a dozen deputy assistant administrators and several dozen division directors. It should be added that the assistant administrator had been employed by an oil company as a trainee for less than a year, while one of the division directors with "industry experience" had merely pumped gasoline while working his way through college.

What is disturbing about these findings is that more experienced officials were not put in positions of responsibility in the FEA. The Federal Energy Administration was called upon to distribute crude oil and refined products in order to minimize dislocation of the economy at a time when the economic well-being of the nation and the industrialized world was threatened by the Arab embargo and OPEC price hikes. The United States was faced with a form of economic warfare. Yet it sent into battle its greenest troops. Its seasoned soldiers were suspect and, for this reason, were confined to barracks.

Nowhere has the absence of qualified and competent staff been felt more strongly than in the drafting of price and allocation regulations. One does not have to be currently employed by a major oil company to do the job. It helps, however, to have some experience in crude trading and product distribution. Contrary to the impression created by critics of the industry, to be an academician or an economist is no substitute for experience in buying and selling oil. The trading of crude oil and refined products is very nearly an art form, requiring an understanding of pipeline systems, quality differentials, the names and locations of producers and refiners, refinery mixes, and a number of other aspects of the process that can be obtained only by working in the industry. During the embargo, especially, there was a national need for qualified individuals to ensure reasonably equitable distribution of oil, while at the same time minimizing the impact of the Arab embargo on the U.S. economy. Yet, because of the widespread suspicion of the oil industry, qualified personnel did not participate in the emergency effort. Instead, regulations were written largely by officials without industry experience—some of whom actually professed antiindustry biases.

Federal policy during World War II and the Korean War was quite different. Then the government also assumed responsibility for the pricing and allocation of oil, but high-level executives from the industry, with an intimate knowledge of its workings were brought in, in effect, to run the program. Because the industry was not then the object of widespread hysteria and distrust, it was able to work cooperatively with the government to meet a national emergency.

The oil industry was prepared once again to provide skilled manpower in 1973. In planning for an emergency the government had created and maintained the Emergency Petroleum Supply Committee, a group of over 200 industry executives, 60 of them in key positions in their companies, in the event that government intervention in the supply and distribution of oil once again became necessary. The committee met every year to work out hypothetical supply and distribution problems. After the embargo was declared, the administration considered activating the committee, but was deterred by a Justice Department ruling that raised antitrust problems created by legislation enacted since the Korean War. Perhaps more important, soundings on Capitol Hill indicated strong opposition and the likelihood that the administration would be subjected to even harsher criticism about its industry connections. The Emergency Petroleum Supply Committee is now a dead organization.

Another program intended, among other things, to provide industrial talent to the U.S. government has also been subjected to congressional attack. Under the Presidential Executive Interchange Program young executives from industry spend a year in government while a comparable number of federal civil servants spend a year in industry. The interchange program became the subject of controversy in 1974 because four oil industry junior executives serving in various government departments happened to be reorganized into the Federal Energy Office when it was created. Subsequently, one of these executives, an employee on leave from Phillips, was charged by several congressmen with having inserted the so-called "double-dip" provision into FEA allocation regulations.[31] These congressmen also charged that this provision netted Phillips substantial profits. The incident was investigated by staff members from several congressional committees and was the subject of public hearings by a subcommittee chaired by Congressman Dingell. The hearings disclosed that Phillips did not benefit at all from the "double-dip" provision.[32] Nor

31. Because of a fluke in the regulations, oil companies required to sell crude oil under the allocation program were allowed to recover part of their crude oil costs twice, once from the refiner-buyer and once from their own customers. In fact, the regulations were ambiguously written, and the extent and nature of the provision were never entirely clear. It was removed from the regulations several months after its insertion.

32. Although Phillips did not recoup any benefits from the "double-dip," it "banked" some costs arising from this provision. Banked costs were not passed through to consumers in the form of higher prices, but reserved by the oil companies for possible pass-through at a future date if market conditions permit. Market conditions have not permitted and, as a result, industry "banks" have grown steadily over time.

was the Phillips employee's responsibility for the double-dip established. The FBI and the Justice Department declined to investigate the matter further because there was no evidence that any crime had been committed. And, despite charges by several congressmen that the industry had made billions of dollars from the double-dip, an FEA audit revealed that the actual amount was $40 million, an average of .0005 cents per gallon during the period in which the double-dip was in effect.

Nevertheless, the Presidential Executive Interchange Program has probably been destroyed as an effective means of hiring qualified personnel from the oil industry and, possibly, other industries as well. As a result, in the event of another supply interruption the government is now less likely to obtain personnel knowledgeable about the oil industry and its operations.[33]

There have been several instances in which individuals have been denied jobs with the FEA for no other reason than their background in industry. For example, the services of Russell Cameron, a nationally respected expert on synthetic fuels, were lost because of John Sawhill's concern over his connections with the oil industry and the probable hassle with Congress they would create. Duke Ligon's confirmation by the Senate as an FEA assistant administrator was delayed for months because of family interests in the oil industry and his past employment by a major oil company. He had worked for less than a year as a trainee for Continental Oil. Ligon has since resigned. The only other assistant administrator with industry experience was Melvin Conant, a former employee of Exxon. Conant had received a fixed severance fee and no longer has any ties with Exxon. Nonetheless, his nomination went to the Senate only after considerable delay by the administration and was approved only after prolonged debate and sharp criticism by some members of Congress. Of ninety senators voting on Conant's confirmation, thirty-five voted against it simply because of his background in industry. In February 1976 Conant also resigned to return to private life. At present, few high-level FEA officials have had any experience in the energy industries.

The failure of the government to place qualified persons in key positions has resulted in a number of incidents that would be comical were it not for their possible serious impact on the U.S. economy. Early in 1974 an FEO employee phoned the American Petroleum Institute to ask the

33. For reporting on the "double-dip" controversy see *Platt's Oilgram*, September 27, 1974 and October 3, 1974, and the *New York Times*, September 26, 1974.

technical definition of the unit of weight used by the oil industry called the "Platt's Oilgram." [34] There have been frequent instances of administration blunders, especially involving price and allocation controls, that reflect the lack of expertise. The Federal Energy Office's first buy-sell list for crude oil, published on January 22, 1974, contained an unknown refiner—the Ingot Oil Company—which, apparently, had been formed simply to obtain an allocation from the government. This error was not discovered until the list was published in the *Federal Register* and other oil companies protested vigorously. In May 1974, after substantial pressure from several airlines and their trade association, the Federal Energy Office ordered a number of refiners to increase their yields of jet fuel by 6 percent. The oil industry's compliance with this directive was physically impossible, however, unless production of unleaded gasoline was reduced. Several refiners were faced with a Hobson's choice between disobeying either an FEA or an EPA directive. Finally, in 1975 the FEA drafted a regulation requiring truck stops and service stations to post the lead content of their diesel oil. The regulation was sent to the *Federal Register,* but was later withdrawn when an FEA official realized that diesel oil contains no lead additives. There have been many other instances of arbitrary and sometimes silly rulings by the Federal Energy Administration stemming largely from ignorance of oil industry operations.

The nation has allowed suspicion of the oil industry and especially of the major oil companies to cloud its vision. Concern over conflict of interest is legitimate. However, this concern must be balanced against other national interests, particularly in a crisis situation created by foreign producing countries. Then, more than ever, the services of competent and experienced individuals are needed.

Federal energy programs during the past three years have been marred by a continuing conflict between a need to achieve greater energy self-sufficiency and the congressional demand that the government regulate the pricing and distribution of oil and punish the industry for alleged wrongdoing. The government cannot ensure reasonable invulnerability of the U.S. economy and continued freedom of action in foreign policy while, at the same time, satisfying congressional demands for ever greater restrictions on the oil industry. Nor can the nation obtain energy

34. Readers of my footnotes need not ask this question.

self-sufficiency if the services of experienced and competent individuals are denied or lost to the government. Unfortunately, it has been the punitive personality of federal energy policy that has dominated. As long as this emphasis continues, it is unlikely that the objective of reasonable self-sufficiency in energy will ever be achieved. As Pogo used to say: "We have met the enemy and he is us."

13

Federal Government Energy Organization

William A. Vogely

The organization of those portions of both the executive and legislative branches of the federal government concerned with energy has been in a state of flux for a number of years. With the enactment of the legislation [1] establishing the Energy Research and Development Administration, the Nuclear Regulatory Commission, and the Energy Resources Council, organizational arrangements have been improved in the executive branch. Further, the emergence of new leaders in the House of Representatives at the beginning of the Ninety-fourth Congress has shifted the power base on energy matters in the House.

In this chapter the energy organization of the federal government as it exists in the summer of 1975 will be examined. Following that is a discussion of the major issues in organization and a look at some probable alternatives.

Executive Branch Energy Organization

The basic shape of executive branch energy organization is the concentration of energy policy making within the framework of the White House staff headed by the Energy Resources Council. This council, created in 1974, has a limited life of no more than two years, and if the proposed Department of Energy and Natural Resources is established in the meantime, it will expire upon that establishment. The council, by legislation, consists of the secretary of the Interior, the administrator of the Federal Energy Administration, the administrator of ERDA, the secretary of State and the director of the Office of Management and Budget, plus other officials as designated by the President. The ERC is the focal point of energy policy recommendations to the President, replacing the ad hoc committees and energy czars of the Nixon years.

---

1. All legislation mentioned in this chapter is cited serially in Appendix A.

Budget decisions and legislative proposals are coordinated at the White House level by the Office of Management and Budget. This office, which serves as a direct agent for the President, has extremely broad powers and responsibilities, but has no direct charter for energy matters. Nevertheless, depending upon the incumbent President, it can play a major role in determining energy policy and federal actions in the energy area.

The actual federal operations and programs in energy are carried on by cabinet departments, independent agencies, and regulatory commissions. Many, in fact most, cabinet departments are to some extent concerned with energy issues, and most regulatory agencies are also involved. A count of energy organizations done by the Senate Interior Committee in 1973 identified nineteen such organizations, not counting the separate bureaus and units within each of the cabinet departments. Since the date of that survey, three new agencies have been added to the list—the Nuclear Regulatory Commission, the Energy Research and Development Administration, and the Federal Energy Administration; and three have died—the Atomic Energy Commission, the Office of Emergency Preparedness, and the Office of Science and Technology.

In some of these agencies energy is a matter of major concern on a continuing basis; in others energy questions are more peripheral, though because energy is at the moment a problem at the top of everybody's priority list, the distinction between major and minor involvement appears somewhat arbitrary in some cases. The cabinet departments of Interior, Transportation, Treasury, and Defense have major programs in the energy area. The departments of Agriculture, Justice, State, and Commerce, while they have energy responsibilities, can be assigned a more secondary role in the energy power structure. Of the independent agencies involved, the Federal Energy Administration, the Energy Research and Development Administration, the Nuclear Regulatory Commission, the Environmental Protection Agency, the Federal Power Commission, and the Tennessee Valley Authority have a central concern with energy questions. Other independent agencies with lesser responsibilities include the General Services Administration, the Interstate Commerce Commission, the Council of Economic Advisers, the Federal Trade Commission, and the National Science Foundation.

Department of the Interior

The Department of the Interior is the major cabinet department in the energy field. Its basic responsibilities in energy flow from the responsibility for managing the public lands and the publicly owned energy resources both within the land area of the United States and on the outer continental shelf. Further, the responsibility for managing the water resources west of the Mississippi, which lies with Interior's Bureau of Reclamation, places the department in a strong position with respect to hydropower development, and it markets all federally owned hydroelectric power. The department, acting as trustee for Indian tribes, is also involved in the energy resources on tribal lands. Finally, the scientific agencies of the department are responsible for energy resource analysis and information, and the Bureau of Mines operates the most important energy data system in the federal government.

Two assistant secretaries at the Department of the Interior have primary and major authority in the energy area—the assistant secretary for Land and Water Resources, who oversees the Bureau of Land Management and the Bureau of Reclamation, and the assistant secretary for Energy and Minerals, who oversees the four power administrations, the Geological Survey, the Bureau of Mines, and the Mine Enforcement and Safety Administration. In addition, the assistant secretary for Program Development and Budget, the organization that constitutes the major analytical arm of the department, also has a major influence on energy policy analysis.

The Department of the Interior was created on March 3, 1849, merging the General Land Office, the Office of Indian Affairs, the Pension Office, and the Patent Office. Its energy responsibilities have been established by a long series of congressional acts, some of which give authority to specific bureaus and agencies within the department. Over the years, functions of a housekeeping nature have been removed and other functions have been added, so that now the department is basically the custodian of the nation's mineral and other natural resources.

The Bureau of Land Management manages the publicly owned land and mineral resources. There are many acts that underlie the bureau's statutory responsibility, but the major ones for our purposes here are the Mineral Leasing Act (1920), the General Mining Laws Act (1872), the Outer Continental Shelf Lands Act (1953), the Acquired Lands Mineral Leasing Act (1947), the Multiple Mineral Development Act (1954), and the Geothermal Steam Act (1970).

Under the terms of this legislation, the energy resources owned by the federal government are made available to the economy through a leasing procedure, with the exception of uranium, which is locatable under the mining laws.

The Bureau of Mines was established by an act of May 16, 1910, as an agency to conduct inquiries and scientific and technological investigations into the mining, preparation, treatment, and utilization of minerals and to disseminate information concerning minerals. Its major responsibility in the energy area now is the providing of data. Functions previously performed by the Bureau of Mines in energy research and in coal mine health and safety have been transferred to other agencies as described below.

The weekly, monthly, quarterly, and annual data on energy production and use flow from the Bureau of Mines statistical system. It is not, of course, the only agency involved in the energy data system; but it has historically provided the very basic information concerning energy production and use.

The Geological Survey has two major energy functions. First, it is responsible for the classification and inventory of energy minerals on federal land, and for providing the basic energy resource data about the United States and the world. Second, it has been given responsibility for the regulation of mining on federal lands, including operations on the outer continental shelf.

The Mine Enforcement Safety Administration was broken off from the Bureau of Mines in 1973. The organization took over the administration of the Federal Metal and Nonmetallic Mine Safety Act of 1966 and the Federal Coal Mine Health and Safety Act of 1969. These acts provide for federal inspection and standards of safety in coal and other mines. This agency therefore has an important input into the technologies of coal mining and plays an important role in the cost of such mining.

The Department of the Interior contains four power administrations, each of which is unique. By far the most important from the point of view of energy is the Bonneville Power Administration, which manages and markets the hydroelectric power generated in the Pacific Northwest by the major dams of the Columbia River and its tributaries. The Southwestern and Southeastern Power Administrations are marketing agencies for federally produced power from Bureau of Reclamation and Army Corps of Engineers hydroelectric projects. The Alaska Power Administration is in structure more like Bonneville, in that it manages hydroelectric facilities in Alaska.

There are other Interior agencies which have relatively minor impacts on energy. These include the Bureau of Indian Affairs, which advises the Indians on the management of their energy resources, and the various staff analytical offices of the department which provide advice to the secretary on energy policy matters.

The Federal Energy Administration

The Federal Energy Administration was created first by executive order as the Federal Energy Office and then by act of Congress in the spring of 1974. It has taken over responsibility for energy crisis management from the Department of the Interior and the Office of Emergency Preparedness. From the Interior Department the FEA took the duties and responsibilities of the Office of Oil and Gas, and it has been assigned responsibility for carrying out the functions mandated by the Defense Production Act and the Energy Supply and Environmental Coordination Act. The basic legislation establishing the FEA provided for a life of two years, at the end of which time permanent decisions are to be made with respect to energy organization.

The Federal Energy Administration operates the emergency allocation scheme; controls oil imports under the President's oil import system; has responsibility for developing the conservation program of the federal government; and operates a subsidiary data system based upon the primary data collected by other federal agencies, as well as data collected under its own auspices. Although there is nothing in the law which so requires, the head of the FEA has in practice been the chief line official to whom the President has turned for advice on energy matters.

Energy Research and Development Administration

ERDA was created by the Energy Reorganization Act of 1974. It was established as the central energy research and development agency within the federal government and had transferred to it major portions of the duties of the Atomic Energy Commission, the energy research activities of the Department of the Interior, the solar and geothermal responsibilities of the National Science Foundation, and alternative automotive power systems research from the Environmental Protection Agency. Further, ERDA was given a special assignment with respect to the helium program as it relates to energy, although the program is managed by the Department of the Interior. ERDA became operational on January 19, 1975, and was created in response to an administration proposal for the establishment of a separate R&D agency within the context of the proposed Department of Energy and Natural Resources.

The Regulatory Commissions

There are two major energy regulatory commissions—the Nuclear Regulatory Commission and the Federal Power Commission—and two other commissions that have peripheral impacts on energy, the Federal Trade Commission and the Interstate Commerce Commission.

The Nuclear Regulatory Commission was established by the Energy Reorganization Act of 1974. It took over the regulatory responsibilities previously lodged in the Atomic Energy Commission. This commission exercises basic authority over the licensing and safety of nuclear power stations. In addition, there is an Office of Nuclear Regulatory Research which is to develop studies for the use of the commission in its regulatory activities.

The Federal Power Commission is mainly concerned with the nation's electric power and natural gas industries. Under the authority of the Federal Power Act (1935) and the Natural Gas Act (1938), the commission is responsible for the regulation of rates for wholesale interstate sales for resale, by both electric power companies and natural gas pipeline companies. It also regulates the rates for sales of natural gas by producers to natural gas pipeline companies, and certifies natural gas pipeline companies' facilities for construction.

The Federal Trade Commission and the Interstate Commerce Commission both have limited nonspecific responsibilities in the energy area. The Federal Trade Commission's interest in energy stems from its responsibilities under the antitrust laws. Pursuant to this general authority, the agency investigates significant issues associated with the competitive availability of alternative energy sources. The Interstate Commerce Commission has as its primary role in energy the provision of an adequate supply of railroad hopper cars to those mines upon which the utility companies are dependent for their coal supply. In addition, the commission exercises certain jurisdiction over companies engaged in the interstate transportation of oil and other commodities (except natural gas) by pipeline. Common carrier oil pipelines are subject to the rate and service requirements of the Interstate Commerce Act and to its reporting and accounting requirements. It should be noted, however, that oil pipelines are not subject to the certificate of necessity regulations, or to procedures and regulations concerning abandonment.

Other Concerned Agencies

The Environmental Protection Agency was established under Reorganization Plan No. 3 of 1970, effective December 2, 1970. The agency affects federal energy policy indirectly through its program activities and by setting and enforcing environmental quality standards relative to the use of the various fuels. The major legislation under which the agency establishes standards which influence energy use are the Atomic Energy Act of 1954 relating to radioactive safety, the Clean Air Act as amended, the Federal Water Pollution Control Act as amended, and the National Environmental Policy Act of 1969. In addition to its regulatory functions, the agency also conducts and contracts for research in various areas relating to the provision of clean energy.

The Department of Defense plays a relatively minor role in energy policy formulation, as it is largely a consumer of energy. However, the Army Corps of Engineers is responsible for developing the economic hydropower potential of the nation in the construction of multipurpose water resource projects. The marketing of the resulting power is turned over to the various power administrations of the Department of the Interior. In addition, the Office of Naval Petroleum and Oil Shale Reserves operates the Naval Petroleum Reserves in Elk Hills, California, and in Alaska.

The major energy responsibilities of the Department of Transportation involve public safety in the transportation of fuels. It administers a series of laws having to do with the transportation of explosives and other dangerous articles; it establishes common carrier motor rates under its general authority; and it has specific responsibility for oil pipeline safety and natural gas pipeline safety.

The Treasury Department, because it administers the tax laws of the United States, has major impacts, of course, upon the energy industries, but the department has no specific energy responsibilities. It is worthwhile noting, however, that representatives of the department sit in at top-level energy discussions, at least under the Nixon and Ford administrations.

The Tennessee Valley Authority was established in 1933. Its general purpose is to conduct a program for the use, conservation, and development of natural resources of the Tennessee River drainage basin. The TVA power system is the sole source of electric supply for about six million people in an area of 80,000 square miles covering parts of seven states. The system includes extensive hydroelectric development, and large-scale fossil and nuclear generating plants. The authority is a major buyer of coal in the eastern United States. Although it is of great significance as an energy supplier to its area, it plays a minor role in federal energy policy.

Other cabinet departments which have an effect on energy as part of their major missions are the Department of Agriculture, the Department of Commerce, the Department of Justice, and the Department of State. Since energy is an important industry in this country, a major source of our commodity imports, and a significant factor in our international relations, all these departments have units concerned with energy policy, but they do not have specific legislative authority giving them responsibility in the energy area.

Many other agencies affect energy policy in their own spheres of influence. Among these are the Council of Economic Advisers, the Council on Environmental Quality, the General Services Administration, the National Science Foundation, and others. Some counts of the federal agencies that have an impact on energy have gone as high as sixty-six.

Congressional Energy Organization

There is no clear energy organization within the Congress. When energy legislation is introduced in Congress, it is distributed to committees for hearings and related action. During the Ninety-third Congress, thirteen Senate committees, seventeen House committees, and two joint committees became involved in various aspects of energy legislation. On the Senate side, they were:

Aeronautical and Space Sciences
Agriculture and Forestry
Appropriations
Banking, Housing, and Urban Affairs
Commerce
Finance
Foreign Relations
Government Operations
Interior and Insular Affairs
Judiciary

Labor and Public Welfare
Public Works
Rules and Administration.

The House committees involved were:

Agriculture
Appropriations
Armed Services
Banking and Currency
Education and Labor
Foreign Affairs
Government Operations
House Administration
Interior and Insular Affairs
Interstate and Foreign Commerce
Judiciary
Merchant Marine and Fisheries
Post Office and Civil Service
Public Works
Rules
Science and Astronautics
Ways and Means.

The Joint Committee on Atomic Energy and the Joint Economic Committee were also involved in energy legislature.

There have been substantial changes in the power structure in the House of Representatives since the Ninety-fourth Congress convened in January, 1975. With the retirement of Congressman Wayne Aspinall at the beginning of the Ninety-third Congress, and with the emergence of the Democratic caucus, the effective power in energy has to a certain extent swung away from the traditional committees and has moved toward some younger men. Effective energy policy leadership in the House now lies with Representative Mike McCormack, using the Science and Astronautics Committee as his base; Representative John Dingell, Interstate and Foreign Commerce Committee; Representative Al Ullman, chairman of the House Ways and Means Committee; and Representative Phillip Burton in his role as leader of the House caucus. This is not to say, of course, that the traditional committees do not still exert very great influence; but it is to point out that regardless of the structure of the organization in the legislative branch, very often the real power lies with individuals.

An illustration or two would be useful to lay out the procedure and indicate some of the apparently strange assignments. The Department of the Interior is responsible for administering the outer continental shelf under the OCS Lands Act of 1954. Congressional surveillance of this program has traditionally belonged to the House and Senate Interior and Insular Affairs Committees, which exercise oversight of the Interior Department. In addition, the annual budget has been defended before the Senate and House Appropriations Committees. However, when the administration of and the leasing policy on the outer continental shelf became an important issue, the House Judiciary Committee held a series of hearings on this matter. They exerted jurisdiction on the basis that the Outer Continental Shelf Lands Act, because it dealt with international waters, had originated in the House Judiciary Committee. Another example: since the Constitution provides that all revenue legislation must originate in the House of Representatives, all those aspects of energy policy that relate to taxation, import taxes, or tariffs fall within the primary jurisdiction of the Ways and Means Committee.

Organizational Issues and Problems

The above had made abundantly clear that the energy organization in both the executive and legislative branches is highly fragmented and of an extremely ad hoc nature. Within neither branch is there any organization with continuing chief responsibility for the major aspects of energy policy. The major cost of this situation, in terms of efficiency, is that there is no continuing professional staff devoting themselves to energy matters, to advise the policy makers on the technical and economic aspects of energy policy issues.

This is quite unlike, for example, the situation with respect to tax laws. Congressional groups concerned with tax matters include, in addition to the Ways and Means Committee in the House and the Finance Committee in the Senate, a Joint Committee on Internal Revenue which maintains a staff of experts on the Internal Revenue Code and taxation in general. In the executive branch the responsibility for tax policy is concentrated in the Treasury Department, where a specific Office of Tax Analysis maintains a similar professional staff, and within the Internal Revenue Service there is another professional staff dealing with tax administration.

No similar situation exists in energy. Take, for example, an issue which impinges upon energy supply in a very significant way—the regulation of the prices of natural gas at the wellhead by the Federal Power Commission. On the administration side of this problem there is the Federal Power Commission, which administers the Natural Gas Act; the Department of the Interior, which is responsible for federal leasing of gas, issuing of right-of-way permits for gas pipelines over federal lands, and the health and safety regulation of gas production on federal lands and the outer continental shelf; the Council of Economic Advisers, which is concerned about the impact of deregulation on the problems of inflation and overall levels of economic activity; the Department of Commerce, which is concerned about natural gas availability for industrial users; the Federal Trade Commission, which is concerned about the competitiveness of the natural gas industry; the Environmental Protection Agency, which is concerned about the environmental impact on air quality of the deregulation decision, as well as the National Environmental Policy Act requirements impinging upon the decision; the Departments of State and Treasury, since natural gas is imported from Canada and Mexico, and liquified natural gas from overseas; the Energy Research and Development Administration, since the future price and availability of natural gas have a major impact on the viability of synthetic fuels technology based upon coal; and several others whose interests are more peripheral.

On the congressional side, directly involved are the House and Senate Committees on Interior and Insular Affairs, because of their responsibilities for overseeing the leasing of federal lands including the outer continental shelf, and the Senate and House Committees on Commerce, which have taken primary jurisdiction in this matter since they are the committees which handle the Natural Gas Act. In addition, several other committees in Congress become involved in various aspects of the problem.

Quite obviously in such a situation, many diverse positions with respect to natural gas policy will be developed and require reconciliation at very high levels on a political rather than an analytical basis. Within the Nixon administration, this problem was handled by moving the decision on natural gas to the then existing Energy Committee in the White House. Now the Energy Resources Council would take care of the divergent views within the executive branch and present a proposal to Congress. On the congressional side, both the Senate Commerce Committee and the Interior Committee had their staffs examine the issue and published reports, although the issue is in the former for final action.

One can duplicate this example for every policy issue on energy supply, as within the federal government there is no focus for energy policy in a single responsible agency, with an adequate staff to analyze the widely divergent views coming from the various agencies involved.

Energy Organization Proposals

The issue of organization for energy has been a lively one since 1971. President Nixon that year submitted a proposal for executive reorganization which would have established a Department of Natural Resources as the premiere agency in energy policy within the administration. This plan was modified in 1973 to call for a Department of Energy and Natural Resources, with a separate administration for energy research and development.[2]

Congress has also been very active in the energy organization area since 1971. Series of hearings have been held on the administration proposals and on various alternatives. As a result of these actions, there have been substantial changes in energy organization, the most important of which were the creation of Energy Research and Development Administration, the Energy Resources Council, and the Nuclear Regulatory Commission late in 1974. In addition, the Federal Energy Administration was established in the spring of 1974 with a two-year life. The President has abolished the Office of Emergency Preparedness and the Office of Science and Technology, whose energy-related programs and functions have been distributed throughout the government, principally to the General Services Administration and the National Science Foundation.

The Energy Reorganization Act of 1974 calls for the Energy Resources Council to present to Congress, through the President, a proposal on energy organization by July of 1975. No such proposal has been submitted, and President Ford has simply requested an extention of the life of the Federal Energy Administration. The major issues that must ultimately be faced are:

(1) Should there be a cabinet department primarily devoted to energy or one which covers energy and natural resources?

(2) Should energy research and development be conducted under a separate administration; and if so, should the planning and budgeting of that administration be under its own control or under that of the responsible cabinet department?

2. See Appendix B for relevant documents.

(3) Should there be a permanent council on energy as part of the executive office, similar to the Council of Economic Advisers?

(4) Should the regulatory commissions dealing with energy be consolidated for greater efficiency?

(5) Should there be established within the federal government an organization to explore for, and perhaps develop, the federally owned energy resources of the United States?

An Energy Department?

Should there be a cabinet department with responsibility only for energy, or should energy be included in a department with broader responsibilities for all natural resources?

The administration's proposals have called for a single Department of Energy and Natural Resources. The department proposed by the President would absorb the Department of the Interior; it would also include major portions of the Department of Agriculture; control of the civilian planning operations of the Army Corps of Engineers; and the National Ocean and Atmospheric Administration, the scientific agency in Commerce, which would be combined with the Geological Survey into an administration dealing with the earth and meteorological sciences.

Much of the political opposition to the Department of Energy and Natural Resources stems from the proposal to incorporate into it the planning functions of the Corps of Engineers and the scientific functions of the Department of Commerce. For this reason, serious consideration is being given to a new proposal of substantially less scope, i.e., a department based primarily upon the Interior and Agriculture functions, with no attempt to fold in either NOAA or the Corps of Engineers civilian planning functions.

Conceptually, the cleanest approach would be a comprehensive DENR as proposed in 1973. In addition to having a clear responsibility for natural resources policies and programs, such an organization would bring together the planning functions in water development of the Corps of Engineers and the Bureau of Reclamation, and the pork-barrel aspects of trade-offs that now exist would be minimized.

On the scientific side, there is a great deal to be said for combining the National Ocean and Atmospheric Administration under the same roof as the U.S. Geological Survey. The earth sciences are intimately entwined with the oceans and the atmosphere. Such a reorganization would make possible a higher quality pursuit of the scientific objectives of the federal government.

Nevertheless, the greatest urgency is to establish a clear responsibility for energy policy within a cabinet department. It is only with such a clear assignment that the competitive and diversive nature of energy policy development can be corrected. If the inclusion of the more politically sensitive elements of the reorganization proposal will tend to delay any action, then a case can be made for a more limited plan.

As this chapter is being written, it is not clear what the administration will propose. What is clear is that a substantial reduction in the number of players in the energy policy game is a high order of national priority.

Energy Research and Development

At the time that the Department of Natural Resources was initially proposed, energy and development was conducted by both the Interior Department and the Atomic Energy Commission. The major issue which surfaced early in the 1960s was the relative emphasis on the various energy sources and the division of research funds among them. For a variety of reasons, in part because of friendly cooperation between the Joint Committee on Atomic Energy and the AEC, the bulk of the federal energy R&D budget for many years was given over to nuclear power research, with very little money devoted to coal and minuscule amounts to oil. In the early 1960s this issue was faced by the science adviser to the President, and a report was issued which called for a reexamination of the priorities and an increased effort in fossil-fueled energy research and development. Although this report did have some impact on budget priorities, situations of dual control in both the executive and the legislative branch over energy R&D stategy persisted.

President Nixon, in his proposal for a Department of Natural Resources in 1971, suggested handling this issue by giving the secretary of the Department of Natural Resources control over the research budget of the Atomic Energy Commission. This would have been accomplished by having the AEC submit its research budget proposal through the Department of Natural Resources and by having a senior official in that department responsible for the development of the research strategy.

In 1973 President Nixon retreated from this concept, and proposed a separate energy organization—the Energy Research and Development Administration—which was established by Congress in the fall of 1974.

The question now is whether the separation should be maintained or whether research and development should come back under the auspices of a major cabinet department.

There are two major issues involved: first, the size of the federal budget for energy R&D, and second, the distribution of that budget among the alternative energy research strategies. From a strictly organizational point of view, it appears that the establishment of ERDA has solved the second problem. The trade-offs among competitive energy R&D proposals will now be handled by a single administrator, and he will be responsible for creating an optimum balance of research expenditures.

On the issue of the total size of the research and development budget, it does make a difference whether ERDA will operate under the umbrella of a cabinet department or as an independent agency. If it were part of a cabinet department its budget would be examined within the context of trade-offs between energy R&D and other natural resources programs. Such balancing would have to take place at the Office of Management and Budget if it remained an independent agency, and could not be as adequately staffed as under the alternate proposal.

Council on Energy

The Energy Reorganization Act of 1974 established an organization within the White House, but its members consist of administration and cabinet officers. A proposal introduced by Senate Democrats and being considered in Congress is for an independent council with members appointed by the President and confirmed by the Senate, like the Council of Economic Advisers.

This proposal, in a sense, competes with that for a Department of Energy and Natural Resources. If energy policy is made the primary responsibility of a major cabinet office, then there is little to be gained and much to be lost by establishing a competitive organization in the same policy area advising the President independently. However, if the creation of the DENR is not in the cards, the proposed energy council has much to recommend it over the Energy Resources Council that now exists, because that organization cannot build up an adequate professional staff to guide policy makers. The actual analytical studies will be done within the organizations of the Council members, and the White House group cannot attract and maintain a highly competent, highly professional staff. However, an energy council patterned after the Council of Economic Advisers could do precisely that; thus, whether or not the creation of such a group is a valid proposal depends upon how Congress reacts to the establishment of a Department of Energy and Natural Resources. If DENR is established, there will be a continuing need for an ERC of the present mold in the White House, to coordinate the department's interest in energy and natural resources with those of the other cabinet departments and independent agencies.

The Regulatory Commissions

As indicated earlier, there are two major regulatory commissions dealing with energy, and the issue is whether they should be reorganized into one body for greater efficiency. A similar situation existed before the Atomic Energy Commission was dismantled, and a study of the pros and cons of combining it with the Federal Power Commission was prepared at the request of the White House by Commissioner William O. Doub of the AEC. The study concluded with the recommendation that consolidation be carried out, but this proposal was superseded by the Energy Reorganization Act, which established the Nuclear Regulatory Commission.

Fundamentally, there is no reason to believe that the problems of nuclear safety are related to the pricing of natural gas. The problems of the regulatory commissions flow from the inherent difficulties of regulating economic markets in the case of natural gas, rather than from diverse responsibilities and overlapping jurisdictions in the two commissions. There appears to be no overwhelming increase in efficiency to be derived from combining them. Moreover, neither commission has played a major role in determining energy policy. Thus, if energy policy is clearly made the responsibility of a cabinet department, there appears to be no reason for further consolidation in the regulatory area.

Government Energy Corporation

There is a substantial move in the Congress in 1975 to change the basic system under which the United States develops its federally owned energy resources. As explained in the chapter in this book on federal leasing, such resources are now developed by private industry under leases granted largely on a competitive basis. Some members of Congress are seriously considering the establishment of a federal corporation to develop at least a part of these resources and to explore the unproven lands prior to leasing them. The philosophy is that the federal government can then establish a yardstick for pricing and costs, can directly control the exploitation of the resources, and can take the economic rents thereon for society as a whole.

This issue is, of course, much larger than one of organization. It would involve a fundamental change in the institutions surrounding the development of the federally owned resources on the outer continental shelf and of the coal resources in the west.

Overview of Energy Organization

The previous sections have described the existing organization for energy in the federal government and looked at some of the emerging issues. However, it would be very easy to overestimate the importance of organization to national energy policy making. Each President, in fact, establishes a method of operation which relies heavily on trusted advisers regardless of the organizational structure. For example, at this writing President Ford clearly is depending upon Frank Zarb as his major adviser on energy, although the chairman of the Energy Resources Council is the titular head of the energy policy organization. This situation is, of course, not unique to energy. Henry Kissinger ran the foreign policy of the United States from his position as national security adviser to President Nixon and has continued to run it as secretary of State.

However, there are now important shortcomings in organization which should not be overlooked. The two most central elements now lacking are clear assignment of responsibility and the providing of adequate policy staff resources. The need for the former is obvious—the current situation clearly demonstrates the dangers of not accepting it. The second need is for continuity in dealing with the complex issues of energy, which only a professional staff can provide. As William Johnson points out in his chapter on crisis mangement in this volume, a major problem with the Federal Energy Organization was its lack of energy expertise. A high-level professional staff in energy cannot be developed in quick response to a crisis or within the context of a temporary agency. The development of such a staff requires a firm foundation in an established agency that can provide promotion opportunities and positions of prestige and power to career civil servants. The current energy organization of the federal government militates strongly against the development of such a staff. On the contrary, it clearly emphasizes the duplication of staff efforts in competing organizations and the generation of instant staffs containing instant experts in response to shifting responsibilities.

Organizational effectiveness could thus be improved if the government were restructured along the following lines:

(1) Within the executive branch, a cabinet-level department with major responsibility in energy and other natural resources should be created. The energy problem is currently the most severe problem in natural resources, but it differs only in degree, not in kind, from the general problem of managing nonrenewable natural resources. Data systems and expertise that apply to the energy area are transferrable to the other commodity areas, and great efficiencies in staffing and data collection can be brought about by combining all natural resources under single cabinet-level department. Therefore, something like the Department of Energy and Natural Resources is a preferable solution for the executive branch.

In order to facilitate trade-offs between short- and long-run problems, the Energy Research and Development Administration should be a part of that department, not an independent agency. There are major advantages in getting the federal funding trade-offs balanced prior to submission of budgets to the Office of Management and Budget. Such a system reduces the conflicts at the level of the total budget and permits more competent staff management of these decisions.

(2) On the legislative side, there is need for a Joint Committee on Energy and Natural Resources to replace the Joint Committee on Atomic Energy. Such a joint committee, which would have subject matter responsibility for natural resource issues and policy, could develop a professional staff and provide expert advise to Congress in this most complicated area. This committee, however, should not replace the Senate and House committees in overseeing the Department of Energy and Natural Resources or appropriations. It should function like the Joint Economic Committee and the Joint Committee on Internal Revenue, as a professional committee looking at substantive issues, not at organization and management.

Conclusions

Organizations can make a job easier or harder to accomplish, but there is no simple optimum way to organize for a job. The energy organization of the federal government has made the job of energy management harder, rather than easier. Moves to centralize energy and natural resources responsibilities, to formalize the coordinate process within the White House structure, and to provide Congress with a professional staff, can make the formation of energy policy more rational and the performance of energy programs more efficient. This is the end result we should seek.

Appendix A
Legislative Citations in Order Cited in Text

1. Energy Reorganization Act of 1974—Public Law 93–438.
2. Department of Interior, 1849—9 Stat. 395; 43 USC 1451.
3. Mineral Leasing Act of 1920—261–263, 283–286 30 USC 181 *et seq.*
4. General Mining Laws Act, 1872—30 USC 21 *et seq.*
5. Outer Continental Shelf Lands Act, 1953—43 USC Seds. 1331 *et seq.*
6. Acquired Lands Mineral Leasing Act of 1947—30 USC 351–359.
7. Multiple Mineral Development Act, 1954—30 USC 521.
8. Geothermal Steam Act of 1970—30 USC 1001 *et seq.*
9. Organization Act of Bureau of Mines, 1910–30 USC §§ 1,3,5–7.
10. Organization Act of Geological Survey, 1879—43 USC 31(a).
11. Federal Metal and Nonmetallic Mine Safety Act, 1966—30 USC §§ 721–740.
12. Federal Coal Mine Health and Safety Act of 1969—30 USC §§ 801–878, 951–960.
13. Federal Energy Administration Act of 1974—Public Law 93–275.
14. Defense Production Act of 1950—50 USC app. 2061–2166.
15. Energy Supply and Environmental Coordination Act of 1974.
16. Federal Power Act, 1935—16 USC 79(a) 825r.
17. Natural Gas Act, 1938—15 USC 717–717w.
18. Atomic Energy Act of 1954—42 USC Secs. 2073, 2092, 2111, 2133, 2134.
19. Clean Air Act of 1970—42 USC 1857–1857L.
20. Federal Water Pollution Control Act as amended, 1972—Public Law 92–500, 86 Stat. 816.
21. National Environmental Policy Act of 1969—42 USC 4321–4347.
22. Naval Petroleum Reserve Act of 1920—10 USC 7421–7438.
23. Explosives and Other Dangerous Articles, 1948—18 USC 831–835; USC 834.
24. Natural Gas Pipeline Safety Act of 1968—49 USC 1671–1684.
25. Tennessee Valley Authority Act of 1933—16 USC §§ 831–831dd.

Appendix B

1. Office of Science and Technology, Executive Office of the President, *Energy R and D and National Progress* (Washington: U.S. Government Printing Office, 1964), 437 pages.
2. The White House, *Papers Relating to the President's Departmental*

Reorganization Program (Washington: U.S. Government Printing Office, March 1971), 288 pages.

3. ——, *Papers Relating to the President's Departmental Reorganization Program—Revised* (Washington: U.S. Government Printing Office, February 1973), 311 pages.

4. United States Congress, House of Representatives, Government Operations Committee, Hearings, HR 9090, July 24, 25, 26, 31, August 1, 1973, 284 pages.

5. ——, Senate Interior Committee Print, *History of Federal Energy Organization*, Serial No. 93–19 (92–54), 1973, 59 pages.

6. ——, Senate Interior Committee Print, *Legislative Authority of Federal Agencies with Respect to Fuels and Energy*, Serial No. 93–2 (92–37), 1973, 236 pages.

14

Beyond the Crisis: Transitional, Efficient, and Ultimate Resources

Nicolai Timenes, Jr.

The typical planning horizon for energy projections and policy since the early 1970s has been the year 1985. Prior to the autumn 1973 oil embargo imposed by the Organization of Petroleum Exporting Countries (OPEC), the popular focus had been on business as usual. The embargo itself shortened, rather than lengthened, that perspective. It is difficult to consider events toward the end of the century while sitting in a queue at the local gas station. The most comprehensive recent analysis of the nation's energy future, the Project Independence Report,[1] concerns itself principally with events through 1985. Concern with what some would call the short term is legitimate, given the pressing nature of the nation's energy problems and the important influence of near-term energy considerations on the economy, employment, and the inflation rate.

Nevertheless, the present situation is largely the result of trends in energy policy and in exhaustion of traditional resources which have long histories. Also, decisions made today will determine the shape of the nation's energy markets in the next decade and possibly the options available for the years beyond as well. One need only consider the long lead times involved in implementing the most immediate decisions: eight to ten years for construction of a nuclear power plant, three to five years to open a new coal mine, three to five years to develop a new field on the outer continental shelf, and perhaps longer to bring that field to near full production. Similarly, much has been made of the potential of new and emerging technologies. However, research is a time-consuming, sequential process; implementation of fruits of research on a large scale requires

1. Federal Energy Administration (FEA), *Project Independence, A Summary* (Washington: U.S. Government Printing Office, November 1974).

time, the commitment of significant resources, and perhaps institutional change as well.

There is a small but increasing literature on the analysis of alternative energy futures beyond 1985. Some analyses (those prepared for the Club of Rome, for example) serve to alert the public to future dangers, such as exhaustion of traditional resources and rise in pollution levels or other undesirable effects.[2] Some are designed to show the impact of new sources or the future market penetration of existing sources (many of the Project Independence studies fall into this category). Still others seek to show the potential impact of alternative strategies, often with a clear preference for a particular strategy. (The report of the Ford Foundation's energy policy project is appropriately entitled "Exploring Energy Choices." [3]) Each of these studies has an underlying ethic, at least implicitly. In some instances, the underlying assumption is that the maintenance of environmental quality is the highest objective of energy policy; in others, the maintenance of a stable economy or continuation or improvement of material life-styles is the desideratum. Whatever the objective, all such studies share a common conclusion: that projection of past trends is a poor way to predict likely futures.

Many future projections (those cited are among the least guilty) suggest or advertise solutions in terms of nontraditional energy sources which are claimed to be cheap, plentiful, harmless to the environment, and so forth. Fusion and solar energy are frequent subjects of such laudatory treatment. Many analyses of alternative futures also imply fundamental changes in the underlying forces and institutions that shape energy markets.

It is the thesis of this chapter that the future is not deterministic. The futurist who argues, for example, that by the year 2000 solar energy will provide 40 percent of all home heating in the United States indulges in rhetoric to make a point. It is not correct to say "will" in this context; rather, one means "could" or "should," or perhaps both. The futurist

2. Donella H. Meadows, Dennis L. Meadows, Jorgen Randers, and William W. Behrens, III, *The Limits to Growth: A Report for the Club of Rome's Project on the Predicament of Mankind* (New York: Potomac Associates/Universe Books, 1972). Technical description of the underlying models is contained in Dennis L. Meadows, William W. Behrens, III, Donella H. Meadows, Roger Naill, and Erick Zahn, *Dynamics of Growth in a Finite World* (Cambridge, Mass.: Wright-Allen, 1974).

3. "Exploring Energy Choices: A Preliminary Report of the Ford Foundation's Energy Policy Project" (Washington: The Ford Foundation, 1974).

deals in conjecture, makes assumptions, and shows the consequences of those assumptions.

But what if other assumptions prove to be the ones adopted by society or resulting from research?

The point is, we do have choices. We will be able to exercise those choices over the next decade or so, and the actions taken in that decade will strongly influence the shape of the nation's energy markets through the end of the century.

The critical questions for making those choices include the following. What futures are possible, in the sense of what sort of energy markets or mixes of supplies and demand are feasible? Which of these should we strive to obtain, based on some value system which balances economic, environmental, quality of life, and equity considerations? What resources can we tap? How will technology aid in achieving the nation's long-range energy goals? How will the alternative futures be determined, in two senses: (1) what models best represent the relevant institutions, and (2) what institutions and mechanisms will be employed? What changes in life-style will be acceptable? And, finally, and perhaps most important, how will these issues be decided and who will decide them? This chapter attempts to address these questions.

The use of energy resources has followed a classical pattern of discovery, understanding, development, exhaustion, and abandonment. While some energy resources, such as wood and hydroelectric power, are clearly renewable at least up to some point, nevertheless their importance has tended to shrink in the face of limitations in total energy potential and rapidly rising energy consumption.

To consider how such patterns might change in the future, it is worthwhile to review the status of the various potential energy resources and technologies in four categories, which may be termed traditional sources, transitional technologies, efficient technologies, and ultimate technologies.

These categories may be defined by the state of knowledge and extent of implementation or development to date. By any of these criteria, coal, oil, natural gas, and hydroelectric power are traditional sources. It also follows that the economics of these resources are proven. These are also the resources—particularly oil and gas—whose growth potential is limited.

The remaining three classes are only beginning to be tapped. Significant technological and economic questions attend development of transitional technologies although it is clear that each is at least technically feasible. Nuclear fission is included here, not so much because of economic uncertainties as because it has only begun to make a significant contribution to the nation's energy supplies. Geothermal technologies and those that produce synthetic fuels from coal and from oil shale are also in this category. More work is needed to demonstrate their economic viability and their technical applicability to a broad variety of resources. These technologies may, however, be expected to be the first to supplement traditional sources. Their resource targets are largely untapped, but still clearly finite.

A third category, here dubbed efficient technologies, includes those whose application is more remote and for which there are yet significant technical and economic uncertainties. Included here are the nuclear breeder reactors, particularly the liquid metal fast breeder reactor which is now the subject of intensive research, and advanced power cycles such as magnetohydrodynamics for generation of electric power from fossil fuels. In each case, the efficient technologies offer promise of extracting much more of the heating values of fixed resources than do the nearer-term transitional technologies.

All the technologies in the first three groups, however, must draw on existing resources which, while perhaps not yet adequately measured, are known to be finite. (A possible exception is geothermal resources, although there is some evidence that they can be drawn down locally.) The fourth group of technologies, here called ultimate technologies, includes those which offer promise of liberating energy supplies from difficult resource constraints. Several of these are often termed the "exotic" sources. The most important are nuclear fusion, which offers the potential of deriving massive amounts of energy from minute amounts of deuterium and tritium, which are components of sea water, and solar energy, in which the power of the sun is harnessed directly to do useful work. The limits upon implementation of these technologies—other than the economic—are perhaps less obvious than the limitations on other, more traditional sources.

It will be useful to consider each of these groups in turn. Despite abundant reserves, the consumption of coal has declined as a fraction of total consumption, sinking to 17.9 percent in 1973.[4] The position of coal in

4. U.S. Bureau of Mines, press release, "U.S. Energy Use Up Nearly 5 Percent in 1973," March 13, 1974 [source for this and other 1973 energy use statistics].

the nation's energy markets has been eroded by a number of factors: through the early 1970s comparatively low prices for imported oil, convenience and economics in home heating, and, toward the end of the 1960s, rising costs and declining productivity associated with implementation of health and safety standards in a chronically dangerous occupation and, finally, imposition of stringent air quality standards. Per unit of energy, combustion of coal releases more oxides of sulfur and particulate matter into the atmosphere than that of any other fuel. Sixty-five percent of the coal consumed in the United States in 1973 was consumed by electric utilities to generate power. One-third was used in industry, and only 2.2 percent in other applications. Even in the electric utility industry, there has been a trend away from combustion of coal and toward increased consumption of fuel oil, as a means of reducing air pollution.

Together, oil and gas accounted for 77.1 percent of the nation's energy consumption in 1973. As oil and gas are often found in the same geologic provinces, or are even associated in the same deposits, the consumption and supply of these resources are closely linked. Both are now seen to be in short supply domestically.

Considerable controversy attends the extent of such resources. For example, estimates of the crude oil and natural gas resources of the United States as of December 31, 1970, prepared by the U.S. Geological Survey, show 2,892 billion barrels of which 52 billion were recoverable and identified. These are among the highest estimates of resources published anywhere.[5] However, only 450 billion of the 2,550 billion barrels of undiscovered resources were estimated to be economically recoverable. Forty-seven percent of these were estimated to be offshore. A recent report by a committee of the National Academy of Engineering,[6] adopting a different estimation technique, reached a conclusion of much smaller reserves, at least in onshore provinces. Shortly after that report, the Geologic Survey released new estimates—prepared using different techniques—which are now among the lowest published.[7]

Until there has been much more exploration, especially in the less de-

5. P. K. Theobald, S. P. Schweinfurth, and D. C. Duncan, "Energy Resources of the United States," Geological Survey Circular 650 (Washington, 1972).

6. "Mineral Resources and the Environment: A Report prepared by the Committee on Mineral Resources and the Environment (COMRATE), Commission on Natural Resources, National Research Council" (Washington: National Academy of Sciences, February 1975).

7. Betty M. Miller, and others, "Geological Estimates of Undiscovered Recoverable Oil and Gas Resources in the United States," Geological Survey Circular 725 (Washington, 1975).

veloped areas, this debate must remain academic. The trends, however, are clear: with current consumption of petroleum products in excess of 6 billion barrels per year, reserves, and then resources, of petroleum economically recoverable using current technology will be exhausted within a matter of decades.

It is the nature of this exhaustion which is at issue. The optimists claim that the combination of technological advances and the functioning of market mechanisms will cause additions to supply, constraints to demand, and efficient allocation of the available resources in such a fashion that the transition away from dependence on oil and gas will be smooth. The pessimists suggest that the finiteness of the oil and gas resources, together with imperfections of market and other institutional mechanisms, may combine to cause precipitate changes and painful dislocations, such as those suggested by the systems dynamics models.[8]

The heavy dependence on fluid hydrocarbons of the nation's energy economy, coupled with increasing reliance on imports and the insecurity of those imports, has led to sentiments for shifts away from oil and gas consumption as a policy objective. "Project Independence" and other energy initiatives are, in essence, designed to steer the economy away from increasing dependence on imported oil and toward other fuels and reduced consumption.

While the situation with respect to natural gas may be less visible because it is less tied to developments on the international scene, it is nonetheless quite similar. Because the interstate natural gas market is regulated by the Federal Power Commission, some instances of scarcity have been met through curtailments of certain industrial and other large-scale uses. Although such curtailments are perhaps less obvious to the individual consumer than some other methods would be, they are nonetheless good indicators of a market out of balance and of a declining resource.

Hydroelectric power is environmentally and economically appealing; essentially no pollutants are emitted into the air, there is no radiation hazard, there may be relatively little water quality impact, and operating costs are low. Nevertheless, some 36.5 percent of the existing potential hydroelectric power in the United States has already been developed,[9] and provides less than 4 percent of the energy consumed in the United

8. E.g., Meadows et al., *Limits to Growth.*
9. Federal Power Commission, "Hydroelectric Power Resources of the United States, Developed and Undeveloped, January 1, 1972."

States. Thus we can expect little significant additional help from hydro-electric power.

It is now appropriate to turn to the transitional technologies, those for which technological and economic uncertainties remain, but which are technically feasible and tap large existing resources. The nation's resources of coal and oil shale are still very large relative both to current consumption and to other resources.[10] The problem is that combustion of coal in the traditional form may be environmentally unacceptable, and that oil has yet to be produced from shale on a large scale.

There are several approaches to developing clean fuels from coal. First, and in a sense most obvious, is to clean up the effluents from the coal combustion process. A variety of add-on processes for control of air pollutant emissions and effluents to the water are being developed. A lively debate surrounds their reliability and economics. Although at least one widely distributed report asserts that stack gas cleaning systems could, indeed, be reasonably and reliably employed in the near future,[11] further research on refinements of existing processes and development of new processes is underway; yet there is no rush to adopt stack gas cleaning technology. The reasons are at least in part institutional: electric utilities have long been inherently conservative and risk averse, loath to embark on ventures that offer anything but the highest level of reliability.

While add-on control for stack gas cleaning is likely to be employed to at least some extent in the coming decades, add-on technologies tend to be, in the long run, unsatisfactory. Thus research is directed toward developing fuels or processes that are inherently clean. Such an investigation is current research on fluidized-bed combustion. In this process, crushed coal is burned in a bed of ash and limestone that is "fluidized" with air. The limestone reacts with the oxides of sulfur that result from coal combustion to form a solid, which may be disposed of with the ash from combustion or may be regenerated, producing elemental sulfur or tractable sulfur compounds, thus reducing air pollution problems in the combustion of coal.

New methods of burning coal directly for electricity or process heat

10. Theobald et al., "Energy Resources."

11. Final Report: Sulfur Oxide Control Technology Assessment Panel (SOCTAP) on Projected Utilization of Stack Gas Cleaning Systems by Steam-Electric Plants, submitted to the Federal Interagency Committee: Evaluation of State Air Implementation Plans, April 15, 1973. Another review of the state of research is contained in James T. Dunham, Carl Rampacek, and T. A. Henrie, "High-Sulfur Coal for Generating Electricity," *Science,* April 19, 1974, pp. 346–351.

will be of little comfort to the household, commercial, and transportation sectors that now consume 45 percent of the nation's energy. These sectors rely heavily on oil and gas, and automobiles and other capital investments may not be readily convertible to other energy forms. For this reason, the conversion of coal into synthetic gases and liquids become attractive. So, too, do oil and gas made from oil shale.

Technologies to produce oil and gas from coal and shale have been known for many years. The basic chemistry of development of synthetic fuels from coal involves combining the carbon (C) in coal with hydrogen (H) to form methane (CH_4) gas or other combustible gases or liquids. In the process, any impurities present in the coal can usually be taken out for convenient disposal. Large-scale production of synthetic fuels from coal has occurred in various places around the world since about 1910, with particular application in economies under considerable pressure and with limited indigenous resources of oil and gas—such as prewar Germany.[12] Coal is now being gasified in Turkey, India, South Africa, Scotland, Morocco, Yugoslavia, and Korea.[13]

Synthetic fuels from coal and oil shale have not, in the past, been competitive with oil and gas from traditional domestic sources or with imports. That situation may be changing; for example, the estimates for Project Independence suggest that oil from shale might well be competitive at oil prices of $11 per barrel, although not at $7 per barrel. If the oil producing cartel continues its current policy of maintaining world oil prices at the higher levels, then a synthetic fuels industry may quite possibly emerge. The major stumbling block to implementation, aside from the level of price, is the expected stability of that price. Inasmuch as these world oil prices are many times the cost of production and delivery, the producing countries have the option of lowering them, thus rendering synthetic fuels production uneconomic.

Various steps, including oil import quotas and guaranteed purchase agreements, have been suggested as means of ensuring development of a synthetic fuels industry. With the heightened awareness of vulnerability arising from the 1973 embargo, it is possible that the government may make some such incentive or guarantee available and foster the creation

12. Federal Energy Administration, ''Project Independence Blueprint, Final Task Force Report: Synthetic Fuels from Coal,'' prepared under direction of the U.S. Department of the Interior, (Washington: U.S. Government Printing Office, November 1974).

13. Arthur M. Squires, ''Clean Fuels from Coal Gasification,'' *Science,* April 19, 1974, pp. 340–346.

of a synthetic fuels industry a matter of public policy. Several proposals to provide federal incentives for synthetic fuel commercialization came before the Congress in 1975 and 1976.

Synthetic fuels from oil shale are a particularly interesting possibility. Resources of oil shale in the United States are vast, compared with resources of traditional oil and gas and with national consumption.[14] Until quite recently, shale oil was considered marginal in terms of economic recoverability. Some 80 billion barrels have been estimated to be recoverable at prices of $4–$5 per barrel—although those price estimates are now almost certainly too low. These deposits are concentrated in Colorado, Utah, and Wyoming, and are in the comparatively rare shales yielding thirty gallons or more of oil per ton. After several unsuccessful attempts to interest industry in developing oil shale over the years, the Department of the Interior in 1974 leased four tracts on the public lands in Colorado and Utah for very large initial bonus payments, possibly signaling the beginning of an at least modest shale oil industry, although subsequent events have suggested a tempering of enthusiasm.

Major problems stand in the way of the development of a synthetic fuels industry. Removal of uncertainties concerning world oil prices may reveal the importance of other constraints to synthetic fuels production, such as rapidly rising estimates of cost, potential environmental impact at the points of extraction and conversion, and competing demands for water in arid regions. The major attractive deposits of both coal and oil shale are on public lands in the West. Coal gasification, coal liquefaction, and oil shale are very large consumers of water. Water is comparatively scarce in the West, and there are increasingly pressing demands for the available supplies. Also, many of these technologies are still comparatively inefficient in their use of the total heating value within the coal and shale. Disposal of massive quantities of spent shale is a special concern.

Geothermal energy is another potential transitional source. Geothermal "hot spots"—areas in which the earth's heat is available particularly close to the surface—occur throughout the country, but are most prevalent in the West.[15] Although the extent and nature of geothermal resources is as yet poorly understood, there are commercial applications of geothermal energy at several points throughout the world, including the

14. Theobald et al., "Energy Resources."

15. L. H. Godwin, L. B. Haigler, R. L. Rioux, D. E. White, L. J. P. Muffler, and R. G. Wayland, "Classification of Public Lands Valuable for Geothermal Steam and Associated Geothermal Resources," Geological Survey Circular 647 (Washington, 1971).

Geysers in California. In most instances these facilities make use of "dry steam" resources; the employment of more prevalent, lower temperature hot water systems, some of which include high concentrations of corrosive salts, poses serious technical and economic problems.

Finally, we may also consider nuclear fission to be a transition technology. The current generation of light water reactors uses a few percent of the energy in the uranium feed. The uranium feedstock is used once, and the radioactive wastes from the process pose grave waste disposal problems. Despite a modest amount of reprocessing, the Project Independence Report, based on estimates by the Atomic Energy Commission, predicts that by 1985 existing and planned nuclear power plants will have consumed 352,000 tons of U_3O_8 (uranium ore). The Atomic Energy Commission estimates that the United States has 520,000 tons of uranium reserves producible at a cost of $15 per pound or less, and an additional one million tons of potential resources producible at that price. While improvements in efficiency may be anticipated and additional resources may be made available at higher costs, it is clear that uranium resources are not inexhaustible in terms of the current fuel cycle.

Thus, it is important to consider the promise of efficient technologies. These are, generally, technologies which may be employable to extend the life of existing resources such as uranium, coal, and oil shale.

Perhaps the most interesting and controversial possibilities in this area are breeder reactors for nuclear power plants. Most uranium occurs naturally in the form of U-238. The U-235 isotope, which occurs naturally as 0.7 percent of natural uranium, is the basic nuclear fuel. Thus total energy recovery from current reactor systems is limited to about 2 percent or less of that potentially available from natural uranium. A breeder reactor is one that produces another isotope which can, in turn, be used as a fuel. The liquid metal fast breeder reactor (LMFBR) would be expected to produce enough plutonium Pu-239 after ten or fifteen years of operation to provide start-up fuel for another reactor of comparable size. Current estimates are that an extensive breeder reactor economy could lead to the use of 60 percent or more of the total energy in uranium.[16] If successful, then, breeder reactor research could imply perhaps a thirtyfold increase in our effective resources for nuclear fission. The objections that have been raised focus on potential risks to public health and safety and

16. U.S. Atomic Energy Commission, "Proposed Final Environmental Impact Statement: Liquid Metal Fast Breeder Reactor Program" (WASH-1535) (Washington, December 1974).

the potential availability of less costly and more environmentally acceptable alternatives.[17]

Somewhat less spectacular increases in efficiency of use of indigenous resources may result from the so-called advanced power cycles. Magnetohydrodynamics, in which fossil fuels are heated to become plasmas, and the electric power derived directly from the plasma, may ultimately yield efficiencies of up to 60 percent of the energy content of fossil fuels, compared with perhaps 40 percent for the most efficient modern steam electric generating plants.

The LMFBR, magnetohydrodynamics, and other advanced power cycles are the subject of continuing federal research. A major commitment has been made to the LMFBR, involving hundreds of millions of dollars in research monies per year. Given the major technical problems which must be overcome, commercialization of neither the LMFBR nor magnetohydrodynamics is expected before the early 1990s. The schedule for research, development, and implementation of breeder technology has been the subject of a particularly vigorous debate, the outcome of which is far from clear.

The traditional, transitional, and efficient resources just described may help extend the life of known resources well beyond the horizon of current concerns but not, perhaps, beyond the lifetime of children born today. Thus, the search for what we may call ultimate sources. These are the energy sources with potential for removing energy markets from the constraints of clearly finite resources.

The prospect of solar energy has begun to capture the public imagination. Collecting the heat energy which falls upon the earth each day from the sun and converting it to useful work promises, like hydroelectric power, to be an endlessly renewable process. The Project Independence review of the question concluded that six technologies have been proven technically feasible: (1) solar heating and cooling of buildings; (2) solar thermal conversion, by which the heat from solar energy is transferred to a working fluid to generate electricity; (3) wind energy (highly efficient windmills); (4) conversion of solar energy to the production of plant biomass (organic matter) and the subsequent conversion of this biomass to a variety of fuels; (5) harnessing the thermal gradients which occur naturally in the ocean to produce electric power; and, finally, (6) use of photovoltaic electric power systems to convert incident solar energy directly

17. *Ibid.*

to electricity. Of these, solar heating and cooling of buildings and the use of windmills seem closest to useful application. The Project Independence Report suggests that as much as 1.5×10^{15} BTUs of equivalent fossil fuels could be produced from solar heating and cooling systems by 1990, and 2×10^{15} BTUs by wind conversion by that date, with possible additional contributions from some of the more remote technologies as well.[18] This could amount to as much as 2.4 percent of total U.S. demand in that year. For such results to be achieved, an aggressive research and development program must be successful, and appropriate incentives must be introduced for the implementation of the new technologies.

Limitations thus far have included problems of storing solar energy; its incidence on the earth does not usually conform to the pattern of energy requirements, thus necessitating batteries, heat sinks, or other energy storage devices which add to system expense. Photovoltaic conversion has been successfully applied in the space program, where irregularities of energy supply due to atmospheric interference do not obtain. Photovoltaic cells, though readily available, are extremely expensive for large-scale application. Important questions have also been raised about the area required for the collection of solar energy necessary to match the levels of electricity consumption to which the nation has become accustomed.

Controlled nuclear fusion is another important potential source of virtually inexhaustible power. The current nuclear power systems—and the breeder reactor systems referred to above—derive their energy from splitting a large atom into neutrons and other light nuclei. In these cases, the sum of the masses of the products is less than the mass of the original large nucleus, and the difference is converted to energy. That energy—or some portion of it—can then be captured and converted to do useful work.

In the fusion process, the opposite occurs. Two nuclei are fused together to form a larger nucleus and other products. In certain cases, the mass of the products is less than the sum of the masses of the constituent parts, and again the energy may be converted to do useful work. In order for fusion to occur, the colliding nuclei must be brought together—and this is the source of the problems which are now the focus of so much research. The nuclei are accelerated to the plasma state and must be confined long enough for reactions to take place. Experiments are being con-

18. Federal Energy Administration, "Project Independence Blueprint, Final Task Force Report: Solar Energy" (Washington: U.S. Government Printing Office, November 1974).

ducted with a variety of magnetic and laser devices, and basic problems of physics and engineering involving high temperatures and pressures, intense magnetic fields, and so forth, remain to be solved. If those problems can be solved and technical feasibility of controlled fusion demonstrated by, say, the early 1980s, then fusion reactions could begin to provide commercial-scale electric power in the early 1990s.[19] Fusion processes could use as a fuel deuterium, a natural isotope which constitutes 0.015 percent of the hydrogen present on earth—for example, in sea water. While literally finite, the deuterium, and hence fusion, resources are in effect inexhaustible.

Development of technologies will have a strong influence on the shape of the nation's future energy markets. As was noted in the preceding section, only the traditional sources employ technologies whose economics and reliability are fully known. It is known that each of the transition technologies will work—that synthetics can be made from coal and oil shale and that geothermal power can be harnessed (at least in the case of dry steam). However, whether these technologies can profitably be applied to a broad range of resources on a large scale has yet to be proven. The energy produced by these resources is almost certain to be expensive by recent and current standards. Far less certain, at present, are the economics of the efficient technologies. While they may be efficient in terms of use of the resource, they are as yet many years away from commercial implementation. Further, research in these areas is likely to become increasingly expensive. Finally, the technical feasibility of the ultimate technologies—especially nuclear fusion—has yet to be proven.

Research in these areas will not be cheap. The costs are so vast, in some cases, as to be beyond the capacity of the private sector to absorb. For example, the Energy Research and Development Administration has asked for $392 million for research on nuclear fusion in fiscal year 1977, alone; this research has been underway for many years but will become more expensive as installations come closer to commercial scale.

The federal government has recognized that, if such research is to be done in a timely fashion, federal funding will be required. Accordingly, energy research has increased severalfold in recent years. Clearly, the budget process will influence the availability of technologies for the pri-

19. U.S. Atomic Energy Commission, "Draft Environmental Statement: TOKAMAK Fission Test Reactor Facilities, Princeton Plasma Physics Laboratory, Princeton, New Jersey" (WASH-1544) (Washington, January 1975).

vate sector to implement. One choice in particular deserves careful attention: that of the liquid metal fast breeder reactor. There are many alternative approaches to constructing breeder reactors. Selection of the LMFBR for intensive research not only preempts the available research funds, but virtually ensures that, if LMFBR research is successful, that technology, rather than others, will be the one implemented in the first generation of breeders. Alternative approaches will simply not have received the funding required to bring them to the same state of development.

Federal research in nuclear power was an outgrowth of weapons development. Civilian reactor technology also benefited from work on reactors for naval vessels. Until recently, federal support of research on nonnuclear energy has been modest. Research by the Bureau of Mines on oil shale retorting in the 1940s and 1950s is a cornerstone of current oil shale technology—but the funds for those research efforts never exceeded a few million dollars per year.

With the government doing the research and owning many of the important resources—notably oil shale and western coals—and increasing public dissatisfaction with the nation's energy situation, there are increasing calls for yet heavier government involvement in energy. The use of controls, subsidies, or institutional mechanisms such as government corporations could all add further to the impact of federal action on the nation's energy market.

Various models have been suggested for predicting the nation's energy future. Those most popularly used fall into three broad categories: (1) projections of past trends; (2) restricted projections, taking into account certain important limiting factors; and (3) economic models which reflect certain balancing mechanisms.

For many years, projections seemed appropriate. Demand continued to grow in a reasonably well behaved fashion which could be shown to be related to population, gross national product, and certain other key indicators. A principal characteristic of projection models was their expectation that energy prices, and in particular relative prices, would continue in historic patterns. The fruits of technology were such that energy prices generally tended to decline, and thus to stimulate growth in demand. An example of this point of view is the 1970 National Power Survey of the Federal Power Commission,[20] which projected a fourfold increase in

20. "The 1970 National Power Survey: A Report by the Federal Power Commission" (Washington: U.S. Government Printing Office, December 1971).

electric power generation capacity in the twenty years from 1970 to 1990. Often such projections are quite detailed, providing breakdowns by sector of the economy and nature of the fuel.[21] The post-embargo Project Independence Blueprint, though focusing on the period up to 1985, analyzes two cases for the years beyond. A "base case," in which overall energy consumption grows at a rate of 2.5 percent per year to the year 2000 and beyond, and a "conservation with a major shift to electricity" scenario, which projects approximately a 1.6 percent per year overall growth rate, are presented.[22] It is less than clear how such growth rates are to be sustained if reliance is to be placed upon traditional or readily available alternative resources.

The restricted projections attempt to take the dwindling of resources into account. Perhaps the most widely known of such models are those prepared by the systems dynamicists.[23] In their World Model, all natural resources are aggregated and supposed to be finite. A function that related capital expenditures for natural resources to the fraction of those resources remaining attempts to account for scarcity; nevertheless, overall pressures in the model are such that the existing resources are rapidly exhausted, leading to precipitate declines in quality of life, economic well-being, and so forth. The structure of the model is such that the catastrophic result is independent of the actual amount of resources available, but rather is caused by the finiteness of those resources.

Such models have been used to treat highly aggregated groupings of conventional, transition, and alternate sources, defined somewhat differently from the way we do here.[24] A difficulty with the systems dynamics models, at least, is the very high level of aggregation, which tends to obscure the market and other mechanisms that many feel will be important determinants of both intermediate steps and ultimate results.

Dissatisfaction with the functioning of the first two classes of models leads to a desire for models that better reflect the operations of actual mechanisms. Research in these areas has been led by economists. However, the traditional economic construct, which involves balancing supply

21. Walter G. Dupree, and James A. West, "United States Energy Through the Year 2000," U.S. Department of the Interior, December 1972.

22. FEA, *Project Independence Report,* p. 430.

23. Meadows et al., *Limits to Growth.*

24. Andrew Ford, "Environmental Policies for Electricity Generation: A Study of the Long Term Dynamics of the SO_2 Problem," submitted to *Energy Systems and Policy;* Roger Naill, continuation proposal: National Science Foundation (RANN) Grant #GI-34808X, "The Role of Coal in the Long-Term Management of U.S. Energy Resources."

and demand, depends on a reasonable knowledge of supply and demand elasticities—the rates of response of supply and demand to changes in price. Measuring such elasticities for the short run is extremely difficult, and numerous attempts have met with only limited success. Moreover, even if it were possible to measure elasticities applicable to present energy markets with some confidence, it would be impossible to project such elasticities far beyond the region of observation. Market structures may change; life-styles may change, implying unknown shifts of demand in the manufacturing and service sectors of the economy. Supply poses even more difficult problems as new technologies are introduced, tapping resources which are not now exploited.

Nevertheless, several interesting attempts have been made. Notable among those that attempt to estimate the market penetration of advanced technologies are those of Alan Manne and William Nordhaus. Manne accepts a long-term energy demand growth rate of approximately 2.5 percent per year, and then attempts to meet that demand by using a linear programming model. The model operates with an objective of meeting projected energy demands at the minimum discounted costs for capital investment, fuel, operating, and maintenance to the year 2030.

Manne's results are most interesting. They may be viewed in the context of the four categories developed above. The contribution of traditional sources in this model (which takes account of resource depletion) is expected to decline after 1985.

The transitional sources become increasingly important in the transitional period, with contributions by the light water reactor (the current generation of nuclear reactors) peaking in the year 2000, and synthetic fuels from coal introduced about 1990, with both declining essentially to zero by 2030. An interesting anomaly here is that the contribution from oil shale increases monotonically throughout the period. Manne shows the fast breeder reactor contribution as rising rapidly from its introduction about 1995 to dominance of the electric sector two decades later. The advanced technologies (which we have called the ultimate technologies) come into play about 2015.

An interesting aspect of the Manne model is his treatment of the nonelectric sectors. He acknowledges that some increase in demand will continue in the oil, gas, and synthetic fuel sectors. This is handled by the introduction in 1995 and rapid rise to dominance after 2010 of hydrogen, generated through what he terms "a promising but unproven process for thermal chemical production of hydrogen through HTR's (high temperature nuclear reactors) coupled to fast breeders.'' [25] The importance of this result is clear: many candidate "ultimate technologies" focus on production of electricity in stationary installations. We must expect that many energy applications will not be amenable to direct use of electricity, and some mechanism such as that assumed by Manne to be so important will be necessary if demand for nonelectric sectors is to continue to grow—or even to be sustained—during these periods.

Similar considerations prompt the analysis of Nordhaus.[26] He seeks also to minimize the discounted costs of meeting a set of final demands through the year 2120, on the assumption that there exists a "backstop technology [that] may well be extremely expensive relative to current technology; nevertheless, if it exists, it assures that the planning problem has at least a feasible solution.'' Nordhaus's example is the nuclear breeder reactor.

The computational algorithm (which depends heavily on prices involving "royalties"—akin to rents and a reflection of presumed scarcity) is such as to suggest rapid shifts among energy sources; there is no provision for smoothing. Yet Nordhaus points out that his use of a discount rate of 10 percent—one which is widely accepted for such calculations—implies just such rapid shifts. It further implies that the introduction of synthetic fossil fuels and the "backstop technology" (our transitional and ultimate categories) will occur later than most other estimates project and that rapid depletion of existing resources will continue.

The central issue with all these types of models is not how well they predict the future, but how they reflect possible institutional mechanisms and decision processes, and what those processes will or should be.

This leads to the consideration of the role of institutions.

The economist likes to think in terms of the efficient functioning of the free market. In a free market the price mechanism acts to call forth additional resources and new technologies as they are needed to meet demands, constrains demands as resources become scarce, and efficiently allocates available resources to their best uses. Transitions are expected to be fairly gradual, and dislocations minimized.

25. Alan L. Manne, "U.S. Options for a Transition from Oil and Gas to Synthetic Fuels," December 1974 (work supported by National Science Foundation Grant SOC 75-05288).

26. William D. Nordhaus, "The Allocation of Energy Resources," *Brookings Papers on Economic Activity,* No. 3 (1973).

The difficulty is that the free market is a far from perfect model of reality. Considerable controversy attends the extent to which competition actually exists in the energy industries, particularly on the supply side. One need not make a detailed examination of hard-to-obtain data, or take a moralistic position, to conclude that there are certainly regional imperfections and considerable reluctance to innovate in areas where innovation might render obsolete extensive existing plant and equipment.

Government actions also create market imperfections. In addition to the usual regulatory functions, subsidies, import quotas, and other factors which perturb the market, the government plays an important role as owner of major fractions of the nation's energy resources, is the nation's largest consumer, and conducts a research program.

The functions of government with respect to the leasing of resources and to the stability and level of prices are discussed elsewhere in this volume. As we have noted, the federal government has a major role in research and development, particularly where there is little incentive for major private research expenditures. There may also be instances in which the government duplicates research in the private sector. Finally, government research along a particular avenue may preempt a whole area. A company faced with the existence of an extremely expensive government research program along one technological avenue is unlikely to pursue another technique independently. Time lags are extremely important. Research underway now is unlikely to bear fruit in the form of commercial implementation for at least ten or fifteen years; much federal energy research is even longer term.

Despite the important role of the government in research and in energy policy, it is the private sector which ultimately will implement any new technologies. That sector, confronted by the desire for profit and the need to stay in business, must necessarily take a short view. Only when individual companies band together, each contributing relatively modest funds that aggregate to a significant effort—as in the case of the Electric Power Research Institute (EPRI)—are at least some industries likely to provide important alternatives to federal research strategies.

Are these existing institutions adequate to cope with planning for futures beyond the turn of the century? The political process serves at least implicitly to reflect national and international decisions concerning the desired shape of energy futures. But it is not clear that the body politic perceives the long-run implications of short-term policies. With members of Congress up for reelection every two years, and many federal officials in responsible positions serving even shorter periods, their natural focus is the short term. Decisions on matters discussed in this chapter can have little practical outcome during such short time periods.

Implicit in many energy futures are fundamental changes in life-styles. A conservation ethic would be reflected directly in the real gross national product, and in material well-being. An all-electric economy, or some approximation of it, would also represent fundamental changes. The difficulty of long continuing to provide fuel to the transportation sector at current levels of activity has been noted.

For example, if conservation is to be a national policy, should the installation of air conditioners in automobiles be outlawed, or should each individual be given an "energy budget," so that he may decide whether to have an air conditioner in his car or to keep his house five degrees warmer in winter (if that trade can be made)? It is all too tempting for the bureaucrat to seek neat solutions which necessarily imply the imposition of an abstraction of his own choices upon the system as a whole.

The implications of conservation choices may be relatively clear to the individual; the choices among technologies for central station generation will be far less clear. If future energy choices are to be acceptable, then the body politic must be educated now to the realities and potentials of the situation and brought into the decision process to the greatest extent possible.

It is clear that energy markets beyond the turn of the century will be markedly different in shape and composition from those of today. The technically feasible will probably become dominant. The shape of possible futures will become clear only slowly, as the fruit of research now underway becomes available.

It is clear that there will be market changes. It is also clear that the economic and environmental costs of certain outcomes could be very high indeed. There is still time to make extremely responsible choices. The scope of options will shrink with the passage of time. Indeed, very little can be done today to make significant changes in the shape of the energy markets before 1985. Eight to ten years are required for the construction of a nuclear power plant, three to five years to open a mine. Research is an inherently slow process.

It is clear, to this writer at least, that historic rates of growth in energy consumption cannot be allowed to continue unabated. Even if those rates are moderated to an unprecedented degree, new technologies will be needed to provide energy supplies from resources not now tapped. There are many such exciting technological opportunities. Yet the economy may demand more of the technical community than it can produce. There is no certainty that new technologies will quickly become available to provide energy in the quantities and forms demanded at costs to the economy and the environment which will be deemed acceptable. For the years beyond the turn of the century, current models and projections show an increasing gap between what we know can be provided and what we expect is likely to be demanded. To fill that gap, we now have little more than a pious hope that unproven technologies can be made to succeed.

It is most important to begin now to address the complexities of these future energy markets, to do research, and to inform the public of uncertainties as well as facts, so that wise, rational, and equitable choices may be made.

Index

Library of Congress Cataloging in Publication Data
Main entry under title:

Energy supply and government policy.

Includes bibliographical references and index.
1. Power resources—United States—Addresses, essays, lectures. 2. Energy policy-
—United States—Addresses, essays, lectures. I. Kalter, Robert John.
II. Vogely, William A.
HD9502.U52E54   333.7   76-15836
ISBN 0-8014-0966-7
ISBN 0-8014-9159-2 pbk.